EDUCATION IS DEAD

─────

REFLECTIONS ON A FAILED PUBLIC EDUCATION SYSTEM

L. SALVATORE SCARPITTA

MULTI-SERVICES PUBLISHING

Education is Dead

Reflections on a Failed Public Education System.

by L. Salvatore Scarpitta

Educationisdead.com:
email@educationisdead.com

Multi-Services Publishing:
info@multiservicespublishing.com

STOLEN CONTENT

PLEASE REPORT INSTANCES OF CONTENT THAT MAY HAVE BEEN STOLEN OR PLAGIARIZED FROM THIS BOOK.

Contact us at:

stolencontent@educationisdead.com

Or try the website at:

EducationIsDead.com

...or notify the publisher.

As with all technology, websites and email contacts may not always be available.

BOOKS BY THE AUTHOR

Partial list of other books by the author:

The Cartainos: Men of Passion • Men of Stone.
　　The epic generational true story of an immigrant family putting down roots in America. If you like a story that you can stay with for a while, become involved in this one.

Killers Are Fatherless: The Real Cause of School Shootings, Serial Killings, and Gang Murders.
　　Too often fatherlessness is mentioned as a possible problem among school shooters and other killers, before ignoring it and moving on to other topics of more interest to the media. This book doesn't let that happen.

Additional details on these books can be found at the end of this book and on the publisher's website.

EDUCATION IS DEAD

REFLECTIONS ON A FAILED PUBLIC EDUCATION SYSTEM

Multi-Services Publishing
multiservicespublishing.com
SINCE *1989*

CONTENTS

PREFACE

This book does not take a detailed, data-driven look at education as do many other books. It assumes you've already seen plenty of data reflecting the state of public education today. So, after noting some of the general situation today, I'll be observing, commenting — and telling a few stories.

Regardless of my observations, thoughts — and stories — the point will be repeatedly made that the current education system is no longer fixable. Being brevity-challenged, I'll be rambling more than many of you might like. But the point will still be made: *Education Is Dead.*

As were so many others, I was brought up to love America. I didn't even notice it happening to me. Being American was simply who we were.

When I was young, my parents didn't talk about the country much. (The topic just doesn't come up a lot with young children.) But, when they did talk about it, their respect and firm connection to America came through to me. Both of my parents loved the country. They had both benefited from the opportunities in America.

Both had been raised by single parents, by their mothers, although my father also had a close connection to his father.

Although he was born in America, my father came from immigrants who worked hard to become part of the country. Mostly, they succeeded.

As did others who came, they wanted to be part of the American Dream. They may not have been able to define it, but they understood its importance in their lives and in the lives of others. Find their full story in the epic book: *The Cartainos: Men of Passion • Men of Stone.*

Although too many wrongly think that it is, the American Dream has never been solely a dream of financial success. It is not about owning a big home and a couple of nice cars.

The true American Dream is that of Freedom and Liberty, the *opportunity* to succeed, not necessarily the success itself. *The opportunity.* It's the opportunity to let the goodness that is within you strengthen, grow, and emerge to touch others. The American Dream doesn't promise success. It only promises the *opportunity.* Rich or poor, whether we finally obtain it or not is — nearly — fully within us.

Not long ago, a focus group of foreign students from 16 countries highlighted the changed reputation of America in the world.[1] Students observed that America "is not like it was in the past." One said that the American Dream doesn't exist anymore. Rather than wanting to come to America to study, some now talk about going to China instead because America has changed so much — for the worse.

Another focus group participant noted that "there are no more shared principles or ethical norms" in America today. That observation is particularly damning. Understand that these were *outsiders* from other countries making these observations. This is more than just sad. It's frightening. These international students may not know it, but they are reporting early evidence of the decline and fall of America.

Can America turn these things around? Unless something unexpected happens, it appears to be increasingly unlikely.

When the American Dream and its principles are seen as gone by non-Americans in the world, it truly may be foretelling the death of America. There is sometimes more objectivity in seeing a problem from afar than being in the middle of it, as the American people are today.

Many maintain an optimistic attitude that America can recover, that *"the American people"* will step up and save it. I want to believe that that may be the case. But the common mantra that "the American people" won't let it happen, that they will *"see right through"* what has been happening has been chanted by naive politicians and some in the media for years. Just because we want things to be a certain way, doesn't mean that they are that way or will be in the future.

Large numbers of "the American people" don't really understand what's happening and where it can lead. Worse, those who do understand, don't know what to do about it. At this one moment, it's unlikely that things can be turned around at all. Most good people await coming elections and hope that things might be changed then. But many have observed "issues" in recent elections that have some people concerned about that traditional vehicle of change.

Even if significant political changes can be made in some areas, the death of the public education system would not be able to bring the country back to a time of health. Any changes would still likely leave the current damage securely in place. Things don't change quickly. In spite of best efforts, sometimes things can actually get worse.

Ongoing damage in the country includes many recently changed beliefs and ongoing social condemnations. Much of this has been at odds with the original foundation and values of America as were still in place not many years ago. This has been especially damaging to those who are easily influenced at schools and universities.

I apologize for not taking an optimistic view of the future of America as so many others do. I am only here to report what I observe and pass on my concerns. Even I hope that things might quickly turn around. But the longer it takes, the less likely it can be brought back to health at all.

Sometimes people just have to take off the blinders of their naïveté to look at the dangers and failures around them. They have to look at the workings of world history over the centuries. They must also take seriously the observations of those in other countries as they now look in at America to understand that things might be happening they aren't even seeing.

Legal immigrants who came to America and became citizens are sometimes the strongest supporters of America. They know why they came, and they don't want to lose the country they worked so hard to be part of. They know the alternatives to the freedom of America and don't want to see their new country change to become the same as what they left. They know how easily that can happen.

Perhaps something will surprise us and the country will rise up and respect itself and its own Americans again. Perhaps it will regain its place in the world as the powerful and (mostly) united country of beloved principles and liberty that it once was. But right now, that is not looking likely.

Countries end. Empires end. America, as we have known it, may end, too. Some are looking ahead, concerned that that might already be happening. Some who are looking at America inside other countries see hints of that now.

The potential demise of America today is not simply a political thing where people on both sides can disagree, but everyone continues forward anyway. It's not simply a moment of disagreement.

As even that earlier focus group correctly showed, America is now looked upon in a bad light by many people in other countries today. Those other people are drawing their own conclusions based on what they're seeing. And they're not good.

***

The ones who most strongly developed and strengthened my love and caring for America weren't my parents. They were my teachers. It started in elementary school, continued through high school, and then on into life.

What happened to bring that about? Among other things, we recited the Pledge of Allegiance, *everyday* in class. "Stand up, face the flag, hand over heart, ready begin: '*I pledge allegiance to the flag...*'"

Today, young students are allowed to "opt out" of the Pledge of Allegiance. Incredibly, some politicians are now deriding the Pledge of Allegiance, calling it racist.

For decades now, enough time for multiple generations to have grown up, the Pledge of Allegiance has been optional in public schools, if it's said at all — and oftentimes, it isn't.

However, the fading of the Pledge of Allegiance, by itself, is not the only reason for the loss of patriotism. Formerly, there had also been affirmative and positive teaching about the country by teachers. Students could see America in their teachers, some of whom were models of patriotism themselves.

But, in most classrooms today, all that has changed. Now students notice what is too often the rare teacher who loves America —and says something about it to students. That's not a recent observation. It's been happening for years.

Some teachers seem to treat patriotism as they do religion: they had better be careful showing it or talking about it in the classroom. It might offend someone.

Those wanting to destroy a country can begin by tearing down respect and love for that country. Then they turn it fully around and teach students and citizens why it is actually a bad country, why a newly-designed one is needed — and why they should lead it. This can be part of a process that other countries might use to tear down our country: destruction from within. Is that what's happening? Things are now so divisive, it almost feels as though it might be orchestrated.

An article titled, "Criticism of the Pledge of Allegiance," presents a number of criticisms of the Pledge of Allegiance. A criticism in the article from others actually suggests that "the pledge itself is incompatible with democracy and freedom."[2]

For far too many people, patriotism is already gone. Disdain is arising in its place. Finally come those who are willing to step up and "save" the country — even though some of them are responsible for the loss of patriotism in the first place. Once they and the false teachings they espouse are accepted as true, it's all but over.

Many people feel there is nothing wrong with being negative about patriotism, the flag, and the country. They point to things they claim justify their negative feelings about what they think has often been a bad country. The widespread nature of this negativity is a major and relatively recent change. It is destroying America. Distressingly, some people sound as though the loss of America might be a good thing.

The "old America," beloved and defended in the past, seems gone, or on the way to being gone. It's already almost a thing of past history — and America's newly created history is not being kind to what went on before.[3]

***

In early March 2023, a poll was conducted by the Wall Street Journal and NORC.[4]

In part, we can compare the poll to numbers from 1998. In that earlier poll, 70% of Americans said that patriotism was *very important* to them. But, in 2023, that number was nearly half of that. In March 2023, a mere 38% said that patriotism was very important to them. Note that an additional 35% said that it was "somewhat important" in 2023.

With patriotism declining among those once saying that it was "very important" to them, we now see that schools are "succeeding" in damaging how our children feel about their country. Is that smaller number what one would expect to see in a nation even just likes itself?

If increasing numbers of the American people no longer feel a need to care about and protect their country from potential enemies, is it any wonder that we continue to have so many leaks of sensitive government data?

Consistent efforts to remove God from American public life has done the same thing to religious belief, too. The importance of religion — as being "very important" — dropped from 62% (1998) to 39% (2023). An additional 20% said that it was "somewhat important" in 2023.

Tolerance of others was felt to be very important by 80% of

those polled in 2019, but just 58% in 2023. That's a substantive drop in just over four years.

According to the poll, Democrats are less than half (23%) as likely to report that patriotism is "very important" to them as opposed to Republicans who reported that patriotism is "very important" to them at 59%. (Independents were at 29%.)

What one value increased from 1998 to 2023?

The importance of *money*.

These are just examples of the trends uncovered in this one poll.[5]

Downward movement in the numbers away from former American virtues and values were especially notable in younger generations.

Many people are not concerned about such trends, especially as relate to the younger people polled. They say that these are just expected differences as new generations take their place in society and exert their influence in America.

"Nothing to see here. Move along."

But that is not the case. These trends have been seen elsewhere in history. If this continues, the road does not end in a good place.

✱✱✱

From the time I was little, I heard teachers tell us, *"This is America. You can do whatever you want!"* Again and again I heard that. I wasn't alone hearing it. I was just a small student cog in the classroom wheel, but so many others grew up hearing the same thing.

Doing whatever we want wasn't something we could do just because we're individuals and can do it if we want. What we were told by teachers was almost always linked to America: "This is *America*; you can do whatever you want." Later, some began to change it a bit saying, "This is a free country; you can do whatever you want." There are lots of "free" countries, but there is only one America. There's a difference — or at least there was in the past.

Although it meant that my life would be more difficult, I believed what my teachers told me. I believed that this *is* America and I *can* do what I want. Others, whether they were told that same thing or not, also believed it. As did I, they also lived it, although each path was different. Whether any of us achieve our dreams or not, we have all lived the opportunity America gives us — but only if we choose to take it.

Some stepped back and chose not to participate. They ignored the many possibilities for their lives. That was often a loss for them. People who did pursue it, no matter their race or economic status, grew to become far more than they once were. Success was possible for anyone with guts and a dream because *"This is America. You can do whatever you want."*

Those tearing down America today will point to those who did *not* succeed. They'll point to those in poverty, those whose lives are difficult. And they'll blame it on America. Those people want others to see America as a failure.

But it isn't.

Or at least it wasn't a failure in the not-too-distant past.

For some young (and old) people just struggling to survive, any American dream might seem as though it doesn't apply to them. It's certainly not easy and some may never get there. Remember, it's the opportunity, not a guarantee of getting anything. But it's there for everyone nonetheless.

You'll find success in America among all races and creeds, rich and poor. But success and dreams don't happen by themselves. People have to try. They have to take what they want into their own hands and *make* it happen, or at least put themselves in a place where it *might* happen. Remember, success isn't necessarily defined by financial success. There are many other forms of success and of dreams fulfilled. People often define success from their own personal desires, not understanding that others may be different.

The American Declaration of Independence lists rights of "life, liberty, and the pursuit of happiness." It doesn't guarantee that we will obtain happiness. It just says we have the right to *pursue* it.

Interestingly, from 1849 through today, the Constitution of the State of California has unfathomably said that not just pursuing happiness, but actually *obtaining* it is part of that right. To me, that makes no sense. How can a government promise people the right to actually *obtain* happiness, to actually BE happy? To whom does one go if something interferes with that right, if someone *isn't* happy? Perhaps, I'm missing something here.

> With emphasis added, the Constitution of the State of California says: "ARTICLE 1 DECLARATION OF RIGHTS: SECTION 1. All people are by nature free and independent and have inalienable rights. Among these are enjoying and defending life and pursuing *and obtaining* safety, *happiness,* and privacy."

Some dreams are indeed difficult, not just to achieve, but to keep. Some entail great difficulties in one's life, even though the dream itself might bring great accomplishment and fulfillment. We all hope that financial success is also part of their dream, but, for many people, that isn't always the case. Dreams can be different.

My dreams became dreams for the Adventures of Life. I didn't know which direction my life would be taking. I didn't do much advance planning. (As an aside for others, I recommend doing such planning.) I just seemed to follow one thing after another as things came in front of me.

When I was serving in the U.S. Navy, an officer who was my boss told me that I was a dilettante. That's sometimes a negative thing to say about someone. It suggests the person just dabbles in various things without really becoming a professional at anything. As I thought about it, it fit me. I actually did become professional at several things in my life, but the observation was that I did do many things, though not necessarily in depth.

For me, it was constant learning and a constant adventure as to what would be next in life. But there's no financial security in that kind of life. My teachers hadn't warned us about that. They probably should have. They simply and repeatedly said that this is America and we could do whatever we want. And there is *so much* to do!

When you move from job to job and place to place, you don't build up much security, either life security or financial security. One day, you stop working. Perhaps you retire.

So, if someone is thinking about doing *everything,* I don't recommend it. Even when young, you should be thinking about building income, saving for retirement, or saving something just for emergencies. Of course, that's just a thought. You can do whatever you want — well, within reason. Perhaps you'd better check the small print on that first.

I ended up with knowledge and experience in a lot of things and I did become professional at a few. That allowed me to counsel, caution, teach, and encourage others. My life experience helped me to direct others to a life where their own dreams might be pulling them — or to redirect them if their road looked lost. But those choices are in others' hands. They aren't really up to me.

Each person is unique. Yet we're also not. Inside each of us, we all have a lot in common.

The freedom that has allowed us to do what we want in the past has begun to look bleaker, even frightening at times. Things have been changing.

In the end, life worked out for me. But the journey was insecure. I didn't know where my own road was going or how it would end. Actually, I'm still on that road.

Education is key to all of this, even without college. Many of the most successful people in America didn't complete college.

So America gives you the *opportunity*. You have to make something of that opportunity. Some do. Some don't.

There are countless touching and powerful stories of people coming from families in poverty to success, even to national or international fame. Some we know about. Others we don't. But America has allowed their lives to move in directions they would never have thought possible if they had been born elsewhere.

In my case, that belief in America where "You can do whatever you want," didn't take me down a road to remarkable success in business or financial security. In fact, it took me down a difficult road. Looking back, it would have been better had I picked a different path. A different path might not have actually been *better*, but at least it might have been easier! Yet, in spite of difficulties, *life is good*. In fact, struggles are what make life *life*.

The problem was that, as I already mentioned, since I could do whatever I wanted, I wanted to do *everything*. In the end, I didn't do everything, but I did do a lot. This book's *About The Author* lists only a very small piece of that. If I had just stayed with one or two things, I might have developed more predictable security, financial and otherwise, in my life. But I kept seeing exciting things to do. Too many things! Even in my life today, I already see I won't have time to do all the other things that I *still* want to do.

Right now, it's time for me to write books. As one might predict, I'm not writing in just one genre. My books, both in progress and completed, vary remarkably. That makes it tough to find traditional publishers who normally want predictable, consistent authors in one genre (one category of writing) so that readers will want to follow them.

But hey, this is America! You can *write* whatever you want. You can *do* whatever you want (well, within reason).

Many years of my life were spent in education. I have not liked what I've seen in public education. That's not because some good things aren't going on, or because there aren't good people giving themselves to their students as teachers and administrators. There are many of them.

For me, two of the best and most rewarding years of my life were as principal of a small school. I worked with a staff and teachers about whom I really cared.

Nonetheless, I've been a consistent advocate for school reform. However, although being an advocate is good, it's not good enough, because making significant reforms to fix education is all but impossible.

***

Like many other people, I didn't like school much when I was a student. I was actually a high school drop out. I dropped out of school one semester before finishing high school.

School was oftentimes frustrating and sometimes difficult for me. At times, it seemed like a waste of time. (Sometimes it was.) I wasn't the best student, even though I definitely learned a lot. I've always really liked learning, I just didn't particularly like school. That will sound familiar to many others.

All that ended up being a good thing for my students when I

surprised myself by later becoming a teacher and administrator. I absolutely understood students who were also frustrated with school, who also wanted to quit. I got it. And I did everything I could to try to encourage them and keep them from leaving school.

No one can always be successful in everything, but we must always try. I'm sorry whenever I failed as a teacher, because students rely on their teachers. Teachers are so important in the lives of our students, communities, and the country. We can never do enough for others.

But back to America.

After a few years, it had been drilled into me: America is a special place and we can do anything. We were also told we would have to work hard. Only then might we be able to do what we want. Laziness doesn't get it.

Knowing all this was really a great thing! There was so much to do! I could do one thing, and then move on and do something else! That sounded great!

As one example, I didn't sign up for just one military service. I signed up for two — though not at the same time, of course. There was so much to do in life! This is America! We can *do anything!*

It wasn't just teachers who told us that. Others did, too.

Life is good!

Regardless of what I chose to do, I knew that I could do it — even when I couldn't. But failing is okay. After all, this is America! We can fail, too!

Many of the most successful entrepreneurs failed multiple times, often through business bankruptcies, before finally succeeding. It's all part of being able to "do anything" in America.

Whether in life or in business, you try. You fail. You learn. Then you try again. Failing is part of the learning of life. But don't give up! Learn more, then do more.

There are many things we can do that don't entail starting a business, things that are still challenging and exciting. My first jobs were as a paperboy and cleaning dog runs. Those were exciting ways to make money for me! No one stopped me. I had supportive parents. I could try anything! Well, okay. Not always.

As parents should do, sometimes they would step in to guide

me to something else. That was especially helpful when I was young. When we grow older and enter the world on our own, we begin to make our own decisions, often different from what our parents think might be best. Sometimes, we find we were wrong. Other times, our new paths take us to exciting places that neither we nor our parents would have imagined.

This concept of choosing your own direction in life might seem normal to Americans. *Of course,* you can do whatever you want (if you work hard to get it)! But in other countries, you can't. In America, you can rise from nothing to be a great success.[6] There are many examples of that.

However, recently, there has been a change in how teachers and schools look at the country. Many are not teaching the importance of America anymore. (Some aren't teaching the basic academic subjects adequately either.)

The Pledge of Allegiance isn't required in most places today. Nor is patriotism even considered a respected virtue by many people. Patriotism is optional. After all, many are now saying that America is racist today — and has always been racist.

> People who repeatedly insist that America is racist are either ignorant of the facts, or they're lying. There is no denying that racism exists. Nonetheless, especially in relatively recent times — and especially with the varied and broad numbers of people who are American — America has been one of the least racist countries on the planet.
>
> What should be of great concern, it appears that some people have been *intentionally* feeding and encouraging racism in America, even in contexts where it hasn't existed. This is very serious. Turning Americans against Americans adds to pressures which can bring down the country.

Although education, in the past, has helped to build and strengthen America and its citizenry, its purpose is not solely to develop patriotism in future adults. It is not limited to establishing a commonality of shared values with other Americans, although it should do both of those things. Education is actually key to everything. It offers keys to all of life.

Those of us who served in the military, who took an oath, who pledged fidelity to the country and its Constitution are now demeaned by some people for that very fidelity. America and its flag mean little to many people today.

Although I like to hear it, *"Thank you for your service,"* is just something to say to veterans, rather than something people truly understand and feel.

Many people rant about "Constitutional rights" while knowing almost nothing about either the Constitution or the rights within it.

For me, I was taught in school that America and its flag were things to be respected, that they were something special. They still are.

"This is America. You can do whatever you want!"

But something has changed.

ABOUT THE AUTHOR

So you'll know something about who's talking to you, here's a little bit about the author.

For nearly 30 years, the author (that's me) has had experience in many areas of education, as both a teacher and an administrator. Broad life experience in many other areas adds to that. Here is a partial listing of the author's education experience:

• Teacher and administrator at the elementary, middle school, and high school levels. Worked in multiple schools and school districts in two states. Certificated and taught at the community college level in California.

• Certificated as both a teacher and administrator in multiple subject matter and administrative areas.

• Masters degree in Educational Administration.

• Taught classes partially including full courses in Social Studies (history, government, economics), Mathematics, Writing, English as a Second Language (ESL), Life Skills, Basic Computer, Keyboarding, Cinema, Latin, Driver Education (classroom), Driver Training (behind the wheel), as well as being certified as a Motorcycle Safety Foundation Instructor (although without often actually teaching motorcycle riding), and more. Also worked as a substitute teacher in various schools and subjects.

• Designed and conducted animal behavior modification classes at multiple schools and venues.

• Designed and taught accredited classes not previously offered at schools, including at the community college level.

• Designed and taught non-credit community services classes for adults at multiple schools and colleges.

•Provided leadership and design work for a charter school conversion proposal.

•Spearheaded obtaining accreditation for a previously unaccredited school, just the second school to obtain accreditation in its district at the time.

•Designed and taught private group, as well as one-on-one classes and courses. Previously held a California Private Post-Secondary Certificate of Authorization for Service authorizing teaching in Writing (English) and Mathematics in private post-secondary schools (vocational schools for adults) in California.

•Presenter at multiple conferences, colloquia, churches, and seminars. Among other topics, presentations included information learned from unique experience in the practical application of the learning phenomenon of reminiscence (hypermnesia) as a learning methodology.

•Named an Outstanding Options Teacher, for CCEA [in former] District XI in California.

•Broad and extensive additional life experience outside of education has helped the author to see this situation from afar, as it really is today: beyond broken, and seemingly unfixable. That additional experience only partly includes service in both the U.S. Army (enlisted) and the U.S. Navy (officer).

***

Here are two other books by the author:

The Cartainos: Men of Passion • Men of Stone.

Killers Are Fatherless: The Real Cause of School Shootings, Serial Killings, and Gang Murders.

See the Multi-Services Publishing home page for more information.

PART ONE: WHAT'S THE PROBLEM?

"THIS IS CHAPTER ONE."

Think of this as an Introduction that is so important, I had to call it Chapter One. Note that all footnotes are available as endnotes at the back of the book.

Education in America is broken.[1]

Perhaps you've heard that before.

This is not a casual observation. Don't think that this is something that affects educators and students, but not others. It affects the whole country. It affects the entire world.

Both recent and current generations are in deep trouble. But it's more than that. A broken system has the potential to foreshadow the end of America, not only as it once existed upon its historical foundations, but even as it is today.

So what I'm going to tell you is important.

Let me be a bit clearer: I'm telling you that, in my opinion, and at all levels, the public education *system*, as we expect it to work — as it *should* work — is dead.

I'm not alone in this. You can find other books and articles that use that very word — *Dead* — to describe education as it is today or as it is expected to be in the foreseeable future.

In this book, I will not be presenting to you a study. I'm not relaying to you various facts obtained from learned educators and researchers. Too few people have learned from, or even believe such studies, although they absolutely should. Beyond that, few understand the depth of what is happening — although they see it unfolding right in front of them — and that includes educators themselves.

Worse, people don't care. Sure, some might say, *"Oh, it sounds bad!"* but then continue on their way, assuming that it doesn't impact them. They might think that some interested politician or enlightened educator will (or at least should) take care of it.

But consider this. Such people have had countless years to do that without success. In fact, many things are significantly worse today than in the past. Of course, people say that in almost every generation. But, today, it's gone well beyond what concerned observers have seen in the past. It's highly unlikely that anyone in a position to make changes today will be able to move forward with anything meaningful. I don't blame them. As things are now, it's simply not fixable — by anyone.

In this book, I'm going to tell you what I've seen, how I feel, and a bit of what I've done. That will not only include observations about the concepts of school and education, but also about the *product* of that education in the citizens,[2] voters, and political strength of America.

Whether my observations are entirely accurate or just mostly accurate, the breadth of my nearly 30 years of experience in education, as well as many years outside of it, are such that I feel well-qualified, both in having these opinions and in passing them on to you. (You may have read a bit of that experience in the *About The Author* section after the *Preface* to the book.)

Those who want less opinionated, more traditional studies on the deficiency of the education systems in America can easily find numerous other books on the variety of problems found in America's schools, universities, and in education generally. This isn't one of those books.

On the other hand, try searching for substantive books and studies that *defend* the education system. Try finding substantive support for why education is actually working today, not why it's important (we all know that it is), but that it is actually *working* — perhaps even *why* some think it is working *effectively*. Maybe your luck in finding that defense of education, especially in public schools, will be better than mine has been.

The truth is that we don't need more books, we don't need more studies to uncover what the country has known back and beyond many decades. We've got plenty. I'm not going to waste time putting together more of which there is already enough. It hasn't done any good in the past and it won't do any good now.

Even back in 2008, *Strong American Schools* released an analysis that said, *"Now is not the time for more educational research or reports or commissions."* [3] I fully agree with that. It's time to stop distracting people with interminable studies and investigations that bring us little that is new.

I have no illusions that my words here will bring about changes, even were it possible to fix things. As I'll repeatedly say, education today is no longer substantively fixable. The time when that may have been possible is now gone.

Some will say that my personal experiences don't reflect the actual state of education today. Indeed, I'm certain that things in this book do not fully reflect education everywhere. Nonetheless, I believe those things reflect enough of the situation that they go well beyond merely a cause for great concern. If the country would open its collective eyes, it would see what some might consider to be the death of America as we have known it.

Is there anything that we, as a country and a society, will be able to do about all this?

I want to think there might be, but I am doubtful that there is. More likely, I'm simply letting you know those things which likely foretell our downfall as a nation.

In many places, test scores are down, again. Some have reached the lowest level in decades. From Baltimore, come reports that a number of K-12 schools, at all levels, had *no* students proficient in math *at all. None.* But math wasn't the only problem.[4]

Although people like to point to Baltimore as an example of the failure of schools, Baltimore schools are not alone.

Was the problem that Baltimore schools did not have enough

money? They reportedly had more money than the national average in per pupil funding. But, although money is important, only rarely can it solve fundamental educational problems. A lack of money is not the primary problem in American education.

In his recent book, *The Marxification of Education* (2022), James Lindsay notes that 94% of students at schools in Providence, Rhode Island, are failing mathematics and that *"86% cannot read or write at grade level."*[5]

However, even ignoring Baltimore and Providence schools, there are countless other examples of schools failing to educate their students throughout America today — schools in Illinois have recently been mentioned once again. (Such failures of education are not all in public schools.)

Some schools feel that standardized tests must be the problem — not the failures of teaching and student learning at their schools. Some of them rationalize that such tests might be racist and, therefore, not accurate or reliable. In some places, schools prefer not to give standardized tests to their students at all. After all, no tests, no failing students.

Only with a strong and united decision to change things, especially in the political realm, might we save not just education, but current and future generations of Americans — and the country itself.

But I don't see that happening.

Sound serious? It's actually even more serious than it sounds.

Will I give you the solution to all this? Will I tell you what changes are needed to fix it? Probably not. So why waste time reading a book that won't let you know what needs to be done?

It's because the message here is different.

Numerous other books discuss problems in education. Most of them offer solutions to "fix" things. Have things been fixed? No, they have not been. There has been plenty of time to do it. Why, then, are things still broken??

The reason things aren't fixed is that public education is no longer fixable.

Did you personally take the advice of those other books and studies as to how to fix education? Did you move forward to implement their suggested solutions? (I'm kidding. I know most of you haven't read any of them.)

Precisely what good has it done to come up with solutions that won't be implemented? Even when they are implemented, the vast majority haven't been effective, workable solutions, no matter what their proponents claim.

This is not a positive book. It's not even a warning. Warnings are for bad things that might come in the future so that people can avoid them or stop them from happening. People have rarely heeded warnings about education. No, this is not a warning.

It's already too late.

So you'll hear from someone who has had a fair amount of varied experience in education. You'll hear my thoughts and opinions, my observations, and some of my concerns. Take them or leave them, as you wish.

But remember: I'm not alone in this. Many others feel the same way. They try to come up with solutions just for the sake of having solutions. Books are supposed to present a problem, but then offer solutions. But solutions-for-solution's-sake won't work.

I'm not presenting a lot of specific evidence in this book. You'll find plenty elsewhere, if it's important to you.

I'll also not be providing specifics as to the times, places, schools, or people in the stories I'll be telling you. People tend to attack specifics of stories, while missing the reasons for telling them in the first place — assuming I even have some overriding reason, that is.

Such specifics won't matter for what I'm going to talk about. I'm not trying to "prove" anything. This book is simply my opinion on the state of public education in America.

Let me clarify that when I refer to "education," I mean *formal* education. That primarily occurs in schools. Less commonly, it can happen elsewhere. But here, I'm only talking about formal education in public schools. It is within that definition that the title of this book lives. Many can't even agree on what education is and what it should be doing. A later chapter talks about that.

"Learning" is different. Learning occurs everywhere all throughout our lives. That's what formal education is supposed to be providing, although in a more structured, efficient, and effective way. It's primarily the effectiveness — accuracy, fullness, balance, usefulness, and efficiency — of formal education with which I take issue. As an understatement, schools today are rarely either effective or efficient.

I don't care that the schools that *you personally attended* were good. I don't care that the schools your children went to, or are going to today, were good or are good (or you assume that they were, whether they actually were or not).

Of course, there are still some great schools in America. There are still some great classrooms with great teachers. There are bright spots in almost every school. But there aren't enough of them to create an educated citizenry who will be able to keep the country strong for much longer.

I'll also be telling you just a few of the many stories I have. Some of those stories will support the contention that *Education is Dead*. Some won't. Some might even appear to make the opposite case. Regardless, I'll be sharing a few of those stories with you just because I might feel like it. Sometimes an author just feels like telling some stories. So I do. Maybe some will be of help in this after all.

But don't be misled. The state of public education in America today is as bad as I say it is. It's waiting for you to fix it: YOU. But since most of you don't realize the extent of the problem, or even that there *is* as serious a problem as I tell you here, you're not likely to do anything about it — even if you could. After all, that's someone else's job anyway, isn't it? What do you know about fixing education? You might just make it worse!

How can you even know anything about these things? After all, readers are often products of that very system. And it's hard to know what you don't know.

Some alternatives to the current public education system aren't necessarily great either, by the way.

Is what we have now and what it's becoming better than nothing at all? If it is, it's not by much. We would be slowly sinking even further to the depths below many other countries in the world, except that many of them aren't doing particularly well either. We're already beyond being in real trouble.

For a short time, we remain fortunate that some students are still receiving an adequate education, most often not in the public schools. Those increasingly fewer numbers of educated Americans might help to save the country before it's completely gone. But time to act is limited — and we're likely already beyond those limits. In many, even most places, education is effectively already dead.

But let me give you another troubling observation. *With or without a dead public education system,* at the time of this writing, America is in deep trouble. The survival of the country that existed when it was founded, the country that existed after World War II, the country that existed not long ago, as the vagueness of time is sometimes measured... the survival of America is in serious jeopardy. Regardless of the education quagmire, unless something unexpected happens to turn it around, the United States of America, as it once was, may not survive.

The issues that lead to that observation are discussed in other books and in other places. Here, I will just be concerned with the state of its education system.

Now let's turn to begin with the real Chapter One...

1. THE REAL CHAPTER ONE: THE POLITICS OF EDUCATION

Although the things in this chapter are very important, even critical, they're not the main focus of this book. Nonetheless, in many places, they're destroying the country. Therefore, I'm going to get the basics of these fundamentally political issues addressed upfront. Then I'll move on.

Many books today are ruthless as they go after education for the politics and social agendas that have been inserted in many schools and classrooms today. It's good that such books do.

However, although their concerns are fully justified, they're also making a faulty assumption.

Their assumption is that, if schools can just get rid of all of the destructive socio-political interference, they can finally return to what schools are supposed to be doing — actually educating students.

But that premise is flawed.

It assumes that, after eliminating the social and political machinations of recent years, teachers can again teach substantively, hopefully even passionately, and students can once again begin to learn what they're supposed to be learning. After all, that's the bottom line of what schools do, isn't it?

Sadly, many public — and some private — schools weren't

providing a good education even before the currently damaging social politics entered the schools. It's not likely such schools will be providing a good education even after (or *if*) the current social and political interferences finally go away.

I'll say that again. Even if such ideologies are eliminated, learning in schools is not likely to be significantly better than it had been.

Nonetheless, I cannot proceed without addressing this particular elephant wandering the room. So I'll put the issue on the table, although, perhaps, surprisingly briefly.

Lots of other books and articles have been specifically targeting these issues in depth today. They're sounding the alarm to let you know about these things. My suggestion is that you get involved to *try* getting the things that schools should not be doing out of schools. (Good luck with that!)

Will succeeding at that make schools better again? Well, perhaps it will make many schools — especially public schools — less dangerous to the country than they've become today. It will remove what are mostly twisted or false understandings and teachings. But it won't fix education itself.

Most people have heard of the lower scores students have been getting on standardized tests, especially since the COVID pandemic. They've often heard of our lower educational placement in the world. Perhaps they've also heard that, in too many schools, some high school *graduates* are functionally illiterate.

That means that they can't fill out a job application; can't read or write beyond the level of a lower level elementary school student; can't do much basic math. They simply don't know things. How did they graduate anyway? We'll talk about that again later on.

That's not true at all schools, of course. But it's true at far more schools than people know. Years ago, those students would not have been allowed to graduate. Are they responsible for their failing? Many times, yes. Schools are not solely responsible for everything that goes wrong. However, other times, we can indeed point a finger at the system that was supposed to educate them. Regardless of responsibility, the outcome has been the same. They and we are in big trouble.

Note that I primarily refer to public schools in this book. But these issues often extend to many non-public schools, too. After all, these socio-political beliefs are brought in to those non-public schools by educators crippled by their own "education" in the broken system. They arrive already carrying some damaging, deeply held beliefs within them. Therefore, not all, but many of the teachers themselves are already broken. They might be good, even wonderful people, but many should not be teaching our children.

Should we start getting rid of countless teachers en masse? We can't do that. We don't have enough solid replacements for them. Schools would be closing without any workable alternatives.

***

Here I'll list a few of the politically-charged issues causing concerns in the country today.

Those of you who might not accept that these things are problems — or maybe wrongly support them yourselves — are welcome to just skip over this (second) first chapter and start your reading at Chapter Two. But remember that just because you disagree (or agree) with something, doesn't mean that others feel the same way. Many people feel and believe quite differently from each other at this particular moment in the country today.

Here's that short list:

1. The teaching and promoting of Critical Race Theory (CRT) or similar social designs.

Even in schools that maintain they're not teaching it (by name), it's often taught in the day-to-day teachings of other subjects in the classrooms. There will be more on this further below.

2. Subject matter changes.

Another serious issue are the several questionable changes to previously accepted teachings, especially in history and other social sciences. The introduction of the 1619 Project — also briefly discussed below — is one of special concern. However, there are also other things that are changing history — and even changing other subjects. Historical revisionism has always been a danger. I'll discuss that separately later in the book. But that, too, is in increasing evidence today.

3. Social engineering.

Societal changes are normal over time. But when they become so radical as to alienate or endanger society or vast numbers of people in a relatively short period of time, they should be eliminated. That's especially true when they are forced on people, especially on children.

People today have expressed concerns about the forced integration of the LGBTQ+ agenda. Most people in America have always supported a "live and let live" philosophy. But that doesn't seem to be enough anymore. One side appears to want to *enforce* its agenda on others.

Those who push back on such agendas are accused of hating or trying to stop others from living their chosen lives. In reality, they simply want to stop such agendas from being forced on them, or their children. Other than that, people can (mostly) do what they want.

Such "forcing" partly encompasses indoctrination at schools without substantive support from parents and the community.

Other issues that have been recently raised as serious concerns today have included biological males playing against biological females in sports, as well as using the same restrooms and locker rooms.

In addition, parents across the country have shown up at school board meetings to protest, not just those things, but also access to reading materials — in both classrooms and school libraries — which they judge (generally correctly) to be fully inappropriate for their children.

Increasing numbers of parents have been vocal about such books and materials in K-12 classrooms as well as at school libraries and the children's sections at public libraries. This is a serious issue. Those who make the case that such books and materials are fine for children, even an asset, in K-12 education actually have a nearly impossible case to make in support of those materials. Minimally, they have been misled.

4. Parental displacement.

Many, if not most, complaints today have their origins in the LGBTQ+ agenda. For example, in recent years, there has been a strong push to support school children of all ages in their often-incorrectly perceived desire to change their sex/gender. Data consistently show the problems to which such support can lead.

Encouraging children to consider "changing" their gender is a serious issue. Such actions damage the accepted morality of the community, trashes the responsibility and authority of parents, and can destroy the bodies and lives of children who are enticed or encouraged to go through such processes.

Of special concern is that parents are often *intentionally* left out. Children are advised not to talk to their parents — not to trust their parents. That does wonders to support the already weakened nuclear family in America (yes, that's facetious). School staff then move in to replace parents by providing life-endangering support... and "guidance" for children.

According to a February 2023 article, a Missouri bill under consideration at the time of this writing proposed prohibiting *"school personnel from affirming or encouraging sex orientation changes in children in middle school and under without parental permission."* (Other states have comparable bills under consideration.)

One might correctly wonder why high school students — most of whom are still considered "children" within the control and responsibility of their parents — would be left out of the bill. Parents actually still provide guidance and control over their children even beyond high school. Most love their children for a lifetime.

A 15 to 18 year old is still too new in their world experience to make decisions about changes with lifelong consequences on their own. Even older adults benefit from multiple opinions before making serious healthcare decisions.

If high school "children" can make such decisions, perhaps they should be redefined as adults. But that would be a mistake since their life experience at those ages is still too limited to understand the ramifications of deciding to try "changing" their gender. There has already been documentation and personal testimonies of serious and lasting physical and emotional damage associated with such attempts.

The proposed, but controversial Missouri bill is said to address *"a common situation across America."* Is this something we want to be "common?" Why are schools involved in this anyway? Exactly what does it have to do with (traditional) education? When parents send children off to school, they assume education will be taking place, not something this serious.

It's appalling to me that so many entities and individuals actively oppose the Missouri bill and others that are similar. So, if a young child of these objectors came home one day to surprise their parents as a totally different gender, having undergone life-altering surgery and taking puberty blocking drugs, parents or others not even involved would have no problem with it?

Regardless how they personally feel, why do some educators object to parents being able to watch over and take care of their own children? People should certainly have the right to make choices for their own children, but not for the children of *other* parents.

The proposed bill (its final status is not known at the time of this writing) notes that *"School authorities have taken the initiative to help children change genders… Often, these actions have happened without the consent or knowledge of parents."*[1]

Throughout history, bypassing parents has been a mark of fascist, dictatorial regimes.

One of the great gifts given to parents is their children. When others step in to supersede parents, it can have negative, some-times irreversible effects — not only for the lives of their children, but for the parents themselves. School staff who set these things in motion won't be around to see that. They only have your children with them for a short time. Then school staff can move on with their own lives. They may not even remember your child. But the damage they encouraged can last a lifetime.

Those are examples of some things that have caused deep and serious divisions in the country today. Data show that the vast majority of educators today are politically liberal (left) in their thinking and beliefs. After all, they themselves have been taught by others with similar beliefs in their own education. Therefore, it would be natural that they try to pass on their own personal beliefs to others.

But doing so has led to what have increasingly become dangerous divisions in the country. The word "dangerous" should be taken literally. There are already enough other bad actors involved today to make that word the correct one to use even outside of issues with education.

Outside of schools, such "bad actors" include terrorists, cartels, other criminal organizations, and many individuals, but also other nations. I'm not suggesting that educators are part of those things. Nonetheless, some of that can make its way into schools at all levels.

We are currently seeing increasingly open attacks on the social, political, and moral fabric of what the country used to be. Yet we further add to such dangers by destroying ourselves from within our own education system.

As part of all this, the job of actually educating students, at all levels, has already been severely damaged even beyond the likely irreparable harm we have seen even before the various political and sociological agendas came up.

Interestingly, I believe the socio-political problems now in schools have a chance to be mostly fixed in the future. Mostly, but not entirely. The remnants of the problems will be because legislatures cannot legislate and courts cannot compel teachers and other educators to *think and believe* differently, although it has been tried in other countries. Like all of us, our educators are human beings.

We can't dictate how they must personally think and feel when they're in their own classrooms. They're not programmable robots.

Yet today, numerous studies and polls have shown that the vast majority of educators are on just one side of the political spectrum, that of strongly liberal Democrats (see the polls). Even if we can officially ban the divisive issues mentioned above, much of it will remain in the hearts of educators, even those teaching our youngest students. We don't have enough balanced teachers to replace them, even if it were possible — and it's not.

Regardless, I feel more hope that those things might be able to return to something better in the future — depending on which politicians come to power and how strongly parents themselves stand up against them. I have more concerns concerning the underpinnings of traditional education itself.

In other words, education is indeed dead — but not solely as a result of the current social and political machinations. Those might be the nail in the coffin, but the body in the coffin of education is effectively dead already.

So although you'll hear the above issues mentioned again, know that they are not the primary focus of this book. This book is concerned with today's foundations of traditional education itself.

Why aren't we educating our students fully and properly? Even though most of us still think that we are, have we ourselves — who may have long ago finished our own education — been properly educated in the first place? And if we have not been, how can we even judge?

I'd like to say that this book will answer those questions and provide solutions as needed. But that's not likely to happen. In most cases, the possibility that we can "fix" education is now so slim, that it's truly already too late.

***

A momentary aside: Let me not fail to mention the power of the teachers' unions, especially in support of such political and sociological agendas. These unions include the national unions (the

NEA and AFT), but sometimes local ones, too. The national unions generally do not represent the majority of teachers in the classrooms, though they do represent some of them. Local unions are more directly involved with the lives of teachers.

Teachers have almost no power to change the direction of their enormous national unions. Teachers are often at their mercy — watching their union dues go to agendas that don't even help them, and with which they may not even agree. But the power of the unions can sometimes set the direction of teachers' educational lives.

That can be done through influencing legislation, by using their power in the courts, or by influencing the public. The national teachers unions normally don't negotiate at the school or district levels for teachers. Local unions do that.

Fortunately, union intrusion into classrooms doesn't always happen. In some schools, teachers can just be teachers, almost as though the unions weren't even there — except for taking their dues.

As long as teachers feel appreciated, supported, and cared for by their district, and especially by their local administrators, teachers can be very happy teaching. It's a rewarding job.

Good teachers love to teach. It's a special passion. Students love those teachers. Everyone does.

On the other hand, many teachers are just happy to have a job — any job. Perhaps some can find other jobs that are much easier than teaching has become.

1a. DANGEROUS TEACHINGS

As with other sections in the book, if this section holds no interest
for you, feel free to skip it and move on to the next chapter.

In this part of Chapter One, I'll expand and add a bit more to
some of the important things just mentioned.

Biases exist in all people, including teachers. However, K-12
(that's kindergarten through 12th grade) public school teachers
must not allow strong political, sociological, or religious biases into
the classroom such that they will interfere with healthy and accurate teaching.

Nonetheless, there are many subjects where what may seem to
be a biased presentation to some people, is actually an accurate
presentation of the facts to others. As just one example — and as
already discussed in the preface — a positive embrace of patriotism
should not be considered an unwanted bias. Even though some
appear to disagree today, it has been a value shared by America
since its birth as a country. If one thinks otherwise, why live in the
country?

Things that create unity and express shared values, even when a
small minority of people disagree, are not destructive biases. In
fact, they're just the opposite. Of course, there will never be unani-
mous agreement on most things. But, far more dangerous — as one
example — would be to present values of other countries that are
fully contradictory to the values of Americans as being equal in
value to those widely accepted in America.

As another example, some might feel it is biased to teach the
Holocaust without concurrently making a case that there are
supposedly legitimate concerns about whether it actually took
place at all. Presenting the case made by Holocaust deniers as
merely being another opinion that could be potentially legitimate is
not unbiased teaching. It is educational malpractice.

It's the same for those denying the moon landing and similar
concrete events of history. Even though some holding opposing
views might complain, there is no educational value in presenting
false, even dangerous teachings, other than to refute them. Insisting

that "both" sides be presented equally, when one side has nothing to do with reality, is foolish. Other than to refute them, such "teaching" of two sides equally should be anathema to education.

Teachers who personally hold false and dangerous views, as determined by the actual facts of history in context, are another matter entirely. Such teachers can provide additional evidence of the failure of the education system.

University professors are a different matter. Many have what some might label as "extreme" biases. But it's college. They can have such biases — really, we all can — but professors should try to ensure that students know such opinions are that professor's personal biases which might rarely be held by others.

Of course, to make this more difficult, college students are not necessarily the best judges of what are biases that shouldn't be accepted, and statements and opinions that actually should be believed, and learned. Learning to know the difference is, in part, what college is all about. Unfortunately, students don't always get that right. (Neither do some of their professors.)

However, K-12 students are different from college students. Our younger students don't understand that they can have different opinions, even if the teacher tells them that they can. Very young students won't always understand that other opinions even exist unless they are carefully presented. Almost all such students are simply too young to separate the power of a teacher's personal beliefs, most especially in sensitive areas, from a properly balanced educational presentation.

This is not to say that, like everyone else, teachers cannot have and express their own opinions. They can. But they need to do it as a professional *teacher*, not as an advocate of a controversial social, political, or religious position. This is especially critical when teaching elementary school children, but even all the way through 12th grade. In spite of what many think, even high schoolers are not fully ready to distinguish between bias and fact.

College students should be better able to separate personal professorial biases that might be part of a general presentation of the subject matter. Sadly, even many college students are not yet mature enough to do it.

That case can be made for many full adults, too.

Regardless, from the times of Socrates, Plato, and Aristotle, education has taught examining multiple sides of thought, science, and life. To present only one side of all things in the world can be as bad as making the impossible attempt to present all sides totally equally.

Education isn't easy. That's why knowledgeable, capable, and caring teachers are so valued. There will always be wonderful teachers — especially at the K-12 level. But there are simply not enough of them.

We'll take a brief look at three of the dangerous school indoctrinations we mentioned previously. It's important to realize that, even though some originally had recognizable names, the names of some are now different today. They may not be known by their original names. Nonetheless, their beliefs and teachings are quietly integrating into many classrooms today.

****

CRITICAL RACE THEORY.

Let's start by taking a quick look at Critical Race Theory. Some have identified this as an offshoot of the more general Critical Theory, which we don't discuss here.

From the Britannica.com website, we find some insights into this movement:

> *Critical race theory is an intellectual movement and a framework of legal analysis according to which (1) race is a culturally invented category used to oppress people of colour and (2) the law and legal institutions in the United States are inherently racist insofar as they function to create and maintain social, political, and economic inequalities between white and nonwhite people.*

It adds:

Critical race theory evolved from the critical legal studies movement, which examined how the law and legal institutions serve the interests of the wealthy. It was also influenced by the insight of (then) radical feminism that forms of domination and oppression may be exercised or manifested in seemingly innocuous and largely unnoticed social practices.

On the other hand, at News.Columbia.edu, we find this:

"Critical race theory and the essential scholarship it has advanced may challenge many long-held views, but that is what makes this work so urgent and necessary," said Columbia President Lee C. Bollinger (LAW'71). "I could not be more proud that it is taking place at Columbia. This is, after all, what makes universities such vital institutions in society."

At Imprimis.Hillsdale.edu, we find this taken from a lecture delivered at Hillsdale College on March 30, 2021:

The Department of Homeland Security was telling white employees they were committing "microinequities" and had been "socialized into oppressor roles." The Treasury Department held a training session telling staff members that "virtually all white people contribute to racism" and that they must convert "everyone in the federal government" to the ideology of "antiracism." And the Sandia National Laboratories, which designs America's nuclear arsenal, sent white male executives to a three-day reeducation camp, where they were told that "white male culture" was analogous to the "KKK," "white supremacists," and "mass killings." The executives were then forced to renounce their "white male privilege" and write letters of apology to fictitious women and people of color.

To try summarizing the damage of Critical Race Theory (CRT), we can say that, rather than working to eliminate racism, it defines many additional things as evidence of racism. Worse, it appears to assign blame to the entire white race in America, regardless of actual support or lack thereof for Blacks or other races. It defines white people as being inherently racist. It wants them to "recognize" their inherent racism, apologize, and make concrete amends.

It doesn't eliminate racism. It *causes* racism.

It is not necessary to actually use the name, Critical Race Theory, when promulgating this philosophy. For its proponents' purposes, it's only necessary that its principles are faithfully taught. Some educators have been caught saying to change its name in order to continue teaching it, and that is what has been happening.

CRT enshrines racism, especially towards white people. Yet it has been an American principle for a long time that bias towards *any* race is racism. In many cases, racism is banned by both law and morality.

This is dangerous to the American culture and country. Children learning and practicing such racism as they grow up will continue to pass it on as adults. Most dangerously, these things can later be passed on as these children become teachers themselves.

In the case of white children, they are taught that the faults of racism are traceable to their "privilege" personally — even if they don't quite understand what their teacher is talking about.

This is increasingly widespread. In some cases, its teaching is even *required* by the government in its own departments. Today, its tenets can be found at all levels of education, from pre-school on up.

Those who support the tenets of CRT don't often respond to criticism other than by denying or ignoring any issues raised. They move on to talk about something else. Many have said that it isn't actually being taught in schools at all, other than at universities or specialized schools. (It was once said to just be seen at law schools.)

Should this be a concern at all?

Absolutely, it should be. It has the potential to destroy the country by pitting one race or one class against another. It has already been doing that. Those who disagree might want to look more closely at what CRT specifically teaches and at how it's being taught.

Although it's being banned in places, it can be difficult or impossible to eliminate. Remember that Critical Race Theory, or CRT, is often not taught under that name, especially since there has been so much pushback on it. Sometimes it is being taught under no name at all. It becomes difficult for anyone to ban something that purportedly doesn't exist.

Through teachers who strongly support its beliefs, it can metastasize into other forms. It can then become so closely integrated into day-to-day teaching of all subjects that it is no longer easily recognizable. In that way, it continues.

Many Chinese-Americans see frighteningly close parallels to how China's Cultural Revolution began and progressed. Also noted are its clear Marxist dangers.

Critical Race Theory is among the most dangerous elements that have been introduced to America's schools. The alarm is sounded by many people, but will that be enough to stop it? It is too easy to teach without identifying its elements as part of CRT. Only by careful attention to what is being taught in the classroom might this be identified in its coming new forms and eliminated.

Most Chinese immigrants who came to America for its freedoms do not want to see happen in America what happened — and is still happening — in China. It is frightening to many of them. Too many already see things that too closely reflect precisely what happened in China — much of which is still happening there today.

CRT has gained a foothold so quickly in America that one might suggest that China itself has been involved in its influence and spread. Although definitive evidence is still missing in those potential involvements, it is not missing elsewhere. Indeed, it appears that China has had far greater involvement in the influence of American schools and, especially, universities than most people know.

Among other sources, see Mike Zhao's book about this: *Critical Race Theory and Woke Culture: America's Dangerous Repeat of China's Cultural Revolution* (2022; Liberty Hill Publishing).

****

THE 1619 PROJECT.

This reframing of American history has brought out strong feelings on both sides of the proposed framework. It says that America's founding was actually at the arrival of a ship in 1619 with more than 20 slaves from Africa on it.

At criticalrace.org/1619-project, we find this summary of the 1619 Project:

> *The central premise [of the 1619 Project] is that America was not founded in 1776, or in the early colonies, or when the Constitution was ratified. According to this new interpretation, the functional founding of America occurred when the first enslaved Africans arrived on the North American continent. Further, the authors claim, the colonists fought the Revolutionary War primarily to protect the slave trade. First published in August 2019 by New York Times Magazine, the 1619 Project "aims to reframe the country's history by placing the consequences of slavery and the contributions of Black Americans at the very center of the United States' national narrative." Activists have proposed the 1619 Project as history curriculum in elementary, secondary, and higher education.*
>
> *In response, a growing number of historians, scholars, and critics have written about some of the logical fallacies, false equivalencies, and historical errors in the 1619 Project.*

At its introduction, the year 1619 was referred to as "the true founding" of America. Sometime later, both the New York Times and Nikole Hannah-Jones, its author, changed that, but only after a lot of pushback on that divisive and wrong statement.

Here is a statement related to the 1619 Project in *The New York Times Magazine* on August 18, 2019:

> *What if, however, we were to tell you that this fact, which is taught in our schools and unanimously celebrated every Fourth of July, is wrong, and that the country's true birth date, the moment that its defining contradic-*

tions first came into the world, was in late August of 1619? Though the exact date has been lost to history (it has come to be observed on Aug. 20), that was when a ship arrived at Point Comfort in the British colony of Virginia, bearing a cargo of 20 to 30 enslaved Africans. Their arrival inaugurated a barbaric system of chattel slavery that would last for the next 250 years. This is sometimes referred to as the country's original sin, but it is more than that: It is the country's very origin.[1]

There are numerous articles and books refuting this reframing of American history. They are clear that it is *not* the correct foundation of the country.

There has also been pushback on the claim and credibility of anything purporting to be the unbiased historical competency of Nikole Hannah-Jones. In an earlier college paper, she allegedly wrote, *"The white race is the biggest murderer, rapist, pillager, and thief of the modern world."* Such blatant racism is an integral part of her beliefs and is also part of the 1619 Project.[2]

People frequently write things that have no foundation in fact, or has behind it some seriously damaging thinking. Here, that is racism itself.

The fact that such writings exist and have always existed is one thing. It's certainly people's right to write whatever they want with their own opinions, as I do here. However, when such wrong, damaging, and blatantly racist writings find their way into multiple K-12 public schools as a supposedly legitimate part of their classes, we must take action to protect our children and the country.

- We must immediately push back to stop these things and to remove them from public education, especially at the K-12 levels;
- We must also consider declaring education dead, as I do here, especially where schools continue to promote these things. Consider what you will find in this book, as well as the past decades of data, before you do. Parents must do all they can to correct such falsehoods in their children who have already been exposed to these kinds of damaging indoctrinations.

The 1619 Project is but one example of recent ways to promote divisiveness. Instead, we must promote an understanding of the commonalities in this country and of the respect and acceptance of others. Those were things that this country used to work towards, and should still be doing today. Sure, the country has had and still has problems. But enshrining problems does nothing to solve them. Nor does it help to promote caring along with a national commonality and morality among all Americans.

Fully changing the history of the founding of America is not education. We don't have to deny that certain events may have occurred, but we must fully push back against things that create divisiveness and hurt the shared pride and history of the actual founding of the country.

The President's Advisory 1776 Commission was created to push back against this. It's January 2021 report, simply called *The 1776 Report*, is available online. When President Biden took office, he immediately shut down the commission.

★★★★

CRITICAL GENDER THEORY is less well understood by many people, especially parents. This was touched on in the last section. It suggests this concept:

> *"Gender is a sociological concept, that is based on the fact that relations between men and women are socially and culturally constructed. The theory of gender holds that there is a socially constructed sex based on differentiated social roles and stereotypes in addition to anatomical, biological sex, which is innate."*
>
> *Elsewhere, we read, "Biological differences should not be denied, of course, but those differences should not be a fate."*[3]

This is a formalized concept and teaching that sheds doubt on the strict biological nature of male and female beings. A tangent but related belief, and actionable addition, is that of pushing for child transgender support in transitioning to another sex/gender. Some schools have had explicit policies so that any discussions an educator might have with a child about this are kept away from any awareness or involvement of the child's parents.

Some K-12 public educational institutions have indeed specifically written such secrecy into its guidelines. A failure of parents to act in "support" of the child's desire to change has, at times, been referred to as abuse.

Actually, any abuse is on the other end of this where young children are supported, even without the knowledge of their parents, in making life-altering bodily changes. In some cases, this can involve the permanent removal of still developing body parts of teenage children when doctors and others work to (try to) change a child's gender from one to another.

These things do not belong in any school. Some don't even belong outside of schools. They're damaging wherever they're found. Congress has recently been involved trying to give parents rights in a number of educational areas including being told when discussions with their child occur at school.

Life altering gender-changing decisions should be made when the child is no longer a child. Yet, even then, so many negative outcomes have already been reported that, in most cases, it should be anathema at any stage of a person's life.

Many people suggest that, both in and out of schools, *"Children are being fed 'propaganda' to convince them to undergo such 'severe' treatments."*[4]

I'd better mention that some parents, not just schools, are pushing, encouraging, or allowing their children to change genders. Some are taking their lead from what they hear from others. It likely won't be for many years until such parents see what serious harm was done. (Of course, they may also be ensuring they won't have any grandchildren.)

Money is certainly being made by hospitals and doctors who are involved in these procedures, some of which are now done on preteens. There is much on this topic elsewhere. It's brought up here as ongoing evidence of public education's involvement in some *non-educational* and often damaging activities which are today seen at increasing numbers of schools.

Note that teachers who refuse to keep parents in the dark about what is going on with their children, often due to their personal religious beliefs, have been fired. California is one such state where this has been seen.

****

SEXUALLY EXPLICIT MATERIAL.

One more thing. Sexually explicit reading materials are in both classrooms and school libraries today. Some include library novels with sexually specific materials that can be arguably categorized as soft or hard core pornography — however that may be defined. These are materials that are widely rejected by parents. They should not be permitted in schools at *any grade level*.

Such materials are widely available outside of schools, so they are easily available if parents inexplicably want it for their children. But there is never a legitimate educational purpose to have this kind of graphic material in drawings, photos, or books *in any school — but especially at the K-12 level*.

I'll add that increasing numbers of these materials have already found their way into *children's sections* at a number of public libraries.

This has recently become a major topic of parental concern at school board meetings (public libraries, too). Videos show some parents being cutoff as they tried reading from some of the books that are available to young children at school. Yet, though available to children, such graphic excerpts are effectively prohibited at some school board meetings where adults are primarily in attendance.

The perennial problem with banning pornography is defining exactly what it is. Justice Potter Stewart's famous 1964 comment, *"I know it when I see it,"* actually describes reasoning commonly used by most people today — and not necessarily just for "obscene" materials. (Does the cultural concept of obscenity even still exist today?)

While Justice Potter's comment may not be good for judicial writings — its subjectivity is quite imprecise for a Supreme Court ruling — it is how many people do judge things in everyday life. It's how parents often make (non-pornography related) judgements about what their children see and do.

But here, we need something more concrete. After all, I once heard someone judge a piece of well-written prose describing a non-sexual, gentle romantic kiss (with fully clothed people) to be pornographic. I would hope that judgement might be excessive, even for most conservative people.

Nonetheless, because of the audience in schools, the definition for these things must be more restrictive than it would be in other settings. I won't be wading in to such a definition here, but what most parents consider pornographic, or inappropriate for their children, simply does not belong in schools. Parents should have a strong say in this. These are their children. In almost all cases, their opinions should hold sway. Although there are those who will strongly argue otherwise, there is truly no substantive and justifiable educational value in any of this.

Health and biology classes can certainly present a simple, straightforward presentation on specific biology to students of appropriate age. However, dragging it on by sinking into "performance art," adding unnecessarily explicit graphics, and using other materials of legitimate parental concern have no place in K-12 schools.

> An aside: I just mentioned health classes. I suggest that all subject matter of these classes, including textbooks and materials, be monitored for the *accuracy and appropriateness* of the information they're presenting, not just related to any sex-related material.

Not too many years ago, sexually-explicit material was not an issue at all in schools. Anything along those lines simply weren't in schools at all, yet education was provided to students anyway. Therefore a lack of what many parents consider pornographic materials did not hurt education.

On the other hand, the presence of much of this — especially, but not exclusively, library materials and novels — can hurt the solid development, maturation, and what should be an appropriate societally-shared morality among children. Wrongly-focused parents who feel their young children should be allowed to see and read whatever they want are easily able to do that at home without forcing its availability on others.

It's easy to get this material outside of school. It's almost impossible to keep such materials away from children once it's available in school libraries — or in actual classrooms.

Although others clearly don't understand this, such material really can do damage to children, even to older ones. But let's look beyond children.

There are plenty of *adults* whose addiction to pornography has destroyed their marriages, along with other damage. It's a serious issue among many adults. Some have entered counseling for it.

If it can be that serious for adults, why in the world are we offering these materials so early to our children as though it's normal and good?

No matter what agenda-laden people want to argue, there is no educational value offered by it. Added to that, there are massive numbers of parents who simply don't want it in schools. A small group of agenda-pushers should not override those parents.

(Eliminating classic works of literature that *should* be in schools is another issue. I'm not discussing that separate issue here.)

Hopefully, more educators than we are aware quietly support parents at schools where all this has been happening. But, too many others, including school librarians, are doing the opposite. Some actively promote these materials, even to very young students.

****

The above discussions are relatively brief on these few, serious topics. However, all this should be a flag as to what is happening. None of these indoctrinations belong in schools — or elsewhere.

But why bring up all these things unless I'm going to do a fuller presentation on them? It's because I must acknowledge their existence and, with many others, issue the warning. That's what I've done. It is indeed serious.

However, for many people, these things are the crux of what is wrong with schools today. For those, much more about these things can be found in other books and resources.

Remember that, in addition to the potentially permanent damage to students and future educators, in both body and mind, these things involve usurping the authority of parents to raise their own children.

The fact that agendas such as these are now being actively promoted in schools across the country — there will certainly be others introduced in the future — is yet another compelling reason why we can clearly say that *legitimate education* is dead.

More than that, many schools are not just dead as institutions of learning, they have become *actively dangerous* to your children — and to you.

When a country's education system works to tear down the country in which it exists, it has clearly become an enemy of that country.

These kinds of damaging indoctrinations have been part of even worse happenings in authoritarian regimes in the world, even down to today. Where evidence of such regimes is seen in one form of indoctrination, others easily follow.

This is just one reason why education is no longer functioning. However, this book primarily looks at the other reasons.

***

How can we keep minority-held "extremist" biases with the accompanying frameworks for indoctrination out of schools? It's tough when we find out the true animus of some educators, especially those involved in the hiring process.

For example, in 2022, a Connecticut elementary school administrator appeared to be caught on video saying, *"…if they're Catholic — conservative…You don't hire them,"* apparently adding, *"If someone is raised hardcore Catholic, it's like, they're brainwashed — you can never change their mindset."*

In the video recording, the administrator apparently says that he does not hire people over the age of 30. (They're likely to be conservative.) He appears to clearly say that he does all that he can not to hire anyone with politically conservative leanings. In the video, he appears to be very outspoken in not supporting the educational concerns of conservative parents.[5]

Although this is far more common at *all* levels of education than people know — pre-school through college — it is rarely caught on tape as convincingly as this administrator appears to have been.

A February 8, 2023 report in Canada's *National Post* reported that a 16-year-old 11th grade high school student was arrested when he returned to school after being told that he could not be there. His crime for being told to stay away? In accordance with his Catholic Christian beliefs, the *National Post* reported that the student *"believes there are only two genders, that people can't switch genders, and that male students shouldn't use girls' washrooms."*

In an interview, the student said, *"I got suspended for comments made during a class discussion."*[6]

But what is particularly surprising is that this happened at a Canadian *Catholic school.* The Catholic Church accepts what the student believes so, if the facts of this story are correct, this appears to be particularly egregious. Perhaps there is more to this.

These things point to the pervasiveness of these teachings in schools today — and not just in public schools. Although a number of non-public schools are still educationally strong, others can also have serious educational deficiencies.

2. CAN AMERICA LAST?

Let's start with this:

> "*Freedom is a fragile thing and is never more than one generation away from extinction. It is not ours by inheritance; it must be fought for and defended constantly by each generation, for it comes only once to a people. Those who have known freedom, and then lost it, have never known it again.*" –Ronald Reagan.

The "one generation" to which Reagan referred (above), is the time period of a generation. It does not refer to a particular generation per se, although, depending on the generation, it could refer to that, too. Either way, we must question whether we are today living within the "one generation." We must wonder whether we are now living through the extinction of our freedom, or whether we can succeed in defending that freedom for one more generation.

In this chapter, I'm going to discuss an issue related to that concern. Does the death of education mean the eventual death of America, too?

As this chapter begins, some might be thinking that none of this relates to the main subject of education. It absolutely does.

Defending freedom cannot be done without an educated electorate who understand what freedom actually is. There is credible doubt whether an understanding of liberty and freedom exists among enough Americans today.

> An aside: One recent consideration and discussion has been that, through the development and support of select school-related socio-political and other programs, or by proxy attacks on others — including a broader attack on the fabric of America (note China's intrusiveness through TikTok, as just one of several examples) — it is likely that China may not only be clandestinely undermining education, but actively targeting the total demise of America itself.
>
> One decorated historian sees additional dangers in the current period in America. As have others, he offers a comparison with China's Cultural Revolution under Mao Zedong (1966-1976). Some have even been warning of a possible first-strike nuclear attack on America.[1]
>
> Based on my knowledge of history and of events taking place at the time of this writing, as well as with my background in the military, I caution that such possibilities should not be dismissed lightly.
>
> Of added concern, China's education system is still functioning. Ours is not.

***

Can any country survive for long with a truly broken education system?

None can.

As we previously heard, a bad education system directly damages people and their families. It can damage all aspects of their lives. On a broader level, it damages culture and society. Beyond that, it can take down countries.

Even if public education can be brought back to life, it's unlikely that the majority of people currently involved in it can do it. They and their predecessors have tried to get it working right for decades, actually far longer. Not only is it no better, it's become worse.

Let's pause for a moment to look at a list of things that have happened in oppressive regimes throughout history. It's a list of things that we don't want happening in America. The bottom line is that a badly flawed education system significantly contributes to each of these things. A reinvigorated and ethical public education system might be able to fix it — were it possible to save public education — and that is beyond doubtful.

Those who only want to get back to talking about education, be patient. We'll be there soon. But what you must understand is that everything here directly relates to education. It all does.

Totalitarian governments are authoritarian and oppressive. They endeavor to run all aspects of their country. They are not democratic. They do not tolerate dissent. Let's begin by looking at what has been seen in many totalitarian governments:

1. Formerly accepted books, even literary classics, are banned from schools and libraries. Reading or even just possessing such books can have dire consequences.
2. Book burning has taken place when books go against changing societal or governmental values.
3. Statues of past heroes and others whom the people had valued are torn down.
4. History is revised to suit what powerful, agenda-driven people, including those wielding absolute governing power, want to be taught. That rarely reflects the fullness of what happened. Historical revisionism replaces *actual* history. Both today and in the past, this has happened far more often than most people are aware.

5. Whether by voluntarily cooperating or by being compelled to do so, the news media offers just one side, twisting or entirely omitting truth. This often goes hand-in-hand with changes in history and with a direct control of education in schools.

6. Universities prohibit speakers and books that do not support newly demanded, frequently changing norms. Only professors who closely adhere to those norms can freely teach and speak. Most others must teach or speak with caution, even trepidation. Classroom teaching is sometimes regulated to conform to governmental or new societally approved norms.

7. There is a government takeover of the kindergarten through high school education system. The government dictates its own mandates and teachings in textbooks and classrooms. Schools at all levels can be forced to follow legislated or dictatorial demands designed to enforce the personal desires of dictators or groups of people wielding power and influence. Textbook publishers are forced to include the government's one-sided policy demands. Such revised textbooks seldom provide a balanced and accurate presentation of their subject. New laws, based on such beliefs, give added force to such mandates and changes. The protests of parents are often ignored. Sometimes, concerned parents themselves can be arrested.

8. Businesses conduct business only when the government allows them to open, and only when meeting standards that may have nothing to do with the business. Those not conforming are arrested or financially ruined. Many businesses must stop operating.

9. There is flagrant corruption in elections, if elections happen at all. Election processes are changed to benefit those doing the changing, not to the neutral benefit of voters themselves. Those running for office might be running their own elections.

10. Penalties/punishments/condemnations are doled out for unapproved speech, business activities, even wrong thinking should someone find out that you have expressed unapproved thoughts or opinions. Such consequences may be inflicted directly by those people who disagree with those unapproved thoughts or opinions. Punishment can also come directly from the government itself.

11. Children are told to report on and turn in their parents. Neighbors also turn in neighbors. In both cases, the reporting may be for simply exercising what had previously been valued rights.

12. People and their families may be attacked in their homes, possibly losing their jobs, for "wrong" voting — or for supporting unapproved causes. The government itself can heavy-handedly intrude into homes of non-violent and innocent people, wrongly arresting them in front of their frightened children and spouse.

13. The clandestine monitoring of speech and behavior by the government — both on and offline — widely occurs, violating laws which supposedly prohibit such actions.

14. People are attacked for *past* speech and behaviors, occurring decades in the past, even when they were children or teens — and even if it had been fully acceptable at the time. New laws and notions of what is acceptable can punish, even criminalize, past behavior. Statutes of limitations are thrown out entirely. Additional repercussions can come from the government, or from people wanting to handle these "transgressions" on their own.

15. Former rights of the people are gradually taken away, first unofficially, then formally. Those include but are not limited to free speech and freedom of religion.

16. Wherever possible, dissent is crushed and punished.

17. Many entirely innocent people are locked up in prisons. Others spend many years in prison for what were

previously minor crimes. Trials to convict them are
sometimes in what are effectively kangaroo courts of law.
To "prove" their innocence, many people lose everything
they have, including their homes, their families, and
sometimes their lives.

Even though the above list was originally meant to apply to current
and historical situations in other countries, many of you undoubtedly recognize many or all of those things taking place in America
today.

At the time of this writing, instances of *all* of those things (and
more) are indeed happening in America. As just one example,
weren't people at one time supposed to be innocent *until proven*
guilty?

As said before, many immigrants and refugees from totalitarian and authoritarian governments, including China, will
readily recognize those things as elements of something much
worse coming. Much of that was "normal" in countries from
where they came. Most learned how to survive within the
cultural and governmental abuse and control where they previously lived.

Legally or otherwise, many escaped to make their way to
America.

Even though this is America, upon arrival, many immigrants
still expected corruption. After all, isn't that what defines all
governments? Many are genuinely suspicious of the American
government when they first arrive. I've seen that in immigrants
myself. After all, it's what they've always known government to be.
Eventually, most have been relieved to find that America is
different — or it used to be.

Today, America's culture has been moving away from what it
was in the past. It's been moving dangerously closer to those other
countries from which so many immigrants were able to leave — or
escape.

People are not putting all this together in their minds yet. It's
not likely they've heard that entire list (above) publicly reported in
recent years. But, in full or in part, each item in it has been repeat-

edly reported in America. Let's take a quick look at just one point on that long list.

When protestors first tore down statues in recent times, those doing it said they were doing away with monuments to slave owners. That wasn't true. Also torn down were statues honoring people who fought *against* oppression, *against* slavery.

America's Founding Fathers, including George Washington, Thomas Jefferson, even Abraham Lincoln, all came under attack. Responding to this new agenda, some cities called for and approved renaming schools which had previously been named to honor the great leaders and founders of America.

Whether they knew it or not, those who tore down statues were not doing it so that slave owners would not be remembered. They were tearing down the foundational history of the country itself.[2]

In other countries, statue desecration or removal sometimes accompanied the takeover of those countries and their governments — and the start of another. Those new countries and governments may eventually become ruled by tyrants. Under their new oppression, people lose all freedoms. Many suffer and die. History has shown repeated instances of this.

Throughout history, such governments have done all the above things to their people and more.

Currently, the American people are doing it to themselves.

Note that totalitarian and authoritarian governments are different things, although both operate in opposition to a healthy democracy. However, especially in recent times, the terms are sometimes used interchangeably. "Totalitarian" has sometimes been used to describe a recent shift in America where just one political position is allowed. Those on the other side of that position are persecuted. But America isn't fully there yet. Perhaps there is still hope to turn it around.

Some dangerous people demand that people on the wrong side of whichever position is currently allowed, be fired. Too often such dangerous, anti-American people succeed as companies capitulate to their demands. Such people's actions attack what is enumerated in the American Constitution's Bill of Rights.

Sometimes, these people have shown up at the homes of those

with unapproved thinking to threaten and harass them — and their families. That behavior certainly appears to slant towards totalitarianism. One significant difference is that totalitarianism is practiced by governments. In recent times, it sometimes seems to originate from the people themselves.

Those doing these things have been indoctrinated that their position is somehow right and just. A large, seemingly controlling number of American people don't appear to know what they're doing and where all this is heading. Or perhaps they've been manipulated by people whom they don't even know exist.

Those who do not learn from history are indeed doomed to repeat it. But note that that refers to the *mistakes* of history. The things of history must also be learned so that we can keep good things going when we see opportunities for that. But we can know neither the good nor bad of history without studying it. Further, we can only learn from *actual* history, not revisionist history.

Many in the media seem to be heading in a direction that supports the loss of American ideals. If that continues, any replacement government, or foreign takeover, will not have much left to do. It will largely have already been done for them.

In very recent times, concerns about "socialism" have been widely discussed. Some excellent books point to its development and the accompanying concerns over it.

Yet, in spite of those denying it, wrongly pointing to other countries in the world with purportedly working socialist systems (they aren't really working), there are already elements of socialism in place in America. Increasing numbers of politicians and people support it. Socialism is a problem in itself. Worse, it is a step closer to authoritarianism and then totalitarianism.

Although totalitarian governments operate on the other side of socialism, the things that both share are concerns even before a full move beyond socialism. However, I won't be discussing these things in detail here. It would take an entire book to do that.

But there is good news here. There are already plenty of books with information and warnings about a potentially coming American socialism. Such books are available to read today.

Regardless, we have to ask ourselves why people who have torn down statues don't know that the people of history should be understood in the context of their times. Isn't that how we would want those in the future to understand *us?* Shouldn't those taking part in these activities have been taught these things somewhere? Where should that have happened?

Yes, they should have learned about all those things. It should have happened *in school.* That is what education is supposed to be doing. It is a failure of education when legitimate history isn't being taught.

But that's what has been happening, isn't it? Or do some people understand all those things, but intentionally choose to ignore them? Are they supporting someone's different, but dangerous agenda?

Could it actually be their longer-term intention to overthrow the government, whether through violence or by some silent scheme? That is an extreme suggestion and one I am hopeful I don't have to believe. On the other hand, looking at history, it is part of the road where all this has led before.

Therefore, I can only go along with the first suggestion: a failure of the education system, especially in middle school and high school. That failure includes not only failures to teach things of great consequence, but can also include a conscious twisting, ignoring, and even fabricating of the facts of history. Morals themselves have long since been relegated to the bin of impermissibles.

This failure is not recent. It has been happening for many decades. However, its failures have recently accelerated. Most people don't see it. Most people assume that they are themselves competently educated. After all, most have already completed school and have been taught all they need to know. But people can't know what they don't know.

Of course, there will always be some bias in education because there is always a normal, hopefully mild bias in teachers and books. However, especially in kindergarten through 12th grades, efforts should be made to present the subject matter as unbiasedly as possible.

Most people feel that any bias should be on the side of support for the country, rather than in actively tearing it down as appears to be happening in too many places today. In the past, teachers were not as openly political and biased as they have been in recent times. That is especially true at the universities. Multiple studies have shown that there is now an enormous imbalance of political views in university classrooms. We heard about this earlier.

Why would educators feel that it's legitimate to teach things that tear down the country when democracy and the Bill of Rights continue to exist? That will eventually lead to the total loss of the country itself.

Of course, education is tasked with passing on subject matter knowledge. But, in the past, it has also given students an understanding, even pride, in the foundational rights, liberties, and freedoms of America. Why would students ever want to support America — let alone serve in its military or give themselves to others in service to their country — when they only hear teachers demean it? We destroy ourselves by allowing education free rein to do that.

On and around December 20, 2022, articles in the *Daily Mail, the Washington Examiner,* the *New York Post,* the *Independent,* and many others pointed to a new (California) Stanford University guide designed to eliminate "harmful language."[3] Among other disturbing suggestions, the university recommended not using the term "American." They reportedly called it too imprecise and not in accordance with its Elimination of Harmful Language Initiative. (They prefer using "U.S. citizen.") Needless to say, U.S. military veterans, along with countless others, strenuously objected to the elimination of the word "American."

Note that the terms, "America" and "American," will continue to be used in this book.

The country isn't perfect. It will never be perfect. No country ever has been. But that doesn't justify failing to teach actual history or creating and teaching a false or twisted narrative. Such narratives cannot build faith in and caring for the country. Why is this happening?

We now see large numbers of the population missing key components of knowledge, understanding, and respect for their own country. In large part, those things were supposed to have been provided in their education. In the extreme, some of that potentially misled population may even then be led into anarchy or into open revolt against their government rather than using long established and peaceful processes to make changes.

***

Many countries exist for just a short time, although that time is sometimes measured in centuries. Some are conquered. Others simply change so much that they are essentially new countries.

Looking at what is happening today, one can be forgiven for observing that America may be next — or at least among several countries that have lost the foundations upon which they stood in the past.

Although America can still recover, the chances of its doing so are becoming less likely if it continues on its current destructive path.

Destruction of a country can be done using means which are seemingly directed towards legitimate issues, but which are actually designed to cause internal strife. Focusing on these other issues can hide what is actually happening.

Those involved in promoting divisiveness — potentially instigated by other countries or ideologies — don't know that they're actually being manipulated. They can cover their tracks by accusing their opposition of doing what they themselves are doing. The accusation is often enough. Evidence is not needed.

Enemy countries know that the best way to destroy a country is to destroy it from within. In the past, even the United States has done the same thing in efforts to make changes in other countries. As have other countries, the U.S. has previously attempted to support discontent and protests in those countries in which it wants to bring about change. During wartime, it's what PSYOP [Psychological Operations] units of the military do. It's an important component of the military.

But when it's happening to us, people have no idea. They don't have the training or awareness to recognize what is happening.

Although book burnings are still rare here, they have been happening in America nonetheless. What is not rare is the banning of certain books and movies deemed unacceptable by private corporations that sell books. Those bannings are effectively *digital* book burnings. Just like real burnings, people know which ones are being digitally burned or banned. They understand that, if they don't avoid unapproved books and videos, they may suffer consequences.

Those books, videos, and movies don't necessarily contain anything terrible, just words, ideas, or images that contradict the political or sociological agendas of the banning entities, or of outside people supporting those entities. Sometimes, this includes American corporations. More specifically, these books and videos contradict the ideological agendas of the *individuals* who are in a position of influence and power, including owners and administrators of those corporations. It can also include aggressive "customers" with their own agendas.

But it's even worse.

Often, the public, *even the authors, publishers, and video producers themselves,* have no idea what even caused the digital burnings and bannings. People might hear they contain some generically categorized "hate speech," but which are unidentified, or identified only using definitions made up by those doing the bannings.

If an author or publisher is lucky, someone might tell them what was the specific, flagged concern in the digitally banned book or video. Most companies don't want to give actual specifics since that can lead to defenses of the materials or lawsuits made easier because the author or producer victim knows what caused the banning.

All of this has a chilling effect on writers and video producers. More generally, it has a chilling effect on what was formerly known as "free speech" since no one is exactly sure what led to the digital burnings in the first place. Numerous other companies, schools, and groups may then pile on to the bannings and burnings.

Note that here, I do not refer to those inappropriate books that parents want banned from K-12 classrooms and libraries. Those are a different issue.

***

Many feel the divisiveness in the country has been the worst in 150 years. Not many months prior to this book being written, words were being heard that most had assumed — and had hoped — would never be heard again — words such as "civil war" and "secession."

While those things remain highly unlikely at this moment in time, the mere mention of those words spoken in seriousness is cause for grave concern.

Regardless of its imperfections, America has been the best country in the world. It may have become a cliché in some circles, but America truly has been a beacon of freedom. If it were not, millions of immigrants would not be coming. They come because of the goodness and strength of America. People don't run to tyranny. They run to freedom. They also come for the chance at a better life.

But, at this particular moment, America is not the country it once was. Will its people be able to stop this new momentum spiraling away from its founding principles? At this moment, I am not hopeful.

Is this all part of what one television commentator worrisomely called *"late empire insanity?"* Is the "empire" of America now in its late stages of final existence, as some have already suggested? When we look back at the history of the decline and fall of past empires, there are certainly reasons to be concerned.

***

The loss of a healthy education system is just one part of the broader package and pattern of the loss of the principles upon which an earlier America had been founded.

Even though the country's potential loss would be of much greater importance, here I only offer witness to part of that loss: the loss of a competent public education system. That can extend to some non-public schools, too.

Nonetheless, I'm well aware that, unless things turn around, the much greater loss of the country itself may indeed be on the horizon.

Today, it seems that many Americans don't want to be an American at all.

2a. THE DEATH OF COLLEGE EDUCATION

As you will also read elsewhere in this book, colleges are a mess. But, since this chapter talks about political considerations, it's the right place to bring up something especially important.

Universities used to be places where students could consider and debate multiple sides of issues raised in classes. That has always been one part of the process for developing open-minded critical thinking skills. Students could develop respect for others even though they all held opposing views. They realized that they could engage in (respectful) discussion and debate with those with whom they disagreed, while still sharing in things on which they did agree.

Many welcomed the back and forth discussions. In the end, students could still hang around together and share social activities. Most could remain friends regardless of different points of view on life.

But no more.

Today, it is increasingly impossible to debate multiple sides of an issue on many college campuses, whether inside or outside of a classroom, because vast numbers of professors today hold immovably to one side of the political spectrum. Students who disagree with such professors can see their grades drop — or worse.

Such students learn that they must keep their views to themselves if they expect to make it through school. Sharing their views with the wrong professors, or the wrong students, can be dangerous to their college survival — even to their physical safety. Learning itself can fall by the wayside. Students holding minority positions acquiesce to what they have to do and (temporarily) believe so they can finish their required classes and get a degree. No learning, just college survival. That's a lot of time and money for so little.

Therefore, full and sincere discussions and debates of sensitive topics rarely happen. Students are pushed into understanding that there is really just one acceptable side of a whole list of political and sociological topics. They also learn that it is not only acceptable, but sometimes all but required to reject even listening to the side of a topic with which they have learned they must disagree. Some students learn that it is not just permissible, but sometimes demanded to attack — even physically — those holding impermissible views.

All colleges are not like this, but enough are for this to be of serious concern. Frankly, I have become concerned about this issue even among some conservative colleges.

This is not what a college education used to be. Too few of those who have not attended college, or who completed their college education many years ago, realize what has happened. At the end of an expensive college education, many parents today wonder what happened. They wonder from where what they see as the corruption of the thinking, beliefs, morals, and behaviors of their children have come.

By then, it's too late. Such changes can last a lifetime. They can lead to losses that too often include a loss of family and friends.

People used to think that so-called conservative colleges, even religious colleges, are safe havens from the one-sided political indoctrinations so much in evidence elsewhere. But that is not always the case.

Even such "safe" colleges can employ teachers whose thinking and beliefs align more with "unsafe" colleges and universities. Some colleges are still academically and culturally safe — but it's not easy for many people to definitively know which is which..

One article of December 7, 2022 was titled, *"Zero GOP Professors in nearly 3 Dozen University Departments across Multiple Schools, Survey Shows."*[1]

That article referenced an article in *The College Fix* of November 29, 2022.[2]

The College Fix examined the following universities: The Ohio State University, University of Nebraska-Omaha, University of North Carolina-Chapel Hill, University of Georgia, Cornell University, University of Oklahoma, and the University of Alaska-Anchorage.

Departments that were particularly analyzed were "primarily humanities departments."

Even though six of the seven states are considered Republican (New York is not), 92% of professors were Democrats. Just 8% of professors identified as Republican. In recent years, other studies have reflected similar figures.

What was sometimes a significant number in the study, other professors identified as something different, or were not overtly politically affiliated at all. The affiliations of some others could not be determined.

Nonetheless, the absence of one of the two major political parties in America can only do damage to a balanced education. That not only applies to the two dominant parties, but to the political beliefs of some smaller political parties.

One must also ask why university departments, along with Human Resources departments, are not hiring more conservative professors as an academic and sociological balance for their students.

In some cases, professorial applicants have been required to sign "diversity statements" forcing them to accept a political position about which some may strongly disagree. (Note that the name, "diversity statements," is often a euphemism that doesn't necessarily have anything to do with actual diversity.)

Regardless, that leaves students without an understanding of an entire side of political belief in the country. Political parties among educators were never evenly balanced, but what we see today is an extreme that has already done likely irreversible damage in its failure to provide a balanced education to students. Students' college-developed beliefs are especially influenced by work in the humanities which have a particularly egregious imbalance.

Some of those students, now indoctrinated with a single political belief, then go on to become teachers at all levels, including in K-12 schools. K-12 students then develop their own one-sided thinking.

Jennifer Kabbany, editor-in-chief of *The College Fix* said:

"We've already seen the retiring old guard of classically liberal professors being rapidly replaced by budding scholars trained up in critical race theory and diversity, equity and inclusion dogmas."

That same College Fix article found that at the University of Alaska, Anchorage, "Democrat Professors outnumber Republican ones 14 to 1."

"Democrats outnumber Republicans 98 to 1 in Cornell humanities departments."

Democratic professors outnumber Republicans by a ratio of 16 to 1... (at) 14 humanities and STEM [science, technology, engineering, and mathematics] departments at the University of North Carolina at Chapel Hill.

"Five out of eleven University of Georgia humanities departments have zero Republican professors."

Separate surveys of colleges outside the seven listed here showed data often indicating similar imbalances.

One Republican professor at the University of Alaska had, in part, these comments:

"[In my opinion], the left has killed the liberal arts. They've replaced serious study of serious books with propaganda, intellectually light curriculum and grade inflation. Faculty in the liberal arts can't give a persuasive defense of the liberal arts anymore."

That professor added that the faculty bias then *"...shows up in students."*

Well, of course, it does.

In an article from 2019, *The College Fix* began with this observation: *"A survey of 1,000 Republican and Republican-leaning college students has found that nearly three-quarters of them have withheld their political views in class for fear their grades would suffer."*[3]

Note the terminology selected by the Alaska professor (at his request, he remained unnamed in the article): The left *"has killed"* the liberal arts. He may or may not have meant that literally. However, since this book talks about education being dead, his choice of words is revealing. It may not merely be a figure of speech by those who understand the situation in education today.

Addressing another seemingly racist judgment by some, one educated commentator wrote:

> "...there is nothing about race that makes someone smart or stupid, but there is something about the college experience — and whites are much more likely to go to college — that impairs the ability to think independently. Quite frankly, *many students have been intellectually raped by their professors.*"[4] [Emphasis added.]

***

Note that it is not simply the policies of colleges themselves that lead to students being indoctrinated in just one side of many issues. The fault also lies with the students themselves.

Beyond that, it further lies with the K-12 education/indoctrinations these students just completed, especially at the high school level.

A student poll reported in March 2023 by the Art & Science Group, a Baltimore-based consulting firm, found that one out of four high school students applying to colleges specifically excluded applying in entire states, regardless of the character of particular colleges in them. They applied to colleges situated in states with whose politics or sociological positions they agreed. Many more states were excluded by liberal-leaning students than by conservative-leaning students.

Although students have made such judgments in the past, in light of the strong divisions in America today, this becomes of added concern.[5]

To have so many students emerge from high schools with such pronounced, potentially immovable political views, does not bode well for openness to discuss and consider other viewpoints. It also cuts off potentially healthy relationships with others with whom they disagree on one or more issues.

Taken with everything else, this does not bode well to regain the formerly (mostly) united country of America, with its formerly (mostly) shared values, as we move into the future. Hard lines have already been drawn.

There is more on colleges later in the book.

2b. WHAT IS AN EDUCATED STUDENT?

Let's pause to consider the loss of well-rounded, educated people.

There's a difference between becoming an educated person and just "learning things." Today, while doing only a bit of the second (learning things), most students are really doing neither. Even when "learning things," such things are often separate and disconnected from everything else.

Students can babble such "things" back to teachers and parents. They can even demonstrate a grasp of them on exams. But rarely do they know the actual worth of what they've learned in their personal life, or in any connection with the whole of life in the world.

Really, I'm doubtful that large enough numbers of students in years past did either.

Students go through school motions for many years. But they often come out at the other end with what might be described as a least common denominator of life. They don't see that. They spent all their time being directed how and what to learn — being *taught*. Now, at its end, they finally know — well, they actually just "assume" — that they are, at last, a learned and educated person!

But they're not.

Indeed, this country has not put out truly educated and learned people for many years, if even then.

There are certainly educational exceptions. Catholic schools hung on to actual education far longer than did others. But, today, even they appear to be a mixed bag. In fact, in his worthwhile book, *Designed to Fail* (2005), Steve Kellmeyer refers to the significant collapse of the Catholic school system, especially including its formerly strong religious education, but also beyond.

Some other special schools can still put out (mostly) well-educated people. But public schools, where the vast numbers of Americans are educated? Rarely.

Only in scattered bastions do we find real education still being handed down. But there are now so few as to be ineffective in trying to push back against the overwhelming tide of educational mediocrity. Actually, the term "mediocrity" may give more credit to student graduates than their learning and preparedness for life warrant. (Can most graduates even define the word?)

Worse, defining what makes an "educated person" is no longer what it once was. *"Good!"* you say? *"Things are different! Life requires different skills and thinking today! Students today are indeed educated!"*

Of course, things *are* indeed different. Necessary skills today are different. But that is not how a truly educated person should be defined. Critical elements of an educated person are missing today.

"What are those missing elements you insist are missing? I say that nothing important is missing at all!" you and others might argue back.

Today, I'm not normally going to tell students to pursue a degree in the hard-to-define liberal arts or humanities. But I'm not going to tell them not to, either. If they are independently wealthy, it's certainly a worthy degree to consider. However, if one has to get a job and earn real money, such degrees can make life tough. There are fulfilling jobs one can get with such degrees, but they are often limited or low paid jobs — or such degrees must be combined with other more practical degrees or training.

The military is likely to use almost any college degree as part of its requirements for its officer corps. However, most people aren't entering the military today. Of course, there are other options for liberal arts graduates in addition to teaching. But, from a practical perspective, such degrees can make life harder.

Anyway, as we learned in the last chapter from that unnamed university professor, *"...the left has killed the liberal arts."* Therefore, being able to complete a liberal arts education, let alone a classical education, is very unlikely today, even when enrolling in a program by that name.

Why do I even bring this up?

> *"The term 'liberal arts' has long been used to describe the education of the mind, as opposed to mechanical or occupational education."*[1]

That's an important description because educating the mind — an important part of being a full, educated person — is often lost in many majors. Training a person to have an "educated mind," with the ability, interest, and excitement to learn and think improves a person's quality of life throughout all of life. But it doesn't often give people a good income. Although, with luck, having an "educated mind" can get a student into an occasionally good or interesting job, realistically it will only rarely make such students the money that they will need in order to have a good and secure life today.

How do we instill those qualities in our students without sacrificing the practicality of a "real" job or running a successful business? There is barely time in school for what are considered the basics, barely time for those classes that will give the skills necessary for people's lives today. How can more be squeezed in?

Within the current design of education today, it can't be. The current design has long since passed its limits and has been failing. So we resign ourselves to teaching "things," rather than developing what used to be fully educated students.

Do I suggest, for example, returning to the fundamentals of a classical education? Although I believe that such education can develop better rounded students than we have today, it is neither possible nor practical within today's system.

On the other hand, people today are missing the things that such an education can give, the "education of the mind." In many places, quality teachers no longer even exist to provide the benefits that such education used to provide.

On the other hand, listen to this: It will now make no sense to anyone when I say that some of the most valuable classes I took in high school, that helped me in later life — actually throughout *all* of my life — were my years taking Latin and Greek. Not just any Greek either. Nothing seemingly practical at all. *Homeric* Greek, the form of Greek that Homer used to write the Iliad and Odyssey. It's not even spoken in Greece. What good can that possibly be!

Furthermore, I didn't even do well in the classes, getting an occasional "D," well, more often some "Cs," and less commonly a "B" or two. Is it possible the value I got out of these classes were different from what the teachers evaluated when assigning grades? Yes, that's quite possible.

Clearly, the classes weren't always easy for me, nor were they for others. Yet the value to me, both practically and as a thinking person, was — and still is — immense.

As it should be, the value of such classes is beyond the intrinsics of the subject matter itself. Grades do not always reflect learning — at either end of the grading scale.

The traditional study of Latin and Greek is often thought to be tied in with religious or Christian studies. However, that is not always the case. My own Latin and Greek studies were quite secular. They just taught the languages, generally reading and writing only. (Note that language study is only one part of a classical education.)

I know most of you won't understand why I would say those two classes were of such value. Certainly, there are those who debate the value of a classical or liberal arts education today, especially on the side of those supporting its continuing existence. However, the tradeoffs in pursuing such degrees today generally leave us with a no-win scenario.

Today, I would only rarely recommend classical degree programs to incoming college students trying to decide on a major. That is even though, in my view, such teachings can be immensely valuable, truly close to indispensable for a fully educated person.

However, if education were not dead today, I would likely give different advice to new college students — assuming we still had something called "college" in a completely new education structure.

Nonetheless, I would still consider a classical education for many high school students.

Students today are truly missing an opportunity to move closer to becoming a fully "educated person" by missing the understandings and thinking they were formerly able to get as part of a classical education. There's not much to be done about that today. Only a few schools offer something of classical substance and many of those schools suffer from weaknesses in other areas of education.

Too many schools today can't even handle the teaching of basic skills: English, math, history, science, government, keyboarding.

Therefore, without a new system (which likely isn't possible), can we seriously talk about including what seem to be impractical and esoteric teachings, too?

Without a new system, we cannot. Importantly, as noted before, few of today's teachers would have the ability to effectively offer such teachings anyway. That's especially true among the newer generations of teachers and professors.

Students assume that, if they want to learn something, some teacher will step forward to teach it. But that's not always true.

Even though some teachers might do it, there's no certainty that such teachers even know what they're talking about. In many cases, when something is gone, it's gone.

That includes the ability to think and to understand the importance of a functioning, well-grounded morality. That includes the presence and understanding of personal virtue.

When the last native speaker of a language dies — as happens too frequently among native Americans — that language is lost and does not return. Such is the same with other areas of knowledge in education. It is already too late to regain much of the good we had in the past. There are only rarely competent teachers left to teach us, regardless of what some might say about their own competency.

Although educators and non-educators alike are happy to say they know what one is, defining a truly "educated student" today is generally an exercise in futility.

3. A NATION AT RISK

A reminder that all footnotes are available as endnotes at the back of the book.

In April 1983, the groundbreaking report, *A Nation At Risk*, was released. It offered a grim picture of both education and the direction of America as a result of education's failures. Among other things, it said:

> *"The educational foundations of our society are presently being eroded by a rising tide of mediocrity that threatens our very future as a Nation and a people."*

It went on to say:

> *"If an unfriendly foreign power had attempted to impose on America the mediocre educational performance that exists today, we might well have viewed it as an act of war. As it stands, we have allowed this to happen to ourselves. We have even squandered the gains in student achievement made in the wake of the Sputnik challenge. Moreover, we have dismantled essential support systems which helped make those gains possible. We*

have, in effect, been committing an act of unthinking, unilateral educational disarmament."

It gave us serious additional insights:

"Our society and its educational institutions seem to have lost sight of the basic purpose of schooling, and of the high expectations and disciplined effort needed to attain them."

"That we have compromised [our former commitment to schools and colleges] is, upon reflection, hardly surprising, given the multitude of often conflicting demands we have placed on our Nation's schools and colleges."

A Nation At Risk's observations are still true today, perhaps even more so.

Finally, these next words, also quoted from the report, suggest what caused, or at least significantly contributed, to the failure of this country's education system as we delayed reforms and, in the end, failed to implement anything effective at all:

"History is not kind to idlers."

And that is exactly what we have been.

This report was released in 1983! Why have some people just assumed that things have changed for the better? Indeed, things are far worse in many areas of education. Education was teetering on death in 1983 — actually even earlier. Yet people blithely go on as though nothing too serious is going on today?

If we take *A Nation At Risk* seriously — as we should — we have long since passed a time of recovery. Things either get better or they get worse. They don't stay the same. Education today is hanging by a thread, and I'm being kind saying even that.

Terrel Bell was the Secretary of Education under President Reagan. It was he who put the commission together and selected those who would be on it.

Among the members of the commission was Glenn Seaborg

(1912-1999). He was a Nobel prize laureate and a key contributor to *A Nation At Risk*. Glenn Seaborg described the work of the commission:

> *"There were about a dozen public hearings, panel discussions and symposia, including testimony from some 250 experts, and about five dozen commissioned papers by educational experts, to help us formulate our conclusions and recommendations."*[1]

To that was added the personal knowledge and experience of the commissioners themselves. While that might not be the data that those criticizing it wanted to see, it does not at all sound as though a dearth of substance was used to arrive at their conclusions.

It seems clear to me that some who have criticized the report — as many have done — apparently ignored the report's substantive sources used in its preparation, as well as of the many competent members of the commission.

Complaining about supposedly not having enough professional educators (teachers) on the commission is another red herring. The makeup of the commission was substantive. Indeed, a number on the commission did have substantive teaching experience. I suggest that a different makeup would have led to a weaker report.

The criticism of *A Nation At Risk* has itself often been rife with errors and biases. Some clearly appear to have their own agendas. I reject most of the criticism that has softened, delayed, or muted its serious warnings. They are still valid today — except that things are even further along in the failing of public — and some private — schools.

Reading *A Nation At Risk* still has great value today. In spite of whatever flaws it might have — as does any report — most of its observations are as accurate and concerning today as they were then.

One article critical of it said, *"American education achievement was not then declining and the nation's economy continues today as the most powerful in the world."* It postulated, *"Can a report that is wrong, result in new policy conditions that are right?"*[2]

The author of the book now in your hands feels that the conclusions in that article seemingly critical of *A Nation At Risk* are wrong, as are other negative critiques. However, the observations of the good that has come from the report, regardless of its purported failings, are shared by others.

In that vein, James W. Guthrie succinctly said:

"My view of [A Nation At Risk] in retrospect is seldom, maybe never, has a public report been so wrong and done so much good."[3]

Numerous others have also criticized it. *The Manufactured Crisis* (1995) by David Berliner and Bruce Biddle is one. The Sandia Report (1990) has an interesting history and is another. One complaint about *A Nation At Risk*, shared by others, isn't just about purportedly missing data, it's also about wrongly interpreted data.

As already mentioned and as will be mentioned again later, the book in your hands has chosen to include few data points. The use of such data in the past, for decades and beyond, has proven nearly worthless when we look at how few substantive improvements have come from publicizing such data.

While some reforms and improvements have indeed been made at all levels of education, it has been far from enough. Sometimes, things have been made worse. All that has allowed the deficient state of education — and therefore the country — to continue. Quoting and re-quoting data, whether old or new, will do no more good now to fix what has become an unfixable system than it has in the past.

We don't need to be taking more "honest and comprehensive" looks at American public education today. We've been "looking" at schools forever. None of those looks have resulted in reforms needed to give America a strongly functioning education system.

Fortunately, there are those who continue to sound the alarm raised by *A Nation At Risk*.

One report referred to researchers from Stanford and Munich who…

"...came to a disturbing conclusion: 'the percentage of American students in the U.S. class of 2009 who are highly accomplished is well below that of most countries with which the U.S. compares itself.'"

It added:

"This report offers a dire warning: we are not preparing our students to enter the workforce with the skills they need in the new millennium."[4]

That is still the case today.

Some people make the excuse that much of this happened in the past, but that things are somehow different today.

If they are, they're worse.

One 2019 article said:

"Thirty-six years have passed, and in 2019, the nation is still at risk."[5]

In 2009, a writing *by the U.S. Department of Education itself* said:

"If we were 'at risk' in 1983, we are at even greater risk now."

It does not whitewash the situation when it starkly adds:

"On a strictly domestic level, our performance at the high school level is as alarming as it was at the time of A Nation at Risk, *if not worse."*[6]

Another attack on *A Nation At Risk* said:

"One problem: The landmark document that still shapes our national debate on education was misquoted, misinterpreted, and often dead wrong."[7]

However, based on what I know — even acknowledging that certain data in *A Nation At Risk* may be less than perfect — I must disregard such misguided comments.

Since *A Nation At Risk,* there have been numerous other reports and efforts to bring about change including the No Child Left

Behind Act of 2001. However, along with other efforts, *No Child Left Behind* failed because, together with other programs, it did not address — it did not know *how* to address — the foundational problems in education and schools.

Most such problems are in the classrooms themselves, problems of which are then compounded by often unsatisfactory directives from above. Combine that with a lack of support from legislators, courts, and, too often, administrators, and we see systemic problems that not only have not been fixed, but likely *cannot* be fixed.

Many recommendations in *A Nation At Risk* have only partially been addressed over the years. Most concerns found in *A Nation At Risk* are still largely or fully valid.

The dire warnings of the report have increasingly become part of education's accepted reality today. The "rising tide of mediocrity" has already risen.

3a. COMMENTS ON TEST SCORES AND COLLEGE ADMISSIONS

Many supporters of the current system point to what they feel have been rising test scores over the years as well as increases in college admissions. (Here, I'm ignoring the test score drops during and after the COVID pandemic.) It's sometimes hard to understand where these people are actually getting their figures, even when they tell us.

Indeed, a case can be made that academic scores and world rankings are *improving* from previously very dismal scores and low placements in the world. However, such "improvements" are sometimes gauged over many years.

Improvements at that pace are nothing of which we should proudly hold up as comfortable improvements. Mere *improvements* over many years are not enough. Only *competency* is enough.

In some cases, I'm even likely to dispute whether the quoted statistics were valid in the first place. I won't spend the significant time needed to fully address this issue. But I'll throw out a couple of thought items.

First are test scores. Teachers and schools know how important some school-wide standardized test scores can be. For some tests, there has been a lot of pressure put on teachers and schools. In some places, teachers' pay has been linked to student scores.

How can we be sure that all students take these tests seriously? I believe that many do. However, for those students teachers know will do poorly, it's sometimes quietly mentioned to them that test day might be an ideal day — to stay home.

Test protocols often know that happens. Therefore, they set up "encouragement" for schools to have maximum turnout for the tests. Some insist that students who were absent take it upon their return. Nonetheless, depending on the tests, that isn't always done.

Beyond trying to keep struggling students home on test day, there are other students who absolutely don't care about tests — especially because they effectively have no affect at all on their grades.

Some intentionally answer incorrectly, sometimes just creating patterns on their answer sheets. Some test designs can recognize such invalid tests. Others don't. Even when test proctors personally witness students not seriously taking the test, just filling in answers randomly, some tests don't allow such direct observations to invalidate tests. (That's because some teachers will try to invalidate student tests whom they know will do poorly.)

Of course, those kinds of actions by students who don't take them seriously will likely lower test score averages, whereas absent students might raise them. Also raising test scores are those students who are able to cheat during the tests. In cases where tests are particularly important, some do.

Then there is the consideration expressed by some that student scores should be set against a standard of learning. They should be able to know and pass material considered necessary for them to have learned. I add that all this is quite subjective. Few can agree on most lists of required learning.

When scores are bandied about to the public, scores are presented as compared to other students or to past years of the test's administration. Therefore, if a student gets 50% on a test deemed to contain material that all students should know (some aren't configured that way), it would still be considered a good score if it were better than what the student had previously scored — or if it were better than those of other students — or of students in past years.

Even though no tests are perfect, I support testing. Yet to solely point to what might be somewhat higher scores one year versus past years on rotating tests isn't necessarily determinative of the quality of education.

Some might suggest that I am going against the tide when I suggest that test scores alone are not determinative of whether anyone's education has been a good one.

Next we look on the college side — although the above discussion relates to colleges, too. If one looks back many decades, one finds that most universities rarely had remedial classes for incoming students. Therefore, it was indeed more difficult for many applicants to get into college.

Because college entrance requirements were judged unfair to many students, things loosened up. Students who were clearly not ready for college work were accepted anyway with the requirement that such students take remedial classes to bring their skill levels up to college level. *Of course, their high schools should have already prepared them in the basics of math and language skills before they were allowed to graduate.* But that didn't happen. It's still not happening.

So more students start college today compared to when higher standards were enforced. I'm not saying that's bad. I'm just saying that one can't say that K-12 education is better now because more students are starting college.

Further, professors today — and for many, many years now — more commonly give higher grades. That's for a couple of reasons. First, many students who often weren't ready for college in the first place would be failing their classes. Except in the most egregious cases, teachers don't like to fail students. That also discourages students. But there's another reason.

Many colleges today allow students to evaluate their professors at the end of the course. It doesn't look good if professors consistently get bad student evaluations, even if undeserving (of course, too often professors really can be bad).

Regardless of such evaluations, it doesn't look good if a professor fails too many students. It's felt that a high level of failures, or too many low grades, is a failure of the professor as an effective teacher, rather than the fault of non-studying students. In some cases, that can endanger a professor's job, especially if they don't yet have tenure. Really though, many students just don't take college seriously enough to put in the time needed to succeed. Therefore, it's not necessarily the fault of every professor who sets and expects high standards of students.

This was less of a problem years ago. But, today, with less prepared students entering college, it can be a serious problem for students, teachers, and for learning the subject matter itself.

In order to judge education, I believe that test scores are helpful — although not necessarily determinative — and I'm not dismissing them. In addition, considering other academic factors and performance, generally in high schools, can be helpful, too.

But, in many cases, none of that is helpful at all.

My bottom line regarding testing is that I don't think that test scores alone, even with classroom grades, are adequate to more broadly judge the status of education in schools today.

But you're now asking what I think *would* be adequate, aren't you? The answer is that things are a mess. There isn't really a good answer to that question anymore.

4. A DANGEROUS ROAD TO TRAVEL

Our most critical failing in education is at the kindergarten through high school level, more simply referred to as "K-12." Schooling through the high school level remains the foundation of everything we are as a population. It is far more important than college.

College is where critical thinking, a high level of unbiased academic learning, and effective job skills, *are supposed* to be developed, although that isn't always happening today. It hasn't always happened in the past either.

The true foundation of an educated person is built — or *should be built* — in high school and before. That's why students who drop out of high school are of special concern.

A book from 1971 by Everett Reimer suggests that one of the significant core functions of schools isn't necessarily education. Very importantly, schools provide custodial care for children. That's likely even more applicable today. In other words, schools provide "cheap" childcare. Many people already know that. How else could they go to work? Or "have a life?" Here is part of what Reimer said:

> *Custodial care is now so universally provided by schools that it is hard to remember earlier arrangements. Children must, of course, be cared for -- if they really are children, that is, and not just young members of the*

community taking part in its normal productive and social affairs. Most youngsters still get along without special care, all over the world, in the tribal, peasant and urban dwellings of the poor.[1]

However, today, few children of *any* age can be fully trusted alone at home. It doesn't matter what trusting parents believe (yes, of course there are exceptions). Since they exhibit less responsibility than same-aged children do elsewhere, many need supervision almost up until the time they leave home. Schools provide that.

But is custodial (child) care what most believe is the primary function of schools? Or, perhaps wrongly, do we all assume that it's education? Regardless, taking care of our children may be the main function of schools today, as it was when Reimer wrote about it — and as it has been for many decades and beyond.

***

Although the foundation of my own English came in non-public elementary schools, it was solidified in a 10th grade high school English class. William "Bill" Lenihan — one of the few non-author names you'll see me mention in this book — was the English teacher that year. (He was also an assistant coach at the school.)

If I recall correctly, he was not even an English teacher. He was a Social Studies teacher. But they needed an English teacher and assigned the class to him. We later heard talk that he hadn't really wanted to do it.

He is another example of why I feel the credentialing system is broken. I don't know whether he was credentialed for English. It wouldn't have been necessary in the school in which he was teaching. However, to this day, I'm grateful for his take-no-prisoners approach to teaching it. His example influenced me even many years later as I began my own teaching. I still remember some of his precise words from the class.

I was never a great student. I may have gotten a B in the class. I certainly didn't stand out. But my life strengthened tenfold because of that one class.

Thank you, Mr. Lenihan.[2]

***

Throughout the years, I learned that grades often don't reflect true learning, nor do they reflect academic or personal growth. A's certainly don't, nor do lower grades for many students. Some of the classes I got the most out of weren't rewarded with A's.

In some of my favorite and most important classes, I was given C's. Yet, to this day, a number of those have positively affected me and my life. On the other side of that, the A's I got in other classes did not reflect the waste of time many such classes were.

***

Great teachers are so important in our lives. Most of us really haven't had many of them. But they can make such a difference to us and to the world. Really good teachers aren't often treated as such. They rarely know how much what they have done has so positively helped their students years, even decades later. All teachers should be treated much better than they are by their students, by parents, and by some unsupportive administrators.

On the other hand, I also don't forget that there are some teachers who shouldn't be teaching at all.

That one 10th grade English class literally set me up for the rest of my life. As I recall, I had just one other English class after that. It was a required class in a community college program. One additional required English class. That was it.

That last English class at college may have polished me a bit, but I'm sure I would have been fine without it. (Yes, I know I'm still not perfect. Some of you likely notice that, too.) So that last 10th grade class in high school… and one in college.

Perhaps all that explains why my writing here lacks the power of Herman Melville (author of Moby Dick). I eventually became a high school drop out at a different high school or I would have had to take one final English class in 12th grade. But I wasn't present in school to take it.

Many years ago, remedial classes weren't always part of colleges as they are today. The massive numbers of remedial classes at almost every college across the country for countless years attest to the long-term failure of the public K-12 system. More than just a failure of education, it's also been a political and sociological failure.

Even today, many students don't complete high school. (I didn't.)

Yet, as bad as many schools are today, some are beginning to question whether it even matters any more.

Beyond K-12, universities are also a mess. I'll talk about those again later.

Five things are issues here, especially in the critical K-12 years:

(1) *Not enough learning is happening;*

(2) *Wrong learning is happening;*

(3) *When learning is happening, it happens too slowly;*

(4) *Political and sociological indoctrinations are happening;*

(5) *Among those who remain in school, too many students appear to have given up. So have some teachers. They're just going through the required motions.*

All that's not always true, of course. There are still good classes with good teachers. Lucky students can still experience substantive learning in those classrooms.

Is there any subject area where incomplete and wrong learning is most obvious? It appears that the various social studies classes are most impacted. These especially include history and government... and sometimes economics. In colleges and some high schools, this can extend to sociology, psychology, and related subjects.

I recently noticed a Google search for *"Was Socrates a real person?"* Knowing about Socrates, Plato, and Aristotle is a pretty basic part of history, so I followed up. Is it actually true that people aren't being taught — or don't believe — that Socrates existed? Is it even important that they don't know it?

Yes, it is.

A website by Donald Robertson takes this on directly. It starts by taking note of the "…surprising number of people out there [who] are unsure whether Socrates *actually existed or not* (emphasis his)." Robertson says that some people "…seem utterly convinced he's a completely fictional character."[3]

I'll add a thought that might be a bit disconcerting: I'm hopeful that some of those people aren't teachers.

If you are one of those wondering about this question, Robertson's excellent webpage will be of help to you. (Yes, Socrates was a real person.)

Although social studies classes may be the most egregious purveyors of wrong or incomplete information, they are not alone in failing to properly educate students. English and language skills in students are often terrible. However, schools have even failed students and society in failing to teach basic arithmetic and other math skills.

But how can I possibly ask people to accept the levels of alarm here without extensive studies on the education system throughout the country? *"Research! Studies! Let's get the facts first!"* you demand.

Here's why that's a dangerous road to travel…

Not just for years, but for many decades — and beyond — educators and researchers have studied what's been going on in schools. They have provided facts — or at least the "facts" that came from their studies. They were important. Many added suggestions on how to improve things.

Educators and non-educators have often come up with what are (purportedly) new programs to improve things. Often, those running such programs make substantial money.

But here's the problem: nothing has worked. Sure, some things showed promise. Some may have showed promise in school pilot projects with later success in real schools. There may have even been things that might have worked more broadly if they had been more widely disseminated and implemented.

But they weren't.

So we're left with studies that few people have read and on which no one took effective action. Even if people did try to take action, most of what has been suggested or tried just hasn't worked.

Some things might have seemed to work to improve learning. But nothing substantive enough happened to make broad and significant improvements to classroom learning. Even among the workable programs, nothing that would have "fixed" things and led to significant improvements was transferred to the broader public education system.

But some of the programs, education materials, and training many companies provided did make lots of money.

So what we *don't* need are more studies. I love data and information, but not just for the sake of having data and information. Something positive and concrete must come from it. As a result of such studies, changes must take place to actually improve things, to *significantly* improve things.

That hasn't happened. Anyone demanding more studies is making a conscious effort to ignore what's already in front of their face: a horribly failed education system with past studies that have been forgotten or ignored for years.

This should be obvious to anyone who takes an objective look at what's going on. One does not have to hold a graduate degree to look at education and determine that it isn't working.

It simply isn't.

5. THE CANARIES OF EDUCATION

For many years, canaries were brought into coal mines to protect coal miners. If the birds became sick (or died), it was a warning to the miners.

According to a Smithsonian Magazine article of December 30, 2016, the use of canaries in mines began in 1911 and ended in 1986. Canaries were able to "detect carbon monoxide and other toxic gases before they hurt humans." Observing the canaries protected the miners. The canaries could sense the otherwise undetectable deadly gases well in advance. If the miners noticed the birds were sick or had died, they knew that danger was present. They had to evacuate the mine immediately. If they ignored the sick or dead canaries, people could lose their lives.

Interestingly, one early reviewer who actually supports the observations made in this book, suggested that it is unnecessary to explain what a canary in a coal mine is. He said, *"Everyone knows that!"* Indeed, there are surely readers who feel parts of this book look down on them, treating them "condescendingly," as though they are missing a basic education. Those thinking that way had better think again. After all, isn't that the concern of this book? People no longer know what used to be considered "obvious" not many years ago.

When I began to point that out to the reviewer, I didn't even have to finish. He immediately understood and withdrew his suggestion.

Thinking that because *you* know something, that everyone else must also know that same thing cannot just be wrong, it can even be dangerous. It discards the understanding that education has not been doing its job.

Never assume that because you know something, that others do, too. Nor should you assume that because someone takes extra time to explain something, that it is aimed at you or meant to be demeaning of you. That is often a common, but wrong assumption.

Instead, many authors make that very mistake by assuming that their readers all have what they feel is common knowledge. But we can't know that. We should not assume what our readers or listeners actually know. Media hosts and commentators often do that.

Now back to the canaries.

***

I have what I feel are canaries of education. My canaries are specific topics that warn me of the lethal current or upcoming failings of education. Others may have different canaries that give them their own look at danger in education. I'm sure that other canaries do exist.

Here are just two of my canaries:

> *(1) Lack of full knowledge of nuclear weapons;*
> *(2) Lack of a complete understanding of the Holocaust*
> *along with its importance for the present and future.*

These are both important topics. If you don't know why that is, perhaps you need to attend a full and appropriate presentation on each of them yourself — if you can still find competent teachers for both topics. Sadly, they aren't easy to find.

If I see recent high school graduates who know little or nothing about even one of those topics, I know that other things in their education will also be missing or perhaps had been given short shrift in their schooling — subject matter coverage that was inadequate.

When I talk to recent graduates who had been competently educated on those two topics, the graduates generally know other things, too. But note that, today, the competence of graduates is often a credit to one or two specific teachers, rather than to their education generally.

When I notice that my canaries are not well or (sadly) have died, I immediately assume that the entire system at their school or district (or state) is likely also failing.

It's hard to pick just a couple of canaries that can reflect the status of education today. But, for me, those canaries consistently reflect a sick, dying, or already dead education system. I carry those canaries with me. That is why you'll notice how often I mention those two topics in this book.

Are students able to become well-educated even lacking those two things? Possibly. But I haven't seen it. Can students become knowledgeable about those two topics but still be poorly educated? Definitely, yes. For example, although I taught both topics when-ever I could, my students often had serious weaknesses in other classes, or throughout their schooling, that I couldn't fix. By teaching these things, I was only able to fix those particular things. In most all cases, students should have already learned such things before even coming into my class.

Today, my canaries are sick, actually beyond sick. Early warn-ings by canaries are supposed to help us to save ourselves and others. In this case, those others are students in the public educa-tion system. But those students aren't being saved. They are being restrained in an inadequate public — and sometimes private — education system. They will be suffering consequences of such inadequacies throughout their lives. It won't just affect them. It will be affecting the whole country.

Knowing the warnings are being ignored, I tried to save my canaries by teaching those two topics almost no matter which class I was teaching. It wasn't easy. Actually, it wasn't possible. I was generally able to do it with the atomic bomb, but not necessarily with the far more comprehensive subject of the Holocaust.

But let me add that this book does *not* judge the entirety of the public education system on those items alone. Those are just two of many things that lead to the understanding that education is indeed dead.

We'll move forward now to take a closer look at these two canaries.

6. NUCLEAR WEAPONS

Let's start by looking at the atomic bomb (the A-bomb) and the hydrogen bomb (the H-bomb, also known as a thermonuclear weapon). Both of them are nuclear weapons, but thermonuclear weapons are many times more powerful than the original atomic bomb.

Do you have a pretty good understanding of what those weapons are?

That would generally be a foolish question. Anyone over a certain age knows what they are. Anyone around during the Cuban Missile Crisis knows. Anyone around in the earlier years of the Cold War knows. But that sure leaves out a lot of people today.

When I was in elementary school, probably around 4th grade, we were taught about those things in the classroom. Fourth grade. Actually, even 3rd graders learned much of this so perhaps I learned about them there, too. I can't confirm how much younger the teaching went in school, but we all pretty much knew what atomic bombs were, how they destroyed things, and how they killed people.

We knew that there was more than one kind of radiation associated with the bombs. We learned how to protect ourselves. We learned what kind of materials and even how thick they had to be to protect us from various radiation. Fourth grade. Maybe younger.

It was necessary to learn such things because there was a credible fear that such weapons could be used in the world and might even be dropped on American homes and cities. The Soviet Union had them. We had them, too. We both still do — but so do too many others.

Tensions in the world were such that, in light of the existence of such weapons, concerns for the survival of America, the Soviet Union, and the world were real things. There were legitimate concerns for the survival of the human race itself. Those concerns are still with us but, today, most people truly don't know it.

Those who are *not* over a certain age, those who were *not* around during the Cuban Missile Crisis, who were *not* around during the early years of the Cold War may know almost nothing. Sure, they've heard the word. They know it's a really big bomb. They *might* have seen photos of atomic bomb blasts, perhaps even when used on Japan at the end of World War II. But they don't *actually know and understand* what one really is, and how frightening they are.

For people to assume the ones in existence won't be used, or that terrorist groups or enemies of America — perhaps China, Russia, or some other enemy — won't obtain and use them, is dangerous and foolish.

Atomic (nuclear) weapons are one of the WMD's: Weapons of Mass Destruction. The other two are biological and chemical weapons. But their power pales next to nuclear weapons.

In the past, policy decisions were made with Weapons of Mass Destruction (WMD's) in mind. Or, at least, they should have been. Not too far in the past, politicians, even presidents, were elected based, at least in part, on how well they might protect us from the use of such weapons.

Today, most people don't actually know what they are and why we should even be concerned. They often elect people for frivolous reasons. Nuclear weapons are not among those reasons.

Here are some stories.

Many years ago, I was a fairly new teacher at a junior high

school in the Los Angeles Unified School District (LAUSD). A junior high school was defined as including Grades 7, 8, and 9. Later, junior high schools became middle schools. Middle schools generally include Grades 6, 7, and 8. Ninth grade moved up to high school.

At the time, I was teaching math to middle schoolers on what was designated as an Emergency Credential. That means I wasn't fully qualified as a teacher because I hadn't yet taken the required teacher training classes at college. But, because they were short of teachers, my college background was enough that they let me temporarily be a "real" teacher anyway, pending progress taking a lot of required classes in the future.

> An aside: Some years earlier, when I began teaching at a community college, I had not completed a single college class when I walked in to teach on my first day, let alone having earned an actual college degree. At night, I would be teaching. During the day, I would be sitting in the same regular classes as some of my students.[1]

I had already worked as a substitute teacher for a time in the L.A. Unified School District. I liked teaching. But I was always a bit amused that they let a high school dropout (me) teach. Sure, I eventually went back to school, though not to high school, but I always smiled a bit at that. Maybe that was what was wrong with education: They let ME teach!

So I was teaching math classes the same as any other teacher. I often had over 200 students every day. Most classes had around forty students or so. At least on one day, one of my classes hit 50 students. These were junior high school students, often considered some of the most challenging to control and teach. In many places, the newest, least experienced teachers got the toughest classes. Nonetheless, I really enjoyed my students. It was an honor to be a teacher.

By the way, my college degree was not in mathematics which were the classes I was hired to teach. I never even liked math much. As with other things, math wasn't always easy for me. But there I was, teaching it! I was an excited new teacher with a whole lot of sometimes rowdy and challenging students.

My own background meant that I related much more easily to math-phobic students. I did everything I could to make it easier for all of my students than it had been for me.

But enough of that. Let's return to the atomic bomb.

One day, we were told we were going to have an earthquake drill during our homeroom classes. We were to go over what the students needed to know in an earthquake emergency. Great! I was always one who wanted to be prepared and to know all I could about such disasters. By that time, I had completed time in the US Army. Chances for survival are always better for those who know more. "Luck favors the prepared."

After the earthquake drill was over, there was some extra time. I thought it would be wise to go over other possible emergencies. So I asked about atomic bombs. I asked, "How do you recognize if an atomic bomb has gone off [been detonated]?"

No response.

I reworded it and asked again.

I waited.

An answer finally came, "Uh, a big noise!"

No. That wasn't right.[2]

I spent a bit of time talking about it. As I did, it was clear that students weren't actually sure what an atomic bomb was at all.

This was not long after the Cold War had ended. Did such weapons matter anymore?

Yes, they did and they still do today. Terrorists would love to get their hands on nuclear weapons. If they haven't already, they are likely to get them in the future. There are still thousands of missiles with nuclear armaments in Russia. North Korea has continued to develop theirs, although some small progress temporarily slowing that down came under the Trump administration. But it was indeed temporary. Under the Biden administration, the approach to North Korea changed. Under the new Biden policy, North Korea again began testing potential nuclear weapon delivery systems. Their dangerous rhetoric ratcheted up again.

Iran has moved forward with such weapons, especially after the sanctions on Iran imposed under President Trump were removed by the Biden administration. It is possible that, by the time you are reading these words, Iran may already have their own nuclear weapons. Iran is a dangerous nation.

A number of other nations currently have these weapons. There are current concerns about China. But, besides China, others include India, Pakistan, the United Kingdom, France, and Israel.

It just takes one wrong person at the wrong time to send one anywhere they want. It just takes one wrong person to physically place one in the middle of a large city. As long as they are in the world, they threaten the planet's survival — and it's not likely they're going anywhere anytime soon.

Most people don't understand that. People used to understand these weapons, but no more.

How do those in the media have the ignorance or arrogance to discuss these things when they know, or should know, that enormous swaths of people have no idea what they even are? It's likely because so many of them don't know themselves.

They can invite me over. Perhaps I can help them out.

Some months later, or maybe the next year — I can't remember which — I was able to go to an Emergency Preparedness presentation put on by the school district. The principal had become aware that emergency preparedness was important to me, so he sent me as the school's representative. The presentation was about surviving earthquakes. Earthquake preparation is certainly important! People are far more likely to be impacted by an earthquake than by a nuclear weapon. Of course, that doesn't mean preparation for various other emergencies isn't also important. Does it?

Apparently, it does.

Still being a relatively new teacher, I asked the school district's head of Emergency Preparedness after the presentation about being sure students have at least some basic information about nuclear weapons. His response?

He laughed. He thought it was ridiculous to be concerned about such things. Okay, well I was a pretty new teacher anyway. Still, for someone *actually responsible for emergency preparation for an entire school district* to laugh out loud when asked about it, seemed more than a bit out of place to me since I actually did know about such things. Minimally, it was very disconcerting. Earthquakes are not the only possible disasters requiring advance preparation.

But that's not what I really want you to know.

After my homeroom class in which we had the earthquake drill and in which I talked to my students about atomic bombs, I went to lunch. I visited another teacher to ask something and brought up the fact that my students didn't even know what an atomic bomb was. To me, they were definitely old enough to have at least learned what they were, even if nothing else. So nuclear weapons by themselves weren't the issue for me. It was the fact that they didn't know a thing about them at all.

The other teacher sympathized with my obvious concerns as I talked to her. Then she said, *"Oh yeah. Wasn't that what blew up the building in Oklahoma City?"*

I was taken aback.

On April 19, 1995, Timothy McVeigh and Terry Nichols used a truck bomb to blow up a federal building in Oklahoma City. At least 168 people were killed. More than 680 others were injured.

It was *not* an atomic bomb. If it had been, and depending on its size, deaths may have been counted in the millions.

The teacher didn't know that. She didn't know what an atomic bomb was — at all.

A credentialed teacher.

And she's not alone. There are many teachers who, likewise, don't know what one is, how they kill, or what we can do.

As an aside, many dismissive and naive people say, it won't matter anyway, we'll all be dead.

I admit to being disgusted when I hear the naiveté of that. That is not necessarily true at all. Listen to the many survivors of Hiroshima and Nagasaki. Although their injuries were significant and often fatal, there were many survivors. Assuming one is far enough from the center of the blast, there are indeed things to do to maximize survival.

If teachers don't know what many feel should be such a basic thing (like just knowing what one is!), how can they teach students to know those things, let alone instill a sense of importance about them.

Is this in the history books for both teachers and students? Increasingly, textbook presentations themselves are inadequate. Some teachers say some topic has been "covered" simply because they *assigned reading* on the topic.

How often do students actually do all of their assigned reading, even in inadequate textbooks? Not often enough. What if an important topic is covered in class, but a student is sick and absent? In some cases, that student will *never* be exposed to the topic. The student may never be able to learn it again. Textbooks are not enough. Even when they do cover something and haven't either intentionally or unintentionally changed something they shouldn't have changed, the coverage is often too brief to actually educate students. Many schools have moved away from traditional paper textbooks because of their enormous costs. However, options aren't necessarily as good.

As with too much else, even today's news media makes the naive assumption that people know about certain things — including about nuclear weapons. But not only do the people who listen to them not always know enough, many of the younger reporters themselves don't really have the full picture of what nuclear weapons are. They are all products of a broken education system.

This is not good for reporters. But it's worse for teachers. Unknowledgeable teachers ensure unknowledgeable students. Unknowledgeable students become future, even less knowledgeable teachers, not just concerning nuclear issues, but about many other things, too. Once this starts, it's difficult, no, likely impossible, to reverse. Barring something unknown, future generations will remain unknowledgeable.

I was shaken when I realized the full extent of the loss of this knowledge.

For every year after that as a teacher, I made an hour long presentation on nuclear weapons using videos and my own background. My personal background didn't just include my "4th grade" education, though a surprising amount of that has stayed with me. It included my background in CBR: Chemical, Biological, and Radiological training (later called NBC) in the U.S. Army.

I determined that, as long as I could do it, no student would make it out of any of my classes without having that presentation. It didn't matter the subject matter of the class. I knew that if they didn't get it from me, they would likely never get it at all. Every single time, students were surprised and fascinated (and scared, as we all should be) as they learned about nuclear weapons: atomic bombs and hydrogen (thermonuclear) bombs.

Although the majority of my students did learn about them, few others anywhere else did. If you are of a recent generation, you might know of their existence and small bits about them, but nothing more. That isn't enough. Not only might you know little or nothing, but coming generations will know even less.

I spend some time on this single topic not merely because it's intrinsically important, but because it's an example. We all expect teachers to know things. After all, they are teachers! But they know less and less because education has been teaching less and less — and too many don't know that has been happening. Some do not even know what a nuclear weapon is! When will this stop?

It won't.

It's not being fixed and it's not likely to be fixed in the future, or not until one is next used in war. Instead, we're most likely to hear exactly what I did when I so naively asked about it: laughter, derision, and then simply ignoring it.

Let me be clear about this. The issue here is not just nuclear weapons, although that should be critical knowledge to have. It is a vast array of knowledge that is not being taught, or is being taught wrongly in many subject areas at schools. It is the fact that even teachers don't know these things.

I once learned detailed information about this topic in third or fourth grade. Today, students do not substantively learn about them at all. That includes college level students. It includes full adults, who are out in the world. It surely includes politicians, too.

The issue today is not simply not having learned what should be basics in education today, but even the outright denial of basic tenets of science and other subjects. Suggesting that one's sex is merely "assigned," rather than outright determined at birth is one of those errors of biology we have seen even among — *especially* among — those who are college educated. (Who do such people suggest has been doing that "assigning?")

****

Fortunately, when less educated people don't know something — even some teachers, as we have seen — we can go for help to those with a higher level of education. For example, we can ask lawyers about something that is in their area of legal expertise.

Or can we?

On January 26, 2023, a nominee for the U.S. District Court for the Eastern District of Washington — a lawyer and already a sitting judge — was asked some basic questions by a United States Senator. The first two questions were quite simple. Even properly educated high school students would — or should — know the answers.

The senator asked the nominee to describe what Article V of the U.S. Constitution does. The nominee's answer? The lawyer nominee, a sitting judge, didn't know. *"Article V is not coming to mind at the moment,"* the nominee replied. (Article V deals with the process of amending the Constitution.)

Unperturbed, the same senator asked a much easier question concerning what Article II does. The lawyer nominee, a sitting judge, didn't know that one either. The nominee responded, *"Neither is Article II* [coming to mind at the moment]." (Article II deals with the Executive Branch of government.)

How does a judge not know the U.S. Constitution?![3]

But it's even worse.

How could the American Bar Association have given her a "qualified" rating? How could a president nominate someone who doesn't know the basics of the Constitution?

This nominee was put forward by President Joe Biden. In the past, other nominees have also put in poor performances at Senate hearings. At least one withdrew his name from consideration after a poor performance. At the time of this writing, the Biden nominee had not withdrawn her name from consideration. Hopefully, that will happen.

One concern throughout the country is that people are too often not held to high — or at least to minimum — educational standards of knowledge by those who might evaluate them. That is also an indictment of those evaluating such nominees and determining they are "qualified." It's clear that even the evaluators don't have enough education or competence to competently evaluate someone else.

I don't expect people to be perfect. I'm certainly not. Nonetheless, it might appear that some are not held to any educational standards at all. How would such a person have graduated from law school without such a rudimentary knowledge of the US Constitution!

Education is dead.

7. THE HOLOCAUST

The years moved on. I found myself fully credentialed and teaching at a small high school in the San Fernando Valley. It was also part of the Los Angeles Unified School District. One day, our English teacher at the time returned from a visit to what is now called the Holocaust Museum LA in Los Angeles.

Each year I was at that school, accompanied by my instruction, students at the school watched extensive videos to learn about the Holocaust. For several years, the school took a field trip to the museum after the presentation. As the school's Social Studies teacher, I put together the extensive presentations about it at the school. (I also taught a variety of other subjects there.) The principal was a strong supporter of my instruction on the Holocaust. So were the other teachers.

The students, there because they were at risk of dropping out of high school, were quiet as they watched the video presentations and listened to me. Many students were aggressive on the streets when they were not at school. A number were involved with gangs and drugs. But they were always moved by the videos of this terrible event.

Learning about the Holocaust, especially as they watched multiple available videos taken at the death camps, gave many of these students a perspective they hadn't had before. A number came away with a stronger understanding of life, injustices, and of personal sacrifice. It was always worthwhile. As good lessons do, it taught lessons beyond the topic itself.

My presentation not only consisted of multiple videos, but also of careful commentary that I added to the videos. It was a minimum of two hours, perhaps a bit more. But, if scheduling allowed and I felt my students were up to it, I added another one to two additional hours on another day. It was all valuable.

Their feedback was consistently strongly positive. In most cases, it did change how they looked at life and how they might treat others. I don't know how temporary that inner appreciation for life was. I don't know how temporary it might have been in helping some to stand up for others, or if it lasted throughout some of their lives. But there is no doubt that they were affected. It also opened them up to discuss related topics. It's what school is (supposed to be) all about.

Knowing and understanding the Holocaust is truly important. Living and teaching the mantra and commitment of "never again" should always continue forward. But, judging by the events since the Holocaust, including those of today, that is clearly not happening.

How can we be sure that something so terrible never happens again? Even today, there are those who deny that it even occurred in spite of overwhelming evidence, including videos, surviving witnesses, and physical evidence. Millions of non-Jews were also killed by Hitler's Third Reich during World War II, but the Jewish people were especially targeted. They have consistently carried the torch to keep alive the memory of the Holocaust. But sometimes it falls to others to do it.

Those who do not learn from the past are condemned to repeat it. Learning history is critical if simply for that one reason.

The English teacher who returned from his visit to the Holocaust Museum LA had missed the trip a day or two before. He had not been there and wanted to be sure that he experienced what his students (indeed, almost all students at the school) had experienced. So he went on his own.

Upon his return, he told me this story.

As the English teacher had been studying the exhibits, he overheard a couple of university graduate students, also visitors, talking. One asked the other, *"Did you know about any of this?"* The other student said he had not known about it.

The students were not talking about the Holocaust Museum. They were talking about the Holocaust itself!

***

A January 2023 National Poll conducted by the University of Massachusetts Amherst reported that 30% of African Americans agree that "Jews still talk too much about what happened to them in the Holocaust." Compare that to 19% each of Latinos and Asians and 15% of whites.

This is a concern because many Jews who were actually closely involved with the Holocaust don't necessarily even talk about it. This is not a Jewish issue alone. It is a significant issue for the human race.

Often forgotten are the millions of non-Jews who were killed in the Holocaust. Therefore, even though Jews were specially targeted, they were not the only ones marked for extermination.

That large number (30%) of African Americans who feel that Jews talk too much about it is of special concern. Younger people (18-29) among all races are also likely to agree with that same statement: 24%.

It is very likely that, since the Jews were more widely known to have been particularly targeted, that there was simply an assumption that Jews must be talking about it more. In reality, although the Holocaust is indeed often referenced today, there was no accompanying question as to how many Jews the respondents may have known or could point to whom they had heard in the media actually "talking" about what happened. That had apparently been the real point of interest.

Therefore, why did they agree with that statement? My guess is that respondents may not have actually known who is doing the talking about it today rather than (necessarily) judging their understanding as an indication of rampant anti-semitism.

This is yet another issue involving the failure of education. The fact that other races answered differently does not suggest to me that education is without blame.

I am not Jewish. However, as possible, I undertook in all my classes to be sure that my students had a full and correct understanding of this event. I never heard a single student complain that they were tired of hearing about it. None ever said that the Jews talked too much about it. Even at the high school level, few knew anything of substance about it other than, perhaps, the name and a general description of what it was.

I am fully convinced that their fuller and detailed knowledge of what happened as a result of my presentations would follow them throughout their lives. Because I also discussed what led up to it, I believe they will be more aware of a similar progression in the future should they see it develop. Sadly, they are likely to be alone in that recognition.

At all levels, that poll is yet another indictment of the education system. Once again, it points to the failure of the education system to correctly teach and contextualize the Holocaust itself.

Younger people would likely have been taught by younger teachers, who may themselves have only been taught a partial or inadequate understanding of the event.

Note the earlier observance of the graduate level students who apparently knew nothing about it at all.

The disparity between African Americans and other races is of significant concern, but it is not the only concern brought to light in the poll.[1]

*****

How can students make it through high school and at least four years of college never having been taught about the Holocaust? How many others also know little or nothing? And what did those graduate students intend to do when they finally finished their graduate program? *Teach??* Let us hope not.

Sadly, as we just heard concerning the teacher who did not know what an atomic bomb was, too many teachers today, even though most are really good people, don't know some basic things. This is a point worth repeating.

Some teachers today, especially new ones, are coming from the broken system where not enough education — or wrong education — has been taking place. They then turn around and teach other students what they have "learned." Their students will then turn around and do the same.

Adding to the lack of education, too many teachers now feel that their *opinions* are as valuable as facts. All of us have opinions and, if based on facts, it is not bad to have them.

Unfortunately, the facts upon which many teachers have based their opinions have often been wrong, incomplete, or missing altogether.

How can a teacher have an opinion on a war today that could escalate to a nuclear conflict if that teacher doesn't actually know what nuclear weapons are and the damage they can do? It's no problem to have an opinion. They are everywhere. But how helpful are they to the generations of students for whom teachers are responsible?

***

Here is a final observation as I end. Responsibility to teach about the Holocaust often rests with non-Jewish teachers.

One time, I went to the library at the Los Angeles Holocaust Museum to check out some Holocaust-related videos to show to my students. I asked the librarian which ones she might recommend. She didn't know. She hadn't seen *any* of them. She couldn't. The event was still too traumatic for her as a Jew. She was certainly not talking about it "too much."

A Jewish administrator at a school where I taught was very supportive of my ensuring students knew and understood the event, but was personally unable to attend any presentations. It was too difficult for her to witness the event via the videos and my presentation. Those two are not alone. For many Jews, especially for those who lost family or ancestors, it has remained difficult.

So when a poll asks whether Jews talk too much about the event and get so many responding that they do, I have to take issue with the observation, or *assumption*, by the respondents. I must also express a potential concern with the design of the poll itself.

I'm sure there are Jewish teachers who are perfectly capable of some level of presentation, hopefully together with actual videos of the event which I feel are critical. But I don't think that we can always count on finding those teachers.

Therefore, in many places, the responsibility for strong and thorough presentations on the Holocaust will have to rest with non-Jewish teachers for at least a while longer. Really, that is how it should be. This is far more than "just" a Jewish event.

8. GIVE US MORE STUDIES!

In spite of what I said earlier, some of you might *still* be thinking:

> *"You can't make a case that the education system is broken just because a few people don't happen to know about a few history topics that people don't even care about today. And would it matter if a teacher in math or physical education or music didn't know about those things? It wouldn't! You'd better come up with more facts before your case can be made! None of those examples seem that important to me! Where are the studies to support your concerns!"*

I have presented just two of many, many examples of critical information that *all* teachers, indeed, all people should know. So why don't they? Teachers can't pass on to students what they don't know — or don't believe — themselves.

However, as I have said from the beginning, there are countless studies, books, and talks about the serious problems in education. Have you read them? What has come of them?

Nothing.

So all I am doing here is presenting what I know, what I have seen, and what I have experienced. The experience of others may be different. I have read a number of books and studies with strong arguments calling attention to the failing education system. Those who could do something either haven't read them, don't agree that serious changes are needed, or don't care — as long as they can keep their jobs. Even when they know that something needs to be done, and really want to do something, they're not in a position to do anything about what needs to be fixed.

I feel less that I am sounding an alarm than giving a prognosis that education is effectively already dead now.

Okay. Not everywhere. As I have said, there are still some bastions of good schools and actual learning that still exist in the country. But, under increasing social, judicial, and government pressures and mandates, and especially under the new cadre of "socially and politically correct" teachers, even those bastions of good schools will likely have a temporary future existence.

So I don't mean that *all* education is fully dead everywhere. But the results of what we see in most schools, especially in most public schools, are so bad that I feel justified in generalizing as I do. Many successful people have become well-educated not because of the system, but in spite of it.

People feel that actual *learning* mostly takes place in schools. But it doesn't just take place there. It also takes place in the home, in life, out in the world, and in every other place. "Learning" is part of formal education, but it is different.

"Formal" education doesn't always take place in the world, although plenty of *real* learning does. We all want to trust schools when we want to educate ourselves or our children. Most people still trust schools. But should they?

Many parents like to think that their children are in a good school. After all, "They're getting really good grades!" Okay, then— Congratulations!

Sadly though, judging the quality of a child's education by what grades a child is getting, rarely lets anyone know what that child is actually learning. Parents can often be wrong in judging a school to be a good one, but it's too late by the time they find that out.

After all, many of today's parents were brought up in that same broken system. So, if what's being taught in their children's schools is what they themselves learned, it must be good. Right?

It's already too late. The broken system is now perpetuating itself.

9. HISTORICAL REVISIONISM

What is education for? What is its purpose?

That question does not have a simple answer. Here are a few answers to consider:

"To learn things."

It's generally the bottom line in education, isn't it?

To teach students to think and reason carefully based on information and life experiences. (Some call that critical thinking.)

Thinking and reasoning well isn't as easy as many think it should be. Some of that comes simply from maturing — getting older and more experienced in life. But such skills are what many employers feel is a primary reason to hire college graduates. Indeed, that's why some don't require any specific degree at all, as long as the applicant has completed any college degree.

"To be able to read well, write well, and do math."

Countless people in America still can't do those things well.

"To be able to function productively in society."

A lot goes into that. Education is just one part.

"To be an informed and involved citizen."

Enormous numbers of people don't understand how their own government works. Without that understanding and without understanding the history of their country and the world, citizens can't knowledgeably vote or fully participate in their government.

Informed citizens can be effective in determining a good direction for the country and their community. Ignorant citizens can take their country in wrong, even dangerous directions.

Knowledgeable citizens can agree or disagree with each other, but they do so with what should be a defensible foundation of knowledge or experience.

Citizens with minimal background about their country and of the history that preceded their own lives might talk vigorously with those with whom they disagree. But they might also be less helpful in supporting the direction their community and country are going. In a later chapter, I'll bring this up again.

"To learn, preserve, and carry the lessons of civilization forward."

Are all the achievements of civilization preserved in the education of younger generations? That sounds like a lot of responsibility for an education system to take on! Isn't it?

"To distinguish between truth and untruth."

Like beauty, is truth actually in the eyes — or mouth — of the beholder?

"To distinguish between right and wrong."

That's an important thing to learn. But, as related to public education, among some people, it is controversial and open to discussion. Nonetheless, there should be some morality in common to all in a nation. One would also think that there should be some respect and nurturing of personal virtues.

"To learn the lessons of history so that the mistakes of the past are not repeated."

Related to the Holocaust, the important mantra of "never again" is dependent on learning and understanding history. Related to the loss of liberty and freedom, an ignorant nation will lose itself and its freedoms just as others have.

"To understand shared values that may be needed to preserve and defend democracy and freedom."

These were part of the original foundation of America. Today, they are looking different as we continue to move to the future. Why has it changed?

"To become interiorly richer and better people."

"But wait! You mean education is supposed to do ALL of those things? That can't be! It's too much!"

Of course, it's not too much. It's what good education does — or what it *should* do.

Is public education successfully doing all those things today? Overall, it is not. When we look closely today, "education" sometimes seems to be doing exactly the opposite of all that.

Let's consider some of the benefits both students and society can and should be getting from some of the basic subjects in K-12 education (kindergarten through 12th grades). These critical adjunct benefits are not what most people would put first on their list:

1) Math is critical in building *self-confidence,* not just in math, but also in other subjects, and in life. Secondarily — and calling this just "secondary" will sound nonsensical to most people — it allows people to function in contexts requiring competence with numbers and problem solving.

In different contexts, sports, public speaking, and other things can also build self-confidence. But math is special. It is also available to a large number of people. We'll consider this again in Chapter Ten.

2) Social Studies — History, Government, Economics — becomes *a foundation to develop thinking, understanding, and competent decision-making in life.* It allows people to think at a forest level, rather than just sidle up to the trees. Social Studies history courses can provide us with a common, shared history and story. Among citizens and residents, it can and should develop a set of shared values, and an educated ability to run the country.

3) Finally, *language* — reading, but especially writing and speaking — is *power.* Success in leadership and life is far easier for people if they are comfortable and highly competent in language. Success is possible without it, but it is far more difficult for those who cannot effectively wield the power of the common language. Fluency in multiple languages is even better. Language is power.

Foundational to all education is truth, even though it can take different forms in different contexts. Is what we are being taught actually correct? In the past in other countries, but even today, totalitarian governments have altered the teachings of history to influence its current, but also its future generations. People then get angry at other countries and people because they have been told false things about them. They were not taught the truth.

In other cases, countries try to erase their past history when it makes them look bad. So they create a new history. Some create false histories of other countries in order to galvanize their own people against those countries.

When a country is taken over by a totalitarian regime, books are destroyed or rewritten to favor that new regime. For example, many in China and Korea are very concerned about Japan changing its history in schools, ignoring or rewriting what Japan did to those countries in the past.

China has reportedly had an increased influence on the contents of American textbooks, starting at the earliest grade levels. What might be revisionist content can support the Chinese Communist Party's agenda.

How can people make informed decisions when wrong or intentionally false information is taught? Much damage is done when information is left out entirely. Educators in the United States used to feel that wasn't happening. They felt that America's education system taught objective truth, especially about history. Of course, there are always unintentional errors but, overall, the system and the people in it tried to teach truth. They tried to accomplish all the things we mentioned above as being objectives of education.

In large part, that is no longer the case today.

The former "truth" of things is not necessarily the same "truth" we learn today. Did we have a new enlightenment that has allowed us to make changes to past truth? Overall, we did not. Former truth is still today's truth. It just isn't taught that way anymore. Of course, research or new information might contribute to adjustments or corrections to the information we have. But the actual truth of history should remain as it has always been. Truth should be truth.

For example, was George Washington *actually* the first American president? We weren't there. We didn't meet him personally. So just exactly how do we know that? Nonetheless, we universally accept that fact of history.

After all, we read about Washington in books! But, who wrote those books? Did they lie to us, or was it an actual fact? Or has it been subject to politically inspired changes? Should that be a "truth" that remains? Or, as has happened in other parts of history, is it subject to change?

George Washington was indeed the first U.S. president.

In which subjects are false changes most likely to occur?

History is number one. But it also happens in many other areas including political science, English, even math and geography!

"Geography?" you ask. How can there be misinformation taught there? And what about math? You can't change objective principles and teachings of math, can you? Math is math! Actually, people are indeed changing things in ways that have nothing to do with a subject's objective lessons.

The question I'm asking is, what has happened to education? Students are now thinking and acting differently based on wrong or missing information. They have especially been taught such things over the past few decades (although not necessarily in math). They think and act differently because of political indoctrinations in classrooms that often have nothing to do with the subject matter itself.

Few would dispute that people can do what they want in their own lives as long as it doesn't negatively affect others. After all, it's their life. However, mandating or indoctrinating *others* to do the same thing, even in the face of strong, even factual disagreements, is a completely different matter. Yet this has too often been done, even through government legislation. It also appears through textbook and school mandates.

Today, some agenda-rich people do try to get others to live their lives, even their personal lives, in ways which the agendas of these total strangers dictate. That's inconsistent with freedom. Those few should not dictate how others live. That includes not being forced to support life paths which are objectionable to those being forced onto those paths.

Most countries have some level of a shared cultural morality. But there are often those who want to tear it down.

The intrusion of political or sociological agendas by government or by non-educationally-competent entities should be challenged. Such intrusions can result in changing teachings or classroom materials and is rarely legitimate. (Normal, impartial educational textbook reviews, *by those competent to do it,* are different and are necessary.)

Such intrusions are certainly illegitimate when they involve promoting teachings solely originating from changing political or sociological realms, especially when they include committing what some may feel is the academic crime of historical or sociological revisionism. Such revisionist behavior damages individuals, education, and, by extension, the future of the country itself.

Even if it takes many years, those people who can dictate and control what is happening in schools, including what is being taught, will eventually control the nation. A healthy, properly functioning public education system is critical for a free country. Increasingly, that is too often not true in America.

At one time, local communities had a say in what was going on in their children's schools. Increasingly, that input and control has been taken away by entities further and further away from those communities, specifically by some large school districts, the state, or the federal government. Unfathomably, even agendas from other countries have been considered *by those other countries* for required inclusion in the curricula of American education. What's going on here?

***

Educators are aware that not all parents or community members can do a good job monitoring the day-to-day intrinsics of education in schools. Many in the community suffer from the past failures of education themselves. In addition, there are some basic understandings needed by those involved (educators as well as those in the community) if they are to effectively watch over education.

Even though I say that those educators who have been in a position of policy and oversight have failed to fix education — along with politicians and others — those in the community, including parents, can also fail by unintentionally heading down a wrong path. Many parents — but also others in the community — can feel strongly about wanting to change/fix public education. Many times, they are correct. But other times, what they adamantly insist on doing can unknowingly make things worse. Reinventing the wheel without enough experience can lead to repeating the same mistakes that crippled education in the first place.

I'm definitely on the side of parents who are trying to get harmful indoctrinations out of the schools. I also support parents who correctly want to see books and materials which are inappropriate for *any* K-12 student, removed from classrooms and school libraries. It's amazing to me that there has been so much debate on that point. Just a few short years ago, almost no one would argue in support of K-12 students having access to some of the materials now found in many schools.

All involved with education should look at what has failed in the past so that those same things aren't done again. Unfortunately, records of failed attempts of the past are rarely kept. We can't easily know some of the many things that have been tried before today, sometimes years or decades before. Efforts to try what are really the same or similar failed "reforms" of the past, sometimes just with different names, often fail as they had failed before.

Educators themselves often don't know that. Only educators with decades of experience will be able to recognize that some of the various "new" programs and purported reforms are the same as similar ones they saw fail in the past. It's almost impossible for parents or community members to know about them.

Nonetheless, some things are obvious on their face, such as enforced requirements for damaging, politically-driven agendas — especially those that either have no basis in fact, go against the founding principles of the country, or go against successful educational methodologies of the past. In the first two cases, parents and community members are as good, often better, than professional educators are in urgently calling for change and reform. But judging success or failure of educational methodologies is not easy, even though some people — even some educators — might think that it is.

***

It's finally time to talk about historical revisionism.

This is what happens when schools, publishers, or others, change the history that students are being taught so that it is different from what actually happened. This is often done to inculcate students with political or sociological agendas that some group, government, or individual dictates must now be taught — regardless of the objective truth of events, history, and life.

One way to tear down a country is by getting rid of its past, in particular by demeaning or eliminating its past heroes and its previously respected founding fathers.

Without them, there are few, if anyone, left whom we can hold up with pride as a nation. Without heroes and a proud history, a country's original founding principles and beliefs will not survive. It then becomes easy to take over that country by people or countries with bad intents. We must be particularly vigilant that those tearing down the country do not do so from within the country itself. Such people are often those holding political or financial power in the country.

News and social media can also work against the country. We have discovered that some in the media are intentionally doing that.

When honors (statues and namings) are withdrawn from America's foundational heroes, including George Washington, Thomas Jefferson, Abraham Lincoln, and others, we find ourselves in the same position as other nations where the same things were imposed on them by tyrannical governments.

There is one appalling difference today from the past corruption of other nations. Certain other nations have changed their histories to make themselves look good as well as to support new regimes that have taken over. America appears to be changing its history to actually make itself *look bad*. That is more than just wrong. It is dangerous.

Those doing the changing say they are simply "correcting" or making clear the things of the past. But they're not. They're corrupting the facts of history to make America look bad. These are people who appear not to like their own country.

Recent historical corruptions seem to particularly focus on "racism," but also on anything else they want changed to match new agendas. They do this not just by adding or changing things of history, but also by leaving out key foundations and under-standings.

History shows that countries often collapse from within. There-after, outside enemies and nations can easily move in and take over.

That doesn't necessarily mean an outsider's military would occupy the country — although that is certainly possible. The takeover may happen more subtly — and in broad daylight. The "new" country will then follow the wishes of those who have perpetrated the takeover. As elsewhere in history, those involved use rational sounding arguments for what they're doing. They capi-talize on the naiveté and poor education of the population. Such a population can be easily misled. People don't recognize what is happening until it is too late. Even then, they might not understand what just happened.

Even though others might see what is happening, they are not enough. What follow are words from a December 2020 conference in Florida. They lay out clearly and accurately why history is so critical if we are to survive.

> "When you destroy the past, you eliminate all reference points. If you have no idea what came before you, you have no idea what normal is. You can not understand the consequences of what's happening now if you can't look to the past and understand the consequences of the same behavior in another time. The root of wisdom is knowing what happened before. [The past is] the roadmap. So when you destroy that, you have an entire country that is very easily manipulated."[1]

Just a few weeks later, that same speaker laid out the abuse and destruction of truth in history that observers know is already here:

> "History is a political tool. History is not simply a record of what happened. History is a way to shape the future. History is used to hurt some people and to help other people gain power. History is never neutral." Once truth becomes irrelevant, "Ideology is all that matters."[2]

At that point, history is no longer history. Even some purported "historians" agree with rewriting, reinterpreting, or simply fully falsifying history as long as it supports their preferred ideologies. Yet that places the country in the same company as other countries with whose history and abuses we would not want to be associated.

The use of history as a political tool — a "weapon" is likely a more correct designation — can do irreparable harm. It is almost never justifiable. It means that entire populations believe and live under a structure of untruths. Assuming those are actual truths, they then pass them on to subsequent generations. This means that decisions, including political ones, are made based on false knowledge and understandings. The destruction of history is difficult to reverse. So is the destruction of countries.

Decisions, voting, thinking, and beliefs — including religious beliefs — which are founded on misleading, even fictional histories, can create a dangerous future for the country...and the world.

History must be protected. It must not be manipulated. But, in multiple countries, it *has* been manipulated. Operating within the corruption and failure of American education systems, both public and private, it is happening in America today.

9a. This section is a modified and condensed version of a Digression by the same name found in the 2022 book, *The Cartainos: Men of Passion • Men of Stone,* also by the author. Some comments are added to more clearly connect it to the focus of the book in your hands.

AN "INTELLECTUAL PLAGUE"

In her book, *I Live Again* (1951), Princess Ileana of Romania said that "an intellectual plague" spread through Romania at the end of WWII. After the war, Romania was effectively ceded to Stalin's communists in the Soviet Union (the USSR, of which Russia was the largest part). Romania became part of the Iron Curtain, a group of countries controlled by the USSR.

The USSR was actually the Union of Soviet Socialist Republics. It was often simply referred to as the Soviet Union. It was comprised of Russia and a number of other countries and satellite nations, including Romania.

Why do I have to add that explanation? It's because so many in recent generations don't remember or never learned much about the former Soviet Union other than, perhaps, its one-time existence in history. That no longer seems to matter to anyone who wasn't alive during those times.

But it should. That's especially true if Russia decides to recapture parts of its former USSR self — as it appears to be doing in recent times.

Along with other Iron Curtain countries after WWII, Romania had been cut off from open access to the world.

Do all readers know what Iron Curtain countries were — or even care? I assure you that many no longer know. So goes history. So goes life. So goes education.

After taking control of the country, communists began indoctrinating the Romanian people with their political and socioeconomic beliefs. The communists knew that the key to their control would be through the indoctrination of the children — and the way to reach children is through the schools.

To do that, teachings and histories in conflict with their new indoctrination had to be replaced or eliminated. According to what is laid out in Princess Ileana's book, here is what happened:

- History textbooks were taken outside, put in a pile, and burned. The whole school was taken out to watch the book burning. The lesson was that *"the past and everything taught about it had been wrong and false, and must be destroyed."*[1] Book confiscation and burnings have also occurred in other places at other times in history. Perhaps most memorably were the book burnings in Nazi Germany in 1933. But, more than once, book burnings have taken place in China as well as in other countries.
- Elsewhere, new textbooks were substituted for the old ones. *"It was forbidden to mention any historical events not listed in the text,"* or to change in any way the communist version of those events.
- Esteemed writers and poets were removed from literature books as though they had never existed. Romanian kings and queens — and others of whom the people had been proud — were expunged from textbooks. Pictures of *"Stalin* [infamous leader of the Soviet Union] *and Groza* [the first Communist Prime Minister in Romania] *were substituted."*
- Where books were not burned, students and teachers were prohibited from using them or even just possessing them. *"Lectures were substituted for the texts in all classes except mathematics."*

All that seems terrible — and it clearly was.

But, unbelievably to many, we can find recent instances of *each* of those things happening in history classes *in America,* as well as in other subjects at all grade levels.

Today, these things happen even in countries that purport to be democracies, that still profess to be free.

Perhaps even more concerning, responsibility for these things does not always rest with governments. Agenda-laden individual citizens of current or formerly "free" countries are too often directly responsible for them.

(Temporarily) free and democratic peoples who are involved and supportive of these things rarely have a correct and full understanding of history. If they did, they would never allow history to be changed.

In postwar Romania, the blatant destruction of Romanian history and culture was done openly, in front of everyone. Parents who wanted to preserve their history, culture, and values, were forced to teach their children at home. In some cases, parents put themselves at risk of punishment by violating educational prohibitions.

In addition to what happened under Hitler's Nazis and Stalin's communists, historical revisionism took place under other totalitarian regimes, including in Asia. Books had to contain teachings approved by the government, even if what was being taught was largely false. That meant going against the past traditions and facts of their people's history, culture, and morality.

Frequently, the facts of wars are targets for "reinterpretation." That is understandable. It's difficult for people to acknowledge their own wrongs. But revising histories so that they no longer match the facts should be unacceptable almost no matter what the reason. Otherwise, people will not learn from the past and stand up so that it doesn't happen again.

Today, free people bristle when they hear of forced changes to the cultures and histories of people. Such is inconsistent with the sensibilities and beliefs of a free people. Many Native American peoples will attest to that.

Yet, in America and elsewhere, such "free" people do not see that historical revisionism is already being practiced right in front of them. It's increasingly seen in the writings of new and "revised" textbooks, most notably history and other social science books. How is this possible when concerned people today find it so unacceptable? Do not states or governmental agencies review textbooks for acceptability and, especially, accuracy? Even though history is never fully neutral, surely, the history books of a free people should contain objective and trustworthy facts — or at least as much as possible!

Were textbooks burned today, free people in free countries would sit up, take notice, and demand that it stop. They would angrily move to counter attempts to rewrite history that reflect specific agendas of the government, the authors, and others.

But wait. Those words were written just a short time back. Yet today, books that are no longer considered "acceptable" have actually been burned, both in America and elsewhere. In most places, it is not hidden. It has happened fully in the open. Yet few people are rising up to stop it. Intimidation appears to be preventing large enough numbers of people from coming forward.

Therefore, even in America, history is being rewritten[2].

[Note that I am not referring to those books deemed unacceptable by parents as were previously discussed. That is a fully separate and unrelated issue.]

Changes naturally occur in a living society, but such changes should not require rewriting or obviating history itself. The value of parents' roles in education has been increasingly replaced, often without their knowledge.

Unlike the public pronouncements of the communists and some other countries, shifts in teachings in the U.S. and other democracies are often so gradual that they are not noticed. New generations then espouse the new teachings, accepting them as correct, as the way things should be — as the way things have always been — when in fact their histories, culture, and values have already been reinterpreted and rewritten. They are then being taught to children who will take it all in as fact — and teach it to students of the next generation.

Revisions in the histories of world religions have already led to countless believers accepting religious beliefs and revised histories that simply didn't exist not many years ago. Whether secular or religious, such new histories are often fervently believed by current and recent generations of misled and unknowing youth. As teachers of future generations, they will confidently pass on those same false "histories" and "truths" to those whom they will then teach.

Under both Naziism and communism, if parents tried to correct the wrong teachings of the schools, their own children could turn them in to the government. In many cases, that could lead to their imprisonment or death. Romania was not the only country where this happened.

Today, in the "free" world, many of these changes are being done openly. The 1619 Project would be one example. Other changes may go unnoticed, happening over many years — slowly, subtly, and insidiously. Some American states and school districts might (wrongly) say otherwise, but it is rare that even one person with *competent* and *objective* knowledge thoroughly reads a new textbook in an attempt to confirm its accuracy prior to adoption. Multiple thorough and competent reviews by people on different sides of politics and history are needed to ensure proper textbooks. However, from a practical perspective, that isn't an easy thing to do.

Those few who do "review" some textbooks, but who are neither competent nor objective, are inclined to accept the authors as authorities, seldom questioning the material since they themselves may not feel qualified — and indeed may not be qualified — to make factual judgments. Few working educators actually have enough time and energy to do thorough textbook reviews anyway.

Sending K-12 textbooks back to publishers for factual rewrites or corrections can happen, but it is rare. Too often today, the inclusion of "new facts" (or political correctness) can actually be dictated by states or school districts.

Publishers often write textbooks to meet the requirements of the largest states, their largest customers. California has great influence over the content of textbooks.

Some publishers might release separate versions of their textbooks to support different customers. Others don't.

On the surface, some textbook/historical changes appear to be of little consequence. However, they are not of little consequence. When we begin to accept small inaccuracies as though they were fact, it becomes easier to accept larger ones.

One should not be able to read high school history books and identify the churches and religious beliefs of the authors. Yet, increasingly, that is possible. It is increasingly possible to identify their political beliefs, too.

Religious history, formerly based on secular historical facts, are now changed to match often unsubstantiated teachings of one church or another to which one or more of the authors belong.

Factual changes related to the early days of Christianity, Catholicism, the Protestant Reformation, Hinduism, Buddhism, Islam, and Protestantism may all be changed to suit some authors' personal beliefs (or personal ignorance) with no regard to demonstrable facts. At that point, the damage is done. Such "revised" facts will then be accepted by students and teachers alike. They will be repeated and passed on to new generations with the confidence that these new "facts" are part of correct history.

But they may not be correct at all.

Compare books of today with those used prior to the middle of the twentieth century, the mid-1900s. In places, many no longer match. Some will argue that such "older" history has been "corrected" or "clarified" in the current writings.

But the "corrections" in more recent books can more often be attributed to the politics, religious beliefs, or political correctness of the times, the authors, influential politicians, or some new and destructive movement.

Haven't some countries who enforced new histories also argued that they were simply "correcting" or rightly "interpreting" the facts? Certainly, the Nazis and communists justified their own changes — and they were not alone.

Pick up a high school American history textbook and look at one simple example found in many (not all) history books. Find in it the famous words that Neal Armstrong (1930–2012) spoke upon first setting foot on the moon. He did *not* say, "That's one small step for *a* man, one giant leap for mankind." He *did* say, "That's one small step for man, one giant leap for mankind." There was no article, "a" before "man." Not all, but some textbooks have changed his words.

One can argue that he had meant to say that. One can say that he was supposed to say it. Some have said, unconvincingly, that it was found in the static. Some have even claimed that the original utterance may be sexist and should now be changed regardless of what he actually said.

Whatever the controversy, the bottom line, historically, is that not only did no one hear him say it, but that he simply didn't say it. There was no article "a" in front of "man."

Exactly why, then, would an author of a history book intentionally change his wording? It should be a minor issue to get such an obvious fact of history correct. The textbook author would certainly serve readers by giving the correct phrase and then discussing any controversy surrounding it. But, too many who have changed his words have not done that. They simply print the revised phrase as though it were fact.

A minor issue, you say? Why should we be concerned about a small detail about which no one cares and that really won't affect anything?

It is not that at all. After all, exactly *how many* "minor" historical changes are acceptable? One? Five? Fifty?

In *Footprints in the Dust*,[3] Rick Houston does not mince words saying that Neal Armstrong did not add the article, "a," to his words on the moon *"and to imply otherwise is revisionist history."*

To condemn anything as "revisionist" in what purports to be a history textbook may be among the most damning statements one can make about it. Although not always the case (sometimes it might be), some feel it can label the historian/author as unknowledgeable — even untrustworthy.

Some years back, the author himself compared older American and world history textbooks with more recent releases and noted that certain events or facts of history are described differently in each book; sometimes the basic facts themselves had changed.

The real issue is that, increasingly, changes are not so minor. They extend not only to the basic facts themselves, but to changes in interpretation from how they were interpreted at the time of the events. Judging the past by the continually changing standards of today prevents a correct understanding of the people and events of the past. That is not what history should be about, especially at and below the high school level, but really at all levels of education.

Of course, comparisons and discussions of historical events in light of today's understandings are legitimate and important. But to falsely interpret, revise, or expunge the past — often with some "agenda" by an author, a government, or some group — is destructive to both current and future generations. It can also be disrespectful of those who lived the past. How are people able to learn from the past if they are not provided the truth of the past from which to learn?

"Those who cannot remember the past are condemned to repeat it.[4]"

No one can remember a past they didn't learn in the first place — or learned wrongly.

In the vast majority of cases, we do learn the truth; most of the history that we learn is correct history. The thing is, as much as possible, that should be true in *all* cases, not just in "most" cases.

But it isn't.

We are already on a slippery slope and appear neither able nor willing to stop our slide.

History textbook authors, as well as teachers, have an obligation to teach the truth. I also maintain that books even for general readership that recount history should do so correctly. If they veer away from that truth, they should clearly note it in an obvious place somewhere in their writings. Otherwise, unwary readers might later assume that such facts are the correct ones of history — even when they are part of fictional accounts. Forgetting in which fictional context they learned them, they will pass them on as true history.

Movies which rewrite history — there are a number of them — can do even greater damage because they can make the revised history seem real. I'm not at all saying to ban such movies! But I am saying that we must do what we can so that some don't confuse such non-history for actual history.

Then, of course, there are increasing numbers of people in outright denial of certain historical events — deniers of the Holocaust and the moon landing are but two prominent examples. Some writers today wrongly ascribe that to legitimate controversy. But actual deniers of historical truths are *not* part of "legitimate controversy."

Some readers of these words are already asking for other examples to debate. But this discussion has arisen here only because Princess Ileana described what happened in Romania. Her descriptions should be an alarm and serious warning for the rest of us.

***

At least, we might be grateful that our children are not taught to turn in their parents, as they were taught to do in Romania, the Soviet Union, and in other countries for "unacceptable" activities, including providing prohibited teachings at home.

We might be grateful, were it not that parents today are already at increasing risk that their children might indeed report them for one thing or another — as is often *directed* by schools, teachers, and/or government entities. Too often, they can be reported for activities of which parents may be totally innocent.

Such reporting may appear justifiable in certain cases, abuse being the most notable. However, the potential for the expansion of children reporting on parents for other activities, far less justifiable, is already in place. Already, too many children falsely report, or threaten to report, their own parents out of vindictiveness for some parental action with which they disagree.

According to at least one December 2011 report by National Public Radio, the government has discussed plans to work with the Department of Education to uncover potential home-grown terrorists. Although details were lacking (and while acknowledging the alarming existence of terrorism, correctly defined), such conversations begin to look frighteningly like the times when children were told to spy on their parents in the Soviet Union (and elsewhere), turning them in to the government for some "prohibited" activity or utterance.

The mechanism is already in place for this. If we look at history, we realize that such mechanism may gradually be repurposed for future, more disturbing uses of children monitoring and reporting on their parents. Eventually, that could even be for holding out-of-favor social or political positions.

Yes, we want to protect children. Yes, we want to root out truly dangerous terrorists. Should reporting be expanded to include that? Alas, "terrorist" definitions have changed over time. Even now, it includes those whom no one would have considered to be a terrorist even just a few years ago.

But new generations don't know that.

Many educators have been quite uncomfortable with mandatory reporting requirements in many parts of the country. Such requirements were put in place to provide recourse to protect children from abuses at home. However, many educators see situations involving such mandatory reporting that deeply trouble them.

***

I repeat myself here that people have no way to learn correct history, many parts of which we do not want to repeat. Repeating history has already led to terrible suffering in regimes and countries throughout the world. It is unlikely to stop.

Even worse, educators themselves are often products of that same system. Too many educators now believe that certain revisionist history is actually correct history. After all, it's what most of them were taught as they themselves went through school. Often in good faith, they pass it on. What else can they do? It's all they know.

Many observers point to the prevalence of revisionism on college campuses, but it is far more critical when it happens at the earliest grades, including through high school.

Even when the facts of history may be presented accurately, strong biases by many educators then impugn, twist, and cast doubt on that history.

***

The bottom line is that both historical and cultural revisionism is alive and well and likely in your neighborhood schools right now. Few people are aware of it, even those who should know better. Those can include state and local textbook review boards, committees, and educators at all levels.

Power is increasingly being wielded, and the abuse of power in small things has always led to abuses in bigger things.

It may be better for a free people were books publicly burned more frequently. In that way, all would know exactly what is happening and would, we can only hope, rise up to stop it. [That, too, was written just a short time back. But, as mentioned before, books *are* being burned in places. It does not appear that anyone has wanted or been able to step up to stop it.]

Ensuring that actual history is being taught requires more recent generations to question their own teachings. Many have already been caught up in the distortions of historical "truths."

Of course, many feel that none of this matters anyway.

And it is that indifference that paves the road to our undoing.

Princess Ileana was right to be alarmed.[5]

10. THE CONFIDENCE OF MATH

Math is not merely important for its practical need in life, business, and math-intensive careers. As we learned in the last chapter, it also quietly builds self-confidence in students. Students who struggle with math often do poorly in other classes, too.

Do students have trouble in other classes because the same habits and difficulties causing them problems in math also cause them difficulties everywhere? Or does their lack of self-confidence brought about by struggling in math affect them in all classes — and in all aspects of their lives?

I believe it is the latter.

If you ask educators (especially math teachers) about this, most will agree with the connection between math and student confidence. But, without considering the question, the primary goal of mathematics teachers is to teach the math itself, not to develop self-confidence. That is an important by-product of learning math, not something that can be directly taught. If that isn't clear, let me try to say it a different way.

Students who are self-confident, generally speaking, do better in math. It seems easier for them to learn than for students who have "math phobia," those who *really* dislike math. Of course, the reason they dislike math is because they can't do it well. And they can't do it well, at least in part, because they don't have the confidence, the self-belief, that they can actually learn to do it in the first place. (I'd suggest that might be a Catch-22, but then I'd have to explain what that is.)

Self-confidence is *naturally* developed as students do well in math. However, that should not be confused with the recent injection and promotion of "feelings" in math classes by some schools, as opposed to just teaching the math itself.

Although teachers should be aware and supportive of students who are seriously stressed about math, they don't need to be discussing generic "feelings" in math class. (That might actually be counterproductive.) They just have to help students do well. Any "feelings" of confidence will show up naturally, as a direct result of student success.

Students who really hate math — and that includes adults — actually exhibit physical distress when faced with math problems they are required to solve. They might get mildly dizzy, have tightness in their stomach or chest, even feel mildly nauseous. Most don't talk about such symptoms. All they say is that they really don't like math.

However, if we can get students to be successful at math, if they can successfully solve problems with comparative ease, even with occasional fun, their self-confidence with numbers increases substantially. They feel they can actually learn math. And that self-confidence transfers over to non-math classes — and to life itself.

One of several ways the author developed self-confidence in math students was to teach some non-traditional methodologies. By showing students that, by using some easier methods, they could actually be better than almost anyone else they come across worked wonders with some students. I often taught small pieces from *The Trachtenberg Speed System of Basic Mathematics*[1] to instill confidence and some mental math discipline in many students. It was generally fun for both me and my students.[2]

For most people, math really isn't fun. When it is, students do much better. Once they think that even just a part of math is fun or easy, they begin to know that they really can do it. The problem is often that they are getting one or more pieces of basic *arithmetic* wrong — and they don't even know it.

A number of students have learning disorders, both diagnosed and undiagnosed. Dyslexia remains a common problem in many students — and also in adults. Research into it has been ongoing for many years. Yet students who have it are often without help. Many students don't know they might have it and teachers don't always recognize it, especially minor manifestations of it.

Other teachers refuse to informally diagnose or even suggest a possible learning disorder. That is even if they have seen such struggling students for many years and should know how to recognize it, at least as a possibility.

Since they are not doctors in the field, most teachers insist, as they are told to do, that they cannot diagnose anything at all. Of course, we don't want teachers to willy-nilly tell students or parents that a student definitively has some disorder. Many teachers would get it wrong.

On the other hand, most students don't have access to formal evaluative services, especially in smaller communities or in rural parts of the country. Therefore, they are just allowed to struggle on without help.

If it is an ongoing difficulty without other obvious causes (such as not studying at all), teachers should minimally and carefully raise the possibility of such issues with students and their parents.

Teachers can suggest getting a doctor or professional involved if parents can find one in their area.

Experienced teachers can also suggest to both student and parents that the student consider trying different learning methods which the teacher might suggest. Some teachers do know about such options.

If they have time, a good resource for both parents and teachers might be the school's Special Education teacher(s) to see what they suggest.

Some schools in the country might have specially funded programs to address certain disorders and are might willing to talk to teachers. Special Education teachers at the student's school or at other schools might also be resources.

Unfortunately, many doctors themselves don't always have enough experience in the full range of learning disorders. Too many doctors just default to prescribing medication rather than finding non-drug alternatives — that is, if alternatives are even available.

Since some students can be overmedicated today, it's good to talk to the doctor about alternatives that might also work. However, in many cases, prescription drugs can be the correct choice. This decision is best made between parents and doctor. Of course, the child is involved in this, too.

I'm not giving medical advice here. See a doctor for that.

But, if teachers do nothing, students are left hanging because no outside help is available. It leaves many students on their own and in academic survival mode (cheating instead of learning).

Teachers are the frontline resource. If what a teacher tries in order to help a student seems to be working, it is certainly wise to bring it up and discuss it with both students and their parents. If something isn't working, it should be dropped so that something else can be tried instead. Regardless, both students and (caring) parents should be involved.

Nonetheless, teachers don't have the time or ability to discover or diagnose every single problem in every class, especially in large classes. But, when a problem might be recognizable, teachers should consult with others and try *something* that might be of help. Doing nothing is to abandon students entirely who may have already been struggling for years.

Without success in class, especially in math, students of all ages (including adults) will continue to lose confidence. Especially in math, they will not be able to learn what is being taught in class — without cheating. And many — likely most — students with certain learning disorders have learned that they must cheat to survive academically. They've become quite good at it. If there might be a legitimate learning disorder involved for which the student has no help, it's not necessarily their fault. It's a failure of the system.

Survival cheating is far more common than people think. In most cases, no one but the student knows they're doing it. But sometimes, good teachers can catch it.

I'm not talking about cheating because a student didn't study or didn't do the assigned work. I'm talking about either an unad-dressed learning disorder, a crippling lack of self-confidence because of many earlier educational failings, or perhaps a legiti-mate, nearly disabling case of math phobia.

> Note that students should not use math phobia as an excuse for doing poorly. Nor should they or their parents blame it on some self-diagnosed disorder when one doesn't really exist. However, such can indeed be a primary cause of serious difficulties in students who aren't even able to identify it. This happens more often than people might know. With the right help from good teachers, involved parents, and others, many students can make good progress in overcoming some learning disorders. With work, they can move themselves towards greater success.
>
> But not always. Sometimes, the only way to move forward is with the help of medical or other professionals. It's important not to give up.

Many students have indeed given up that there might be any help out there for them. They've become tired of parents and teachers telling them that, if they would just get more serious about studying, they would succeed. In most cases, more studying certainly is the answer. But, with learning disorders, it is counter-productive to insist on doing something that hasn't worked. The student needs caring and understanding help in order to succeed. Otherwise, they will continue to struggle and fail throughout their lives and have no idea why.

Many students know that something is wrong, but don't know what it is. Someone has to tell them. In most cases, that's a teacher.

Let's now move on to look at one basic arithmetic test, designed by the author, and administered some years ago to 7th, 8th, and 9th grade students at what was then a junior high school in Los Ange-les. There is little reason to believe that things are much better in similar schools today.

10a. MATH: THE SBAST

For many years, and still today, countless students graduate from high school possessing very weak skills, not only in English (both reading and writing), but also in mathematics. We know this as we look at a variety of test results and surveys. We also note the great number of students who need remedial classes when, or if, they enter college.

Some years before I began teaching in the Los Angeles Unified School District, I taught in two private post-secondary schools. Those are for-profit schools that offer programs training adults for specific jobs. They might get training to work at airlines, in travel, in computers, in business, or in many other fields.

My primary work there was to provide a review of both basic English writing skills and basic math skills for the adults who were beginning their programs. Writing and math skills are needed in almost every field. It was important that students have a working foundation in both.

Schools had learned that many adults, whether or not they had finished high school, had low English and math skills. At the time, I held a California Private Post-Secondary Authorization for Service which allowed me to teach several subject areas, including writing and mathematics, in California private post-secondary schools.

It didn't take long for me to understand how difficult math was for many adults. It hurt me to see so many struggle with math phobia. They had signed up at the schools to learn a trade. But then, many were having to work at something, once again, that they never liked when they took it the first time — and at which they still weren't very good.

I began to write handouts for the way I explained the topics. Fortunately for my students, I had never liked math much myself when I was in school. I worked to find out how I might encourage them, and how to simplify things as I taught.

Many people and schools feel the best teachers are the ones who are best qualified in their subject matter. Too many times, that is completely wrong. Such people might know their subject, but they don't always know how to teach it. The subject may be so easy for them that they can't empathize with students who are so confused and stressed about it.

I have always said that schools need the best *teachers*, not the best subject matter professionals.

I found myself explaining things non-traditionally. I did it to reduce stress and confusion. It seemed to work. More than that, it succeeded because students found they could get math problems right. That often translated to an increase in their level of self-confidence.

The handouts became long enough that I put them together in a book: *Math Is Easy: A Basic Math Review for Adults*. The book, which is not currently in print (but may be back), received a number of good reviews.

One teacher who reviewed the book commented, *"The manner in which the math is presented is superb."* It received numerous testimonials from students, primarily adults, who used it to improve their basic math skills.

***

When I later began teaching at a junior high school (7th, 8th, 9th grades) in Los Angeles, I saw the same stress and confusion in many of my younger students that I had seen in the adults I had previously taught. I knew what was ahead of them if I couldn't help them.

That junior high school had a mixture of low and high performing students. Many students struggled as students do in other schools. Other students did well and were successful at getting a better level of education. A number of students were from families who had not been in the country long. English was not their first language. Many of them struggled both academically and behaviorally.[1] That is too common in many schools.

Based on what a number of my students quietly said to me — especially as several wanted to nominate me for a Jaime Escalante Mathematics Teacher award — I could see that I was helping them. I was, and am still, very touched by their letters.

I am not what is important about some of the middle school

students' nominations and I initially hesitated to use them lest that is what you might think. What *is* important is to understand how frustrating math is to many of them. It's special when we see them change, when we see them gain self-confidence, when they begin to take pride in math, when they take greater pride in themselves, when they begin to look forward to coming to math class.

Those changes in students are what we all need to keep in front of us so that we don't give up on them, so that we care about as many as our energy allows us to do. I didn't take an interest in just a couple of students, but in as many as possible at the same time. There's just so much any one teacher can do, but we have to do our best anyway, even if it's not enough. What follow are samples of what a few students wrote. I only use their initials.

AM:

Here is an excerpt from a longer writing by one student. I don't recall his grade level, but believe that he may have been in 7th grade.

> *"I came into Mr. Scarpitta's class failing math and didn't know the work, so I wouldn't do the work. Mr. Scarpitta saw the potential in me, so he pushed me everyday to do my best. ...I don't think I could have passed math at all if I hadn't had Mr. Scarpitta for a teacher. Out of all teachers I've had for math, he didn't give up, and encouraged me not to give up. Every teacher that has the title of a teacher is not. What I mean is, those who really go out of the way for when they don't have to should be and only should be called teacher. What makes Mr. Scarpitta special is his heart and kindness."*

I'll say again: I am not the special thing in what that student said or what any student says throughout this book. Indeed, most good teachers have students who say wonderful things and who feel they are the best for them. But what is most important is what a *student* needs. Keep in mind that I was not even a fully credentialed teacher at that time. Did I become a better teacher after completing the many required classes of teacher training? I did not. Only a few teacher training classes benefited me as a teacher. Some others were interesting, but they didn't really contribute to making me a better teacher. Most classes wasted both my money and time.

JM:

Here is a touching comment taken from another student's page-long writing. This was not part of a nomination. He wrote it for me in one of his English classes.

> *"You know I would be pleased if you were my father because you are a good person in this school because you help me to learn math and how to do things."*

Many students have difficult lives at home. We'll look at a couple of examples a bit later on.

Far too many students grow up without a father. *The Cartainos: Men of Passion • Men of Stone* has numerous examples of what happens when people grow up fatherless. Along with one other book, it contains an extensive section on the problem of fatherlessness. That other book is, *Killers Are Fatherless.* Both are by this author.

LM:

Here are excerpts from another student. Her full writing was over two full pages long. She had me as her math teacher when she in 8th grade, but she wrote her pages the following year when she was in 9th grade. When she had started in my class, she knew nothing about me except that she didn't want me for her teacher.

She went to her counselor almost daily to ask to transfer out of my class. Her counselor told her, "NO." In the end, she was happy that she stayed. As I repeatedly say (and that's the real reason I quote her here), math builds confidence. Once students have confidence, they can not just do math — they can do almost anything.

It's almost as important to build confidence in students as it is to teach the mechanics of math itself. They must both go together.

> *"I have learned more math with Mr. Scarpitta in one semester* [she had me the previous year] *than I did in 2 or 3 years with other teachers. ... In his class, you don't learn only math. He taught us History, English, and [more]. ... He knew all kinds of shortcuts for any mathematical problem. When I was in Mr. Scarpitta's class I did not realize what a great teacher he was, but once I had another teacher I realized how good of a mathematics teacher Mr. Scarpitta really is. Mr. Scarpitta opened new mathematical doors for me. Mr. Scarpitta told the class to never give up no matter what. ... He always makes his students [feel] like they could concour [conquer] the world. ... He always saw the best in his students, even if they were not as good, like me. I was not a good and fast learner, but he always told me that I improved, even if I did not. That got my confidence high, and I was able to do anything."*

MC:

In later chapters, we'll hear high school students mention that it sometimes seems as if their teachers didn't care about them. It's the intangibles that contribute to student confidence and learning. In all the teacher training classes, no one emphasized the importance of student confidence or developing hidden student strengths. Yet that is what can get students excited about learning — and the confidence that they are able to learn.

> *"When I first came to this school, I was in the 8ᵗʰ grade and the math teachers seemed like if they didn't care. I didn't know anything about math. ... When I came to Mr. Scarpitta's class I said in my mind, what a waste of time. I am going to get an "F" anyways. Well I was wrong! He started teaching me and the rest of the students. ... He is not boring like other teachers. He takes time to help us. He is friendly and understanding. ... He cares about us and he wants us to be something in our future. I know he doesn't do it for the money. He does it because he cares."*

Elsewhere in this book, I mention that, when I hire, I do all that I can to hire for *passion*. No teacher training program can teach that. It's either part of you or it isn't. Teachers without that passion have a more difficult job getting through to students, especially to students who need extra help.

So what can be done to ensure more teachers come with that? Teacher hiring and teacher training programs need to be re-thought. But it's not likely that will happen. Changing anything significant in education is all but impossible.

Today, there are things that we *don't* want to find in teachers who will be teaching our children. Teachers must come *without* the dangerous indoctrination that is part of Critical Race Theory and other dangerous philosophies. They must be without the social engineering that has been spreading rapidly today. This, too, is a difficult quality to ensure is missing.

So many students at all levels today are being taught these things as though they are normal and right. But they're not. They work to destroy not only education, but the country itself — and that is happening today.

In spite of the kind words from many of my students, I never felt that I was capable enough to do all that they needed. Really, none of us are. We can only do the best we can do.

Many teachers are truly far better than I am. They, too, have accolades from their students. But those things are not what are most important. Our job isn't to accumulate accolades. It's to develop students who will become educated and hopefully morally strong adults. We want them to have good lives, to contribute to others and society — as well as to their country within which we all live and share.

***

Teachers (and others) often make assumptions about students. For instance, they assume that students have certain skills. After all, those basic skills had been taught to them *for years*. Basic Arithmetic is one of those. So, if a student has trouble with a new math topic, teachers might not always look at educational basics when the teacher is trying to teach Algebra, as one example. Teachers might wrongly assume it's a problem with the new material in Algebra, when it's really a shortcoming in basic arithmetic.

Even when teachers recognize a problem in basic arithmetic, teachers don't have time to go back and reteach things the student should have learned long ago. They might mention the problem to the student, but then the teacher moves on. After all, they must finish that year's material and there is always more than they have time to cover.

I saw certain students miss some basic algebra problems, not because of the algebra, but because of some basic multiplication or division error. I didn't know how common the problem might be, but I could see that it needed to be addressed. It became clear that it was more common than I had first assumed. We needed to find the full extent of the problem.

I asked the principal if I could develop a test to let us see how widespread the problem was. He was a good principal. He was supportive. The test was called the SBAST ["S-Bast"], the Scarpitta Basic Arithmetic Skills Test. Before finalizing it, I got input from other math teachers.

Although some math teachers felt it would be a waste of time, most math teachers in the school administered it to their students anyway. I then scored the tests and prepared the anonymous statistics so they could be shared. The results were enlightening.

The SBAST presented 100 very basic arithmetic problems. These were the kinds of problems all would assume should have been impeccably learned years earlier in elementary school. After all, without a strong foundation in basic arithmetic, how can a student succeed in *any* kind of math?

Other math teachers had three basic concerns:

The first was that the problems were too easy. Clearly, these teachers maintained, the tests would be a waste of valuable class time. After all, they said, students at that level already knew such very basic arithmetic!

A second objection was that students should be able to

have as much time as they needed to complete the test. (It was timed, but it gave students *plenty of time* to complete it.) My response was to ask how much time do we expect our students to take in order to answer questions this simple?

For example, while waiting in line to checkout at a grocery store, how much time is acceptable to hold up the clerk and everyone behind you while you're trying to figure out what 14x2 is? Or 5x3? Or 12-8? Some things simply have to be known either immediately, or within seconds. That's part of what an educated person does, isn't it? Special education or learning impaired students are sometimes different, but we're testing the general student population here. And, no, saying they can just use the calculator on their cell phones is not an acceptable answer. So the timing of the test was very important.

The last objection was the most interesting. I had set a passing score of 90%. Less than 90% would not be passing. More than one teacher felt that was unreasonable. A passing score should be set lower than that. After all, passing in most classes then was considered to be 60%, a low D. Couldn't I make passing 70% or 80%?

I had already let those teachers review the test. I asked them to tell me which ten problems was it okay that students in 7th, 8th, and 9th grade didn't know. Would it be 9+4? 8+12? 36-11? 2x8? 7x3? 40÷8? 9-4? Or "hard" ones like 150÷10? 36÷12? 37-12? 66÷22?

I told them to look at the 100 questions and find ten that it was all right that our students didn't know. In my thinking, passing should have been 97% or more. I was willing to let students miss a couple due to daydreaming or just a handwritten "typo." We can all make unintentional mistakes. But missing TEN of such basic arithmetic problems by students at those grade levels? How can that be acceptable to any educator?

In the end, most teachers understood that and went along with the 90%. Yet, even after reviewing the test, one or two teachers still insisted that 90% was too high as a passing score; it should be lower. How can one then find *15 or 20* of those problems that *anyone* would say were all right for our students not to know? We needed to know what our students could do.

Passing was set at 90%.

Although teachers of honors classes in 7th and 8th grades gave it to their students, the teacher of the 9th grade honors class did not. Otherwise, the test was administered to almost all students present at the school the day it was given.

A total of 1,380 tests were given schoolwide (breakdown of some numbers may be slightly different due to issues with some tests). Scores were divided into four groups: 90-100 (Passing); and three failing groups consisting of 80-89%, 60-79%, and 0-59%, grouped somewhat differently below.

Here are the results:

SCHOOLWIDE:

PASSING: 750 students — a very low 54% of all students taking the test.

Combined total of the three failing groups (which include scores of 0 to 89%) was a total of 630 students, that's 46% of all students taking the test;

Combined total of the two lowest groups (scores of 0 to 79%) was 409 students — 30% of all students taking the test;

Total for just the bottom group (scores of 0 to 59%): 164 students —12% of all students taking the test.

Here are the scores by grade level:

•GRADE 7:

PASSING: 311—55%;

Combined total of the three failing groups (0 to 89%): 254 students —45% of all 7th grade students taking the test;

Combined total of the two lowest groups (0 to 79%): 166 —29.4%;

Total for the bottom group only (0 to 59%): 68—12%.

•GRADE 8:

PASSING: 310—60.7%;
Combined total of the three failing groups (0 to 89%): 201
—39.3% of all 8th grade students taking the test;
Combined total of the two lowest groups (0 to 79%): 121
—23.7%;
Total for the bottom group only (0 to 59%): 44—8.6%.

•GRADE 9:

PASSING: 129—42.4%;
Combined total of the three failing groups (0 to 89%): 175
—57.6% of all 9th grade students taking the test;
Combined total of the two lowest groups (0 to 79%): 122
—40.1%;
Total for the bottom group only (0 to 59%): 52 students,
an especially embarrassing 17.1% of all 9th graders taking
the test.

One might ask why 9th grade showed the worst passing scores
among the three grades tested. When junior high schools were
reconfigured as middle schools in that district (soon after the test),
9th graders were in high school. Even if a higher number failed to
take it seriously — and we have no data or evidence to support that
at all — 9th grade numbers are still frighteningly low.

Regardless, how was the education system able to teach so
many students without absolutely ensuring they knew arithmetic,
the very basics of mathematics? Even though the SBAST was given
a number of years ago, have things been remedied today? Evidence
leaves us with serious doubts.

Sure, many schools will have scores significantly higher than the
ones here. To me, high enough would be that 99% of all schools at
these grade levels would score 98% or higher. Actually, even much
lower grade levels should do almost as well. Are all students able
to get that at least 98% on such a very basic arithmetic test?

Results were unacceptable when the test was given and they're unacceptable now, regardless of any excuses someone might try to give.

With 90% as passing, students can miss ten problems and still pass. Are *you* able to pick out ten problems you feel it's okay for a 7th, 8th, or 9th grade student to get wrong? Remember, some teachers felt that students should be allowed to miss even more than that because, they said, 90% is too high for a minimum passing score.

Go now to look over the SBAST problems in the appendix at the back of the book.

11. CHEATING & MORALITY IN PUBLIC EDUCATION

Students don't want to fail. Some say they don't care whether they do or not, but nearly all of them really do care.

But how can they succeed at any level of mathematics when we just drag them through it, failing or just barely getting by (often by cheating) — because they can't do basic arithmetic? Clearly, they need help. They need remediation — a refocus on these basics so they can finally get things right!

Understand that many of these students actually understood how to do the math they were being taught, perhaps algebra or something else. I could tell their procedures were right. But their actual answers were wrong! How frustrating for them! They thought they were doing everything right, but their answers were wrong! Why??

It's because they couldn't do basic arithmetic. One small error — let alone two or three — and it becomes impossible to get a problem correct. Students may not even know why. So they experience terrible frustration. No wonder many give up. No wonder they lose confidence in themselves. No wonder they think they're stupid and can't succeed in school, not just in math.

How can we fix it?

Those were seriously bad scores on the SBAST. Students lack of competence in basic arithmetic needed to be fixed. (It's the same for basic competencies in other subjects.) I wanted to take a period of time to focus on repairing this deficiency in our students. After all, there was a large percentage of students who needed arithmetic repair work.

The principal commiserated, but couldn't see how it could be done. Math teachers are required to complete certain things during the school year and there just wasn't time to do the full remediation that was needed. Anyway, wouldn't it hurt students for whom this was not a problem?

The suggestions: Couldn't we just give extra assignments for the students to get their skills up to speed at home? Couldn't we just "fit in" some remediation during class while we moved on to cover what we had to cover? (Move on? You mean continue to move forward while our students continued to fail what we were covering?) A dedicated focus was needed, not just a bit of add-on remediation.

Isn't that what colleges do? Remediation?

No, they don't.

Here's the bad news. Even remedial classes at college generally assume that students can do basic arithmetic. Therefore, struggling students with such basic deficiencies won't necessarily be helped. It's even harder for students with undiagnosed learning disabilities, or students whose disabilities are diagnosed but who receive effectively no help.

An aside: I hear some people wondering why colleges accept students not prepared for college in the first place. Perhaps only the most prestigious colleges might not accept them (maybe) . This has been going on for many years now. I don't see it stopping. After all, don't *all* students have the "right" to go to college (prepared or not, apparently)? Many students today aren't even concerned about getting into a college. In the past, students struggled to do well in high school, not just to get high grades, but to actually learn things. They were proud when they applied and were accepted into a good college, sometimes into *any* college. Today, they just assume — often correctly — that, unless their grades or other things are really, really bad, *some* college will accept them, any college. If they really want to go, they can get in somewhere.

I'm a teacher. My job, my passion, has been to help students to learn and to succeed. I also want them to get excited about learning and about life, to let them feel confident and good about themselves. I may not always succeed, but that has always been my desire. There are many teachers who feel the same way that I do. I primarily do that through the tool of teaching the subject matter of the class.

But teachers were then, and are now, forced to "cover the material" regardless of whether students can succeed at it.

Many struggling students know how to get by. I have already mentioned their prime strategy: They cheat.

Why would they want parents or teachers to tell them — AGAIN — that it's their fault for not studying enough, or for some other reason? Why would they want to embarrass themselves in front of their friends or other students by doing poorly in class? They don't even understand why they're having trouble. They don't know why they continue getting things wrong. So they cheat.

But when students get things wrong, they shouldn't feel that way. Teachers should assume that students don't want to do poorly on assignments and tests. Before students totally give up, before they don't care anymore, teachers should see the red flag waving each time they do poorly on assignments and tests.

If students will let them, teachers need to move in to help. Asking for help, repeatedly, if necessary, is also a good thing for students to do. Sadly, too many students have given up on that, too. When many ask for help, they don't always get it. Or they get some routine answer that really doesn't address their problem.

But if students get answers right — because they successfully cheat — teachers have no reason to help them. After all, they're getting answers right, aren't they? They don't need help!

In reality, teachers can't always help their students. Sometimes, there are just too many who really need help. Teachers need to be able to take time they don't have, perhaps even changing the "required" curriculum to give the truly substantial help many need. So even the best teachers can't always fix the deficiencies in their students. There's just too much happening.

As a new teacher, I discovered assignments and tests were evaluative. They helped me to recognize and diagnose problems in my students. Students looked at their failures as hurtful, as evidence that they themselves might be failures, that they just couldn't do the work.

Yes, often students (and parents) really are to blame — and that isn't necessarily the fault of teachers, schools, or school districts.

On the other hand, often it is.

Cheating is bad because it doesn't let teachers know when and where students have problems. Of course, this assumes that all teachers want to help. Sadly, they don't.

When there are too many students struggling in class, teachers have to consider that perhaps there is something they need to change in their teaching to help their students. Many don't see that.

Many teachers who are very, very knowledgeable in their subject matter can't understand why it can be so difficult for their students. After all, it was easy for them. Why can't their students get it? Clearly, they aren't studying! That's the answer!

Okay. Truthfully, that often is the answer. On the other hand, many times it isn't.

The other reason it's important not to cheat is that *it's simply wrong* to cheat. It's MORALLY wrong to cheat. It's currently one of the few traditional moral standards left in schools.

Oh wait. Isn't it?

Whoops. It's not. Instead, isn't the truth that cheating is not acceptable in schools, not because it's a moral wrong, but because it violates school rules or various codes of conduct? So, it's not because cheating is wrong unto itself, but simply because it violates a *rule* not to cheat. Those are two different things.

Cheating is wrong in schools almost always because cheating violates some class, school, or district *rule* or some college *Code of Conduct* — but not because cheating, by itself, is inherently a moral wrong.

Are there any behaviors left that are prohibited in public schools and universities because they are *intrinsically* morally wrong? Other than a few individual teachers, do public schools teach ANY actual moral standards?

Indeed, there is little or nothing that one can think of that is prohibited at schools solely because it is *morally wrong*. Violations of rules and laws, yes. But nothing that is accepted as societally morally wrong such that it would be condemned on campus. (Okay, yes. Stealing and vandalism are *moral* wrongs. But wait! Are they really?)

I assure you that (almost) anything you might think of which you might consider morally wrong, is either not considered to be wrong at schools today (one doesn't want to be judgmental, after all!), simply isn't taught as wrong, or is just outright ignored.

Schools didn't used to be like that. Even up to the middle of the last century, schools actually taught and enforced a variety of (secular) moral standards. But no more.

But wait, again! There really are some moral prohibitions. We have seen some in recent years. But this new "morality" focuses on constantly evolving social or political speech or behaviors more than on the previous far more traditional morality.

Today, cheating in schools has a new face. Computers, phones, and other tech devices can now do an even better job at cheating. Artificial intelligence (AI) tools such as the relatively recent ChatGPT are still in their relative infancy, but they can already write in such a way that one cannot easily distinguish between AI writings and those of actual humans. Google and others have been working on similar tools.

Such tools are not limited to cheating at schools. They can also be used in the workplace and elsewhere.

However, significant warnings about the current and increasing dangers of artificial intelligence are being given by those who should know. Such warnings should be taken seriously.

11a. MORE MATH: CHEATING HURTS STUDENTS

I needed to find a way to encourage my students not to cheat. I did not need to do it so that I could get upset with them or them with me. I sincerely needed to know how they were doing. Low scores are not necessarily bad. They are communication to allow me to know what I needed to do to help and whether I could do anything at all. With enormous class sizes, a teacher can't help every student directly although, in some cases, some students really do need special help and encouragement.

So in most cases, their communication to me had to be through their tests and quizzes. Students assume it's for a grade that can only hurt them. But it shouldn't necessarily roll out like that. It was not unknown for me to throw out scores on quizzes or tests for the entire class. But I needed to know how they're doing. It's so discouraging for students to do poorly all the time.

I couldn't know how they were doing unless I could see what they didn't know. If too many weren't learning something, it could be my fault. I might need to change something. But I couldn't know that unless I had legitimate results of assignments and quizzes. Cheating denies me what I needed to know to be sure my teaching was on track. It also denies some students from (hopefully) getting targeted help from me — if my time and resources allowed. With large numbers of students, they don't always.

Some of you will be thinking that not all teachers think this way — and that's true.

In addition, no teacher wants to give an A or a B to cheating students, while students who had studied hard get the same or even lower grades. Although there is another side to this argument, most consider that to be a fairness issue for those who did what they were supposed to do by studying and learning the lessons.

Another aside. In some school environments, "friends" and peers of students actively look down on students who get good grades. They discourage their friends from doing well. Some might even threaten such students. After all, these "friends" don't do well. Why should others do well and embarrass them? This is especially prevalent where there are a high number of street gangs attending the school, but it can happen elsewhere, too.

At the time, I had well over 200 students during my five classes, plus homeroom, possibly reaching 220 students per day or beyond.

So, one day, in one of my classes, I gave a quiz.

I reminded them as we started that it was important not to cheat. I walked the classroom making sure they were working and not cheating. Cheating is actually an impossible task to fully stop it, but walking around can help and should be done anyway.

I carried the master test with me with the answers on it. Instead of being sure the answers faced me so that students couldn't see the answers (or leave it back on my desk where it belonged), I "accidentally" left the answers facing out so they could be read. As I stopped to be sure one student or another was working, the answers were in plain sight to students across the aisle who wanted to see them.

A couple of times, caring students tried to speak up to let me know the answers were showing. I quickly cut them off and told them to get back to work on the quiz.

At the end, I collected the quizzes and immediately corrected them. Those who had copied the often blatantly wrong answers from the master "answer" sheet were questioned in class.

"I notice that some of you have the exact same answers as are on this wrong answer sheet. You weren't cheating, were you?"

Caught! A number of students groaned when they realized that they, too, had been duped. Of course, it was embarrassing for them. It was also a bit funny, even for those who cheated. It's really important to establish cheating as unacceptable.

The lesson that day wasn't math. It was cheating.

I gave zeros to the students who cheated along with a little mark so I would remember why the zero and not necessarily hold it against them later — unless they kept up the same thing some other time. I didn't tell them that though.

My objective wasn't really to make the students feel bad, although it didn't bother me if they did. It was fine with me — and they knew it was on them for cheating. In an unhealthy change in recent times, students complain if anyone makes them "feel bad" about anything. More on that in the later chapter on Snowflakes.

The class talked about it for a bit and it was worthwhile. Students noticed that I actually cared about something different. One of the things I cared about — was them.

I couldn't repeat the cheating lesson in any other class. Once done, word goes out. That, too, was fine. Students in my other classes could get the same lesson, vicariously.

Of course, one or two parents complained. Was their concern that I should not catch their beloved and trustworthy children cheating? What was wrong with me! It's still smile-worthy.

In reality, I cared enough about my students to want to know if they were struggling. As I said before, I could only do that by seeing when they were doing poorly. I needed to know that. Cheating hurt them because it prevented me from knowing the facts of what my students could do. It interfered with either changing my teaching, if necessary, or trying to help them as individuals since I couldn't know who really needed help.

When too many students in class did poorly, I could only blame myself. I must have done something wrong as a teacher. Even then, knowing the truth is important. More than once, I threw out an assignment or quiz for the whole class when the scores were so bad that I could indeed only blame myself. Then I started again. I tried to find a way to fix it. I tried to teach it again so they might understand it better. Even doing that doesn't guarantee success. But the eyes of both teacher and students are open.

However, regardless of what I could do, it wasn't enough. Too many students had baggage from previous years. Too many students had serious problems at home. Too many students had problems I couldn't possibly know about.

Of course, just because students in some schools and in some classes struggle doesn't mean the whole system is broken. Does it? So why even tell these stories?

11b. A SATURDAY CLASS

I was still a new teacher, in my first or second year of teaching middle school math. I was working on getting my actual teaching credential. I was still teaching on an "Emergency" credential.

As you have heard, many of my students struggled. Since I, too, had struggled with math in school, my heart told me that I needed to try to make things easier, to encourage them so they might feel better about themselves. Even though they needed to know when they messed up — perhaps by not doing the work or studying at home — it was also important that I not put so much personal blame on students that they would give up completely. Sure, sometimes it's definitely their fault. We should be direct and not take blame off of students when it actually belongs there — as it often does. But, initially, I often look at myself. After all, I'm the teacher.

As teachers, we can teach a topic differently. We can take those students quietly aside and give them sincere help and encouragement. We can call home, not to criticize, but to encourage our students and their parents not to give up, or to get help when things are tough. But we must also be carefully direct when the fault appears to lie fully with the student.

What if half the class needs help like that? Teachers don't have the time or energy in their lives to handle all those students individually. In that case, teachers may need to consider redesigning their classes or trying different methodologies. There really is a point when teachers should examine themselves, as teachers.

But that does not mean that the problem is always with teachers, even when a large proportion of a class is struggling. It could be something else entirely. Assuming they have supportive and caring administrators (they don't always), teachers should reach out for suggestions. They can work with other teachers to develop something different that might work for a teacher's students. Again, even having done all that, there might be something beyond control of the teacher that might still be causing problems.

Teaching is hard. It can be very draining. Teachers can burnout, especially if they are strongly concerned about their students and hurt when their students are hurting. There is just so long teachers can survive without getting consistent support from administrators, parents, and others — or by just backing away for their own survival.

In one class that year, I had a big 9th grade student who frequently displayed a disruptive attitude in class. When not at school, he was hanging around with older teens with gang connections. He was already on the wrong path. He was not good at math and continued doing poorly on assignments and tests. His behavior in class wasn't good. He could be disrespectful.

Other teachers had also reported problems with him and, quite understandably, were not inclined to give him the benefit of the doubt. He disrupted their classes, too. His attitude was a problem for them and for their classes.

Something told me that his difficulty in being successful in math might be influencing his attitude in general. Why? Because math builds confidence. Failure in math, means low self-confidence. Low self-confidence affects all aspects of learning in almost every academic class. I've said that before. It can affect their behavior.

I wanted to spend personal time helping this student, but there wasn't enough time in the day to do that.

Finally, I quietly asked him if he would be willing to come in on a Saturday so that I could help him. He agreed to come. Because this one student would be there, I opened it up to select others whom I knew were discouraged and struggling. I extended invitations to them, personally. In the end, I had probably five or so students who would come. (It's been too long to remember the actual number.)

I told the principal what I would be doing to be sure it would be okay and that we could get into school then. We used a side gate that I would unlock for the students.

Surprisingly to me, the principal seemed surprised and concerned. Apparently, there would have been a problem with the teachers' union if I came in without getting paid. I told him that I really didn't need any pay for it, but he knew he had to get me paid or he would be in trouble with the union. So he got some small amount approved and supported my Saturday classes.

Note that many other teachers have done the same thing. They, too, put themselves on the line to give extra help to their students whether after school or on weekends. They, too, don't need to get paid. For good teachers, it's their life, not just their job. They just need to help their students. I really did far less for far too little time compared to other teachers who have done so much more. [1]

We need much more of that and don't have it enough. Teachers simply can't always do that. In some cases, they can't get such extra time approved, with or without pay. Teachers should be allowed to be creative and do whatever might help their students, within reason. (Some things could actually put some teachers in peril.)

My Saturday class went on for just a few short weeks. But I was able to develop success in these students, especially in the one I wanted to reach. These students absolutely *wanted* to be there Saturday. They wanted to feel good about themselves. They wanted to succeed. When the gate wasn't open, they climbed the fence to get in. Effectively, they broke into school — to learn.

My goal wasn't necessarily to just teach them to be skilled with the math methodologies at class, although we did do that. My primary goal was to increase self-confidence and excitement in my students. My goal was to make them feel good about themselves and to believe they can not just be successful at math, but in other subjects, too. I used math to do that. I saw these students improve, both in math and in their behavior. It was clear they had begun to feel better about themselves.

Well before the end of the year, I had to stop our Saturday meetings. That one student began to get pulled further into gangs. It hurt me to see that. It was as though I had personally failed. To this day, I feel I hadn't done enough for that student — for all of my students.

I don't remember the details now, but it seems to me he may have later dropped out of school or gotten in trouble with the law. Regardless, I saw our personal relationship improve in class and his self-confidence and academics improve. I understood that many difficult students could be reached, especially if we can remove them from their peers so they don't have to posture in front of them.

There are many examples of teachers better than I am doing that very thing in schools throughout the country and throughout the world. Many teachers perform miracles where others have failed.

But, although the lives of countless students are turned around by this relatively small cadre of educators, it's not enough to save education itself. There simply aren't enough of them, nor are there enough of the truly good administrators needed to keep such teachers supported, healthy, and actively helping to save the struggling, special students who need them.

12. WHAT IS FREE ENTERPRISE?

What is America's economic system? Although it goes by other names, basically it's free enterprise.[1] People can and do start, run, and profit from their own businesses. This is a country of entrepreneurs!

Our businesses provide jobs for other people. They produce goods and services, not just for America, but for the world. Americans are among the most creative people on the planet. That's why China and other countries steal the things we create from us.

But do we teach it? Do we actually teach our own economic system of free enterprise?

In other countries, people are always starting businesses. Look at all the sidewalk stands selling things as you walk the streets of other countries. That's tougher to do here. Laws and regulations, you know. It's not that those are wealth-producing businesses. Owners often have little money for themselves at all. But it's *their* business. They didn't get a job working for someone else. They started their own business, as very simple as that business might be.

Someone from outside of America might find it strange that our schools don't teach students how to do that since it's so important to people in this country. Yet students rarely learn how to start and run their own businesses, America's foundational economic structure. Why is that?

Perhaps starting a business is too simple to teach? After all, anyone can do it, right?

Not really. It takes courage and willingness to take a risk. It takes money and lots of time. To be successful, it takes knowledge, which many people don't have when they first start a business.

Schools do teach and prepare students to get JOBS. Students are taught how to work for someone else, not how to start their own business so that others work for them. Huh? Isn't that the economic engine of this country? What's going on? Just what have our schools been doing?

This isn't a new phenomenon. It's been going on in America almost since schools have been schools. The answer is simple. (Most) educators don't run their own businesses. They have what are generally very secure JOBS. They know how to interview, how to put together an old-fashioned resume, how to dress (sometimes), how to apply for and get... *a job.*

Surely, training to start and run a business is at least available in college! We all know people with MBAs, Masters of Business Administration. That's business, right?

Actually not. MBAs prepare students to get higher level JOBS (they hope) in business. *Someone else's* business. Sure, a number can and do start their own businesses. But that's not where you'll find most MBAs.

Teachers rarely have extensive experience in succeeding at starting and running businesses. So how can they teach it? Well, they can. Anyone can teach anything. But can they teach it well and correctly, so that their students will have a good chance to succeed at it?

Especially at the K-12 level, it's just not done. And kindergarten through 12th grade is where it *should* be taught, not simply later at college. Of course, it's also important to teach it at college — but it generally isn't done there either, unless you're in a major that teaches it. But such majors rarely even exist.

Countless astonishingly successfully business owners never

even made it through college. Why should they? They started their own businesses and didn't look back.

Businesses often fail. That doesn't necessarily mean the business owner failed and is condemned to work for someone else forevermore. Quite often, when a business fails, the business owner just starts another business. Failure is not necessarily a losing experience. It's a *learning* experience.

I tell that to new chess players. You only get better when you lose. In fact, if you win all the time, you'll get lackadaisical. You'll stop playing your best. You'll actually get worse!

Many high schools teach economics. That's important. But it's not about how to start and run a business. Many schools have business classes. But they rarely teach the mechanics of planning, starting, and running your own business.

Real teachers love to help their students. If a student personally asks for help starting a business, I know that many teachers will give that student whatever help they can. It's just that they normally don't have enough — or *any* — practical expertise in it. Nonetheless, they can offer good help, even if it means referring a student somewhere else for even better help.

I once had a *middle school* student who started his own video game business. Clearly, his free-enterprise-supporting parents would have had to help. But it also seemed to me at the time that it was the student's idea and the student's business. What did this middle school student do then? He *hired* some of his classmates to work in the store with (for) him after school and on the weekends!

Did he learn that in school? Of course, not. He would have had to do it on his own. Okay, my guess is that his parents provided good help and support. Perhaps they were entrepreneurs themselves.

The bottom line is that, with rare exceptions, America's schools don't even teach its own economic system. Schools pretty much teach how to get jobs and work for other people.

I'm not saying that learning how to get jobs is bad. Of course, it isn't. It's critical to know how to get a job. Even people who run their own businesses should know how to do that.

But where's the other side of that? Where does one find the

fundamentals of starting and running a business in America? Who teaches us how to maximize our chances of success in business? Where do people go if they don't want to work for someone else forever?

Mostly, business owners learn those things on their own. There are some government resources to help them. Some are very helpful. Sometimes mentors are available who do know business. But, basically, people starting their own businesses are often on their own.

Whoops. I might be wrong. You see, schools don't necessarily even teach a lot about how to get jobs either! A good teacher might teach it as part of another class, something like a life skills class. But, in most schools, many students can go completely through high school (and college!) and receive little, if any, specific training on how to get a job as part of any required class. Some teachers do teach it well. But is what they're teaching actually what is needed? Depending on the teacher, it isn't always.

In order to survive in life, including in jobs, you have to be able to read well, write well, do math well, and know some things about society often learned in social studies. Schools do that. Well, schools are *supposed* to do that. Yet, as critical as those things are, students aren't even learning those things very well any more, are they?

I have talked about free enterprise and jobs here. But I want to be clear that at least some fundamental knowledge of economics, generally, is important. It affects everyone's life. Voters need it to understand ballot propositions and what the candidates are telling them. Really, everyone needs it. In some high schools, it's required. In others, it's not.

13. VOTERS SHOULD KNOW HOW GOVERNMENT WORKS

An uneducated electorate (voters) that never adequately learned about how their government works, can easily be used by people with an agenda to destroy the government itself.

One doesn't actually see anyone "destroying" the government (and, thereby, the country). They're often just seen as (significantly) "changing" or "reforming" it. In the end, the result is the same. The country no longer exists as originally founded. That has happened to other countries in history.

Too often, the majority of those "changes" or "reforms" wouldn't be supported by people (voters) if they actually understood, not only the foundations and history of America, but also the errors of other countries in history which put too many of them on the road to tyranny. At times, that led to a total loss of freedom for their citizens. "Reforms" don't always do good things. Looking back, many reforms have been destructive.

> An educational aside: The word "reform" is frequently also used in education. But we can see that "new" reforms are sometimes just repackaged reforms of the past that didn't work the first time — or the second, third, and subsequent times. Reforms can be important. But true reform in education does not appear to be possible today.

Without knowing and understanding history, voters cannot understand whether some change has the potential to put America on a path to bring down the country as we have known it. Truthfully, those who have not learned from the past are indeed condemned to repeat it. That can't be said often enough. But the past can only be learned in a solid education system that doesn't teach "revised" history with continually changing political and social values. But that's what's been happening.

Do legislators know these things? The way a number of legislators have been voting in recent times, one might easily conclude that many don't. After all, most of them are also a product of the currently broken educational system.

So how is it possible that some schools and districts can decide *not* to require U.S. Government for high school students? Or perhaps they might offer some inadequate "dumbed down" version of it with similar results. In a moment, we'll look at one example.

We can't have a functioning and healthy government, *run by our citizens,* if citizens themselves don't know how their own government works. At some level, this problem has always existed, but it's become truly critical today.

It's terrible to say what I'm about to say in today's culture. The suggestion may even violate past court rulings. Nonetheless, here it is:

> *I don't believe that citizens should vote if they don't know how their own government works. It doesn't matter how they vote, only that they know how their government works first.*

America's citizens are supposed to run their own country. After all, it was "the *People* of the United States" who ordained and established its Constitution. That's according to the Constitution itself.

Citizens run the country by voting and, sometimes, by serving in office or in other ways. To maintain a strong country, they must exercise their right to vote carefully. To do that, they must understand how their government operates.

With the right teachers, it's not difficult to learn. But, at some point, it must be learned. Even new citizens must pass at least some small test showing that they know something about the government. That same test is not required of citizens.

This is not some exclusionary literacy test. In fact, with a good teacher, someone can learn the basics of the government even if they don't know how to read or write. (This is all FREE, should that even need to be said.) With a good teacher, the basics of the U.S. government and its Constitution aren't actually that hard to learn.

Voters should understand some basic facts if they are to make logical judgments in voting. They can vote as they choose. That's up to them. But if they don't have a foundation of information about the government, voters cannot make good choices. What are these basic facts, this "foundation of information" that I maintain are critical? Here are a Basic Five that I might suggest. Others would suggest something different:

(1) All voters must understand how their government works. As complex as America's government has become, the United States Constitution itself isn't actually that difficult. It's pretty easy to simplify it further so that voters understand the structure of the country's government. Voters must understand what it means to vote and how to do it. They should understand the three branches of government, what powers they have and don't have, and how they relate to each other. An overview of the Bill of Rights with special emphasis on the first five amendments is also important.

(2) Items of international importance are important because choices voters and their representatives make, affect and are affected by international issues. Number one among such items, one of critical importance, is to actually know what nuclear weapons are. This was discussed earlier in the book and readers should know how I feel about that one.

It's not enough that voters are simply told about nuclear weapons or read about them in a book. People need to see some actual videos of the early nuclear tests, especially the tests of the far larger hydrogen bombs. They should see what happened when atomic bombs were used, not just tested. They need to see videos of the aftermath of Hiroshima and Nagasaki.

If the issue of "weapons of mass destruction" (which include nuclear weapons) comes up in an election, how can a reasoned choice be made if voters have no idea what WMDs are? But wait. In federal elections, especially for president, this issue <u>always</u> exists. Are we actually sure the politicians we vote for understand these things themselves? Even if some say they do, do they really? Is this issue that critical? Yes. It is.

(3) Also mentioned earlier was the Holocaust. Why is that critical? We all need to remember that the decisions we and our politicians make don't just affect others, the lives of millions of people may be in their hands, in *our* hands. When people say that genocide should happen "never again," those words should not be taken as just some nice words that don't really mean much to the world (and to us) today. Do people even know what those words mean anymore? Do people understand what a genocide actually is? Those we elect to Congress or to the presidency may have to face such things in the world. Who do we want making decisions? We all must under-stand what those things are in the first place.

As with nuclear weapons, both students and voters should see the actual videos of the Holocaust. No one can understand the terribleness of what happened without actually seeing it. Books and lectures alone are just not enough. Some have said videos are too graphic. Tell that to those who died.

Do we have a responsibility to others? Or do we close our eyes and say that it's not our problem? When we are aware of millions being tortured and killed, is it *truly* all right to turn away? Some-times America is the only help that the people who are being slaughtered have in the world. We don't want to be the police of the world. But to turn our collective backs on those being killed is to ignore any foundation of morality we used to have. We might ask ourselves what God would say. Even when we knew better, we turned our backs on the Holocaust itself — until we couldn't look away anymore.

The only way to remember those who died, and to teach it as

something that must happen "never again," people today must actually see it. When I taught this, I don't remember one student who didn't seem to become a better human being after understanding the actuality of what happened.

Human life is delicate. Human life is special. Sometimes the past can change people in the present. We want our elected officials to understand these things, too.

Recall, that the nuclear and Holocaust topics are part of my canaries of education that can flag warnings of the failure of education itself. I've seen an increased seriousness and growth in maturity, even in adults, when those same lessons were given. Isn't that what we want to see in voters, too?

(4) In order to make informed decisions as to who will run our country, we need to understand where the various roads might take us. As a surprise to many, the decor at the ends of these roads may have changed, but the actuality of what we'll find at the end of each road is pretty much the same.

Newer generations have already lost knowledge of the former Soviet Union. Even though it doesn't yet exist again in its previous form, the underlying philosophies, methodologies, and history that led to and supported the Soviet Union still exist in countries throughout the world.

Today, people hear the words "communism" and "socialism" thrown around. Many think they know what they are, sort of. But if you ask them to explain what each is and what has happened in countries those systems controlled, most people — especially in more recent generations — would be unable to do so. Yet these issues directly relate to decisions that must be made in America today, and in the future.

Related to that, we can find war at the end of some of the roads our elected leaders choose. Understanding the wars since World War I — their causes, America's involvement, and what happened in the end — can reduce the chances of becoming involved in future wars. Really, America has had a long history of involvement in war. Sometimes, it has been necessary to protect people, the country, and freedom. But that has not always been the case.

We want people to watch over our country who understand all this.

The government and its people had better make decisions carefully. But that can't be done if people don't have an accurate understanding of what went on before. Best is to understand history in our hearts, not just in our heads. There are some very powerful documentaries that can do just that.

(5) Domestically, voters should have at least a basic understanding of economics. Extensive education about economics is not practical. For many, it has been one of the more hated subjects many high schoolers take. But even a short and gentle summary of how economics works might give voters a bit to think about when making decisions.

Today, some teachers don't know enough about some of these things to be effective in teaching them as they were once taught, as they should be taught. There are always exceptions, but finding the exceptions doesn't exonerate public or private education, overall, from their responsibilities to educate the nation.

The current system has failed. It is continuing to fail. These topics may be taught, but the teaching itself is often inadequate, sometimes even erroneous. These are just examples.

None of the (suggested) things listed above are political. (Well, people can make anything political, can't they?) In the past, those of all political persuasions knew those things. It was part of their upbringing. They were considered basics in their education. One reason was that the education of those topics was closer to the actual events in history. In spite of that, there were always some people who didn't have the "basics" inside of themselves. Today, the concern is that there are large *numbers* who don't know what used to be foundational in education anymore.

✳✳✳

There are always those who will say that the things listed above are too much, that they'll take too long to learn. (Are you one?) However, a short, special design for voter training really wouldn't take long at all, likely just a few hours.

People will also say that teaching voters about their government can stop voters from voting. Some will accuse supporters of developing an informed electorate as engaging in "voter suppression." But is it actually our goal to have people fill out ballots just so that we can point to larger numbers of people voting? Or is our goal to be sure the American people are actively and knowledgeably running America? Voters just putting marks on a ballot is not the same as effectively and seriously running the country. It just isn't. That does not disenfranchise voters. It does the opposite.

People "voting" — simply making marks on a ballot — but who are truly clueless about what they're doing, whom or what they're voting for, and about the ramifications of their votes — are not running the country at all.

The real "suppression" isn't about voting. It's letting people think that it's okay if they "can't learn," that it's okay if they remain without education in their lives. There are always very rare exceptions to anything, but letting voters think it's just *too hard* to learn about their country — or about anything else — suppresses them from being happy and from having a better life. Being without knowledge, without education — *that's* the suppression.

Responsible citizenship is not intuitive. It must be taught, protected, and nurtured. Democracy is not served, nor is it healthy, just by counting massive numbers of voters not making the thoughtful decisions they need to make.

Democracy is served when large numbers of active, thoughtful voters actually know how the country operates and the issues that they need to understand to make choices and help to run the country. Democracy is served when people have full and accurate information about candidates and issues. That has not been happening.

Even some elected legislators don't necessarily have the basic background and education they themselves should have. This has nothing to do with which party they might belong. It has to do with the dead education system, public or otherwise. Recent judicial and administrative nominees testifying before Congress have shown themselves to be woefully ignorant of what even some high school students are taught by good teachers. They not only embarrass themselves, they embarrass an education system that left them so ignorant in some fundamentals of their own professions. This, too, is frightening.

War is war. Weapons are weapons. Communism is communism. There are not two sides to some facts that align either with or against the foundational values of America. However, as we heard earlier, there are some who have tried (and succeeded) in creating multiple, often false or twisted histories.

Certainly, I would expect the five suggestions for better voters listed above to be modified. I'm open to that. But *something* should be done to ensure that we have a better educated electorate. Those who think Americans wouldn't be able to learn or understand those things should step back and get a better respect for people. Of course, they're capable. They just need to be given the opportunity.

But people making marks on a ballot, or voting for a candidate because they like their name or their food choices do a disservice to the country. They also dilute the votes of citizens who take voting seriously. Whom or what they vote for isn't the issue. A foundation of voter knowledge so they can participate in running the country is.

> Why do I even have to wish for things such as are listed above?
> There is not one thing there that isn't taught, or *supposed* to be
> taught, in public schools today. Why isn't that being done!

Okay, okay. Sure. If you have high schoolers, you might ask and find that their schools are indeed "teaching" these very things. But wait. Why is it that so many adults don't know, or don't remember enough of any of those things today? Could it be because they were not taught correctly, that they are still being given short shrift? Could it be that, in spite of what you are told, so many things are not actually being taught at all?

We all hope that it isn't true but, as we heard before, not all teachers even know some of what they themselves should know. And, if teachers don't know these things, there is no way their students will know them either.

Most teachers are good teachers and do know their subject — at least we all want to think that. But — and I ask this again — why do so many adults, so many citizens, so many *voters*, not know the five things that were laid out above? That's not all a truly educated person, an educated voter, should know. But voters and the country need to take citizenship responsibilities and our role in the world seriously.

How badly have some schools failed in their responsibility to teach and develop informed and caring citizens? In some cases, their failure is nearly total.

How do many people actually vote? Maybe you've heard some of the following words from your family, friends, or neighbors:

- *"I think I'm going to vote for <u>him</u>! I like his name! I used to have a friend with the same name!"*
- *"Oh, I just ask my daughter to fill in my ballot when I get it at home. She's 13 years old now. I think it's time that she learns how to do it."*
- *"My friends all tell me that I should vote for the lady with the red hair. They tell me she's good. I really don't care so I guess I'll vote for the redhead."*
- *"I just make a pattern of marks when I fill in the ballot, just like I used to do when I took hard tests at school! I don't know any of these people and I don't really care about any of this stuff anyway."*
- *"I don't really know what Congress does. But I don't like that one, the one who keeps running all those really terrible commercials. So I'm not voting for him."*
- *"I always vote. But I only vote for people who look mean. I figure they can get more done because people are scared of them. I like mean people. I think they're cute."*
- *I don't understand how anything works at all. Government is confusing. But I vote anyway so that I can say I voted.*

•*"I don't vote. I don't care. Isn't that good enough? You vote for me, okay?"*

Where do we learn how our country works? Where do we learn what is expected of us as citizens? Do I even have to ask those questions?

Most of us learned about how the American government works in high school, generally in 12th grade.

For most students, it was a required class, at least for one semester. Many of those students have balanced that one semester of government with economics in the other semester that year. As adults, these students would vote more knowledgeably because they know — or should know — how things work.

One doesn't just jump in a car and start driving. They must first learn how the car works and what's expected when they're on the road.

Shouldn't it be the same with running a country? Far too many people feel it puts too many restrictions on people to actually learn how to help run their own country. It's like saying that everyone should be able to drive a car regardless of what they know. It's their right! So here's the key! Go drive it!

The bottom line is that people really should be learning how their country works. Most of us have seen television interviews with random people on the street. The interviewer asks questions about how the country works. People embarrass themselves by knowing nothing at all. Really. Almost nothing! Some viewers laugh. Is it really funny? Or does it scream to us that the American Public Education System has failed both them and us.

Surely, those people took a U.S. Government class in high school, didn't they? We all think that most did — and that makes this whole thing even sadder.

***

Well, at least all schools across the country require it, don't they? After all, it's a basic shared preparation so that we know what we're doing as citizens. Perhaps those people interviewed on the street simply forgot what they learned years ago (sometimes just one year). We all forget things, don't we?

But wait. What if those people never took a government class in high school at all? Can there actually be schools that don't require it?

Indeed there can be. In fact, there may be entire districts that don't require it for their 12th grade high school students.

Students who took a U.S. Government or a comprehensive Civics class in high school assume that everyone else took one, too.

But, if no such class was required when students went to high school, they won't understand why any students have to take one at all. Isn't it just an optional elective? After all, they didn't take it when they were students and they came out fine! Right? (Not right.)

Things become worse when those who never took U.S. Government in high school later become teachers and administrators. They may be wonderful people, but many don't understand why it's necessary to insist on mandatory U.S. Government classes. After all, there are other important classes to take, too!

***

When I was working at one school, I was appalled to find that the district didn't require students to complete a U.S. Government class as part of the graduation requirements for high school seniors. Other schools and school districts throughout the country require it.

I don't know the number of those throughout the country who don't require it, but even one is too many.

Let me tell you about one such district.

I was at a district school board meeting when a board member expressed concern that students might not be learning enough about American Government. It was a legitimate concern. Government classes were not required in that district. Students could take government classes as an elective — in the few instances it was even offered as an elective.

But that's not good enough.

The District superintendent (whom I liked a lot) reassured the board. He told the board member that students can go out into the community to volunteer for activities that let them participate in the community.

After a lot of talking, the board member seemed to be okay. Well, actually he didn't seem fully okay. He still seemed confused. But since the superintendent seemed confident that students were learning it, things were probably okay.

No. It wasn't okay.

There was no formal required education in U.S. Government. Such classes are sometimes called Civics. That can be a simpler form of an actual Government class. Depending on the teacher, they can be excellent, or they can be grossly inadequate.

I was the principal at a district school at that time. In spite of the superintendent having already answered, I couldn't help myself. I immediately jumped in to respond to the board member. I said that on my watch, our high school students *would* be enrolled in a full U.S. Government class.

Enrollment for the coming year was approaching. I determined that I would program the students myself to ensure that we fit in, and *require,* a U.S. Government class. Even more than the concerned board member, I was stunned, just short of angry, that our students weren't required to take a substantive U.S. Government class before they graduated and went out into the world as voters.

But it didn't work as I had hoped. Before I even knew it was happening, an administrator at district headquarters began talking to students and setting up student schedules for the following year. I had already made my feelings known about the importance of a Government class for our high school students. But it was to no avail. The district administrator told me that the U.S. Government materials could just be added on to a U.S. History class.

Nope. That doesn't work at all. Both classes have a lot of substantive information. Combining the two would have meant that students would have been shortchanged in both classes. I was on the losing end of the issue. Senior high school students did not take a U.S. Government class before they graduated.

Few of our graduates went on to college. Even if they did, it would be unlikely they would have taken a Political Science (a college name for Government) class there either.

It was my impression that both the superintendent and the involved administrator were graduates of that same district. Since they would not have taken a Government class there themselves, they saw no reason why current students needed one either.

This is a serious problem and it's not uncommon. Educators with their own shortcomings in education often perpetuate those shortcomings in students. Can that be turned around? Sometimes. But note that I made a strong decision to change things — and failed. An end run was made around my decision for change.

Do those students, now graduates, know how to run their country? Is it really important that they don't have full knowledge of how their government operates while others do?

You already know my answer to that one.

***

Even as these words are written, there are *millions* of people from other countries pouring across the southern American border. This is beyond just being "serious," it's potentially catastrophic to the country. We shall see.

I bring it up for this reason: Some legislators are currently proposing giving these millions of unscreened illegal border crossers amnesty at some point — and adding in a fast track to citizenship. That assumes that they won't be voting well before either of those things happen — and many doubt that they won't be. Even if those legislative proposals aren't put into law now, they might be in just a few years more.

Regardless, will these millions have learned how the country and its government operate? Will they understand its values and goals? Even if they eventually have to take a too-short test on the government at some point, will it be adequate to understand the things I just mentioned? That will be highly unlikely.

However, these vast numbers will further dilute the already weakly-educated electorate in the country. That will continue to leave the electorate open to politicians and others who are effective at enticing, misleading, or scaring voters.

When those are combined with a "news" media that currently twists words and events, that intentionally fails to report on significant events, voters are unable to develop informed opinions based on fact and truth.

This situation leads to the manipulation of voters. That can lead to getting a government not intended by voters if they had been fully informed, if they had been given actual truth. Although people often think otherwise, because of the unhealthy media today, much of America is oblivious to what is going on in this country.

None of this turns out well.

14. THE MEDIA: DO THEY KNOW ENOUGH?

In recent times, many of those working in the news media appear to interpret the Constitution opportunistically. Some have even appeared to show a lack of basic knowledge about it. This is especially true of some of them in more recent generations.

Let's consider why this is important. If a media host is interviewing a guest who makes an unintentional, but egregious mistake, that host should jump in to correct that person. For example, if the guest notes that some tax rate is 35% when it is actually 48% (or vice versa), a competent host should jump in and make a quick correction. Otherwise, listeners or viewers would be left with incorrect information. There would not be bias in that correction. It can be easily checked.

By the same token, if a guest insists that the federal government should take over something that constitutionally belongs to the states, that same competent host should jump in and question or correct that statement. There is no bias in such a correction. It can be easily checked.

The Founding Fathers of the country didn't want an all-powerful central government. That's why the country's original constitution, the Articles of Confederation, didn't work. It went so far in ensuring the central (federal) government had less power than the states that it proved to be unworkable. The same concerns that a central government might be too powerful also existed when our current Constitution was written to replace the Articles of Confederation. Nonetheless, more power was given to the central (federal) government anyway.

When the current Constitution was written, states were still considered to be of primary importance. In fact, at that time, state legislators themselves chose their U.S. senators for their states. Until a constitutional amendment changed it, the people did not directly vote for their U.S. senators. Today, a few rare voices have proposed giving it back to state legislatures to strengthen the power of state governments again.

That mythical media host should either immediately correct, or carefully question the guest noting that the Constitution doesn't necessarily give the federal government the power over the states that the guest proposes. Many things come down to the Constitution on which (almost) all else is based. It's not actually a particularly long document.

In recent times, we have seen a great deal of attacks on the federal government for failing do to one thing or another, even though it's actually prohibited for the federal government to intervene in state powers. We've also heard various candidates for office propose things that are prohibited by the Constitution. These things regularly end up in the courts. Yet, rarely, are such statements by guests corrected, or at least questioned, by media hosts.

There are two reasons that may not be happening. (1) The hosts either have some bias, especially if the guest takes a position they support. Or, perhaps they don't even care what's being said. That's not good. (2) Worse, hosts may not even know there's a potential violation of the Constitution. That's not good either.

Some would undoubtedly say they're not constitutional lawyers and can't make such judgments. After all, there are nuances in some interpretations of the Constitution. There have always been debates and court actions around it.

But nor can it be assumed that the Constitution is impossibly difficult. It isn't.

Any properly educated high school student of U.S. Government should have at least a *basic knowledge* of each article of the Constitution.

Of course, we rarely see media hosts challenging or questioning guests on such constitutional issues.

But, without bringing it up, listeners or viewers would be left with a potentially false impression that what the guest was suggesting is correct and might be easily doable. If, for some reason, the guest's suggestion was actually constitutionally permitted, questioning the guest would be a learning opportunity for listeners or viewers.

Truthfully, I have come to believe that too many in the media today, especially those from more recent generations, often have gaping holes in their education, some even concerning the canary issues discussed earlier. They don't necessarily think they have anything missing, of course. As I've said before, none of us can know what we don't know.

On November 3, 2022, Joy Reid (1968–), a popular MSNBC TV personality of her time, had unusual remarks on the knowledge of many people. She said, in part:[1]

> *"The only people you ever hear use the word, inflation, are journalists and economists. Right? So that is not part of the normal lexicon of the way people talk. So it's interesting that Republicans are doing something they don't normally do, right?, which is not use common, the common tongue, or not use the common English, like they sort of do on their campaigns like they do with crime. But what they've done is, they've <u>taught</u> people the word inflation. Most people who would have never used that word ever in their life are using it now because they've been <u>taught</u> it, including on TV, including in newspapers... They've been <u>taught</u> this word."* (Emphases hers.)

So how are we to take her remarks? Whichever way they are taken is bad for education.

The Daily Mail summarized its understanding of her remarks saying:

"Controversial MSNBC host Joy Reid has claimed that the word 'infla-tion' is not a standard part of the 'normal lexicon' of Americans, and that most people using it learned it from political operatives…"

In many schools, high school students take an economics class. How is it they would not have learned the term, inflation? Vast numbers of people in the country do know what inflation is, or at least have a pretty good idea.

Yet in Reid's remarks, we understand that few, if any, do. We understand that a political party had to teach it to them, apparently making a concerted effort to do so. According to Reid, people learned it, not just from that political party, but from TV and newspapers.

If she is correct, she is pointing out yet another failure of education in America. If she is not correct (most likely), we see the failure of her own education, in part by seeming to feel the word, inflation, is a high brow word rarely used or understood other than by journalists and economists. However, the seeming disjointedness of her own language in discussing this is its own red flag for education in this country. (Reid is a graduate of Harvard University. She has also taught a Syracuse University class in Manhattan exploring race, gender, and the media.)[2]

***

Just as teachers who don't know or don't understand some topic pass their lack of understanding to their students, some in the media pass on, with great confidence, erroneous or slanted inter-pretations of the Constitution (or something else) to their readers, listeners, or viewers. Exactly how much responsibility do deficien-cies in their formal education bear for that? For how much do any shortcomings of Constitutional competence — or perhaps inten-tional bias leading to fully false interpretations — bear respon-sibility?

Neither of those possibilities would be a concern at all if their readers, listeners, and viewers were themselves knowledgeable enough to know what their Constitution, as just one example, actually says and what possible interpretations there might be. But from where would those readers, listeners, and viewers get their understanding of the Constitution? Shall I make a bold guess?

Schools.

I don't mean to just pick on those in the media. Perhaps even worse are the educational holes in some members of Congress.

The American Constitution isn't long. There aren't really a lot of complex confusions in it after one takes into account some language nuances over the years. Such things aren't difficult. Competent teachers can handle teaching it. Although courts have had to provide clarity over the years, the basics really aren't that difficult.

So how important *is* public education?

Crucial. It's crucial. Without it, citizens will continue to be easily misled as many already have been. Citizens run the country. Those in Congress or the White House are there only because citizens send them there. But sometimes we have to wonder if those citizens really understand what's going on.

So the death of the American Public Education system must eventually lead to the death of the country itself — at least as it was once known. Its past freedoms can disappear. So can liberty itself. It's happened elsewhere. It can happen here. Some see that it is already happening.

The bottom line remains: if education isn't doing its job, bad things follow. Those bad things can easily include the loss of the country.

The bottom line is that public education should be the vanguard of truth. It should be a place where the thinking of students is built and nourished based on a true, and correct education. Programs like the dangerous 1619 Project do not meet that standard. Instead, they only serve to further destroy education and, by extension, the country.

15. IMMIGRANTS AND EDUCATION IN AMERICA

The United States was founded by immigrants. Since its founding, it's had a love-hate relationship with newly arrived immigrants over the years. But, in recent times, the issue has become far more difficult and certainly more polarizing.

Under President Biden, the southern border with Mexico was totally opened. That allowed millions of immigrants/migrants to come into the country in a manner that led to little, if any, screening. Less than halfway through his presidency, over five million migrants had illegally entered the country. The pace of migrants illegally entering the country has been predicted to increase significantly even beyond that.

At this book's writing, countless migrants are still flooding across the border. No effective action has been taken to stop it. In Congress, action has actually been blocked as some tried to stop what some have called an invasion. When no action is taken to stop these numbers from coming in and when proposed actions to slow or stop it are voted down, common sense tells people that a fully open border is likely intentional. The migrants are not simply from Mexico. They are from over a 130+ countries. Public education does not have enough resources to understand the cultures and languages of so many children entering schools so that the children can be appropriately educated.

Even though here illegally, once they are here, those countless numbers have been granted many benefits. Among those benefits is the opportunity for their children to attend public schools. Also included are other things given to them that even native-born Americans are not given.

Although Americans also have the right to attend public schools, in some school districts the massive impact of millions crossing the border impacts both the quantity and quality of education for resident American children.

This does two things. First, it puts a burden on schools many of which already did not have adequate funds to hire enough teachers and resources for the educational needs of their local community students. That was even before the influx of these new migrant students. Impacted schools must now find and hire more teachers qualified to teach children who are often unable to speak English well, if at all.

Where that can not be done — due to a lack of funds or a lack of available and qualified teachers — students can only be added to already overcrowded classrooms with less qualified teachers to provide extra support for their needs.

Regardless of what might be said, in many cases, schools might seem to primarily be providing childcare and food services for the new arrivals. Adequate numbers of qualified educational staff, as well as school facilities, are often missing or strained beyond what can be productively sustained.

Increasing numbers of students may be added to classes in the middle of a semester. That can cause disruptions even in classes that might otherwise be functioning well. That is tough and confusing for new students. But it also affects the large number of students already in those classes.

Of course, this is often the nature of K-12 education. Students come and go. Those outside schools normally don't see the complications of a classroom beyond the teaching of the subject matter itself. But this extra and unexpected strain was intentionally allowed when the border became fully opened. Schools are certainly not the only services impacted, but they are our focus here.

At one point, when I was teaching a class of students with limited English proficiency, I had 50 students in one of my middle school classes and that was well before the current millions entering the country.

Even though I loved my classes and my students, I was a relatively new teacher at the time. But even far more experienced teachers reported immigrants who were disruptive, sometimes fully out-of-control.

It can take just a single student, let alone several, to fully disrupt learning in any classroom. That can wear out and frustrate teachers. In some districts and schools, restrictions preventing educators from getting control over classes often mean out-of-control students and classes, no matter which subject is being taught.

Such problems also exist among non-immigrant students. But the significant increase of new students only exacerbate these issues.

It is a serious problem that potentially large numbers of relatively newly arrived immigrants — whose language skills are weak and who may not understand the requirements of their new country — are then thrown in to already crowded subject matter classes in schools. They are combined with the American-born students who had already been in those classes and who possess good language skills and a (normally, not always) better conformance to educational expectations in schools. Some schools might have orientation classes for new arrivals. Others don't.

Actually, new arrivals who speak almost no English are often less problematic than high school students who have learned enough English to interact with others. To be sure, that's not always the case. Many immigrants are great people and serious students. But it just takes a small number to significantly disrupt classes and wear out both teachers and administrators.

Of course, there are plenty of native-born students who are also serious problems in classes. What I'm saying here is that, by adding to already large numbers of students naturally adds to classroom management issues. Immigrant students take extra care fully outside of behavior concerns. I worked with many and loved my students, but I also acknowledge the problems and special needs that can accompany relatively newly arrived illegal immigrants.

Because of the disparity in student needs and behaviors, it's generally the American-born students who suffer the most since the subject matter is normally shifted to be taught in a less challenging manner in order to meet the needs and weaker language skills of these new students.

Repeating myself, I am not saying that all American-born students are wonderful students. They certainly aren't. Nor am I saying that all illegally-arriving immigrant students are difficult students in class. They're not either. Regardless though, the vast numbers arriving have put additional strain on schools and teachers.

It is often logical to separate students in classes designed to support their special needs. But, in some places, court orders and parental complaints have, at times, precluded that from happening.

One Arizona teacher with experience teaching classes of students from Mexico remarked to the author on the terrible difficulty of his students to retain anything taught in class, even outside of behavioral issues. One explanation the teacher tentatively put forward to explain this was that many students had learning disorders originating from their mothers abusing drugs or alcohol when they were pregnant. Of course, that happens with too many non-immigrant students, too.

Nonetheless, the teacher reported that those problems seemed to be far more common in his classes among relatively recently arrived immigrants than among the teacher's classes of American-born students.

Because immigrant parents are also new to the country, they are not familiar with what can be different expectations and methods in American schools than they found in their countries of origin. Language difficulties make communication with teachers difficult. Interpreters are not alway available.

All that can lead to uncooperative, even hostile parents, or parents who think they shouldn't even be involved. After all, isn't it the school's job to teach their children? Why should they be called to help get their child under control or to ensure homework and studying is being done?

On the other hand, some parents of immigrant students can go to the other extreme, administering serious punishment to their child at home well beyond what would be called for. At times, that might be for some relatively minor classroom issue, but for which a teacher needs help from parents nonetheless.

Teachers don't necessarily know that's what parents are doing at home. Often, parents new to the country need guidance and help as to what to do and expect now that they're here. Some immigrant parents can benefit from help from personnel and resources that schools might have so that they themselves can learn the ropes in their new country.

This can be difficult for many already-overwhelmed teachers, as well as for other students and staff.

In some schools, teachers are available who might be familiar and comfortable with migrant students. Some might even speak the language — though not the languages of immigrants from the well over 130 countries from which their students might arrive.

As I said earlier, I really liked my classes of students who may have been relatively new to the country, perhaps arriving just a year or two before I got them.

One reason many became disruptive was their own frustration because they, in fact, did need extra help. Nonetheless, disruptions are frustrating to teachers — and to other students who are there to learn.

The problem is that when a teacher — especially a relatively new one — has multiple classes with over 40 students, or an entire day seeing over 200 students — as I did in my early days of teaching — there are simply limits to what can be done. Some administrators are very helpful and supportive. Others are quite the opposite, blaming all difficulties on the teacher even when things might be well beyond the capabilities of even the most experienced ones.

Nonetheless, I saw the difficulties and complications of all this on the education of *other* students. I could see that other students might not receive as challenging an education as might happen were so many illegally-arriving immigrants not in their classrooms. Understand that this issue can extend even to classrooms in the same school without immigrant students in them.

Many classroom teachers and schools do a very good job teaching *all* students in their schools. However, bringing up a handful of perfectly run classes and schools with remarkable teachers does not obviate what is being said here.

Notably, even the most caring and otherwise qualified teachers can be driven to burnout even in many non-immigrant classrooms. But, add in the extra needs of immigrant students — and their parents — and it can be too much for some.

New, less experienced (or fully inexperienced) teachers are often given classes with behaviorally-difficult, sometimes limited English proficient students. Why wouldn't more experienced teachers be assigned to handle such classes? It's often because they have "already put in their time" teaching particularly difficult classes. They themselves might have been fighting burnout. Regardless, they now have seniority.

So such classes might then be given to (often unsuspecting) newer teachers. In my case, I was excited to be teaching *any* students. I felt a responsibility to do a good job, even for difficult students. Unfortunately, my inexperience when I started out meant that I often didn't know what to do to resolve particularly difficult behavior problems — even though I sincerely wanted to do so.

As previously mentioned, when I first began teaching in public schools, I hadn't yet completed *any* teacher training classes at any university. That might seem to be a serious handicap.

Unfortunately, and as also mentioned before, when I finally did complete my full credential, just a few education classes — if even that — had been of value at all. Some teachers have a wonderful experience taking their teacher-training classes. For others, the classes are not much above worthless.

Extra pay for teachers is often touted as an answer for everything. But it doesn't matter how much a teacher gets paid. It rarely makes things easier in the classroom. That's not to say most educators shouldn't be paid better. In some places, teachers are woefully underpaid. Too often, their pay is dangerously low and should be fixed immediately. It's just that great pay doesn't necessarily equate to great teaching.

***

Let me end with one more thing. All of the above is certainly a concern in that it weighs down schools beyond what they are already barely handling. They juggle it all as they try to offer a stable education for students. But it's rapidly becoming untenable.

With what are now *millions* of illegal border crossings bringing countless more people from a great number of countries, the country's public education system is about to become totally overrun.

Beyond the children, there will be countless adults who will want to take classes to learn English, usually at night. (I taught English to some of those parents.) That means further pressure on the supply of bilingual and other specially competent teachers in various subjects. But they are already in short supply at many schools. Some schools will be completely overwhelmed. Yet they will be blamed when things aren't going well.

Things in this section are still in flux. They may change in the future.

16. WHAT ABOUT ELECTIVES?

Let me take a moment to talk about electives.

One advantage of public schools is that they generally have more electives available to middle and high school students than do non-public schools.

One disadvantage of public schools is that they generally have more electives available to middle and high school students than do non-public schools.

Some say that electives can take time away from foundational subjects including advanced placement (AP) college level classes. Some suggest that can sometimes put students at a disadvantage in applying to some, though not all, colleges. In other cases, colleges maintain that they prefer students with broader backgrounds and interests — though that may not always be true.

I personally recommend considering limited electives if they don't interfere with taking what might be foundational academic classes. I enjoyed the electives I took.

Colleges themselves require electives as part of their own degree programs. While many are interesting, others can be a waste of time. Sometimes they seem to be there just to keep some professors employed.

I enjoyed and learned from my archery and golf classes in

college. Archery stayed with me well past college. There were other electives that I also enjoyed. Could I have lived without them? Of course, I could have. But they are meant to make students better rounded as people. And they do.

In some K-12 schools, sports are electives, although most team sports are extracurricular, taking place after school. For many students, sports is especially important. Because of requirements many schools have to maintain a minimum grade point average in academic classes in order to continue in sports, they can serve as incentives for students to do well in school. Although that's true in theory, it doesn't always work out that way — especially in college sports.

Other extracurricular K-12 — usually grades 7-12 — activities, which may or may not be considered electives, partially include drama, chess, speech, debate, and more. All of these are helpful to broaden students' confidence and overall life skills. I was personally involved in all of those and more in high school. Some can unexpectedly improve student behavior and academic performance. We'll talk chess in the coming section.

Electives can be things that get some middle and high school students especially excited about school. They introduce students to subjects and skills they may have never even considered. In some cases, they can put students on paths in their lives neither they nor their parents ever imagined.

In other cases, they can be a waste of time.

But so can non-elective classes.

But if they can be fit in, I certainly recommend some of them. Even homeschooling parents fit in electives, although some don't even know they're doing it.

Traditional electives primarily include music, art, and shop classes.They might also include specialized PE (physical education) classes. As a young student in middle school, I took two shop classes (ceramics and electric shop) and one music class that taught me how to (barely) play the violin. Those were all in my second semester of 7th grade. Years later, I returned as a teacher to that same school.

I don't remember anything else that I took that semester except for those classes. The violin class gave me just enough competence to be able to play second violin in an orchestra in a middle school class that summer. That was the only time I ever got to play in an orchestra (also an elective). I've always remembered it. It was a great experience. At the final performance of the orchestra for an auditorium audience at summer's end, the teacher asked me to play a piano solo in front of everyone.

Thanks to my mother, I had been taking private piano lessons. I wasn't great at it, but it was apparently enough to play a bit of Chopin's Revolutionary Etude at that middle school concert — along with my second fiddle violin effort. I suppose I wasn't terrible. The teacher didn't throw me out.

Even without being too good, that one violin elective class opened a moment of adventure that I treasure to this day. For many students, music, in particular, is an important part of their schooling. It can then become an important part of life. If a school doesn't offer much in the way of electives, there are often options for such things outside of school. Music and other elective classes are generally first on the chopping block when schools must make cuts because of budget shortfalls and rising costs. After all, they can't cut basic English and math.

Electives can also include some academic subjects, including foreign language, although that's sometimes a requirement, not an elective. I wasn't particularly good at foreign languages either. Besides the Latin and Greek I mentioned earlier, I also took a smattering of Spanish in middle school as well as American Sign Language in college. Most of the language classes I took were required. Not being able to practice those languages regularly, most were later forgotten.

Even though I rarely actually used the languages (other than a bit of Spanish), I felt their study was of great benefit to me. They structured my thinking about other things. They gave me a stronger appreciation and understanding of language, in general. Interestingly, I credit studying the languages I took in high school with helping to keep me out of a war when I later served in the U.S. Army. One never knows where learning will lead.

***

"Shop" classes are electives. For many students, especially those in high school, these classes can put students on an entirely different path in life, sometimes giving them instantly marketable life skills. Even if they don't become professionally involved in welding, carpentry, electronics, auto repair, and so forth, even entry level skills can allow students, as adults, to have the confidence to handle some of their own basic needs at home.

In other cases, these electives provide students with a foundation for later formal training in those skills to earn full certification. As mentioned, some classes can also develop self-confidence in students — like math, only different.

For many years, elective shop classes have been wrongly looked down upon by many people. They have not been considered to be "real" academic classes. Many said that only students who weren't good enough at academics, or students who weren't good enough to get into college were relegated to take such classes so they could at least get *some* job.

That's totally wrong. In fact, although the rest of education is surely dead, elective classes that teach various trades, where they are still offered, are not dead. They can teach students skills that, with more training, are foundational to getting them good paying jobs. In some cases, those jobs can support them for the rest of their lives.

While academically-trained students, including many college students, might later have trouble finding regular work for adequate pay, those with some of these trade skills might make well over $100 an hour. Not only that, it also allows them to be in charge of their own lives, perhaps starting their own businesses and employing others, maybe even some college graduates who used to make fun of those high school electives.

In some parts of the country, fully certified plumbers and electricians, for example, are (almost) always in high demand. Whether academic or not, times can be tough for anyone, no matter how good their skills or competency. But these artisan skills will always be in demand, even in bad economic times. Barbers and beauticians are examples of others who can sometimes find more work in places than they can physically handle. While others look for better jobs, skilled technicians for a variety of complex equipment will continue to be in demand, including mechanics for today's complex computerized automobiles and trucks. Such technicians will need to stay current on new and updated equipment.

Life can be hard for anyone. Some tradespeople struggle in situations where competition, physical disability, or economic downturns can lead to difficulties finding work, especially in certain communities. But, overall, these should be respected skills for students that cannot be easily taken away. *This* education is *not* dead.

Perhaps the biggest problem with learning trades today is that trade schools are now charging abusively high tuitions. As private entities (as most are), they have been permitted to do that. But, as with college students, the debt their students — graduates or not — are left with is often unconscionable.

Barbers, beauticians, and many others should not struggle for years with student debt that may soon rival that of college students, especially when the financial benefits of those skills, even if normally good, still might not justify the excessive tuition. Even when new students sign disclosures from schools saying that they understand these things, students rarely fully understand them at all.

Making things worse, when the government pays or subsidizes such tuition, it only encourages further tuition increases. Government subsidies have also been accused of contributing to enormous increases in both regular college tuition and in healthcare.

But this book is not about all that.

Since we're considering electives, I have one last thing for you.

As other educators have also found, teaching and encouraging students to play chess — hopefully during the school day — can have a positive affect on both the academics and behavior of students. After a while, some even seem to have magically gained more maturity. It doesn't always happen. But it happens often enough to take such changes and personal growth seriously.

Some wrongly think that these results can happen with any game. But it is specifically with chess that noticeable benefits are most commonly seen. They appear to be completely separate from the game itself but, without learning and playing the game, wouldn't happen at all.

To be most effective, chess should be played against an *actual person* as an opponent, not against a computer or electronic chess program. For those who become more serious about it, playing against a computer program is fine. But the more substantive benefits — especially developing appropriate interactions and respect for people — come from playing against real people, under the oversight of a teacher.

Of course, chess can also be an after school activity. That includes joining chess clubs as well as chess *teams.* Teams can play against other schools in tournaments. But here I'm talking about a more direct integration with the school.

Since chess is a tool that can improve both academics and behavior — if done correctly, that is — the more integration with the actual school that is done, rather than simply relegating it to an optional elective, the better it can be. Several times a week is better than just a day or two.

This only works if students enjoy playing and end up doing it on their own, if chess sets are made available, and if it doesn't significantly interfere with actual teaching time.

If the school situation won't allow a tighter integration, it can still be done after school, but many students won't attend, including those who might benefit the most. During the day, you can get most of them involved.

Teachers overseeing this should be competent in chess and supportive of the game. They should understand its seemingly unrelated benefits — which are actually quite related. To get the most out of it, a teacher should structure and oversee play, at least in the beginning.

Respect for opponents should be taught and enforced as necessary. Those struggling with the game should be encouraged and supported. Even non-chess playing teachers should become familiar with it and support its place in education. (As parents do, some teachers will also complain.)

Many parents and teachers don't understand this at all. They absolutely know that time is being wasted by just "playing games."

In reality, chess is something entirely beyond that. *Used correctly,* it can lead to seriously positive benefits beyond the game itself. I have personally seen this when I introduced it to a school of at-risk students. Many others have also seen its benefits —if it is done correctly.

Learning and playing chess can support improvements in academics (I've seen it) with some improvements in attention span (players improve their focused attention when they play the game), as well as potential changes in behavior and maturity (gradual calming that can come with concentrating on the game carries over). It can also develop an increase in self-confidence. So it's more than "just a game."

When chess stops, many students might revert to being less productive, although some might see newly-found positive changes continue.

It is my personal experience that boys seem to like chess more and stay with it longer. Girls tend to learn the game faster and get good at it more quickly than boys do. But they usually don't stay with the game as long as boys do. That's just a generality, of course.

This is also a good game with which to develop a closer relationship with a parent. Most commonly that happens with fathers. I'm not being sexist here. That's just the way it usually is.

Perhaps you've seen one of the several movies about chess and children. If not, try out a couple of them. I particularly like *Searching for Bobby Fisher,* but there are also others.

All this might still seem strange as part of education. But for many, many years, teachers who have been involved with this "game" have often seen similar results.

Sadly, chess won't fix what's wrong with education overall.

17. WHAT DO STUDENTS THINK? PART ONE

We have now looked at several aspects of public education. Much of it has simply been my opinion. But much has not been. Fortunately, we have a few comments by actual past students who, while apparently talking about one thing (the history course they had just finished), were unknowingly pointing to concerns in public education.

These student comments are from just two summer school classes at a large public high school in the Los Angeles Unified School District. For the summers I was there, I taught U.S. History A and U.S. History B — first and second semester American history. Those two courses are supposed to comprise the full history of the United States from its beginning, divided into two parts.

During the year, each part normally takes a full semester to teach. In these summer classes, they were each compressed into six weeks. Students generally took one or the other, but not both. Many students had failed the class the year or semester before the summer. Others were taking it for the first time just to get ahead.

Of course, there isn't nearly enough time in a six-week summer program to cover all, or even half of U.S. History well. Teachers can only do the best they can.

***

At the end of the summer, I asked my students to tell me how things went, to list my weaknesses and ways they felt I could improve the class. I asked them for comments on anything they liked or disliked about the course. Such teacher evaluations are more commonly used at colleges with adult students. However, I've found teenagers often provide respectful, honest, and helpful feedback. They also feel respected for being asked, which they were.

Not only do these evaluations let me look at myself to see if I'm doing things right or need to make adjustments, they also allow the students themselves to reflect on the class, reviewing and summarizing it in their own heads. Evaluations are also a final opportunity to talk to me. They knew I would listen carefully to what they wrote — and I did. That's something that too many students don't get enough of today — someone to listen. Both parents and teachers should be doing that.

It's possible I connected with some because I had dropped out of high school, because I myself often found school frustrating and sometimes difficult. I understood how some of them felt. Does that mean we should hire high school dropouts to teach?

I don't know. Maybe sometimes.

Once students know they're being heard, it's a different world for them. The class becomes more meaningful, no matter the subject. It's especially important to give students with difficult behaviors the opportunity to talk, but, more critically, to be heard. Little by little, I have seen students change. Those who don't may have been already lost. Schools and homes waited too long. Sometimes, you can make inroads, but, by high school, reaching some hardened students is beyond what many teachers can do.

Relying on a single end-of-course evaluation written by high school students would not be enough unless the students had already become accustomed to writing their thoughts…and being heard. That's why, in many of my classes, I had assigned what I called "logs." These were brief daily writings at the very end of almost all daily classes. I might allow maybe three minutes for them. Often, they were just two, three, or four sentences. Some students had a lot more to say — and that was fine. There were no length restrictions on either end.

Although I told students that I was interested in feedback on each particular day's class, I also told them they could actually write anything they wanted to write about. They did.

What was really important about the logs was that I then responded back on the same paper and passed them all back the next day. Sometimes, there was something specific the student would bring up that required a more complete response from me. But mostly, I would make listening noises. "Ah. Yes. I used to feel that way — and here's what I found. Oh. Too bad. Right. I agree. Talk to me if you're confused again and I'll help you."

Listening noises — so that the students knew that I actually read what they wrote. Many students were astounded when they first got them back and realized I was listening. It didn't take long for me to go through them all for one class. However, when I had several classes and maybe 100 to 200 students, I couldn't do logs for all of them. Not only was it too time-intensive at that point (after all, I also had tests and assignments to correct), but there is a point when burnout sets in. Still, they were very important, especially in some particularly challenging classes.

I also found that, if, for some reason, I had to stop students from writing logs later in the class, certain students became very frustrated with me. They *really* wanted to continue. Are you sensing a consistent theme here? Many students don't have enough, or any, people to really listen to them.

Learn from this. If you have children of *any* age, but especially middle or high schoolers, find some way to get them to talk to you — or write to you. Be sure to *always* give them your thoughts, positive only, as feedback. They should know not only that you hear what they're saying, but that you *care* what they're saying.

Talking to your children on a regular — maybe even a formal, scheduled, daily basis — should begin when they're *very* young. Do whatever works for you both. But learn to listen seriously to your children. Hear what is behind what they're saying, not just their words. If you have to correct them or let them know their behavior was unacceptable — it's important to do that when necessary — do it in a different context.

Logs were one of the tools that helped me to diffuse problems in a class and to get students' attention. It was an easy thing to do, most of the time. It also let me keep tabs on whether the class didn't understand something that I thought I had taught to them.

If two or more mentioned they were confused, I would sometimes reteach it in a different way. If three or more said something, I definitely put the blame on me. But I would never have a clue about that if I didn't ask for (nearly) daily feedback. Mostly, they didn't actually talk about the class but, if something wasn't right, they would tell me.

If another student was causing trouble in class and I didn't know it, they could surreptitiously let me know and I could then take care of it. I didn't ask. Students just told me. Sometimes, they even gave me advice about what to do. I always took their advice seriously, even if I couldn't always follow it.

I tried to use logs as often as possible with my high school students — and in some of my college classes, too.

There are countless other comments from my students in other schools, classes, and subjects. Here, I'm just picking two classes over a single summer. I choose these because the student comments go beyond what their words are actually saying. However, the ones from which I quote are not logs. They're part of the more specific evaluations that I asked them to do at the end of the course.

It's important to listen to what these students are *really* saying. Ignore comments about me, personally. Consider them to be comments maybe on teachers, generally. I'm not what's important here. Instead hear what these students are saying about education in general.

Try to feel what they're feeling. Understand where they feel they have been forgotten. Hear their pleas for help. Feel their fears and frustrations.

Many are scared, but they hide it. You should know that they really want to succeed. They want to have pride in themselves. Ask yourself why, as a nation and as individuals, we have failed them. Understand that, when we fail them, we fail ourselves, and we fail our country. These students had hoped for more from education than what they had been given. They had hoped for more — but they didn't get it.

So, to understand even part of what has been wrong with education, you must look beyond their words. You should not simply read the words they hand-wrote (often poorly) on paper.

Not only are things no better since these students wrote these evaluations, in many places, they're worse.

Listen carefully to students today. Some of them may be your own children. Of course, some may be wrongly complaining about issues that they themselves should be solving, that they themselves may have caused. Perhaps they have to study more or behave better. It's possible their attitude needs to change. You can work on that.

But in many, many cases, there truly are things you can sense beyond their words. Whenever possible, education should be a positive and exciting experience. Too often, it's not.

Education is something that should make our lives better. It's something that can even excite us. So, if a student is constantly complaining, look into it.

It's possible there might be something broken, systemically, in their school, in the district, or in their state. Perhaps a teacher could be better. There are many less than adequate teachers (and administrators). But the problems are often something beyond that. Whatever they are, pay attention when a student talks to you about school or college.

The answer to problems at school is not necessarily to go in and complain that a teacher is "mistreating" your child or is doing something wrong as a teacher. That may or may not be true. But teachers already have to put up with a lot, so take care of them when you can.

Nonetheless, if something is going on, you should go in to talk about it. See if something can be worked out. Be nice. Be respectful. And recognize that so much of public (and often private) education is broken that answers aren't always simple — if there are any good answers at all.

I repeat myself: don't attack teachers. Yes, some are really bad.

But most aren't. Some parents wrongly defend their child when what their child is doing in school is indefensible. Parents think they're supposed to defend their child. That's not what a good parent does.

A good parent calmly explores the problems, talks to teachers and others, and comes up with multiple solutions. If their child is wrong, the parent should act like a good parent and instruct, help, encourage, perhaps discipline their child so that their child does things differently, even apologizing if the situation calls for that.

***

If you have forgotten, let me remind you that some of the things in these sections might not seem to support the thesis that Education Is Dead. However, the student comments below show that students had not previously learned what they should have already learned in high school, sometimes even before high school. So some of these comments truly are an insight into education in general.

The inability of these high school students to write well at the high school level is of real concern. But many students were not born and raised in America. English is their second language. Regardless, schools should push and encourage them to improve anyway.

Students here were (mostly) on track to eventually get a high school diploma. Will that diploma mean that they can read and write well? Do math? Know history? Sadly, it does not. And those are not the only deficiencies with which students will graduate. Simplistically suggesting they should just be "held back" until they catch up is almost never a workable solution.

Yet all my students were special. When they were particularly deficient and I knew that my limited time with them would not allow me to correct everything — especially in subjects outside what I was teaching — I was sad.

I was frustrated, because my students were often frustrated, too. Let's move on.

***

One last thing. Here are a few words about punctuation in students' writings.

As much as possible, I have included the students comments *as they wrote them*. (They were all handwritten.) Based on their writings, it will seem to some that many students here might be performing academically lower than other students you might know, at least in their writing skills. Although that is certainly true in many cases, there was actually a mixture of students in each of the two classes whose writings I partially include here.

Even when English was not their first language, there is still cause for concern about their abilities. These are high school students. Most would be graduating at the end of the coming year, or perhaps in two more years.

Regardless of their primary language, sentences generally do end with warm, fuzzy periods, right? Here, you'll notice an absence of periods, actually an absence of punctuation in general — but mostly periods.

Periods let us know when one thought ends and another one starts. Otherwise, we can be confused.

But, before anyone gets too critical, look around and think about this. Have you read the texts on your cell phones closely? Some of you might have noticed a lack of periods in texts you receive — as well as those you might send! Why is that?

In most cases, it's because many people have taken to <u>dictating</u> their texts, without punctuation. Most dictation tools allow speakers to say "period" and the dictation tool might actually insert periods! Or commas! Or other punctuation! Whew! Good news!

But wait. Why aren't we actually seeing that punctuation when we read a text on our cell phones? It's because most people don't dictate punctuation. At least today, it can be obvious who is dictating texts and who isn't. No periods.

Being able to dictate texts and emails is a wonderful thing. One day very soon, all of those apps will be able to guess when a sentence ends and insert periods (or other punctuation) by them-selves. As of this writing, most texting apps don't yet.

Most of us have become pretty competent at reading texts and other communications even without periods and other punctuation.

Many of us can even understand people who have repurposed punctuation. For example, here is a non-question with an unwrit-ten, attached question: "Education is really pretty good today?" That's actually a statement, a declarative sentence. Isn't it supposed to end with a period, not a question mark?

Here's what that wrongly placed question mark actually means: "I think education is really pretty good today. Do you agree?" Saves you a lot of writing by just putting it at the end of the opening statement as we first did. It's not right (yet). It's a non-standard use. But it's working for some people in their informal communications, such as texts and emails.

I bring all this up because, as I'm sure you've guessed by now, you'll see that many of these students' comments don't have enough punctuation. They were written without using electronics, so that is not a consideration here.

I did try to find some punctuation. If a stray mark *looked*_like it *might* be a period, I put it in for you. Sometimes I cheated and put one in when, in spite of the stray mark, I was pretty sure there really wasn't one there. In extreme cases, I did a bit of editing to make something more easily readable. Otherwise, you might not have guessed what they were saying at all. As much as possible, I tried to leave the comments as the students wrote them. None-theless, I put periods at the end of each comment. I couldn't help myself.

If you're listening to an audio version of this, you won't notice most of what I just talked about.

There are a total of just 22 students you'll hear from in these coming two chapters. Most student quotes are just short excerpts from their longer evaluations. In some cases, I quote their entire writing. If, for some reason, you must skip these two chapters, you're certainly free to do so (not that you need my permission, of course). Here we go.

***

"You have a great attitude & demeanor towards you students, because you treat us like young adults, & not like children."

Later in the book, I'll tell you about trying to save a tardy student from being thrown out of summer school. I hadn't realized how much my effort to save the student would ingratiate me to many in the class. This next student hadn't forgotten when that happened.

"The way you teach makes it easy for your students to learn. Your good attitude and laid back views on tardies & other small annoying school policies makes us want to learn."

I certainly hadn't *said* that I was bothered by "small annoying school policies," but it's easy for students to pick up on such things from their teachers. Indeed, I was *very* bothered by some of that school's policies — especially those of the summer school principal.
Here's something that was echoed by many students:

"I learned a lot of things in the six weeks I spent in your class, more than I learned during the actual year of US History 11A & B."

Earlier, I mentioned the importance of teaching what atomic and hydrogen bombs actually are. Here's a mention of that:

"What I found it interesting with the videos on the wars end on the atomic And hydrogen bomb. I learned that the total destruction of the H-bomb. Things that makes me think. That's why you're a great teacher. You make me think. You make me read up in the past, catch up on current events, and wonder where we are heading, hopefully not too another world war."

That student was not alone in his comment on the atomic bomb and on war generally. Isn't that the purpose of education? I tell you that *none* of my students, even those who had taken the same history classes before, knew what an atomic bomb was. They didn't know its power. They hadn't seen actual videos of them and they didn't know the multiple ways they can kill. These were high school students who would soon be going out into the world — and voting — but they knew nothing about the most destructive weapons ever made.

It's only by shaking up students with real facts — hopefully with carefully selected videos, which I use extensively — that schools can change how students think. That can then lead to greater maturity and to making more responsible and knowledgeable choices as adults — and as voters.

***

CM:

This next student had been in school long enough to have at least generally known the Holocaust existed and something about what happened. But, like many other students, the student actually didn't know much or anything about it. She did not have an understanding of its horrors. As evidence of that, here are her comments on the Holocaust. The spelling and punctuation are as they were in her original handwritten comments.

> "<u>Holocaust</u> *Thnx for showing us movies and talking about it I never knew about it know I do Thax to you. So know when people talk about it I won't stay quiet I can acually have a convesation about it and give my opinion."*

***

MS:

Here are extended excerpts from another student. I will discuss some of what she brings up a little later:

"From the beginning I was able to tell that I was going to like that class not only because Mr. Scarpitta's enthusiasm and humor made it fun but knowing that everything he was teaching was for the best, for our knowledge in the future. I admire teachers such as him that even when most people were failing at one point didn't stop them from caring to keep teaching and doing what they were doing but there's only a few of those teachers around, all the other teachers in order for them to pay attention to you, you have to come to them them and ask them personally to help you or teach you more instead of wasting time for a period long."

"Anyways what I learned in class for six weeks then I ever did in any of my previous history classes was more about the Holocaust, more detailed information from the past wars such as; civil War, Indian war, Spanish American war, World War I, World War II, Cold War, Korean War, Vietnam War, Gulf war(…) and all the other things that happened in those periods. I think the best thing with the videos…"

"but I really didn't like how warriors had to end up but if that was the only way to get freedom didn't bless those men who gave their wife for us whether they've volunteered or not. I especially know a lot more about the atomic/Nuclear bombs that I've ever did let wait for them in the future. I think I have more honor for this country my better understanding of what the people did before even though some where bad things such as slavery, prejudice, and some passed laws. I learn some songs such as the national anthem, Pledge allegiance, America, America the beautiful, and the Declaration of Independence (useful thing is people of the US need to know)."

"I want to thank him for me being a student in his class, and given a whole new meaning to history, which you now I care about learning more about history and I ever did, I used to hate history but that all changed."

AZ:

In large part due to past court rulings, it's still difficult in places to put K-12 students into what might still be called remedial classes in places. Separating students according to their abilities has been prohibited in many schools. Some might consider separating students needing special help to be "racist." After all, why should only better performing students be in the more advanced classes?

That sort of bad thinking, supported in most cases either by legislation, district policies or, more likely, court rulings, hurts students. That used to be called "tracking." That became a bad word in education.

Let me add that what I am saying here can vary by location.

To make it seem acceptable, some try to distinguish doing it by renaming it "ability grouping." They might give examples of putting students needing extra help in groups in a classroom so that they can get the help they need. That is misleading.

Tracking itself is grouping students by their abilities. After all, what happens if you have two hundred students who absolutely need extra help? That can't be done simply by setting up a couple groups in a classroom.

In reality, the problem is not just the students. It's the required curriculum. Sure, teachers can separate a few students very temporarily in classroom groups. (Frankly, that can be more embarrassing for some students than other options, including full blown tracking.) But students who are significantly behind can't be brought up to speed quickly enough to handle their actual grade level curriculum. Even if they can be, their former peers have already moved on. They're behind again.

Is there a reason to avoid putting students in a track based on their capabilities? One problem with it is that, once a student was put in a particular track, especially a lower level, they often stayed there. Schools did not always re-evaluate their progress to see if they should be moved to a more challenging set of classes.

Because parents often complained about that, or didn't think their children belonged wherever they had been placed, some went to court. Rulings effectively told schools that all students should have the same access to course instruction and materials. Upper level honors classes were (mostly) not affected. Most other students were assigned to classes of an equal level so they would have access to the same instruction as everyone else. Sounds fair, doesn't it?

Many feel it is not. In fact, many feel that, too, is racist. That is although helping students who really need it was never meant to be racist at all. It was meant to be a caring and good thing as struggling students were helped. However, since data show that many "minority" students have more difficulty than others, they found themselves kept in lower level classes as they waited to "catch up." Sometimes that never happened. It's a real problem.

Then, there's the related problem of courts cracking down on schools who seem to be keeping some students away from grade level instruction. But, many students receiving grade level instruction can't handle it without special tutoring. Some then become frustrated. Eventually, many drop out of school entirely.

In recent years, many schools have found ways around the tracking dilemma. Many have tracked students without calling it that. It's very frustrating for many students who *really need* special help and who *really* want teachers and classes that address their needs. Many immigrants to America have such problems. Sure, they get language help — ESL (English As A Second Language) or other classes — but those classes may not be enough.

Putting such students in mainstream classes is often done prematurely. Mainstreaming is the default way to program students in most schools. Court rulings and legislation might even require it.

However, as students' frustrations grow, so do their behavior problems. They begin to hang around other students who feel the same way. Groups of such students are, or become, part of criminal gangs. Students are comfortable being with others who understand their frustration. It goes downhill from there.

Students who are successful and feel good about themselves have a better chance to avoid gangs, to go to college, and to succeed in life.

Coming up is a high school student who needs help. I wasn't there to know what happened to her, but my guess is that she didn't get the help she needed. Like too many others, she may have eventually dropped out of school entirely.

When I started teaching in Los Angeles, I asked to teach special classes for those students needing to be brought up to speed. (Remember the Saturday class?) It hurt me to see their frustration. But, too often, I wasn't able or allowed to help students needing special help. There just aren't enough teachers to pull each student out separately to tutor them or to teach special classes.

Educators are told that, legally, we don't want to deny students the same learning opportunities as other students have. After all, that would be racist or, at least, bias against lower performing students, wouldn't it?

Actually, it would not be. Many times — assuming there are enough resources — it can be the only effective and caring thing to do. Nonetheless, many parents have gone to court. Changes for *all* students have often resulted. For some students, it's a good thing. For others, it's terrible. Isn't there a balance?

One more thing. Why do so many students say that many of their teachers don't seem to care? You'll notice that many students say that. Others told me in person.

Sometimes, teachers do need to protect themselves from burnout by actually caring a bit less. Caring deeply about each and every student simply isn't possible for long. I have seen that in teachers. It can be exhausting to constantly care, especially when we can't do enough to help our students.

But, what a difference it is for students when they have teachers who sincerely care about them! That's what we all want, isn't it?

These next insights were written by an 11th grade high school student. Was her schooling preparing her to graduate? Did she graduate from high school the following year? I don't know. Here are some excerpts from her course evaluation:

"even do I [fail] this class but I still learn something I head learn aboutn holocaust and other things that I been taking is my other histeor class, even d I did ndF [?] give up but I learn somethny I feil good aboutn myself by not droping this class and when I [take] in next smaster and I would no more better [than] the other student know."

"I felt like what ever you were teachig or telling the Student it was for ar good and you were not [like] the other teachers that they dont care abouth thore student [you] always [care] abouth us [and] you did what ever you could..."

NP:

Here is another student. Listen to what she is really saying. It's not just about her teacher. It's about something more:

"I really wish I had you for regular school. I learned so much in just six weeks imagine two semesters with you. That would be great. I can learn so much from you. I really liked learning about the Holocaust. Even though it was sad I still like to learning about it. I'm People need to know that this sad thing really did happen. It's sad that some people in the world are in denial in think this didn't happen.

"I never knew half of the things you taught me about each war. Before I just thought 'oh, yeah war. Real sad.' Now I know how war was started and what people went through to help our country. Many people died for me. So I could have independence. I really appreciate this effort for me."

"The movies were very helpful. They talked and showed us lots of footage so we could imagine how it really was."

"About the family history. I was going to record it but when I went to it didn't work. I was really mad. So I had to write it. I had a lot of fun talking to my grandma. She just kept talking and talking. And I just kept writing and writing. I hope I can continue this and learn about every member in my family. It's a good way to let family know that you care."

***

NR:

[Regarding her history teacher from the previous year:] "I didn't like how he teach. Because I didn't understand him that's why. I fail his. I really don't want to fail this class because I do want to be able too graduated I'm June. ... I would be the first one to graduate from high, so I want to be able to give that to my mom. I know that means a lot to her. And especially to me. My family thinks I'm going to end up dropping out of school that I won't make. So I want to show them that I'm going to. Well I had fun being in your class"

Did she make it to graduation? I wasn't there to find out. Sometimes students need someone to specially help and encourage them. They need to get academic help they might not even know exists. But, even then, it's tough. You can't help but *really* hope that she graduated. On the other hand, having read her writings, most would feel that high schools are without academic standards to allow students with such low writing skills graduate. Yet, too many without an acceptable foundation in education do.

When people complain that high schools shouldn't let people so deficient in basic skills graduate, they have to realize that these are real people. It's not likely non-graduates would stay in school and keep trying to learn what they couldn't get the first time. They would need non-existing specially designed classes to help those who didn't graduate. Most would quit. Some might consider suicide.

Is it the lesser of two evils to let them "graduate?" Or would the right thing be to ensure that they are actually educated in the first place? If not one, then the other.

This is really hard. Instead of breaking our hearts as we watch failing students with such hope and frustration from afar, we should all do something to help. That should include parents and other volunteers, not just educators. It should include other students, too.

We must try to offer all the extra help that we can if we're going to help students meet the basic standards of high school graduates — which are often too low anyway. Aren't high school graduates supposed to be ready for college? We'd like to think that. But we know that far too many are not.

PM:

Another student. Note that learning about the Holocaust really is important. What if I hadn't taught it? Adequate teaching requires a minimum of a full two to four hours with strong videos and lecture. Would she *ever* have actually learned what happened? Would other students have learned it? Is it as important as I say it is?

> *"What I've learned of this six weeks were alot, personally I didn't know nothing about the Holocaust or what it was, but now I do not. I know that a lot of people were killed, how they were killed and for the reason they were also killed. … you have a lot of patients and don't give up on your students (thank you). You are different than most teachers because other teachers wouldn't off cared or would off just given up on their students. … I really think you should be happy with yourself because we did learn and tried and didn't give up…. thank you for being a good teacher and for understanding us."*

***

MS:

And another mention of the Holocaust… She doesn't say much here, but the recognition of its importance is enough. Clearly that one topic, covered much earlier in the class, had a significant impact on the students. I include these comments because there will be a number of people who still wonder why I listed it as one of the core things educated voters should know. It's not just a bias of mine. It really is important.

> *"I really learned alot about the Holocaust it was really interesting."*

"I really don't like history thats why I took it during summer to get over with it Luckily I got into your class because you changed my whole thoughts about history know I do think that history is important & fun to. Thank you so much for your time & thanks for the knowledge you passed on to me."

(You're really welcome. It's what teachers do.)

***

JA:

After giving examples, including names and dates associated with the history of the atomic bomb, this student said:

"These are things I didn't know before."

Once again, understand that if I had not taught this to my students, combined with excerpts from multiple videos, in most cases (that's *most*, not simply *many*), students would reach adulthood and never actually know what an atomic or hydrogen bomb actually is. There are currently *countless* adults (and too many teachers!) who know little or nothing about it.

Sure, they know it's a big bomb. They might have read about them, maybe seen a photo in a textbook or something brief on TV. But that's a far cry from actually understanding the full power and devastation that define them. Many of the wonderful, but concerned readers of this book, products of the American public education system, don't know enough about them either.

Many in the news media, many reporters and editors, naively believe that their readers, listeners, or viewers understand what these weapons are. They're naive, in part, because many in the media themselves lack a full understanding of what these weapons are. They're really big bombs! We don't want our enemies to have them. Isn't that what blew up the building in Oklahoma City? No, wait. That was a *teacher* who said that.

Over the years, teaching about the atomic bomb was one of a handful of things I taught that truly affected students. That, then, affected other things I taught throughout the rest of the class. I gave the presentation on the atomic bomb regularly, in all of my classes whenever I could, regardless of the subject of the class. I used about 25 minutes of excerpts from multiple videos, stopping frequently for more detailed explanations and teaching. The total presentation was normally around 70 minutes.

Once in a while, another teacher might come in to listen. Why? As I already mentioned, some teachers no longer remember — or more often had never actually learned — what an atomic bomb actually is.

This is truly one of several critical topics in education today. There remain more than enough of these weapons in the world to wipe out much of the planet. So I ask again. Why haven't schools ensured their students know this? Well, for one thing, they don't have knowledgeable teachers and substantive resources to be able to teach it.

To me, high school is the best place to include this. Remember, during the early years of the Cold War, many people learned solid details about them in elementary school, even in third grade. But, as I mentioned, who would teach it today? Knowledge about them is now almost completely lost, even among teachers.

Time for a reality check here. I spend a lot of time mentioning atomic bombs and the Holocaust. Those are not the only things important in education. But there are countless other things that are also missing from the education system, things that are taught wrongly — or not taught at all. My two canaries of education are just the low hanging fruit, the easy ones to mention. But there is much more our students don't know. What I've mentioned and will mention again, are just examples of the situation we're in.

This same student continued:

"The videos we saw were great I haven't seen any of them before they were all great and exciting can't forget some or most of them were sad because many people died to protect this nation. [Then, in very large letters,

underlined, he finished by saying:] *I enjoyed everything. I will miss it."*

Of course, teachers love to hear that. But, more than that, isn't that what we want *all* of our students to think about their education? Why should this be unusual? Many other teachers also have great feedback from students. Many teachers do make a difference in the lives of their students.

The problem is that it isn't happening nearly often enough. We want this to be the norm, not the exception. Otherwise, schools and educators fail. No one wants that. But it's what has been happening.

18. WHAT DO STUDENTS THINK? PART TWO

Here we continue with insights from student evaluations as in the previous chapter. There are things to learn here.

***

CC:

I'm quoting this next evaluation in its entirety. It's not long. That students thought I taught them well is not the point. I am not what is important. The important thing for you to understand is what is important to the students. Such things are important regardless of which teachers they have. These writings are insights, not only into the individual students, but also into certain groups of students as a whole — as well as into education.

It's true that these students were not honors students. Your children may be in schools with a totally different caliber and culture of students, as well as with different teachers, standards, and instruction. But I guarantee you that, even at other levels, schools have been failing our students and, therefore, the country. Here, you're just hearing from this one group. I assure you, though, that they really are representative of countless other students. So take these student comments not as isolated exceptions, but as a window into the much broader education system from their eyes.

I'm sure I don't have to remind you that these are the writing skills of high school students. Some, *but not all*, of the students I quote here are from immigrant families. English is not their first language. Nonetheless, I'm not sure I find that to be a good excuse for their poor English. Who can we blame? By now, you should know it's the schools.

What can schools do about this situation? At the moment, we're not here for that. We're here for something else. But the answer today is likely little or nothing.

"Im not trying to kiss butt but I think your are a really good teacher. You're the only one that I've respected in along time. You understand how to get through to us and I bet majority of the people in here would have failed with another teacher. Its cool how you know that were still teenagers and we still think like teenagers, even though some of us do have a point sometimes. Our generation isn't stupid just sometimes we don't try and mostly cause we have no one to listen and understand, yet you understand and helped alot of us. One proof that I know you understand is because you know the stupiedity of this school and how they run it. If it was my choice and this class'es choice we'd probably vote you principal you should try it one day. I found you as a very fair teacher and I trust that you graded right. P.S. I don't mean your easy and we can walk all over you. Thats not true. Class was cool I like how it was run I liked how we talked and I liked the quiz idea."

CR:
Here is what I thought was a strange comment from a student:

"The only possible suggestions would be to add a greater amount of work."

The student then went on to give suggestions for more work, including a project and essays. More work? Was he being facetious?

Who knows — but likely not. In this six-week long, two-hour a day, five day a week class, I gave LOTS of work to the students. Most couldn't keep up with it.

One student correctly noted that they completed almost half the U.S. History textbook, most of it as homework. Half the book is normally one full semester. (Of course, not all students did the work.) The class had near daily quizzes to encourage doing the near daily textbook reading assignments for homework.(It didn't always work, of course.) They saw many hours of solid, applicable, and mostly pretty good videos with solid learning in them. They had substantive lectures from me to go along with them even as they were playing. I also gave memory assignments and repeatedly quizzed them on the memory work.

Some decades ago, the important learning method of memorization began to be considered bad teaching. Don't we want our students to actually *think* instead of just doing rote memory work, newly enlightened educators said? Memorization is not the only important learning tool that has been thrown aside over the years.

I assigned memory work to students so they could learn things they really do need to know, including patriotic songs. That way, students don't have to hum along with the national anthem when others sing it at some sporting event. They will know it. Others can hum along with them.

Frequently, I recorded and played selected news items for the class from the radio. It's important to get students to understand the importance of current events. (One time, at another school, I got myself in some unexpectedly serious trouble by doing that.)

By themselves, current events are often uninteresting for students at that age. They have to be explained. They have to be put into a broader context. They have to be made interesting.

As I just mentioned, students memorized — and could recite with confidence — the Pledge of Allegiance, along with other patriotic songs — as well as the second sentence of the Declaration of Independence. These are things that America shares as a nation. They link us together. I'm there to create not simply *knowledgeable* Americans — but *Americans.*

After all, if they aren't assigned in school, when will they learn them?

They won't.

Hopefully, they'll remember them. If not, it won't be hard to refresh their memory. After all, they already learned these things once. They'll have the confidence they can do it again.

I repeatedly tested the class on the memory assignments, as well as on other things. Repetition is the only way to ensure memorized items stay with you. The grades weren't important. It was the repeated testing. That's the point of things. Tests can be a learning tool, not just something for evaluation and grading. Learning is more important, is it not?

As one student mentioned above, students were also assigned a family history project. They had to interview an appropriate family member. I gave them training and showed them an example. As I knew, it wasn't always easy for them. Some students mentioned it in their course evaluations. The students who were successful doing it found it to be very valuable. More than one planned to continue family history work after the class ended.

Keep in mind, these were not honor students. As you can tell from their writings, many struggled. But I guarantee you that the things they learned — *really* learned — are not necessarily known even by students considered to have higher level learning abilities. And what will sound even worse: even teachers don't necessarily know these things.

It was a six week class.

This student's end-of-course evaluation continued:

"I think I learned more in 6 weeks than I could have in a year. Usually, we get taught solid facts like dates and events, but [in this class] we learn reasons, causes, effects and opinion. These thing. enhance the course. Not to mention that the two hours were pretty enjoyable. Thanks for a cool six weeks!"

Multiple students lamented that they had not learned things in other classes. The students themselves knew that they should have.

Many teachers would object. They would correctly say that they do teach such things! It's really up to the students to pay attention in class and do the work to actually learn it themselves!

But there's a difference between teaching something and actually *learning* it. A surprisingly high number of students know that they're not learning enough. Many college students feel the same way. Finally, many burn out on their college classes. In the end, they no longer care.

Good teachers have to keep their finger on the pulse of what students are thinking. Only in that way are teachers able to quickly change *the way* they're teaching and even *what* they're teaching. I have certainly had to change. Others should, too.

Many teachers do change when it's needed. Too many others don't.

It's very easy for teachers to fall into the same comfortable teaching pattern they've been using for years. It takes time and effort to change.

***

PS:

> *"I really appreciate Mr. Scarpitta for... actually teaching me stuff that I will actually remember and want to remember. I have not been bored, but actually interested in all the work we have done throughout this 6 weeks."*

One of the things we don't hear enough is that a student *wants* to remember things. *Wants* to remember. They might say they learned things or that they will remember things, but rarely do they add that they really *want* to remember it. That's different and, to me, it's very important.

Here's a bit more. She is clear about what students don't like:

> *"My last teacher was not very clear about things and could not really describe or tell us what actually happened in our past history because all he did was just give us work and never talk about it."*

"I have to let Mr. Scarpitta know that the [videos and lectures] have been really effective for me, but I think for the rest of the class also."

Videos must be carefully selected. They often have to be edited for time, while still leaving time to explain and put them into context by the teacher. No teacher can do as effective a job teaching certain topics as strong videos can do. If something is going to stay with a student, it is often a well-produced video. But good teachers must use them as a *tool* for teaching. They don't just put one on, press play, and figure it will do all the work. Much more is needed and *teachers* have to do that.

***

OR:

Here's a student who would graduate the following year. He wrote:

"You are the only teacher I had [in high school] that really cares about the students. My personal that [thought?] is that, that is a real teacher. Right now, I am very interested in U.S. History. Its very important, I now understand."

It's simple to understand why students feel it is important that a teacher cares about them. Why, I ask, would a teacher *not* care? All teachers cared at some point, at least when they were new teachers. Am I wrong about that? I cannot believe that teachers don't care about their students — at least as they began as teachers. I do believe that not all know how to show that caring to them.

No caring; no learning. Many students agree with that.

I have known many really fine teachers who care deeply about their students. I can't believe that so many students feel that teachers don't care about them. That can't be true, can it?

***

CV:

Excerpts from another student's comments:

> *"You know when I found out I needed to take summer school for a history class I almost died because I thought it was over. But after attending your class these six weeks just flew by so quickly. The two hours in class felt so short so incredibly fast. ... I believe you have an original yet interesting way of teaching. It really brings the interest out in history. I hate history I don't like it but I enjoyed and learned a lot. ... I know you'll be the teacher I'll remember always."*

I am not the issue here. Many other teachers get wonderful comments from their students, too. The real issue is why students don't feel this way in nearly *all* of their classes. If they don't, they'll just barely learn what they need to get by. That's not enough. But that's what's happening, isn't it?

We need more really great teachers. In too many cases, teachers' hands are tied to do what they *really want to do* in order to educate their students. Are there options? Yes. Can they be implemented? Almost assuredly, not. They would be too radical.

As I've said from the beginning, I'm not here to offer ways to fix the current system. Suggestions have been made in the past. Some schools have tried substantively different educational systems and been successful. None of those things have transferred to the larger public sector, or even to schools in the private sector. In other words, talking about what to do about public education has been useless. Nothing has come of it at all. All I can do now is put my opinion of the current situation squarely on the table before you. Gradually, I'm doing that.

***

ES:

I'll also include this next evaluation in its entirety. Here, you see a student who loves learning but who is frustrated with herself — and with an education system that doesn't recognize her different way of approaching learning. The system doesn't allow students like her to succeed. That doesn't mean the assignments she didn't do weren't important. But she needed a teacher to be flexible, or to encourage her to do the full assignments. She talks about grades. I often talked to my students about grades and grading.

When I taught in the Animal Husbandry department at a community college, the first book I required students to read was one about grading in schools: *Wad-ja-get?* Even though it's an old book today, I still recommend it.[1]

Understandably, some of my community college students wondered what that had to do with the Animal Husbandry class I was teaching. I told the adults and the younger adults in class that they were welcome to take a protest "F" if they thought that grading had nothing to do with the class. They all read it. The book is easy to read. It didn't take them long. I myself had first read it as part of the first Educational Psychology class I took. I'll talk more about that class shortly.

As I had also been, many students were changed by reading it. One student later told me that his grades went down in many of his classes because he had read the book. But he learned more and enjoyed his classes more. He thanked me.

Although I (generally) didn't assign it to my high school students, I would still often carefully talk about grading in general, as I did for this class. The student below clearly felt strongly about grades, especially as they can negatively affect learning.

If the American Public Education System were fixable (and it is not), students like this one — really, all students — would have to be heard. So listen to this one now.

As with the other student evaluations, I attempt to include it (almost) exactly as written. This student often uses ellipses (…) in place of periods and commas, or for no apparent reason, so there are a lot of them. Here is her evaluation.

"Mr. Scarpita, I can not think of anything that needs changing in our class... structure...(your teaching structure). One rarely has a teacher with such passion about teaching! I agree that school isn't just about grades... quite frankly I can care less about "a letter" which is supposed to be a symbol of ones knowledge... No letter can exactly state that which runs inside me! All I care about is becoming an educated person. It is unfortunate that grading is so important or though of to be so important... by high schools and colleges... it makes people strive for the grade not the knowledge...

"My experience with my regular school History class was just terrible... There was cheating... (*I feel the grading also pushes students to cheat... I've seen some of the most intelligent students in class cheat*) — I actually knew more than about 4/5 the students in here and I truly felt confident about the knowledge I had absorbed..., but I got a "D.".. It's odd... my behavior that is... I would read given pages... look over the assignment, making sure I understood everything... Then I wouldn't do the worksheets or section reviews... BUT I KNEW EVERYTHING!! I would get A's on the tests... We would have to prepare debates on certain issues & I gave some fiery speeches that left chills running through my body when hearing the words shoot out my mouth... (Guess what I would neglect to do... I wouldn't hand in a typed version of my speech...) I would write highlights... on note cards and deliver my speech quite strongly...

"I really have a craving for knowledge... and I wish more classes were conducted as this class (your class Mr. S.)

"You never seem to give up..., even with students failing, you refuse to give up on them and that is a quality of much value — I wish more teachers would teach, not because of the financial, but fer the love of spreading knowledge...

"Mr. Scarpita ... I thank you."

***

MV:

It's never a good thing to make students feel like losers. I don't think teachers ever want that to happen. Nonetheless, sometimes it happens. I'm sure I may have accidentally said some things I shouldn't have over the years. All of us have said things we later wish we hadn't said or hadn't expected someone to take the wrong way. But it just takes once for students to be affected forever. It happened to me when one of my best teachers once called me a "buffoon" in 10th grade. That never changed my opinion of the teacher though. He still did much more for me than most other teachers have. He remains one of my best teachers. I know he never knew it though. At the time, I'm not sure I did either.

Here's a brief excerpt of another student's comments:

"Overall I think that the class was exciting because of the way you taught us. You never made us feel like losers you said that even if we feel like losers you said that even if we failed we had learned something I hink that we really did. This is why I think the class was good for us. I think I learned more in this class than I had learned in any of all my other classes."

***

BS:

What is really special about this next evaluation is that the student failed the class. Several students did. It really hurts me to fail even one of my students. It's something I didn't have to do too often, but sometimes I couldn't come up with a fair option. Since a number of failing students really did learn things, I wrestled hard to try to find a way to pass them. I wasn't always successful. At least one student apologized *to me* that I had to fail him. Students blamed themselves. They know why they failed. I often blamed myself. Wasn't there something I could have done to help them? Sometimes, there just wasn't. I do *not* want to pass students just to pass them. Some teachers do. It hurts the currently already low standards of education to do that.

On the other hand, *objectivity in grading DOESN'T EXIST.* I don't care what anyone tells me about how "fair" or objective they think their grading is. There's simply no such thing as objectivity in grading. Once I realized that, I looked at grading my students differently.

This next evaluation was in all uppercase (caps). I made it a bit easier for you by removing most of them:

> "HI MISTER! I just wanted to thank you for teaching me alot of stuff I didn't know about[.] Even though I failed your class, I really learned and enjoyed U.S. History B. You teached me so many thing I never new or heared about. For example most of those wars I never even hear about it, the Holocaust, I never knew what that meant.
>
> "I think you shouldn't change the way you teach the class because it's really fun and interesting way to learn about our history. So just don't change. I guess what I'm really tryin to tell you is thanks and not to stop teaching the way you do. But like I said before, 'Even though I failed your class, I really did learn more than you think I did!!!' Thank you."

***

AC:

There are two things to notice in this next student's comments. As did so many others, she, too, mentions the videos I chose. I'm being redundant when I say how important the *right* videos can be, especially in history classes. Some teachers, even parents, don't want to show videos that might be "difficult" to watch. But that's not how learning takes place.

Many years ago, when people were sent to driving schools after getting a ticket, the instructors almost always showed significant videos of the aftermath of actual traffic accidents put together by the National Highway Traffic Safety Administration (NHTSA). Reportedly, some people complained that they were too graphic.

But, if the object was to wake drivers up so they would take driving more seriously and become more careful on the road, my feeling has always been that they worked well. Of course, their benefit may have been just for a limited time (after which drivers should watch them again, to my way of thinking).

I haven't been to a driving school for many years, but I still remember the serious feeling I got from watching them. In my opinion, it was a big mistake to (reportedly) kowtow to those who felt they were difficult to watch. That was the point. No lecture — or anything else — could replace those videos. My personal belief is that they contributed to driver safety.

I bring that up to reinforce the effectiveness of using good and appropriate videos. Of course, some can be a bit of a waste of time. But, sometimes, they're all we've got for certain topics. A big problem is fitting them into the limited class time. More than once (not at the summer school classes), I asked a principal to let me have just a bit more time to finish some especially important presentation that I knew would run long. Good administrators and understanding teachers supported that. During summer school classes, I generally had two hours for instruction. That was immensely more helpful than a mere hour (or 50 minutes) of classroom time.

Of course, I was grateful for the kind comments from students on their course evaluations. I asked for the evaluations. They were not required by the school. Student evaluations are generally required in many universities today.

As you can see, the good comments often relate to the effectiveness of the videos and other resources rather than just to me. If you can make students feel "the pain of people," then history comes alive for them. Students might become better, more caring people. Emotional connections to history help students — all of us, really — to mature and to care about others.

My second point here is something I have brought up before: Many students have difficult lives at home.

Here is the next evaluation in its entirety:

"Thank you very much. I really feel that I have learned a lot from your teaching. The videos on the war had an especial effect on me because I never felt the pain of people in other videos such as yours. As for the Holocaust it made me realize that I might have contributed in happening again

and it made me not to take anything at all for granted and help anyone if I can.

"I think you are a great teacher (even though you don't talk a lot) because it shows that you really care about us and that you want us to achieve something in life as well as understand it. I sincerely loved this class and actually learned something in coming to class. Though I didn't do my family history because I've been having problems with my mother and she wouldn't talk to me. and she was the only one I had to interview but I'm going to make sure I do get things out of her when everything between me and her gets better because she's not an easy person to talk to."

GS:

"In my other class we never saw anything about the Indian Wars so that is what I liked the most because I never knew what those people went through and now I do."

That is a topic many history classes skip through quickly, although it's not the only topic that is given short shrift. I was always aware that if I did not bring up some topic — and teach the topic — that it was highly unlikely my students, as adults, would ever know the facts about those events of history *at all.*

Especially as adults, they are more likely to be drawn in and say something should they hear people take positions based on false or incorrect information. By ensuring our future adults more fully understand our past, they will be able to make better decisions for our future.

Teaching time is always an issue in these things. Time can be taken away for required testing — by districts, states, or the federal government — and for preparation for those tests.

I hasten to add that testing, in itself, is not a bad thing. It is actually essential. Testing is very important to evaluate the effectiveness of what we, the educators, are doing in schools. The problem rises when too many tests are required and when too much time goes into preparation for those multiple tests. I discuss testing in more detail later in the book.

***

AP:

"You have been the most exciting teacher I ever had. ... You are also one of the few teachers that care about education."

This thought has been expressed in other evaluations, and in some of my other classes at different grade levels and across different subjects. WHY do students say this?

"One of the FEW teachers?" I have personally known many teachers who really do care about education. Was this student's comment, echoed by others, just meant as a comment about a small group of teachers? Maybe just a couple of them? I truly hope that was the case. Teachers and administrators who only look at education as a mere "job," and who don't actually care about both education and their students, shouldn't be in education.

***

KE:

Giving students the solid facts of actual history (not revisionist history), with the effects that it has on real people, allows young adults to further develop their own personal morality and their path forward as a citizen and future voter. We need to develop informed and educated voters to keep the country healthy. Right now, we don't have enough of them.

If students learned a personal or shared morality, it was not because I explicitly taught it, but because the lessons of HISTORY taught it to them.

Truthfully, a shared, even a national morality should be part of education as it had once been in the past. Some will say that schools are not the place for that. In some areas, I strongly agree with that — in others, but I do not.

On the other hand, there truly is a shared morality in this country — or there used to be. In recent times, it has come under serious attack.

Part of that formerly shared morality included prohibitions against lying, cheating, stealing, hurting other people, even disrespect for others. Societal virtues include listening and communicating with others respectfully, protecting the weak, helping others when they are in danger, donating time or money to organizations that do good, including churches and charities, and a lot more. We really do have a shared morality. That should be modeled and taught, not *just* in schools, but certainly in them.

Here a student comments on her personal developing morality. Many students will talk about morality, although not by name.

Here, she credits elements of the class for it, in particular the Holocaust:

> *"I enjoyed your class very much this summer. It was very unexpected. ... My favorite [of the videos] I think was the Holocaust one. I think the most important thing I take from this class is a lot of realization about the facts and mistakes of this country and how I truly feel about it morally, and intellectually."*

***

HP:

Inexplicably to me and others, patriotism is increasingly under attack. Those on all sides of the political spectrum used to talk about the importance of the country and their love for it. Yet expressing patriotism today has brought suspicion, political linkages, and condemnations.

Many feel that being "patriotic" is now grounded in the political right wing of the Republican Party. Since such people oppose

Republicans, they also oppose "patriotism" believing it has just become a political talking point of being a Republican.

What's going on here?

If we don't teach and strengthen a shared patriotism among *all* Americans, it may be difficult to ever fully bring back. That also damages connections with each other which are important to protect the country from threats from without — and from within. Why would people participate in the responsibilities of citizenship if they have no reason to care about their country?

To do that, students must learn shared symbols and connections, including patriotic songs and documents. They must also see an example of that in educators. It should never be divisive or pigeonholing to teach or show patriotism. Building patriotism is what we have historically done.

To have a student specifically mention it prompts us to wonder whether or why caring for the country isn't shown and taught by others, especially by educators in schools.

Students actually want to love the country. Where do they learn not to? From whom do they learn that they actually *shouldn't* like it? It doesn't come naturally. It comes from some parents and (recently) from many teachers and college professors.

Not long ago, a U.S. congressman bemoaned the fact that a new congresswoman reportedly said that the Pledge of Allegiance is a symbol of white supremacy and that just *saying* the Pledge of Allegiance can reinforce racism in the country.[2]

How does a country survive when its people are taught that pledging one's allegiance to their country is racist? How can young children develop any pride or respect for their country if they are taught that the Pledge of Allegiance and the American flag itself are symbols of racist white supremacists (however that is defined)? This is crazy.

Sadly, one student observed this:

"Well to tell you the truth you are one of my first teachers who actually taught me well because you care for the United States."

Where are all the other teachers? Where are all the other *Ameri-*

cans? I should not have stood out as being unusual by caring for the country! Of interest, the student also tied in good teaching (at least in history) with caring about the country. That's not something I had previously considered. But the student might have an important insight in this.

19. "HIGHER" EDUCATION CAN DESTROY AMERICA

In an interview on June 21, 2020, John Ellis, Chairman of the California Association of Scholars,[1] said that higher education is now a:

> "...boot camp for political radicalism. It is no longer a place that prepares children to confront the careers that are facing them, the lives that are facing them, with the mental equipment to face new challenges, to analyze the situations, to respond to new challenges they face. That's not happening."

The interviewer interjected:

> "A society cannot survive very long when its children and grandchildren are taught to hate it, to hate every bit of it...We're losing the culture [of America]."

John Ellis continued:

> "The academia is poisoning one profession after another. It's totally poisoned journalism. It's poisoned the teaching in the high schools. High school teachers are all trained on college campuses."

In America, students themselves — purportedly at college to learn subjects of value while also learning how to think critically — now dictate who can speak on campus, what is taught in their classes, and even who teaches them. Their demands are based on their own changing norms which sometimes even they don't appear to understand.

Their demands totally lack the former values with which Americans were once raised. Among others, those basic values included *basic courtesy and respect.*

Do they not understand how they themselves will be treated once these newly accepted forms of poor behavior fully permeate American society? Have they studied [the answer will be: no] what has caused the decline and fall of some of the largest empires in history?

Although significant deterioration in the foundational kinds and strength of values and morals in the history of some past empires may not have always been the primary cause of their decline and fall, they are minimally considered to be a significant factor.

Teachers have been emerging from such college indoctrinations. They now teach at all levels, most concerningly at the K-12 levels. These teachers will perpetuate the newly demanded trashing of America's formerly shared values and morality. They will replace them with the dangers and damage of new ones. Once this permeates the schools for even just a single generation, it's likely all but irreversible for years to come.

Nonetheless, it appears clear that this is the direction America is now on — and it seems to be moving quickly. Apathy and naiveté have contributed to the morass we're currently in that is poisoning the country.

Is an entity outside of the U.S. to blame for the quagmire we are in today? If so, whatever plan they have implemented for the destruction of the country through its educational system appears to be working well.

***

Here's an observation as to the value of a college degree when it comes to success as an entrepreneur.

An article of March 6, 2022 by Isaac Morehouse, CEO of Crash and Founder of Praxis, had important insights. The article was titled: "Why College Degrees Are Working Against Many Job-Seekers."

Referring to how the venture capital firm, Andreessen Horowitz, evaluates entrepreneurs, Morehouse noted one thing of which the firm takes note:

> "One of the strongest indicators [of success with a startup] was being a college dropout."
>
> Morehouse summarizes what such stories tell us:
>
> "A college degree doesn't do a good job of signaling employability... In fact, choosing *not* to get one can be a better signal." [Emphasis his.][2]

Review the college backgrounds of Bill Gates and Steve Jobs. Neither completed college. There are countless others.

Of course, most people don't necessarily want to be an entrepreneur, to start and run their own business. It's not easy.

I'm not suggesting not going to college — although there are other valid paths for those with the guts to take life on themselves. Done properly, there can be many great and rewarding benefits by going to college. However, prospective students had better choose both their majors and the colleges they attend carefully. Importantly, they had better carefully weigh the costs versus the benefits of college. In other words, they had better know what they're doing before heading off to college.

Few do.

Equally few listen to a variety of others to help them plan their future lives and to make practical decisions as to how college might (or might not) help. They figure they already know all they need to know.

The best people from whom potential college applicants might seek life-planning advice are rarely career counselors at the colleges themselves.

19a. "I DON'T CARE WHAT YOU DO! I HAVE TENURE!"

Here are some small university experiences the author had as part of the California teacher credentialing program. These selected stories took place years before the current, far more serious problems at colleges and universities in the country today.

They do not address the truly serious problems brought up in the last section. In part, they show that our education system has been ripe for the picking for some time now. These are just the tiniest hints that teacher training programs have been deficient for some time. Countless other educators have even more significant stories which do not reflect well on the teacher training system.

***

One summer, as part of teacher credentialing requirements, I took an Educational Psychology class on a California State University campus. It was one of the few really excellent classes I took as part of the teacher training program. As is the case with too many students in a world of grade inflation, I got an "A" in the course. In this case, it was deserved.

The class changed how I looked at teaching. Making a real difference in their students is something all teachers want to do in their classes. Too few do that either then or now. This one actually made a difference in my teaching — and in my life.

A bit over a year later, as I recall, I was adding yet another certification to my teaching credential. This one would allow me to teach English as a Second Language (ESL) to non-English speakers. As part of its requirement, the college required me to take...Educational Psychology.

But wait! I already took that class! Not good enough, they told me. That one wasn't part of the program I'd needed in order to teach ESL. After losing the appeal I filed, I signed up to take Educational Psychology, again.

The only difference in the class I signed up for was that it had a special letter after the course number designating it as a class for what I needed. But, what was this! Non-ESL teaching students were taking the same class? They'd signed up for the same class, but didn't need that special letter after the course number. So it had the same course number, just without the little letter after it. Same class. No difference. For me, it would have absolutely *nothing* that would apply to teaching non-English speakers. The other students weren't there for that anyway. And the professor knew nothing about teaching non-English speakers.

But, worse, was how the professor introduced the class on the very first day.

He effectively said:

"Frankly, I don't care much about what you do in class. I'll give you assignments [ones that he'd clearly been using for years]. *You do the work and then present it to the class. Finish the assignments and I'll pass you. I'm tenured and will be retiring soon, so I don't really care what you do."*

Okay. Those may not have been his exact words — it's been a while since I took the class. But they were very close to his exact words.

The class was a waste of time (and money too, of course). It was night and day when compared with the first Educational Psychology class that I took. There was absolutely no reason to require anyone to take such a class a second time, maybe not even a first time. No reason at all. Perhaps it was a fund raiser for the university.

More likely though, those requiring it wrongly thought there would actually be material presented that would make the subject applicable to teaching ESL students and help us as teachers. But, as is often the case, there was absolutely nothing applicable at all. The "professor" didn't even have experience teaching such students.

How often do college students lose their time and money taking or re-taking classes that just waste their time? Far too often. That isn't education. I repeat myself when I suggest that it at least *feels* more like fundraising than education, or is it there to keep professors and staff employed, perhaps as required by contracts? Perhaps I'm being too cynical.

If administrators or curriculum designers actually think there is some value in these classes, they'd better be 100% sure by actually observing the class and talking to students. Giving students evaluations at the end of such classes isn't adequate at all because most of those evaluations aren't adequate.

Frankly, I could have taught the class myself and done a much better job. I would have enjoyed taking it a lot more that way. After all, I'm a teacher! The "professor" did very little actual teaching. When he did, there was little or no substance to it.

What I never forgot was his telling his students, blatantly, that he had tenure, couldn't get fired, and frankly didn't care about doing any more than the absolute minimum. From that point on, I have not been a supporter of tenure. If I had been his boss, and he hadn't had tenure, I would have fired him.

The protection of professors from being fired for having views that are not in favor has been in the spotlight recently. That was the original purpose of tenure and was justified. But, today, students themselves are allowed to pressure professors whose thoughts they don't like into resigning, regardless whether or not the university's administration wants the professor gone. Under serious threats, some professors are forced out even without the involvement of the administration.

Nonetheless, one would think that actually *saying* you don't really care what you're doing in class — including whether or not your students learn anything — should be good cause to fire someone. That's especially true when a professor doesn't even seem to know the subject matter well. But it doesn't necessarily work like that — if they have tenure.

A disturbing report released February 28, 2022 by the Foundation for Individual Rights and Expression (FIRE) said:

> "More than half of faculty (52%) [including almost 72% of conservative faculty] reported being worried about losing their jobs or reputation because someone misunderstands something they have said or done, takes it out of context, or posts something from their past online."

There were numerous other findings of concern in the report. As one example, although 80% of students said that using violence to stop a campus speech was never acceptable, one must then wonder about the other 20%. Twenty-percent of college students is a very large number who refuse to condemn violence used to stop someone merely from speaking on campus. The report is worth reviewing.[1]

Regardless of all that, it seems that professors still need protections in place if we are to ensure academic freedom. But that also assumes such open and free discussions are balanced on both sides of the issues. Commonly today, they are not balanced on campuses at all.

One-sided presentations, supported by others supporting the exact same positions, do not lead to students developing an openness in considering multiple sides of controversial issues taking place in the country and the world.

Too often today, academic freedoms have become academic and political indoctrinations. That isn't education.

Even with a somewhat balanced staff — which doesn't actually exist at most universities; most are top heavy with liberal professors — students can still have a difficult time getting balance in their outlook. Unless they're taking multiple classes in similar subjects, generally in a major, students still just have a single professor in a subject.

So, if a student takes just one history class in college, that one professor's viewpoint is the only viewpoint a student will have, regardless of how many different viewpoints other professors hold at the college. Therefore, it's sometimes disingenuous to suggest than a student's education is unbalanced when it's the norm that students are just exposed to a single professor's viewpoint anyway. Ideally, a good professor would invite others to class to provide different perspectives. I did that when teaching in the Animal Husbandry department at a community college.

Really though, something else has been going on which is of even greater concern: intransigent and societally damaging beliefs and behaviors. That includes being fully closed to people with opposing viewpoints — even resorting to violence to demand and protect their own beliefs, which are too often unsubstantiated in the first place.

Respectful students, productively interacting and civilly debating each other, all of whom have an overriding interest in the joy of learning, are not found often enough in America today.

***

Many, though definitely not all, professors get paid a lot of money to do good things. Unfortunately, too many do little or nothing — or do badly what they do. Students just bide their time so that they can get through the class, hopefully easily, and then move on to something else that may or may not be any better, educationally speaking.

Especially in many majors, much of college really has become a waste of time. Many people, including many professors themselves, don't know that though. There are exceptions (we hope) in some of the sciences, medicine, engineering, law, and a few other programs. But even those can be burdened with extraneous and frustrating classes along with whichever indoctrinations are currently in vogue.

On the other hand, good college programs with great professors are truly wonderful. Students are different people when they finish — stronger, more confident, knowledgeable… *educated.*

That doesn't seem to be happening often enough today.

19b. STOP ASKING QUESTIONS!

As part of that same credentialing program, I took a required teaching methodology class. This was an important class because it dealt with the core methods for teaching in the classroom. I had already been teaching for a couple of years on what was called an Emergency Credential in the Los Angeles School District.

I was working through my teacher preparation program at the same time as I was teaching full time at the same junior high/middle school that I mentioned before. In at least one twelve month period, I took full-time college work at the same time as I was working full-time as a teacher. Others have done the same thing.

Since new, Emergency Credentialed (temporary) teachers generally have little or no training, they could encounter new situations and have to "wing it" or find some mentor who had time to offer help.

As a new teacher, I, too, encountered difficulties in classroom management. ("Classroom management" is a euphemism. It refers to a teacher being able to handle difficult student behavior in the classroom, sometimes seriously difficult.) In any event, I had other questions too. A mentor was available at my school in the guise of another more experienced teacher assigned to help me as I might need. She was very nice and very competent. But she was busy herself — too busy. I was pretty much on my own.

At the time, many students in my classes were not well-behaved. To complicate things, most were children of immigrants who may have been relatively new to the country and whose English was still weak. As I think I mentioned before, I had five math classes and one homeroom class each day. Most of my classes had from 38 to 48 students. One day, one of my classes briefly hit 50 students. (Sadly for my wonderful readers, I repeat myself on occasion.)

So, that was 50 students for a relatively new, inexperienced, and untrained teacher in a classroom containing a number of "behaviorally-challenged" (my term) students. What's wrong with this picture?

250 EDUCATION IS DEAD

On the other hand, don't think that I didn't enjoy the challenge and that I didn't love teaching the students. I did. Math can be so frustrating to so many people, both children and adults and my personally designed instructional materials were put to good use.

I have always said that schools don't need teachers who are professionals in math or in any challenging subject matter, especially at the lower levels. They need teachers who can *teach.*

I've said that before, too. It must be important.

Students must succeed. Teachers must do all they can to help their students even if it means using non-traditional methodologies.

But I have gone way too far afield. Back to the teacher methodology class...

The woman teaching the class had not been in a classroom for many years. Nonetheless, she presented the methodologies with confidence and expected us to regurgitate them on tests.

But those of us who were already out in the real world knew that what she was telling us to do simply wouldn't work with the students we had.

The university methodology class was large. Most students hadn't started teaching yet, so they paid close attention, taking notes that they knew would help them later.

Except they wouldn't have helped them later. The class was being taught outdated and ineffective methodologies by a teacher who was quite confident in her wrongness. That wasn't simply my opinion alone.

Several students carefully asked questions about what if what she suggested didn't work. She gave non-answers. Finally, one student decided to be a bit stronger. He asked the same thing. *"What if it doesn't work? That won't work in my classes."* He was not discourteous. He just wanted to know the answer to his real-life question.

I was not the only one hanging on for her answer. Those of us currently teaching had the same problems, the same questions.

The professor bristled. How dare someone challenge her years of teaching the methodology class! Of course, she hadn't taught real K-12 students for many, many years. Finally, she pointedly told him that these thing do work if he would just apply them *correctly*! She insisted that she had answered him, if he would just listen.

What she wanted him (us) to do was absolutely ineffective. Those of us teaching challenging students knew that. She didn't. She had been out of a real classroom for too long. Sometimes things do change.

Finally, he sat down.

She had basically told him to stop asking questions. After all, she'd already given him the answer!

The course continued. We all just kept our mouths shut, did the work, and waited for the course to end.

She never forgot the student who had challenged her teachings. He even had the tenacity to ask *other* questions! I was with that student as we worked in groups. I had observed him in class. He was engaged, did the assigned work, and was productive. He legitimately wanted to learn to be a good teacher.

His only transgression was that he wanted to understand what he could do with his own behaviorally difficult students so that he could be a better teacher. All of us wanted that.

After the course ended, the teacher gave him a "C." She had effectively failed him. A minimum of "B" was required to pass the credentialing classes. The frustrated student appealed the grade, but to no avail. We knew that student. He was *not* a "C" student.

So credential program students, schools where those credentialed students would later teach, and the profession of teaching itself, all suffered because of that one bad professor.

When I was teaching at community college, I took a summer of classes as part of a cohort at the University of California at Los Angeles (UCLA). A cohort is a group that goes through all their classes together, as a unit. The purpose of the classes was so that I could complete the requirements for a California Lifetime Community College credential. Last I checked, "lifetime" credentials are no longer currently issued in California. Apparently, they were for someone else's lifetime. Colleges later set their own standards.

The UCLA cohort classes were well-taught. They were very good. A solid and helpful teaching methodology class was included. But the classes targeted adult community college students, not the more challenging K-12 students.

Requiring active teachers to take more classes as part of their continuing education is only valuable if the classes they take are actually useful in the real world. More often than not, there is questionable value to those classes.

In the overall scheme of things, the previous stories are just minor incidents. The broader scope of a plethora of failings is the problem.

Some teacher training programs can be excellent. Students emerging from those can be good teachers. They'll have no idea what I'm talking about. They'll think that those things are the exception.

We are brought back to our topic of classroom education as we understand that students aren't necessarily getting what they need from enough of their K-12 teachers, nor are adult students from their professors at college.

We'll talk about teachers again shortly.

19c. WHEN MIGHT AMERICANS NOT BE AMERICAN?

Summer is an ideal time for working teachers to take their required teacher-training classes since they usually don't also have to work preparing to teach classes. I signed up for yet another class on the road to completing the many credential requirements. As part of them, we were required to take a multi-cultural class. I've had to take more than one over the years.

There may have been 40 or 50 students in the class. The first day, the professor/teacher went around the room asking every student their ethnicity and where they actually came from.

When she got to me, I said I was an American.

Bad me. That was clearly the wrong answer. The professor insisted that I identify myself as part of some ethnicity, part of some other culture, some other country.

The professor didn't simply ask where our parents were from. I could have answered that. She wanted to know about *us*. In any event, "American" obviously wasn't an acceptable culture or ethnicity to her.

But it was to me. Actually, not just to me. Being an American is certainly part of a shared society and culture. America is made up of peoples and cultures from all over the world. But we all become one people: Americans. At least, we used to.

I again answered that I was an American. She became irritated. Hoping that I wouldn't find myself in the situation of the methodology student we just heard about who challenged the teacher and lost when it came to getting his grade, I stayed strong insisting that I was an American. After all, I was and still am one.

Why did I insist on answering the question correctly as it applied to me? My grandfather was an immigrant to this country. My mother came to Chicago when she was very young, only speaking Spanish when she arrived.

But both of my parents had made a strong decision that their children would grow up as Americans. They intentionally did not teach us other languages, just English. It was important to *them* that we were *American*.

I was not going to throw that dream away to please a teacher trying to teach some lesson that she felt superseded who we really were.

Of increasing concern, at this present moment, one can identify as almost any ethnicity and be applauded. But identifying as an actual American seems to endanger people at times today. How can that be? The sense of some is that identifying as an American somehow indicates racism towards others. That is totally false.

Immigrants coming to the country are certainly deserving of respect, as are we all, but, somehow, we seem to be told, immigrants are deserving of just a bit more. So why was I somehow disrespecting others (the teacher didn't say that) by insisting that I was an American and not identifying myself as one or both of the ethnicities of my parents? I never mentioned my parents ethnicities. (She never asked.)

If there is such concern about respecting non-American ethnicities, why would we demean those same immigrants who came to America *specifically* to become American? My ancestors came to this country to be part of *America.* They did not come to wave the flag of the country they left — as some immigrants do in America today.

In the name of multiculturalism, it was now being strongly suggested (more than merely "suggested" actually) that those of another ethnicity (my ancestors) must hold onto that ethnicity at all costs — even if their dream in coming here had actually been to join the great melting pot that America was at the time. Something is wrong with this picture, too.

Beyond all that, I had already spent over three years in the U.S. Army during a wartime. I served alongside others of multiple ethnicities. But we all served in the Army together as *Americans.* Later, I also served in the U.S. Navy. More than once, I took an oath to the Constitution — and I was supposed to ignore being an American? More than just taking the oath, I was honored to have administered the oath.

The professor's frustration with me for being proud to be an American did not go over well with me. I was a veteran. I was proud of my parents. Their pride in having their children be an integral part of the United States of America was not something to be so lightly thrown away. She seemed to have respect for none of that. What country was she even living in? And what was her actual job description there?

That professor is not the only one who takes a similar path in encouraging students to consider being an American secondary to their past origins. When America was called a melting pot — it really still should be — it was because countless immigrants came to it from all over the world. They all "melted" together as *one people* with shared values, self-determination — and with freedom and liberty at its core. It was a positive way to look at America and to all of our connections to each other. But, today, that analogy is considered negative, even racist.

It isn't.

I know the purpose of multicultural classes. I've had plenty of classes and training in multiculturalism. I've also had many years working in multicultural classrooms and communities. I always enjoyed the diversity of my students.

But what was the purpose of that particular class and its teacher? I'm not sure I even finished the class. (I'll have to look it up sometime. I remember nothing beyond that first day.) If I didn't finish it, I would have taken a different class to fulfill the requirement. That would probably have been best.

Did classes like that make me a better teacher? They did not. I was already very supportive of all of my students regardless of their origins and have always remained so. There are always exceptions, but I am sure that the vast majority of K-12 teachers feel the same way.

The most important substance of required multicultural classes can often be condensed to just a few hours of instruction and still be effective. I doubt that teachers of those classes, organizations that make their money on multiculturalism, or college and curricular administrators think they should reduce required hours to something that takes up far less time. After all, such classes keep these teachers working, and brings in money for the college. Anyway, such teachers sometimes have nearly worthless degrees themselves. They need the work.

Okay. That's really unfair of me. I apologize. After all, almost every degree has some value, doesn't it? Students generally learn about…something… no matter which degree program they're in. It's just that — with some exceptions that have nothing to do with their degree — some degrees are nearly worthless when it comes to getting a real job and making real money. And when was the last time you rushed to your neighborhood multiculturalism retail store because there was a hot sale on… inclusive vocabulary?

For many today, the primary reason such classes are required and expanded is because university educators strongly believe in the subject matter. Wait. Or is it that, if they *don't* offer such classes, multiculturalists might call the university uncaring and racist? Maybe they're just covering themselves.

Really, states themselves often require them. In same states, they do have more value than in others.

In spite of what some might think is a negative attitude about all this, that's actually not true. The basics of multiculturalism really are important. It's just that it doesn't justify another long and expensive class — sometimes more than one — added to the many classes already required to become a credentialed teacher in many states today. As mentioned, the important foundation for it can often be handled in just a few hours, probably even less.

There was a glitch in the very last required multicultural class I took — yes, another one. The class was online through a state university system in another state. As I prepared to turn in an assignment towards the end of the class, something strange happened. The teacher wasn't there. She'd been there before, but now she wasn't. No response to communications at all. Maybe she was sick? Well, no, she wasn't.

I finally got hold of the department head at the university who broke the news to me: She had quit or just moved on somewhere. Sadly, she failed to tell me, her student, that she wasn't going to be there anymore. I never heard from her again. But wait! I still needed to finish the class so that I could become, yet again, a multi-cultural professional. The department head scrounged up another teacher so that I could finish the required class and move on with my otherwise exciting life.

No matter how I sound, I'm (mostly) not here to disparage

multiculturalism and its classes. Frankly, it's the whole teacher training system that needs major reform. I doubt it will get it anytime soon. Really, things are likely to go in exactly the wrong direction with requirements for even more mostly worthless and expensive teacher training classes.

19d. DO COLLEGE CLASSES PROMOTE VIOLENCE?

Speaking of multiculturalism, I chose yet another class from a *required* list of offerings as I moved on to complete the teacher credentialing program. It was an Asian Studies course.

It began on a California State University campus, but the professor combined it with the same course he was teaching at UCLA, although away from the UCLA campus itself. As I recall, I was either the only, or one of the only non-Asian students in class. I simply wanted to complete the course and move on with my next requirements. I had also hoped to broaden my competency with Asian students so that I could serve them better.

The teacher assigned group projects for presentation to the class. That's a common method of teaching. There can be some benefits but, overall, I have often questioned the effectiveness of group projects for substantive learning. They are often easier for some teachers to assign and grade though.

At least one group, vocally supported by much of the class, presented their project as an apparent way to organize real world community protests over the concern-of-the-day. It seemed to be more than just a classroom exercise.

I found it disconcerting that, as part of a formal course, the teacher himself appeared to support chants that many observers would suggest actually encouraged violence. The chant were not just those of "No justice; no peace!" And burning houses down. They had specific targets in mind. There was no attempt to put any of that into some broader learning context, nor to provide cautions that actual violence should not take place or even be encouraged — as appeared to be happening in that class.

This was a course that was part of a public, taxpayer funded university, actually encompassing two universities at the same time. Is a failure to discourage possible future violence acceptable in such institutions? It was a failure of omission. But the attitude of the teacher during the classes could have easily been mistaken for actual support for demonstrations with the potential to devolve into riotous and violent behavior.

Certainly, this has happened in the past. During the war in Vietnam, many college professors actively worked to support demonstrations against it.

But many might wonder why professors at taxpayer funded institutions of higher learning have protection, especially through tenure, to allow, support, encourage, or just permit by omission of condemnation, violence or potential violence.

I felt uncomfortable in the class, not because of any threat towards me. There was none. My discomfort was with the reduced amount of academics in a class as part of a teacher preparation program — the reason I was in the class — in favor of what appeared to be practice for later demonstrations on the streets. Couldn't that have been separate from an academic class? Again, maybe I'm missing something here.

There are certainly times and places for non-violent demonstrations, even civil disobedience in certain, hopefully rare circumstances. But taxpayers — students and parents who pay tuition — should not be funding the organization and preparation of such events that they don't even know their money is supporting.

***

In support for the title of this section, a March 29, 2023 article reported on a Wayne State University *professor* who was (merely) suspended for purportedly posting on Facebook that *"it would be 'more admirable' to kill guest speakers who hold 'transphobic,' 'racist,' and 'homophobic' views that to just shout them down."*[1]

***

Younger college students, especially students who have only been in school in their lives, are the most likely to be swayed by things that often happen in colleges and universities. Many (likely most) of those can be easily persuaded in any direction their professors want to take them.

Many students with little or no life experience aren't accustomed to challenging their teachers. They can be led in directions that, many years ago, would not be acceptable to most people in education or in the country. Students who do question what is being taught can find themselves in trouble. We saw one example earlier.

In the past, there were always professors who had specific, personal opinions on one thing or another. Their opinions and their college teaching were protected by giving them tenure, effectively protecting them from losing their jobs and letting them to continue teaching what they thought was important.

Most college student have had one or more of those professors. I certainly did. I had no objection that they were challenging different opinions brought by their students. Students were not penalized. Discussions let students hear and consider other points of view, even strong ones. That is how college classes were meant to be. But there is a difference today.

What now seems like long ago, there were once many professors with either alternate viewpoints or who contained their views, just teaching (mostly) objective subject matter in their classes. There's nothing wrong with a college professor holding a strong viewpoint and expressing it — as long as there are other professors to balance their viewpoints.

But today, diversity of thinking and beliefs is mostly gone. More than that, if students openly disagree with something in class, they may harm themselves by risking low grades. In some cases, they will have to drop the class as they face a quiet stonewall against their viewpoints.

But it's worse than simply having a different point of view. In many cases, simply asking a question that *hints* at a different viewpoint — whether the student actually holds that different viewpoint or not — can be sufficient to ruin the student's comfort in class — and possibly their grade.

Over the years, wise students have stayed quiet when they disagreed with a professor. Today, it seems even more important to do that in order to survive at college.

Recently, David Clemens, a law professor at New Mexico State University (NMSU), said that *"twenty percent of faculty members [at his university] identify proudly as Marxists."* That's a large number!

But wait! Do students and faculty even know what Marxists

support? Do they know who Karl Marx was? Do they know how the history of Marxism on countries in the past? Can they easily define what Marxism actually is?

All that should have been learned sometime in school. Was it? Even if you think that you personally can answer those questions, I guarantee you that most people today can't.

Marxism is a political philosophy that does not play well with American democracy. Although it sounds good to some people on paper, in practice, it has failed. History has shown that it has been one factor leading to the destruction of countries and their peoples.

More and more books point to the increasing presence of Marxist principles in educators and, therefore, in schools today.

Without bringing people back to the founding principles of America, such dangerous philosophies can fully take over university thought and teachings. If that happens, countless students will begin to espouse it. Along with other things, it is a serious danger to America.

On the other hand, many students have already been taught from their earliest schooling the respect the knowledge of their teachers. Too many such students are then likely to embrace the positions their college professors hold. There is now far less disagreement with formerly radical positions since such large numbers of college students are already on the same page — and its a wrong page.

Some disregard this, calling it merely speculation or "my opinion." Naturally, they'll express that thought condescendingly and demeaningly. They'll suggest that I should re-evaluate my positions. However, the results that we see in the education system today, including polls about all of this, suggest otherwise.

Students are leaving schools and colleges far less knowledgeable in some (though not yet all) subjects. They also emerge with newer sensitivities making it difficult to productively function within the challenges of life. Many even leave college with mental or emotional sensitivities that put them at a disadvantage in life — and which are potentially harmful to themselves.

Too often, they come away from years at expensive universities unable to get a good job. What's with that? Why do colleges offer majors they know won't allow students to easily get work with reasonable pay?

I loved the one philosophy class that I took. It wasn't a required class. I took it at a community college that I hadn't previously attended. I would have enjoyed taking additional classes in it. But, other than teaching it, there appear to be few jobs directly related to a major in philosophy. Nonetheless, that study can help develop a thinking and well-rounded individual. It can also support jobs not directly related to it, such as the study of law. However, it is in teaching it that many find fulfillment.

I'm not suggesting eliminating philosophy or similar majors. To do so would be a terrible loss.

But students had better know exactly what they'll find at the other end of such degrees. In most cases, students will not find practical moneymaking options after they finish. Colleges aren't telling them — or students aren't believing them if they do. Some students take two majors. Hopefully at least one will give them something practical in their lives.

Of course, some people look at other options and skip college altogether today.

Not long back, I talked to a college student in her fifth year of college. Although there wasn't clarity from that student in what I tried to find out, what did come through was that there wasn't necessarily a desire to work in the communication major she was taking. Why, many might ask, was taking that major in the first place? She's not alone.

20. CRITICAL THINKING?

"We teach critical thinking skills. We think it's important for an educated student."

"Oh!" says the unwary, but relieved parent with a child just starting a new school (maybe even college). *"Well that's a good thing!"*

Yes, critical thinking is indeed a good thing. But, no, it's not being taught, especially at the K-12 level. A few components, if that many, might be briefly mentioned before moving on to the actual subject matter of the class. However, rarely, if ever, does that comprise enough of the structure and components of critical thinking skills, which must actually be *practiced*, to be able to say that critical thinking skills are actually being taught.

But it sounds good to say it's taught, doesn't it?

Sure, an unusual teacher might actually spend some "quality time" actually teaching some fundamentals of critical thinking, but that's pretty rare. K-12 schools often don't have time to teach the subject matter teachers are expected to teach in the first place, let alone adding on something of substance that doesn't seem to fit anywhere. So while some basic critical thinking components might

266 EDUCATION IS DEAD

be introduced by a handful of competent teachers, it's rarely done in such a way that would lead to their competent use in daily life.

More than that, by not requiring a formal critical thinking class for graduation at college — thereby making critical thinking an optional elective for the vast number of college majors — means that even college-educated students will not emerge with an understanding of those skills, let alone be actually able to use *or teach them* to others.

Not every college in the country even has such a class so, it might not be available, even as an elective — even for teachers-in-training.

Are such classes really important? Or is all this a nice-sounding academic exercise?

Really, no one goes to college excitedly thinking, *"I'm looking forward to learning critical thinking skills!"* It's doubtful most college students could even fully know what it even means. They may have heard people say it. They might assume they're learning it. Actually, many already assume that, whatever it actually is, they can probably already do it. After all, it's something that some educators wrongly believe they've already been teaching to students, even in the K-12 years.

Many years ago, "critical thinking skills" effectively became buzz words. The words, *"critical thinking,"* sound good. Educators at the K-12 level — and those who sell programs to them — often say one thing or another will teach these skills to students. Because it's often hard for many to define, it's equally hard to determine if or when "critical thinking skills" have been magically imparted to students — and that's at every educational level.

So the term, "critical thinking," is thrown around liberally as though everyone knows what it is. But they don't. Even teachers, especially at the K-12 level, may not fully understand what it is unless they had a well-taught class on it in college and then practiced and used the skills in their own lives — mostly an unlikely happening. Even if they did, would they have been able to fit teaching it into whichever K-12 classes they're actually teaching — in which they already don't have enough time for the subject matter?

This isn't to say that teachers and students aren't periodically taught basics of logic and decision making, but to call those limited basics by the more expansive term of "critical thinking" is more than just a little misleading. Nonetheless, students at all levels are taught ways to make better decisions, even when they don't know it. But is it enough?

Who knows.

One can correctly argue most people frequently don't make the best decisions in their lives. Even with critical thinking skills, that's not always easy. Most just don't always make well-reasoned decisions about what they're doing. In part, that's why we all make so many mistakes in life.

Of course, things really aren't that simple.

I'm not suggesting that we're incompetent as educated people if we don't have formal training in critical thinking skills. We certainly might not as effective in life than if we knew and used them. But we've mostly survived. We'll probably continue to survive.

So, as a realist, I'm not really demanding that these skills be taught. Colleges have enough other problems handling just the basics. A fully redesigned college educational program could include critical thinking skills. A few colleges do teach them now. But I'm not holding my breath that it will be a foundational part of a college education as many think that it already is now.

The bottom line is that schools and colleges should either get serious about teaching critical thinking skills — or stop lying to themselves and others that such skills are being taught in any meaningful way. Simply mentioning the skills involved in critical thinking, maybe spending an hour or so on them in class, is not enough to actually *teach* critical thinking skills in any sort of meaningful way such that they can be used in the daily lives of students. But even just mentioning the skills involved in critical thinking isn't generally done either.

Beyond all that, many students resist learning things that they have to change their lives to use. Many believe it's an unneeded waste of their time.

Such people assume they know about things — after all, their friends and peers tell them all they need to know about everything — when they really know little or nothing. Making it even worse, unrelenting ignorance is often accompanied by disrespectful and irrational thought, speech, and behaviors.

So today, rather than learning critical thinking — a skill colleges were assumed to have taught in the past — students are developing the opposite skill: irrational, one-sided, uninformed, or wrongly informed decision-making often accompanied by attitudes and behaviors which were totally unacceptable in the past. In fact, some behaviors in young children are so bad that they used to be punished by parents — in the past.

These thinkingless (a new word!) students, college graduates, and non-college-graduate adults base their life choices on some method of ungrounded, unsupportable non-thinking. Worse, they get in positions to negatively affect the rest of us.

They're not the only ones. Too many teachers and professors are now products of that same system, authoritatively spreading what they don't know to others.

College education in America is dead.

Am I going to far? Perhaps. But enough of it is dead to know that colleges aren't doing their job. Worse, in recent times, they're letting some students dictate not only what happens on campus, but even in their classrooms.

Several books can provide a good overview of critical thinking. As one example, see the book, *Critical Thinking* (2020) by Jonathan Huber (The MIT Press).

***

Of course, there are other skills besides critical thinking. Competent language and writing skills are among those.

However, very high numbers of students aren't prepared for college in the first place. Well, that's not exactly right. They're not prepared for college *as it existed in the past*. Many students *are* prepared for college today, but it's a *new* college, a college that prepares itself for today's students, not the other way around. Isn't that a bit backwards?

Many books are available on the situation in colleges today. As just one example, I'm going to quote a small bit from one book: *Academically Adrift: Limited Learning on College Campuses* (2011; University of Chicago Press) by Richard Arum and Josipa Roksa. Here is a sadly accurate observation by the authors:

> *"As policymakers champion increasing access and improving graduation rates, it is appropriate to ask: How much are students actually learning in contemporary higher education? The answer for many undergraduates, we have concluded, is not much."*

That observation is shared by many. The authors offer many insights, along with data and some revealing student comments. They suggest reasons for what's happening regarding both college and critical thinking.

Here, Richard Arum and Josipa Roksa quote Diane Jones:

> *"…Many students who struggle in college lack the preparation and discipline to be there, but our society seems to assume that they belong in college nonetheless," claimed the former U.S. assistant secretary for postsecondary education, Diane Auer Jones.*[1] *It is fair to point out that a sizable proportion of students enter higher education unprepared for college-level work."*

Indeed, many college students are not being well-served by being in college at all. Other preparations for life might be better choices — and even pay more.

As do many books on education, Arum and Roska's book's analysis leads one to believe that changes might be possible, even though the book doesn't seem to say that clearly. It does present observations and data. It seems to assume that fixing what's wrong might result in some solution for the broken colleges. So, if "someone" were to undertake educational repair at the college level, are they likely to succeed?

Definitely not.

Without major systemic changes, colleges — and all of public education — are not only likely to remain as they are, but to actually get worse. Especially in today's political climate, necessary systemic changes are not possible.

Of course, some limited useful "education" is happening at most colleges. But both the worthwhile quality and quantity of it doesn't justify the high price, in both time and money, that colleges demand.

If, joined by this author and others, what Arum and Roska have said about education is true, what is college actually good for? It's far too expensive to turn out products (students) who haven't learned enough. Isn't it the job of colleges to actually *teach enough* to justify their existence?

Listen once again to the earlier answer of Arum and Roska when considering how much students are actually learning in "higher education" today: *"The answer for many undergraduates, we have concluded, is not much."*

That's more than just broken. It's effectively dead.

Does it even matter if we do more research and demand more reports on the issue? It does not. Research, hearings, reports, and more ineffective programs have already been tried without success in changing anything. Nothing has worked to fix it. As much as many people will jump up and down and want to believe otherwise, it's not fixable.

Understand that *countless* observers of education today have made the same observations as have Richard Arum and Josipa Roksa. Students aren't learning much, both in the subject matter they study as well as in the intangibles that are supposed to be part of higher education. Other than a few specialized fields, substantive education is rarely happening today.

"But," you say, "I don't believe this. I refuse to be so negative and give up! Of course, there are ways to fix it! I saw another book once that said someone knew how to fix it!"

Okay then, fine. Drag the dead body of education around with you for a few more years. It will be equally dead then, too.

***

Hard-to-define college skills, such as critical thinking, are actually one reason that many employers still hire college students regardless of their major. Let me say that again. A large number of employers, including the U.S. Military when recruiting for its officer corps, hire college students *regardless of their major* — that is, regardless of the actual subjects students paid big money to study at college. That's often at least partly based on assumptions that students have learned how to think critically — or just to think at all.

They also assume that such students have developed the ability and discipline to learn new skills. While that's sometimes true, it's as often because they've just grown older and more mature as it is because they survived some college program.

Yes, sometimes they do look for specific majors: engineering, medicine, law, etc. But for the majority of jobs, they, along with many other non-military companies, will often effectively take any degree.

In the past, students used to come out of college able to make rational decisions. They made decisions by looking at the facts on multiple sides of an issue and coming up with what they felt were the best choices. Richard Arum and Josipa Roksa agree:

> *"There is at least some evidence that college students improved their critical thinking skills much more in the past than they do today."*

"At least *some* evidence?" So, even many years ago we're not convinced that colleges instilled critical thinking skills in students? Why, then, do people — and especially employers — think, even assume, that college graduates have those skills? Indeed, it's not likely anyone could prove it was even present in most students in the past.

This author certainly agrees. While it's true that many graduates *and many non-graduates* have critical thinking skills at some level, to assume that most graduates have absorbed those skills from somewhere is presumptuous. The assumption is without substantive evidence.

Are critical thinking skills actually important in the first place? It's likely many corporate executives themselves may only minimally have such skills — or fail to use them. Too many may not even be able to define them, let alone have and use them. They don't even know what they are.

However, the question we have to ask ourselves is whether critical thinking skills are really important today.

Since people don't often actually have or use them, likely not. Maturity and additional life experiences, by themselves, lead to at least some ability to think — critically or not.

Well, at least that often happened in the past. It was another reason young people went to elders for advice. Of course, that was many years ago.

Richard Arum and Josipa Roksa used the Collegiate Learning Assessment (CLA) to judge important skills that college students are assumed to be developing *in addition to* their specific subject matter courses. They administered it to 2,322 students enrolled at "a diverse range of campuses" and majors.

Arum and Roksa described the CLA in *Academically Adrift: Limited Learning on College Campuses*. They wrote:

> *"According to its developers, the CLA was designed to assess 'core outcomes espoused by all of higher education — critical thinking, analytical reasoning, problem solving and writing.*[2]*' These* general skills *are 'the broad competencies that are mentioned in college and university mission statements.'"*

Similar mission statements are sometimes mentioned in middle school and high school statements, too. After all, they sound good, don't they?

Really, don't students gain at least part of *some* of those skills — though really rarely enough for later practical use in employment or life?

Let's just skip to a bottom line on this. Arum and Roksa say:

> *With a large sample of more than 2,300 students, we observe no statistically significant gains in critical thinking, complex reasoning, and writing skills for at least 45 percent of the students in our study. An astounding proportion of students are progressing through higher education today without measurable gains in general skills as assessed by the CLA.*

Frankly, even though 45 percent is bad, I believe that number is far too low. Let's look at that again: *"No statistically significant gains in critical thinking, complex reasoning, and writing skills..."*

That's what college *isn't* doing for your children — and for the country.

Am I saying not to go to college? Not necessarily. In most fields, it's all we've got. Is it worth it? Increasingly not.

Even though there are some other options, there really aren't many good ones. Without something to change it, all this continues to lead the country towards its eventual demise. No country can survive without a robust and effective education system for its population. Right now, America doesn't have one.

***

If you talk to many college graduates today, you'll find anything but actual critical thinking skills. You won't even need a test. In fact, you'll often find the precise opposite: making decisions, acting on a set of what they call "facts," without any logical considerations at all.

Today, many seem to make decisions for clearly political or agenda-driven reasons. Even if some decision they're "wrestling with" has nothing to do with politics or some other agenda item, they might be "wrestling" nonetheless.

Actually, students and graduates rarely appear to "wrestle with" decisions at all. They just seem to randomly make them. Any "wrestling" would not involve looking at multiple sides of an issue, evaluating the pros and cons, and coming up with rational choices.

No, the wrestling would actually be because they don't even know where to start. They're trying to come up with *any* answer, regardless of whether it's sensible or even based on a proper set of facts. Others, especially non-college graduates, assume these "educated" people have critically evaluated the facts and come to an educated conclusion. Maybe they have. Maybe they haven't. After all, we do still have a few properly-educated college graduates left.

It's fortunate that Arum and Roska studied this issue using the CLA assessment test. Included in skills they examined were writing skills. That's another important skill people assume college graduates have. Businesses certainly don't want to embarrass themselves by having newly-hired graduates write at the 5th or 6th grade level, do they?

If you're interested in many of the other things in their book, get *Academically Adrift: Limited Learning on College Campuses*.

***

Remember that, unless college professors have prior teaching experience at the K-12 level, they have rarely received training as actual teachers in the same way that K-12 teachers do. Many college professors have no training at all. We'll look at this a bit more later on.

College students know how to get the teachers they want. They ask other students who already had the teachers they're considering whether they're "good" or not.

But what they're often looking for is not truly a "good" teacher, but an "easy" teacher, hopefully one that doesn't give too much work. Is actual learning involved in those choices?

For some students, it is. Some actually look for professors — real teachers — from whom they can learn the subject matter. But while some do that, many others don't. They just want to get through college and be done with it.

The ones who take education seriously — and can somehow *get* that education — are keeping the country alive for a while longer.

Naturally, almost all students assume they are in the well-educated, "competently-thinking" category of students. But the vast majority of such students are wrong.

College simply isn't working.

Of course, critical thinking skills aren't the only purpose for college, right? Students are actually there to learn subject matter skills, to learn something about something.

That's true. That's what they're actually there for.

But even that's not always working well either.

Most colleges with highly specialized programs do still *appear* to be working, at least to outsiders. Those programs include medicine, engineering, technology, some (actual) science degrees, and a limited few others. At least, we all hope they're still working.

Notice I didn't include the study of law in that short list. Law schools have a mixed record. The goal of most law schools is just to ensure their students can pass the state bar exam, not necessarily to actually practice law. Those are generally two very different competencies.

So students, their parents, or the government pay an enormous amount in both money *and time* to get an inadequate education, often just an expensive social life, and a few years to get older during which there might be a bit of normal maturing anyway.

In order to be able to think critically, we must be open to gathering information on all sides of an issue — among other things. However, many college students won't even open-mindedly listen to others so that they can decide whether or not they agree with them, let alone learn anything from a position they hadn't previously understood.

Too often, college administrations have recently supported such one-sided students as they cut off "prohibited" (generally political) speech. — Such speech had formerly been protected as "free" speech. What many do today operates in full opposition to the original intent of a college education.

Learning to debate an issue, while also listening to and considering all sides of that issue, used to be an important advantage of a college education. But no more.

Perhaps critical thinking is overrated anyway. [Yes, that's (probably) facetious.]

21. PARENTS

Parents are responsible for the education of their children, even if they don't actually teach them personally. Parents are their children's first teachers. They continue teaching life lessons to them even while their children are in a physical school. Some do a great job.

Others are terrible.

Some children grow up having never learned respect and caring for others, including for their parents. That's not just sad. At times, it's dangerous to people and to the children themselves. It cripples communities.

Parents are often blamed for being "bad" parents, for not raising their children correctly, for not supporting good teachers as they try to teach their children. (Here, I'm not talking about abusive parents. They're a different issue.)

Here's the problem. How does a parent *learn* to be a good parent? It's usually from their own parents, isn't it? But so many grow up today with just one parent — and that parent might not know how to be a parent either. Some parents struggled through school, perhaps not even graduating. Even if they did graduate, schools don't teach parenting. Of course, many people would be concerned about schools teaching parenting even if they did.

If we put someone in a car who has never learned to drive, never been behind the wheel, and tell them to go to the store, should we be surprised if they immediately get into an accident? No surprise at all. We would expect it. Should we blame the untrained driver for not knowing how to drive?

So why do we blame parents for not raising their children well, when those parents aren't really sure what they're doing? Fortunately, there's something inherent in (almost) all of us that puts us on the right path of parenthood. We just naturally love our children.

In an effort to be good parents, some listen to others — including some "professionals"— who sometimes don't know what they're talking about either — no matter how many studies they quote.

As a teacher and school administrator, it always bothered me when educators felt that the parents are always the problem with difficult students. Many don't see the big picture. Some "children" become parents barely out of high school, sometimes not even finishing it. Did something magic happen to them to instantly make them great parents? Of course, not. Many really want to be good parents for their new children. But some really don't know how to do it.

Some educators need to look at themselves, wondering whether there may have been something more they could have done to help such students to be young parents before those students even became parents. Then, what can we do to support new parents *after* they're parents? But we must also be careful that those who do have good experience parenting don't think that they know everything. We never do.

As an administrator, I would have parents in my office concerned about their children at school. Sometimes they were upset at what they felt was something unfair happening to their child. I always listened. Some were not open to listening to me. They just wanted to vent their anger or frustration. I listened.

More than once as I talked to parents, I moved away from talking about their child and began talking about them, not in an accusatory way, but out of concern for them. Most were sincerely surprised that I had an actual interest in what *they* wanted and needed, not just their child. But I know that we can almost always support children better, if we can also support their parents. After all, *they* are their children's support system outside of school. That system has to be as healthy as all of us can make it. That often entails helping parents themselves.

Some parents had dropped out of high school perhaps many years before. Some had been silently bothered that they hadn't finished high school throughout their lives. I encouraged them to go back, if they were willing to do so. I offered to come up with resources or a roadmap to help them finally finish high school — if they really wanted to do it.

That was indeed something that had been bothering some of them. If I could, I would direct them for help. Even though I'm not perfect myself, I would continue to encourage and support them.

As parents realized that they were important, they might look for a changed pathway in their own lives. Not only would their children benefit (eventually), but parents would look at the school itself with new eyes.

How can we expect parents to be great parents when they have so many personal struggles of their own? We cannot. Nonetheless, they're responsible for their children.

Parents who are healthy, happy, and supported by mentors and people to whom they can go, in confidence, for advice and help, will be great parents for their children. Helping parents helps our children, our communities, and our country.

Some will say that some other entity should provide help, that it shouldn't be the responsibility of schools. Schools have enough else to do. But that's simply wrong. Responsibility to provide help and support rests on all of us. Our students are not students alone. They are part of their family. And that family needs our support. Sure, we can't do everything, but we can do some things. Professionals can do other things parents might need.

Frighteningly, some groups are intentionally working to tear down the core family structure in America. How do I know such things are intentional? Some are quite open about it, even explicitly posting that goal to their websites. Therefore, some people, including educators, can no longer be trusted to help.

Too many don't know or don't believe that this is happening. So the problem is ignored.

In some communities, there are many parents of children in our schools who are first generation immigrants to the country. Limitations in language can complicate things. These parents are also unfamiliar with the culture and the expectations of their new country.

Often, their children learn to manipulate trusting such parents in order to get what they want. Then some take bad paths. Some become involved with drugs, gangs, and violence.

Many situations are well beyond what even the most caring educators can do. We help whom we can. We try to protect ourselves and others from those we can't help. Some might even be threatening to the school, its teachers, and its staff.

But, with rare exceptions, a school is not a center for social services. It's a *school*. There are limits on what schools and educators can do. The default activity of schools — is to teach. Nonetheless, schools must occasionally cross over to provide or find social services support for parents as possible, but without seriously intruding into the domain of parents.

Not all parents are open to help. In fact, some parents are openly antagonistic to teachers and others. As some of us might have been in the past, some parents are a mess. Others can even be dangerous. So now we pivot to look at the other side of things.

***

Some years ago, I was teaching at a small school with students at risk of not completing high school. All had problems. Some were significantly more difficult than others.

One day, after taking away some prohibited item at the school from a difficult student, the student physically threatened me. That happens at some schools more often than parents and the community know. The day was almost over. I discussed the issue with the student but could see that it wasn't doing any good.

Fortunately, his father drove into school to pick up his son. I quickly went outside to talk to his father about the situation. Surely his father would address the issue of threatening teachers.

His father's response was, *"Yeah, I probably would have done the same thing!"*

It was more than just a veiled threat from him. It was then clear from where the student got his attitude. Sometimes gang members are children of other gang members. But threats to educators don't go over well for any of us.

***

Not only do teachers endure threats, sometimes carried out, but they often face intimidation by students who know how to get away with things.

In times past, teachers tried to reprimand students in private. It protected students from embarrassment and took them out of situations where they would stand up for their bad behavior in front of their friends.

One day, I was a substitute teacher at a middle school. One girl was behaving terribly in class. I asked her to stay after class so I could talk to her. After the other students left, she was disrespectful to me. She implied that she would (falsely) report me for inappropriate behavior with her. I was a substitute teacher that day and was not familiar with the students. I didn't address it further. I simply told her to leave. This kind of thing is why procedures changed. Teachers are now told *not* to talk to students in private, but to be sure that others are around.

It no longer matters whether or not students are embarrassed. Teachers must now protect themselves.

Back at that small high school, I had to take some prohibited item away from a misbehaving girl at the school at a break outside a classroom. She was not holding onto it and I was able to simply pick it up. Immediately, she grabbed it, trying to pull it out of my hand. Then she called out, *"Are you trying to rape me?"* ...or words to that effect. I took her to the principal who handled the issue.

Many people don't understand the difficult jobs educators have.

False accusations against educators — or against anyone, for that matter — are very concerning. Few appear able to take strong enough action to stop this behavior in students. But false accusations are a serious concern for many parents, too.

With minor edits, here is an excerpt from a digression in *The Cartainos, Men of Passion • Men of Stone* by the author:

***

Some years earlier, I made a call home about a girl in junior high school (grades 7-9) — she may have been in ninth grade — who had been consistently disruptive in class. The usual interventions had failed. Other teachers were having similar problems with her. I hoped that a call home would not end up with a parent on the other end defending the child, as often happens. I hoped that the parent would work with me to help resolve her defiant and disrespectful behaviors.

As soon as the girl's father answered the phone and discovered the reason for the call, his voice seemed to tremble. The parent was not at all defensive. Instead, he begged for help.

His daughter had threatened to call child services to turn in her father for abuse — again. Her father had not abused his daughter. It was an attempt at blackmail by the daughter.

What he had done was to tell his daughter that he would not loan his car to her older boyfriend so that she could go to a dance with him. He told his daughter that she could not go because her behavior, in general, did not warrant it. She was not only behaving disrespectfully at school, but also at home to both of her parents.

Previously, she had already called child services on her father to get back at him for something else that he wouldn't let her do.

Such false accusations can lead to a negative record for parents and to threats to take away their other children, even when parents are totally innocent. The behavior her father described was consistent with what teachers at school saw almost daily. Since her parents could not control her at home, it was clear that there was nothing they could do to change her behavior at school. They were completely intimidated by her.

The father asked me for help. What could he do?

I told him that, when his daughter was two years old — perhaps even younger — he should establish a structure of age-appropriate discipline and respect. Correct wrong behaviors right away with firmness and love. Don't wait until the child is older. Don't make excuses for a child, or ignore them, thinking that such attitudes and behaviors are cute and not important because the child is too young. Many assume they will get better on their own as they get older. That doesn't always happen.[1]

Of course, it was already many years too late for that.

Even on the phone, the girl's father seemed to hang his head. Almost in a whisper, he said, "Yes, you're right. That's what I should have done." I suggested some resources that might help him but, really, there was no longer much more he could do to turn things around. It was already too late.[2]

***

While we speak of parents whose children have found ways to avoid the parenting they need, we must address one more serious issue.

For unwary parents — sadly, most *are* unwary — social media is replacing them as parents for their children today. Its influence and peer pressures can override the guidance and structure provided by all but the best parents. Social media is a clear and present danger for students of all ages, especially including young adults. Adults of all ages are also at risk. Most don't know the extent of that risk.

Social media is not a competent teacher for your children. However, its use can teach some things. For example, it can teach children how to demean and bully others. It can also allow, sometimes encourage, postings that today can follow and haunt those posting them for the rest of their lives, literally.

Such bad social media behavior damages both your children and their peers. Among other things, some have encouraged others to hurt people online. At times, it can seem as though it has become a competitive sport. That then transfers over to non-digital, "real" life.

Parents, raise your children. Until safer options become available, stop their use of social media, perhaps even yours. As most have seen in recent times, social media companies have far too much power. They can carry your data and conversations, as well as your children's, indefinitely into the future. Watch for other safer and healthier ways to relate to each other online. Even then, be careful.

Because many parents are still untrained or naive about the internet and, especially, about social media, short, basic classes to help parents become competent in this should be put developed.

The power the social media companies wield long ago became dangerous, both for individuals (of all ages), and for the country.

21b. DOES HE HAVE A GUN?

Children/students who don't learn to do what they're told to do by teachers or parents are too often supported by others who feel that adults responsible for them shouldn't be telling students what to do at all. Instead, we should be *asking* or *discussing* things rather than simply requiring compliance. After all, we don't want someone to *feel bad* when we ask them to do something, do we?

That's like saying a small child doesn't really have to immediately comply when running into the street out of reach of parents as moving cars speed by. Compliance means the child might be alive several minutes later. Not requiring immediate compliance truly means the child might be dead.

One day, at a break for students during the school day, the principal came through my room to get me. She had been quietly advised by another student that there was a possibility that a student, a gang member, might have a gun with him.

Why would he have brought a gun? Had he brought it to shoot another student — or a teacher — either during or after school? Who else might be in danger? Could the student be "triggered" by something and simply begin shooting?

We knew absolutely nothing. All we knew was that we needed to safely separate that student from others and search him.

At that moment, the student of concern was sitting in a classroom talking with other students on the break. We needed to go in, separate him from the other students without anyone knowing what was going on, and then handle the situation. The school had no security other than a small group of teachers. We called aside the English teacher in whose classroom the student was sitting to let him know what was going on.

There were about eight students sitting at the table. Those in the room, including the author, calmly told the students they needed to go outside for some believable reason. We were going to waylay the student of concern for a moment as the others were leaving. When the others were out of harm's way, we would be able to address the concern. (But note that the teachers themselves would not be out of harm's way.)

The students all got up to leave. Things were going well. All of a sudden, one of the students defiantly said, *"We don't have to go anywhere!"* He sat back down. When he sat down, *all the others did, too.*

**

That attitude of disrespect and defiance in students is not rare in schools today. Yet there is rarely help for those who have to handle it. In fact, the hands of educators are more tied than they have ever been in the past. In many cases, so are the hands of parents, that is, for those parents who care about doing something rather than just defending their out-of-control children.

For decades, discipline has been gone in countless schools in the country. This is true even where gangs are not substantively present. Although, at times, it can be the fault of some educators, in most cases, it is not a failure of educators if they are unable to handle extreme situations. They were hired and trained to *teach*, not to function as security, and certainly not as law enforcement.

In many schools in the country, students direct profanities and threats of physical violence against teachers — sometimes carried out — even in the classroom. It's a problem that goes well beyond what teachers and administrators are able, *or allowed,* to effectively handle. Dealing with the most serious cases sometimes means an immediate response forceful enough to stop defiance and student violence that can put staff and other students at risk. Calling for outside help isn't always possible. Such help isn't likely to arrive quickly enough, if they're available at all.

Do schools actually have the ability to handle the most serious of these threats and behaviors? Generally not. Indeed, some laws and other restrictions can totally tie their hands. In turn, that can lead to educators, not violent students and their supporting parents, being threatened with legal action.

In many places, the seriousness of this, on its own, is reason enough to diagnose the death of education.

**

That failure to obey legitimate authority had now put eight students and the staff itself at risk should the student choose to use his weapon, if he even had one (we didn't know). Had he brought a gun to shoot someone who was still in the room? Or was it for something that might happen after the school day was over?

It was always possible that a violent feud between gangs was about to overflow onto school grounds. Schools are normally considered neutral territory and that kind of on-campus interaction is generally rare. In this case, we had no idea what might be happening.

We had no choice but to handle things with all students present. We were concerned that, when we tried to separate him, he might suspect something was up and become a problem. We calmly called the student to the next room on some pretext so that we could handle the issue there. We were fortunate that he complied. Once there, we told the student we needed to search him. He allowed it without a problem.

We found no weapon on him. Based on what the principal felt was a credible report, we knew he still may have access to a gun somewhere. Perhaps he had surreptitiously handed it off to someone as he left the room. But there was nothing on him at that moment. The situation was safely resolved — or so we hoped.

I bring this up is for a reason: Had an actual weapon been there, the defiance to authority by the other students could have led to the death or injury of one or more of them had things gone wrong. Rather than instantly obeying authority (we obviously couldn't tell them why we asked them to leave), they were defiant.

It's important that young people — *and their parents* — understand the importance of respect and compliance with authority. Respect for authority is something that will serve them well throughout their lives. Here, others may have been put in danger. It only took ONE student being defiant to pull the other compliant students back to the table.

Although this incident ended well, I never forgot what happened and what could have gone wrong. I have been involved with other security situations at schools. But this particular one reinforced the importance of teaching children respect and compliance with legitimate authority, including to both parents and teachers.

OTHER DANGERS AT SCHOOLS: VIOLENCE

Most of us have seen recent videos of students attacking other students. Fights between students at schools have always existed. Recently, we have seemed to see weaker students simply beaten up. This crosses into serious criminal behavior although, for some reason, it's not always treated that way. In some cases, violence involves gang interactions. In other cases, the violence stands on its own with no gang involvement at all.

One problem is that these violent students are often handled with kid gloves, eventually being sent back to the same school where they may or may not display their violence again. In other cases, such students are placed in the criminal justice system where they are correctly removed from the school.

However, in too many cases where they are not handled by the justice system or where their behavior does not cross some line, schools (administrators) do not have enough tools at their disposal to significantly discipline such students. Even in especially serious cases, there can be difficulty in excluding them entirely from the school. Schools often get the blame even when the responsibility for that failure is beyond the level of the schools. Federal or state laws or court rulings can tie their hands. In order to provide a safe environment, these things must change.

There are options, although smaller school districts without adequate funding often do not have those same options available. Options can include special schools with a special staff in which such students can be enrolled.

But it's not just students who are at risk from such violent "children." Educators and other staff at school are also at risk — and not just from students. Although we also see this elsewhere in this book, we'll take another look at it here.

When I was a principal, some parents threatened me because I had to discipline their children for one thing or another. At least once, students created an unexpectedly dangerous situation for me. But my encounters with such students and parents were really nothing. Many teachers in the country face situations far worse than I did. Some have been killed.

Concerned students, caring parents, or staff would sometimes warn me about things that could be of concern, both when I was a teacher and also as an administrator. Such can be the nature of the job.

Here we will look at the extensive and serious prevalence of this at schools.

****

In 2022, the American Psychological Association Task Force on Violence Against Educators and School Personnel released a report titled: *Violence Against Educators and School Personnel: Crisis During COVID.*

It sampled 14,966 participants includes 9,370 teachers, 860 administrators, 1,499 school psychologists and social workers and 3,237 other school staff members.

There are two things to keep in mind here.

First, as it notes, this survey on school violence was done during the COVID 19 pandemic when many students purportedly received their education at home.

Second, and most importantly, one should not conclude that there was not such violence either before or after the time of the COVID pandemic. There was and there still is.

Here are parts of that report:[1]

"Rates of violence and aggression against school personnel [were] high despite most schools being remote during the time of the survey. One-third of surveyed teachers reported they experienced at least one incident of verbal and/or threatening violence from students during COVID (e.g., verbal threats, cyberbullying, intimidation, sexual harassment). Over 40% of school administrators reported verbal or threatening violence from parents during COVID. These rates of violence are extremely problematic and may contribute to teachers and school personnel wanting to quit or transfer."

...

"Many teachers, administrators, and other school personnel described the violence they face as on-going and pervasive. One educator described their experiences.

'I have been physically assaulted multiple times by students in the building and they know that not only is there no one to stop them, but there will be no consequences either. I ended up in the hospital the last time it happened.'

"Even when many schools were implementing remote or hybrid instruction, there were substantial rates of student physical violence (e.g., objects thrown at participants, ordinary objects weaponized, and physical attacks) against teachers and school personnel.

"Student physical violence rates range from 14-22% of survey respondents.

"School staff (e.g., paraprofessionals, school counselors, instructional aides, school resource officers), a typically unexamined group, reported the highest rates of student physical violence, with 22% of staff reporting at least one incident of physical violence during COVID."

Among other things, this recommended report included these observations:

"School personnel describe violence and aggression from parents and other adults in the school; students are not the only aggressors...

"Parents have been more aggressive and verbally abusive to teachers in our district since COVID. The social media posts by parents are vicious and they don't seem to remember that teachers were already undervalued, underpaid, and overworked before the pandemic. Those feelings have only been made worse by the pandemic."

"I have never had such aggression toward me from the community, the board of education, and my administration in my life. If I could financially quit, I would. The belittling of concerns and

bullying of teachers from other adults has pushed so many of us to a breaking point. I have been called ungrateful, lazy, whiny, entitled, uncaring, heartless, selfish, stupid, and more. By adults."

****

On February 21, 2023, an alleged special education student at a Florida high school became angry when a paraprofessional (generally a trained teachers aide) took away a Nintendo gaming console the student had brought. He was reportedly playing games on it in the classroom.

One report on the incident said:

Surveillance video of the incident, described in the student's arrest report, shows the student running down a hallway after the para-professional (or teacher aide), *and pushing her with such force that she was airborne for 6 to 7 feet before falling and seemingly losing consciousness. The student then kicked her, got on top of her and punched her in the body and in the back of her head "approximately 15 times."*[2].

The student was reported to be 6'6", 270 pounds, and 17 years old. The student also *"made comments that when he comes back he is going to kill her."* The student reportedly continued to display violent behavior even toward a sheriff's deputy as the deputy was writing up the report.

Surprisingly, many will be satisfied to simply give reasons why this may have happened or to make excuses for the student's behavior. However, that does anything to protect educators and other school personnel from being targets of violence, whether from students or from parents.

Regardless of the student's background — his lawyer later called for a mental health examination — there should be no excuses, only effective actions to protect school personnel. That often means permanently removing seriously violent students — and parents. It is of great concern that some schools can be prohibited from taking effective actions, even if they choose to do so. The judge in this case ruled that this student would be charged as an adult.

An aside: Although it's quite clear in the above case, the definition of "serious violence" can vary depending on who is doing the defining. Some people, including many school personnel, will define almost anything that concerns them as "serious," even when there may be school-based ways to handle it. Children who are still growing up will always have behaviors that need to be addressed.

Defining these things correctly is a separate and difficult issue in itself. All bad behaviors should not be defined as "serious violence" when there may be ways to handle things at the school level. Being an educator isn't easy. But, for those behaviors that truly create serious danger, much more effective actions should be taken than can often be done.

Fortunately, although we seem to be hearing more and more of it, most schools do not often have such serious problems.

Nonetheless, schools should have to be concerned about *teaching* — although they're often not doing that well — not just about protecting students and staff from violence. If students in this country — and their parents — would take education more seriously, they might refocus on what will be important in their lives. Too often, that doesn't happen. Schools are forced to focus on this issue — for which few are adequately trained — rather than the education of our children.

For a bit more, see the book, *Killers Are Fatherless: The Real Cause of School Shootings, Serial Killings, and Gang Murders*, by the author.

When parents hear about potentially violent students at school, they naturally wonder why those students are even allowed to be there. Some are gang members. Others are not. Parents wonder why schools are endangering other students and educators, including their own children. Although it can be, it's not necessarily schools themselves which are always to blame.

Each situation can be different. What seems to be common sense is really more complicated. For example, schools are legally not permitted to remove students without special circumstances. That means that, if students have not actually engaged in dangerous behavior, not just a worry about a possible future event, they can't be easily removed. Laws back students. Court rulings back students. Students have a *right* to an education — even students who don't seem to want one at all.

Parents might want such students removed before something serious happens. What parents don't always know is that many teachers and administrators *also* want that to happen. But the hands of educators can be tied.

Even when schools try to take action to protect the school, laws or court rulings can stop them. Covert and unannounced searches of students' lockers — something I recommend be done regularly — are often prohibited due to constitutional concerns. In places where that is a problem, I strongly disagree with it. Things are indeed more complicated than parents think.

Parents should get with educators, lawyers, and politicians and figure out what can be done so that laws, court rulings, and consent decrees don't require potentially dangerous students to remain at school and to allow schools to actively protect students and staff. Some jurisdictions are more amenable to removing potentially dangerous students than others. But where would they be sent?

Therefore, parents should understand the blame is not always on schools who often want to act, but are prevented by forces beyond the school itself. There are indeed alternative schools where such students can be placed. But there are not enough of them.

Most of the country does not have such alternative schools available to which to transfer such students.

I'll mention that such alternative schools have teachers and administrators who put themselves on the line to try to help such students — and keep the larger schools safe. Try to thank and support them when you can. They really do make a difference.

However, even students placed in alternative schools can and do return to the school from which they were removed to threaten or hurt students or staff there. Placing them somewhere else isn't always enough to protect the school that sends them away.

Of course, when such students actually do perpetuate violence, the criminal justice system can step in. That's good, right?

Unless they are charged as adults, such students are still juveniles. They are still treated as *children*. If a court releases them awaiting further proceedings, they are sometimes *sent back to their original school* where they posed, and continue to pose, serious danger.

I have personally seen that happen and, as an administrator — or teacher or anyone else — it makes me totally crazy. Why potentially endanger students and staff because such students have the *right* to be in school? Being a successful student is not always at the top of their list should they return. On the other hand, I have seen some returnees toe the line because they know they have gotten themselves in truly big trouble.

On the other hand, if such a student is fully removed both from school and education completely, what do you think he will do? He will likely join with others — who may or may not still be in school — and become a career criminal on the streets. It's all that society has left for him to do. That's not a good option either, is it?

Some feel that School Resource Officers — someone on campus to protect the school — is the answer to this. Assuming such officers don't back away from danger, as some have, they can be helpful at times. Indeed, some have given their lives.

However, larger schools need more than one, although even that might not be enough. Even one is expensive. Who supplies the funds? In an attack by one or more students, more help is needed quickly than a single resource officer can provide and, unless some of the school staff are also armed, additional help is normally not immediately available. Added to that is the unfathomable policy by many schools that such officers must not be armed. What's with that? Only the school shooters are armed?

As mentioned, many schools and school districts, especially smaller ones, often don't have funds to hire enough School Resource Officers, if they hire any at all. Many voters turn down initiatives to raise property, or other taxes to pay for them.

To avoid unrestricted gang warfare, gangs often look at schools as neutral territory. Gangs have internal rules. They sometimes have agreements with other gangs.

Those who aren't in gangs, don't have any of that.

I'm not suggesting that anyone joins a gang. All gangs are bad. Some are far worse than merely "bad." Most people don't know how deadly they really are. MS13 is one such gang, but there are others, too.

On the other hand, there's this: *Most school shooters who kill large numbers of students and staff at schools aren't gang members at all.*

Again, see the book, *Killers Are Fatherless: The Real Cause of School Shootings, Serial Killings, and Gang Murders,* by the author.

Bullying is a widespread and serious problem at K-12 schools. It can include or lead to even more serious behaviors, generally involving escalating violence. If we are to believe some recent reports, it appears to be getting significantly worse. Bullying involving serious violence is so serious that some bullied children have committed suicide.

There are various degrees of bullying. Those involving very young students are generally very different from those involving much older students. They should be handled using a continuum of discipline. Among older children, the most serious levels involve the arrest of students.

Many schools lack adequate disciplinary tools and authority to discipline such students effectively. Not only are schools different in this, so are the states in which they operate. What is required in one school, district, or state may not be required in another.

The current federal website, *stopbullying.gov*, contains information on the laws, policies & regulations of each state, as well as a variety of other information on bullying.

In many places, law enforcement is seldom involved because, unless there is an actual battery involved, the problem isn't generally considered serious enough to involve the police. Indeed, schools can and often do handle it effectively using normal school discipline policies. Of course, this can vary depending on which state or school such problems take place as well as the level of seriousness.

Bullying and actual physical violence against another student are generally different, although the first may lead to the second.

However, serious or repeated incidences of bullying, and especially anything involving significant physical violence, should be treated criminally, and not handled within standard school discipline protocols. Once again, this can vary depending on the locale and on the details of the situation. It's difficult to make a hard and fast rule about this.

Students of violence should be locked away in order to keep both staff and other students safe. We talked about some of these in the last section. These are not merely bullies. They are "children" of violence. Supportive parents of these criminals should also be penalized — assuming their parents are not suffering from serious threats and intimidation from their own children. In those cases, parents themselves may need help and protection.

Bullying is often difficult to resolve without parental support. However, parents are sometimes part of the problem. Indeed, the cause of bullying at school is sometimes traceable to problems at home. Yet, in too many cases, parents defend their child's behavior.

As one example, while I was working as a principal, one young middle school bully was repeatedly reprimanded and given school consequences. He had repeatedly bullied students (mostly) younger than he was, although generally not physically.

His mother's reaction is shared by many other parents:

(1) She didn't think it was actually happening;

(2) If it actually were happening, she was sure that it was caused by someone else; and

(3) She felt the consequences given to her child were unjust.

She threatened me with various things (in this case, nothing life threatening). She did the same to other teachers and teacher assistants who had also caught her child bullying others on multiple occasions. Parents often don't even take the time to hear what actually happened from the adults involved. Other times, they don't even care.

In spite of all that, I liked this parent. She was positively involved with the school and the community. But, when it came to her own child, she was determined to defend him — and she did.

We eventually made progress changing her child's behavior — at least at the time I was there — but it took some time. I spoke to her many times about it. It didn't take too many talks to understand she felt that she *had* to defend him. That was so that he would think his mother would always love and support him. That is a common reason why many parents support their children, even in situations where there is clear-cut misbehavior on the part of their children.

This is just a small example of what happens in schools — sometimes almost daily — as educators try to get difficult students, including bullies, under control. Some parents threaten physical violence on the teachers or administrators involved who are merely trying to put an end to such behavior.

Unless it becomes particularly serious involving actual violence, getting the police involved is normally a poor option, if an option at all. Especially in some rural schools, police aren't even available to handle bullies, if they're even available at all. With serious violence, police are needed, but sometimes aren't effective at handling this.

I'll repeat that more clearly for those who simplistically think, *"Well, just call the police and let them take care of it!"*

Some school communities *don't have available police at all.* If law enforcement are needed, they might not be available to go to the school for a day or two. Things don't always fit into what those in urban areas, or those in the media, naively assume should be the case.

Cyberbullying (bullying online) is serious. Yet, in many places, schools are prohibited from taking action when such things take place away from school. I strongly disagree with that. Cyberbullying has led to suicides. It can do a great deal of damage to both students and staff.

Whether or not this becomes criminal, schools should minimally be allowed to handle these things under their own internal policies, regardless whether it happens at or away from the school itself. Often due to what I feel are wrongly-focused court rulings, many schools are unable to do that.

My view is that, as long as the cyberbullying shows up at school and targets staff or other students, schools (along with parents and law enforcement) should be able to take strong and immediate action. This is because, since the bullying is online, it can actually *show up at school*, often on both school and student devices.

However, because this can enter a legally sensitive area, my position often does not always hold sway. In many cases, the hands of both schools and law enforcement itself are tied — assuming this doesn't pass into clearly defined areas of criminality, Especially when children are involved, hands of would-be protectors should *not* be tied.

Cyberbullying can do so much damage that stronger protections must be put in place to protect its victims and punish perpetrators — especially those of K-12 age. Although that appears to be addressed in some areas, but it is not enough. There is much more to do.

Why are we permitting something that can lead to the self-inflicted death of our children? No matter their age, don't take your children's word about anything they do online. Find ways to closely monitor what they're doing.

Please stop this from happening!

The government's *stopbullying* website contains, in part, this definition:

Cyberbullying is bullying that takes place over digital devices like cell phones, computers, and tablets. Cyberbullying can occur through SMS, text, and apps, or online in social media, forums, or gaming where people can view, participate in, or share content. Cyberbullying includes sending, posting, or sharing negative, harmful, false, or mean content about someone else. It can include sharing personal or private information about someone else causing embarrassment or humiliation. Some cyberbullying crosses the line into unlawful or criminal behavior.

Sometimes potentially dangerous students, backed by parents who support them regardless of their behavior, "win" as bullying children appear to get away with their behavior. Some cities and schools have ready resources which can be brought in. Other places don't seem to have any resources at all.

It's often too easy to judge schools. But don't do it. Especially in other states, schools may not be able to handle things the same way as yours does. Some really do seem to have their hands tied in how they they want to address this. Others may not want to get involved at all. Those schools who are able to legally and effectively address this, should be held responsible when they don't.

Complications are added when threats made towards educators from angry parents who are supporting their misbehaving children become complaints before the District Superintendent or the Board of Education. Accused teachers and administrators may not even have an opportunity to present the facts of what actually happened. Having no chance to defend themselves, some educators can lose their jobs over it. A lack of due process? It often doesn't matter. The damage is done. In spite of what many readers might think, such things don't always end up in court to ensure that justice prevails.

Things are rarely simple and things aren't always just. Especially when not supported by their administrators, this is one reason why some teachers back away from doing what they should be doing in their classrooms. They back away from strong and caring involvement in their teaching. They might feel it's safer for them, but it's worse for their students, for learning, and for the school.

In the end, students receive a lesser education, communities suffer from lesser educated community members, and the entire country continues to become weaker.

Even though actual criminal laws may be violated at times by both parents and students, charges are rarely pressed. Educators don't like to do that. After all, these are their students and their students' parents. Teachers didn't become teachers to see their students arrested, even when it might seem to be justified. Some correctly fear retribution. Sometimes, an arrest can make things even worse.

When the situation actually does call for such action to be taken to protect teachers and staff, law enforcement itself may not take any action at all. Administrators and school districts sometimes don't react strongly enough either.

Schools must evaluate each incident. Some can and indeed should be handled at the school level. But others must be aggressively addressed using outside resources. That can mean removing potentially dangerous bullies from schools. But that isn't always possible.

Law enforcement needs to take this more seriously. Even when they are called, some well-meaning police simply give the student or parent a warning. They don't realize that students and parents have already had countless "warnings" and, at that moment, the situation has become so serious that the student or parent should be removed or locked up for the protection of other students and school personnel.

Not only do victims of bullying need help and protection, K-12 bullies often need help themselves. There may be things in their lives that have led them to take it out on others. One-on-one counseling with a professional might lead to positive changes in their lives, too.

As with other difficult or dangerous students, federal or state laws sometimes prevent anything but a short-term removal of dangerous or potentially dangerous students. That needs to be changed. As has been noted before, many urban areas have alternative schools in which to transfer such students. Other areas have no schools for alternative placements at all. Nonetheless, effective options are needed in order to handle such students.

Readers here should think beyond badly behaved (or dangerous) students at school. These students go out into the world and bring their bad and dangerous behaviors with them. Many of these children see no problem with it. Businesses and others in their way pay the price. Too often, these children were raised without acceptable social skills, without respect, and without basic courtesy to others. Many of them then carry such deficits into adulthood.

Sometimes, it might already be too late to fix serious parenting mistakes. Yet, in other cases, it isn't. Parents should take quick action to put their children on the right path to adulthood. Learning what a heartfelt apology is — might be a good place to start.

Supportive and involved parents are gold, not just for the school, but for their children. Educators all wish that more parents understood that.

23. TEACHERS & TEACHING

Why do people become teachers?

Aren't there just normally just two reasons?
- (1) They need a job;
- (2) They *really* want to teach!
- (3) Or both of the above.

(1) Many people begin their kindergarten to 12th grade (K-12) teacher preparation program without actually knowing what the job involves. Many assume they know about teachers and teaching. After all, most of us have spent many years watching and (hopefully) learning from countless teachers. But teaching itself can be different. It's often much harder than many people think.

Some people enter teaching because they didn't consider that the academic major they took at college would put them at a disadvantage in finding a job. They may have found that there were all but no jobs in the college major they completed. (Why didn't they know how to find out about that when they selected their major??)

That happens far too often. So now they default to becoming a teacher.

That's not the best way to get teachers. But many enter the field that way. Some love it and are very happy they became a teacher. Others quickly realize they made a big mistake and that teaching is not for them. Some of us have heard stories of brand new teachers quitting within just days or a few weeks of starting to teach, regardless of their years of preparation. They discover it's just too much for them.

Most teacher training programs require candidates or students to quickly get experience in the field, either closely observing, working as an assistant teacher, or perhaps teaching themselves as a substitute or temporary teacher.

After all, who do you want teaching you and your children? Someone who just needs a job and might compromise professionalism for ease of work? Or someone who loves the students so much that they regularly think about them and how to make learning better for them?

(2) Many others become teachers because they have always wanted to teach. They have always loved teaching, even just teaching siblings in their family. For many, becoming a teacher is their first choice for a job, their dream for their lifelong career. There are never enough of these deeply passionate teachers.

However, just like those needing a job (frankly, we're grateful for *everyone* who wants to be a teacher!), teachers-of-passion can still be surprised by the difficulties they can find at some schools. Even some of them can leave teaching more quickly than they ever thought they would.

***

What are these things that can cause many to leave the profession in K-12, even after just a short time? It might happen after just their first or second year of teaching. It can happen much sooner.

There might be other reasons, including low pay. But here are a few others: (1) Teachers experience too many serious problems with students involving classroom management issues; (2) They have problems with support from their administrators at school; (3) It's just not what they thought it would be.

Other issues that might lead to some potentially great teachers leaving the profession. Those can include problems with administrators or with students' parents. They can even include, as mentioned previously, direct physical threats by both students and some parents.

Some teachers who thought they'd get to work shorter hours as a teacher later find that their hours of preparation and correcting papers exceed what they had expected. Of course, many K-12 teachers have learned to simply give less work to their students so they will have less to correct. For those who have a couple hundred students daily, how can they not?

Yet students often benefit, educationally, by doing substantive assignments, whether in class or for homework. Teachers can also identify problems in students' understanding of what's being taught by seeing how students are doing.

Nonetheless, with large numbers of students, it's not feasible to give more than just a few rotating assignments among classes for homework or classwork, some of which can simply be exchanged and corrected by other students in class.

This isn't to say that students can't learn effectively without regular homework. In many cases, they can. But learning is reinforced with assignments at home: homework.

Since I made the mistake of mentioning homework, I might add that, especially in recent decades, many parents complain that their child gets "too much" homework. Clearly, it interferes with the child's *other* lives, whatever those might be (we can take some good guesses there).

In many schools, aggressive parents have intimidated administrators or teachers into not giving much, if any, homework, or just on allowable homework days. Some schools have implemented school-wide policies limiting the amount of homework teachers can give. After all, it's hard for students and takes too much time at home. Students have a life! They can't be doing homework all the time!

What? What's going on with that?

Admittedly, there will always be a few teachers who truly do give excessive work — perhaps wishing their 12-year-olds students were really college students — but I've only seen a few of them. In honors or advanced placement classes, that should not be an issue at all.

If any of this becomes an actual problem, an administrator can address it with the teacher. Well-designed and substantive homework and classroom work (other than group projects), with caring and competent teacher feedback, help students learn.

Nonetheless, if students actually pay attention in class (far too many don't), good teachers can impart an enormous amount of knowledge and skills in the classroom itself.

Most schools today have minimized work that students do. As mentioned, it's easier for teachers — and parents complain less. (Students can complain regardless.)

***

Few people today really understand the classroom management issues teachers and administrators can face. "Classroom management" is often a euphemism that actually means: handling students' bad behavior. Technically, it deals with lots of things surrounding classroom instruction but, for most teachers, it comes down to behavior — or rather *mis*behavior.

Admittedly, there are still many students who are well-behaved and are serious about learning. In almost all cases, they have parents who are involved with them and won't put up with wrong behavior or with a failure to take their classes and teachers seriously.

Parents and educators at such schools can't always understand why teachers at *other* schools can't seem to get control of their classes and their students. If they'd just do this or that, it would all work out!

Worse for some teachers at those other schools are unsupportive administrators. Rather than backing up their teachers when there are problems with very difficult students, they often blame the teachers. After all, those are *their* students in *their* classes; it's *their* responsibility! So get with it or get out! That is the unspoken sense coming from some administrators.

Okay. Sometimes administrators are correct. Some teachers don't want to deal with anything at all. Some teachers find it easier to send the same students "to the office" seemingly everyday. Indeed, some should either get better at classroom management or consider leaving education. On the other hand, administrators also need to get help to teachers when it's needed. Some don't.

Some struggling teachers are simply new to the profession and really do need mentoring and extra help. If they get it, they can be great teachers later on.

But even if more experienced teachers suddenly have problems where they need help, they should get it, too.

Too many administrators are not supportive of their teachers. That's very frustrating to teachers who need support. It can create a toxic atmosphere for school staff.

On the other hand, administrators themselves can be over-whelmed. They can't handle behavior problems in every difficult student every day. Even administrators who really want to support their teachers can't always do it. They have their own work to do, too.

Some schools are fortunate to have the budget for special resources to help in this. That might mean a budget for personnel to watch over such students on occasion in a room dedicated to that purpose. But most schools don't have the luxury of those kinds of resources. That's too bad because many schools really do need that extra support.

✱✱✱

Are some students really that difficult? Isn't it the teacher's job to handle their misbehavior?

Some students really are so difficult that even the most experi-enced teacher can't handle them alone. Such students can be constantly disruptive, destroying the classroom environment and frustrating not only the teacher, but also the other students.

To make things worse, there are limits to what a teacher can do. Those limits might be imposed by the courts or legislatures, usually by those who are often clueless about how serious these things can sometimes be.

Let me not leave out the power and agendas of the teachers' unions, both nationally and, sometimes, locally. Unions do not necessarily represent teachers in the classrooms, although they legally "represent" them.

Teachers have almost no power to change the direction of their enormous national unions. Not only are teachers often at their mercy — watching their union dues go to agendas that don't even help them — but the power of the unions sometimes seem to set the direction of their educational careers. Fortunately, that doesn't always happen. In some schools, teachers can just be teachers, almost as though the unions weren't even there.

As long as they are appreciated, supported, and cared for by their district and their local administrators, teachers can be very happy — teaching. Good teachers love to teach. Other teachers are just happy to have a job. Happiness is good.

***

During one of my early years as a substitute teacher in the Los Angeles School District (LAUSD) — before I worked as a full-time teacher — I was sent to a middle school with a reputation of having difficult students. Middle school students go through changes in their lives during those years. They can be known to be especially challenging. Eighth graders, in particular, can require special attention.

I was assigned to substitute in a classroom so that the regular teacher could be away for some on-campus meeting or required training for the day. Fortunately, she was there when I arrived to brief me on her classes.

She identified one class as being particularly difficult — her 5th

period class, as I recall. She said they eat substitutes for snacks and spit them out. She advised me that I should expect a difficult time. Some substitutes had not been able to handle them at all.

Thanks for the warning!

I wasn't yet a fully seasoned K-12 teacher, but I'd been around long enough as a substitute to be able to think on my own. So, before the school day got started, I went to the office and asked for enough behavioral referral forms for the whole class, maybe 40 or so of them. Those are the forms that are used when a teacher sends difficult students to the office.

The staff in the office looked at me with dismay. They wondered why I needed so many. Didn't I know how to handle a class? Would I be sending that many students to the office? And why was I using up their limited supply of copier paper! What was my problem, they seemed to be thinking, and how did they get stuck with such an untrained, incompetent, and lazy substitute teacher who clearly planned on sending student after student to the office that day?

In spite of their concerns, I got the forms.

After lunch, I placed myself in the classroom ahead of any early arriving students. I was sure to be wearing my most fearsome glare as they arrived. Clearly, some must have thought, they must have been assigned a terrible substitute who looked like he hadn't eaten in a week and was considering selecting one of them for something unspeakable. Would they be able to intimidate me as they had so many others in the past? We regarded each other with chess-like determination.

Perhaps they could be even more creative than I could be in order to do their worst to this new sub — to me. Still, the fearsome glare and occasional snarling lip curl seemed to be working. But for just how long could I keep it up? This was a tough crowd and fearsome glares can work for just so long.

However, before they could figure out how to handle this glaring substitute teacher who walked around like he was actually in charge — could I be mentally unstable? — I passed out the student referral forms to every student.

They knew precisely what they were. With an attitude, one of them asked me why they had to fill them out (though just with their names and the date). I glared back with my own attitude as I told them I was using them to take roll. If they didn't fill them out correctly, or put someone else's name on the form, I wouldn't be able to record their name and they would be absent for the day.

The room was quiet. Would they refuse en masse to fall for my ploy? My glare was still working, but I could feel it waning. They filled out the forms. Quickly, I collected them in order, so that I would know who was sitting where and could select the right form if I actually had to send someone to the office.

It was a pleasant period. Students were (mostly) quiet and cooperative. Together, we handled the assignments left by the teacher. No one went to the office. All was good.

When their regular teacher returned at the end of the day, I briefed her on how the day went. She was pleased that all had gone well. I told her about taking roll with the office referral forms during 5th period. She smiled.

So did I.

***

The most important component of education is the teacher. They do the teaching. Teachers impart knowledge. In the past, if someone wanted to improve the education system, they looked at strengthening teaching. That generally meant giving teachers more training or more college classes so that they could learn more about teaching, their subject matter, and about students themselves.

In most places, teachers might get incentives that move them higher on the salary schedule as they get college units for (theoretically) gaining more knowledge about teaching or their subject matter. That's especially important in subject matter fields that might regularly change, sometimes significantly.

For other subjects, one might question the value of more classes for teachers, other than to move them higher on the salary scale. Of course, that's important. But could there be other ways to do the same thing that didn't require teachers to spend a lot of time and money to take classes that might be of minimal benefit?

When teachers don't know enough about something important or if there are clear and important updates in their field that they can't easily get on their own, it's definitely important to take classes or to get training. But while it's sometimes clearly necessary, it isn't always.

It might not make sense to some people, but more education, more classes, don't necessarily make teachers better teachers.

***

Who do make the best K-12 teachers? My belief is that the best teachers are not the ones with the most subject matter competence. The best teachers are not necessarily the ones with the most advanced degrees or who obtain certifications as master teachers. Of course, some of those are indeed great teachers. But many are no better and sometimes worse than teachers without those degrees and certifications.

My belief is that the best teachers are often those who absolutely *love* teaching and are willing *and able* to actually *teach*. They are teachers who, when they were five years old, would teach things to their two and three year old siblings. As they grew up, they were the ones who always wanted to jump in and help someone do something, *learn* something. At almost all ages, they loved teaching. They are indeed...*teachers* — and that is a proud label. It is elevating and proud when one is sincerely called a teacher.

It's generally far easier to give someone subject matter knowledge than it is to make someone who doesn't like teaching, or is terrible at it, into a teacher. Although teacher training classes can give would-be teachers the techniques, structures, and means to prepare classes, they cannot give anyone the inner passion to be a teacher.

For too many teachers, teaching is "just a job."

For others, it is their life.

During my time as a principal, we had what was sometimes a

challenging class of students. A teacher assistant (TA) was assigned to help out in the class. The TA did not have the subject matter competence the assigned teacher had. But that TA was truly *a teacher.* During times when the assigned teacher was absent, the teacher assistant would run the classes. (Qualified substitute teachers were not always available.)

My observation was that the TA did a better job actually teaching the class than did many regular fully credentialed teachers. Using the available materials for the class, with which the TA was already familiar, she firmly took charge and provided solid teaching for the students. She also had noticeably better control over the students. She didn't put up with any bad behavior with which the regular teacher often had to deal.

One reason the TA was able to handle the class so well was that she knew the students outside of school and they knew her. They knew she didn't put up with any guff or misbehavior. Regardless, the result was a well-managed class with students covering the assigned materials.

It was obvious to me that she really enjoyed teaching. But she had completed little college and really wasn't considered qualified by "the system." To me, she was close to qualified. She just needed strong subject matter support, which would have been available to her by taking a few college classes and getting a bit of help from others. In spite of my encouragement, she chose to remain a teacher assistant.

We had another brand new teacher assigned to first grade. She was one of those who loved to teach. She had indeed been teaching since she was five years old. As do almost all teachers, her teaching techniques improved as she gained more experience. But techniques are not enough on their own. The best teachers have *passion* for what they do. The community knew and supported her. So did I.

***

Give me teachers of passion any day over teachers with vast, advanced subject matter competencies. Ideally, teachers should have both. But passion can't be taught. We do expect teachers to know their subject matter. Some know it better than others.

Most of all, teachers should be able to motivate their students to learn. They must be able to encourage their students, especially students who can become discouraged. They should be innovative. When one thing doesn't work, they should figure out something else that will work for their students.

When I first began teaching at that junior high school in Los Angeles, I did not feel I was qualified at all. Sure, I met the qualifications on paper. But how in the world was I assigned as a math teacher? Nonetheless, I was excited. I loved doing it.

Like so many others, I really didn't like math when I was growing up. Really didn't like it. I do remember getting a Best Boy award in a math (arithmetic) class when I was in second grade. To this day, I don't know how I got that. I credit my mother for being sure I did my math homework and for helping and encouraging me. But it was a struggle.

Indeed, the only class I ever failed was a math class, a trigonometry class during my first semester in 12th grade. I dropped out of high school after that semester.

When I eventually went back to school, to a junior college (now called community colleges), I determined that I would retake that class and pass it. To do so, I re-took some math classes that I had in high school for review. My math classes included both beginning and intermediate algebra. I also took one semester of geometry. Finally, I re-took trigonometry. This time, I passed! I got a "C." Not the greatest grade, but I was perfectly happy with it. I quit taking math after that.

Well, almost. I later took a statistics class.

Nonetheless, during one semester, I had needed one semester unit to maintain my full-time status. I saw a rare class that looked interesting. So I signed up for it. It taught us how to use slide rules. We met for one hour at week at 7:00 AM on Tuesday mornings. Slide rule.

Few people today have any idea what they are. But, at one time, buildings and bridges were built with them. Early on, there were no calculators, and certainly no computers. Perhaps you've gone across an old slide rule made bridge. I found it interesting.

As it happened, that one unit math slide rule class gave me just enough semester units to be certified as a math teacher years later. Huh?

To get the certification in Los Angeles, one needed either 12 semester units of upper division college math classes (upper division meant third and fourth year college math). OR! One could get by with any combination of 20 units of lower division math classes (lower division means the first and second year of college). Of course, other states have different requirements.

Well, lo and behold, I had exactly 20 units! Some lower division algebra and geometry. A trigonometry class. Statistics. And my one-unit slide rule class. Voila! A junior high school math teacher! Because I began public school teaching some years later, I had time to earn a college bachelor's degree, too. But it wasn't in math!

I knew other students who took far more advanced math classes that I doubt I would have survived — I never took a calculus class, for example — but those other students didn't have the right number of units to get certified. I wouldn't be able to say what kind of teachers they would have been, but, subject matter-wise, they would have been far more qualified than I was!

I spend time on that story for two reasons. First, it tells me that one can sometimes get certified while not being totally competent in their subject matter. Second, one can still be an effective teacher, especially if one has a passion for teaching.

And I had that.

I later discovered that, because I myself had not liked math, I totally related to many of my students — and there were a lot — who also didn't like math. As mentioned before, I had already taught basic math to adults at private post-secondary schools. I had seen math phobia and did everything I could to help the phobia go away.

A different teacher for whom math was no problem may not have truly understood the underlying fear and sick-to-your-stomach feeling working with math can cause. I have seen teachers, totally competent in their subject matter blame students for not understanding something after having explained it three or four times.

Fortunately for my students, I was able to explain things using methods they hadn't seen before and that looked easier to them. I also knew that teaching is sometimes just a matter of patient repetition. At the time, most of my students were Latino immigrants.

Students wrote some really wonderful comments about the math classes as they nominated me for the Jaime Escalante Mathematics Teacher award. I certainly felt good about that. (Their first level nominations didn't actually get me very far. The award at the time was generally won by high school teachers.)

I have no doubt that I could not have been as successful had I not struggled with math myself. And as long as I was assigned to lower level math classes, I mostly did fine and survived.

However, should I have actually been a real-life career math teacher? Although I really enjoyed doing it — and even wrote a book on it — I really don't think that I should have been a lifelong math teacher.

But how many other teachers are out there who shouldn't be teaching some subject they barely know themselves and perhaps don't even want to teach it? Too many, I would say. Additionally, not all of those teachers have the passion and teaching competence they should have in order to overcome many student deficiencies. It's not necessarily their fault such teachers are put in positions they shouldn't be in. Nonetheless, it happens.

24. MANY TEACHERS WANT TO GIVE UP

Even though I've said that money is not the answer to many problems in education, it's important nonetheless. There is rarely enough money for schools to hire additional staff, especially at small schools. An on-site security officer can be very valuable. Extra staff can provide security and help with students. Additional certificated staff (especially teachers) can lower class sizes.

You can lead a student to school, but you can't make that student learn. It's a help having more staff.

But where's the money?

Hiring extra full-time certificated personnel is expensive. School districts rarely have money for extra staff. As in most businesses, personnel is the greatest expenditure.

Extra certificated staff can also provide specialized services, such as handling difficult students who are pulled out of class to prevent ongoing disruptions. That allows teachers in their normally assigned classes to actually *teach* their other students. It also allows that "extra" teacher to move these students forward in their class-work. When this is an in-school program, it's often temporary. Students eventually return to their classes.

Some schools even hire trusted substitutes, without a full-time contract, to come in everyday, regardless whether or not they expect a

324 EDUCATION IS DEAD

regular teacher to be absent. That gives administrators someone available to help the school as a whole. Where permitted by states and districts, the better substitutes can be used to watch over students sent out of class for behavioral issues. Many substitutes like that arrangement since they are getting paid more regularly for their work.

Larger school districts can find that it is especially efficient to place these consistently difficult students into a small, separate school at which they can get the attention they need. Staff at those schools can move the education of these students forward while handling their behaviors more directly. Working closely with teachers in the smaller class sizes of such schools can help to change many students' behaviors for the better.

Some administrators put the full blame on teachers for not being miracle workers, not being able to fully control every difficult student in their classes. Of course, some teachers really aren't capable of handling their classes. Some teachers just shouldn't be teachers.

However, in most cases, teachers with problem students (at one time or another, that includes most teachers) just need some extra help and direct support once in a while. In the case of particularly difficult students, teachers *must* have help. If not, a class can completely fall apart or, in extreme situations, the teacher falls apart and finally quits. Just because a teacher doesn't seem to have control over some students doesn't always mean the teacher is at fault — although sometimes it does.

Nonetheless, administrators should want to free the hands and energy of their teachers to do what they're there for: *teach!* Teachers sometimes do need *real help,* not blame, not frustration, and not tied hands (although that is sometimes beyond the control of schools).

Of course, some teachers take excessive advantage of outside help, not wanting to figure out how to get control of students themselves. Some seem to unnecessarily send multiple students out of their classes daily so they don't have to deal with them. A new plan is needed to stop the daily hemorrhage of difficult students out of those teachers' classes.

Certainly in the beginning, teachers should always be given the benefit of the doubt, although not always carte blanche doubt. They do have to step up to the classroom plate. Nonetheless, those teachers who refuse to handle any problem students, even those with minor problems, are a real minority of teachers.

Whatever it is, things must get under control if actual learning is to take place for the rest of the students. In many places, things are always on the edge, never fully under control. Teaching tries to move forward. Student learning may or may not.

How frustrating can difficult students be for teachers? How difficult are classes that are either hard to control (for anyone) or resist all efforts at teaching? How much can teachers – especially truly caring teachers — put up with?

More than once I've had to console and reassure teachers whom I found sobbing on the floor by the wall after their students left their classrooms.

How often will teachers have to cry, so frustrated, before they finally give up? Some just don't know what to do anymore. Even our best teachers can be overwhelmed.

Not only can one or more students be serious problems for teachers (and administrators), but a student's parent(s) might then come in and pile more on the teacher, blaming the teacher and the school instead of their out-of-control child. Even then, plenty of administrators fail to provide the added support many teachers need.

In some middle or high school classes, teachers can exhaust the standard "consequences" and other classroom management techniques they have at their disposal. With some students, it's not always hard to run out of things to try.

Teachers do send problem students to the office, so that either school counselors (when available) or school administrators can handle the situation.

Sadly, this last available option — removing disruptive or disrespectful students — is not always available to every teacher. Some administrators refuse to accept students, blaming teachers because they aren't able to control their classes. In truth, the responsibility for classroom difficulties should fall on teachers. Not all teachers know how to control their students. But, overall, they are generally a small minority of teachers.

The great majority of teachers, even very good teachers, do need periodic support from administrators. Sadly, some administrators don't want to handle these students. Some schools don't have adequate backup plans to handle them. That failing falls on administrators.

Some students are *so* disruptive that none of the classes they are in can function with them present. Near *daily* "issues" with such students eventually leave schools with no choice: the student must be removed from the school so that it can function, so that it can provide education for the vast majority of other students. These are often students who absolutely don't care about causing disruptions.

Some students have no compunction about interrupting teachers, even verbally assaulting them using language that is unacceptable in any context. Even between classes, they may bully other students. Some are entirely out of control.

If possible (and it isn't possible in all schools), such students might be moved to a different class with a different teacher.

But schools can't easily do that. In serious cases, and with the involvement of outside resource personnel (sometimes involving legal resources), such students can be removed from the school beyond just a temporary time. But that is not always easy. It doesn't happen often.

Courts and legislatures often restrict the total number of days a student can be suspended during a school year. This can tie the hands of administrators and teachers. These restrictions were originally put in place for understandable reasons. Some schools used to just send students home, effectively indefinitely, depriving them of their right to go to school. That could be even if there were a way to handle such students in some different way.

Nonetheless, there truly *are* some students who must be removed from the traditional school setting in order to salvage learning and good order at the school.

For example, there may be a ten-day limit on student suspensions, whether students are in a Special Education program or not.

Students can't be removed indefinitely regardless of their daily disruptions to the whole school.

Well before that, parents have been called. Parental conferences have been held (if parents choose to show up). In too many cases, parents may defend their children. Some blame the school, telling teachers and administrators, "Well that's *your* problem, not mine!"

In other cases, parents are very supportive of the school and the teacher, but simply don't know what to do. The student acts exactly the same way at home. Such parents would be happy to do something to make thing better. They just don't know what to do. In these serious cases, some schools might not know what to do either.

A principal might call their district headquarters to discuss the situation. Just as happens at some schools where bad administrators want to wash their hands of such problems, some district administrators do the same thing.

In truth, most such students need special help. They need a totally different learning environment. When appropriate alternative public schools are available for such students, it is best if they are placed there. But alternative schools are not always available.

Some parents and administrators are in denial. They maintain that there are *always* ways to handle especially difficult students. After all, that's what educators are paid for!

Actually, it's not. Educators are paid to *educate*, not to function as constant enforcers of discipline to the exclusion of the greater number of students who are actually there to learn.

***

Here's a story about a dog.

Just as some professional educators, non-school personnel, and parents deny that particularly defiant and disruptive students are too difficult to effectively handle by teachers at school, other behavior professionals have seen the same thing in different contexts.

Okay. I'm going to do something risky now. I'm going to mention dog training. Please don't tell me that children are not dogs! Of course, they're not! However, don't use that as an excuse to avoid looking at and learning about what really are shared principles of learning and behavior. I'm not here for an extensive discussion of that, but I'm hopeful you'll see the point of this anyway.

There are some so-called "professional" dog trainers who deny that truly aggressive dogs exist that can't be handled with proper training techniques — often defined as "love and patience," or by some other equally ineffective techniques. In the same way, some who work with young people sometimes deny that any children pose serious risks. But some do.

When it is suggested that some truly aggressive dogs might attack their owners or other people, some of those trainers deny that dogs would actually do that. (I've personally heard dog trainers say that.) Of course, aggressive dogs do sometimes kill or maim their owners or others. When the topic is pushed, such trainers finally say that only dogs who are mentally sick would do such a thing. There is no option but to put them "to sleep" — to have a veterinarian or animal shelter kill the dog.

Wait! These are trainers who care about dogs? They have effectively said that since their own unremarkable training techniques won't work on truly dangerous dogs (if they even acknowledge that such dogs exist), then nothing will work. Their answer? Kill the dog.

If a truly competent trainer is available, that is almost always the wrong answer. There is (almost) always something that can be done. Although some owners wrongly deny it, it is actually forbidden within the beloved relationship between dogs and human beings to allow any dog to attack an owner — or anyone else.

In the same way, parents, courts, "professional" behaviorists, even some social workers, can deny that the behaviors of some children in schools can reach a level of seriousness, even danger, that many educators know actually exists.

Such people then endeavor to stop educators from taking any action to try to change such behaviors in their students. Although it doesn't happen often, it happens often enough to be a concern for those endangered by the behaviors of such "children."

But back to the dog story.

One day, a Colorado dog trainer whose specialty was working with dangerous dogs, was out in a neighborhood working with an aggressive dog. He was the only dog trainer in that city willing to take on the dog.

Other professional trainers in the city, who were far bigger and stronger than this trainer, refused to work with the dog, sending aggressive dog problems to that one trainer. The others were less experienced and not comfortable working with such highly aggressive dogs.

That one experienced trainer had been successful in working with such dogs. As is often the case, the situation was serious enough that, if the trainer did not succeed, the owners would have to put the dog to sleep. This was truly a life or death matter for the dog.

Regardless of his background, when handling such dogs, the trainer put himself at risk every time he worked to save a dog's life and protect others whom the dog might later attack. It was his job to substantively reduce or eliminate the danger such dogs posed to their owners and to others.

The trainer worked in areas close to the dog's home where the aggressive behavior had to be reliably under control. He used strong but standard corrections, appropriate for aggressive behavior.

That day, as he was out with the German Shepherd-sized dog, a neighbor rushed from a house they had just passed. He had a shotgun. The irate neighbor threatened the trainer that if he did not stop "mistreating" the dog, he would shoot the trainer. The trainer attempted to calm the man and to tell him about the situation. The man was not convinced. The shotgun-wielding man said that he had had dogs his whole life and knew plenty about them. He believed nothing of what the trainer told him.

Shotgun still pointed at the trainer, the neighbor threatened to call the police if he saw the trainer again. Clearly, that was not his only threat. Like too many others, the man would not accept that a dog can pose a real danger to people. He knew that its owners — and obviously the trainer — didn't know anything about dogs.

What the neighbor had wrongly-called "mistreatment" was what would actually save the dog's life. Without work by a competent professional, people would continue to be at risk. It is likely the dog would eventually be killed.

Was using effective methods to get the dog under control "cruel?" Was a caring professional dog trainer involved in trying to save a dog's life a "cruel" person? Most would say that he was not.

Recognizing the better part of valor, the trainer returned to the owner's home. The owners begged the trainer not to give up. They wanted to save their dog. They knew that it presented a danger to people, including to themselves.

The trainer did return to work with the dog, but restricted his work to the owner's back yard. The trainer knew that it was not enough.[1]

There are plenty of people in the world who would prefer to kill a dog rather than use any standard training techniques at all to try to save the dog. Training to stop dangerous behavior and save a dog's life seems more humane than a death sentence to stop that same behavior. Yet many so-called animal lovers/animal rights advocates often prefer death.

Here is a another true story to illustrate the difficulty here. One time, a young adult was training her own dog. Suddenly, she was accosted by someone, also carrying a gun, for "cruelty" as she worked with her dog.

What terrible thing had she done?

She was a gentle, non-violent person who loved her dog. She didn't believe in standard dog training techniques. She didn't even want to use a leash and training collar. So she used food treats to train her dog. The person who threatened her with a gun accused her of cruelty because she was "teasing" her dog with food treats.

The lesson here is that, whether regarding animals or people, the definitions of "abuse" and "cruelty" are often in the eye of the beholder. "Abuse" is often not abuse and "cruelty" is often not cruelty. Those elusive concepts have both been redefined so often over the years that almost anything can now be shoehorned into their definitions.

Allowing that has been a big mistake. What have become people's "acceptable non-abusive behaviors" (if we can even know what those constantly changing norms are) have often created an insidious, even worse kind of abuse. A fuller discussion is beyond this present book.

Children are not dogs. But bad behavior is bad behavior. Plenty of wonderful children who should also be wonderful people as adults instead grow up to be dangerous criminals. We love our dogs and we love our children, but proper, loving, and effective discipline is important for both. Yet schools, parents, and educators are often unjustly attacked by outsiders just for trying to help the children under their care become better people.

***

For some teachers, having no support for difficult students can be the last straw. After so many other frustrations and stresses, some give up on classroom management. There comes a point when some of these teachers stop trying to change students' behaviors at all. Control of their classrooms deteriorates. Learning suffers or dies. It can be exhausting.

In the end, some give up teaching altogether. It's not one thing that leads to that. It's a combination of things. This can be one of them.

As we have said, children are not dogs. But, just as in this story, there are people who deny that some children can be so out-of-control that schools and teachers can't handle them. But sometimes they can be.

Some courts and legislators fail to understand that, too. They can then further tie the hands of schools and educators effectively preventing them from handling significantly disruptive, even dangerous behaviors. They don't understand that, unless such problems are solved, the rest of the school can't function as a school. It can't do what schools are tasked to do: Educate.

Answers are elusive. But this is a legitimate and serious problem in many schools.

Some students can be so difficult that some teachers emotionally collapse under the pressure. Some students physically threaten them. Some parents do, too. You might think they should just call the police and let them handle it. You'd be surprised how difficult that can be. And there can be potentially violent students left behind willing to retaliate for another student's arrest or for consequences given out by the school. Since some students are gang members or are otherwise unpredictable, teachers often take such threats seriously.

For how long do we expect teachers to remain as teachers in such difficult circumstances? That is not what most of them signed up for, is it? They want to *teach*. They want to make students' lives better. Yet even students from so-called "good families" can pose serious problems, serious threats to educators and other students.

One of the most important things I could do as an administrator was try to protect my teachers. That means that I had to put myself in difficult circumstances often in place of my teachers.

One time, I had to ask a big, defiant, and out-of-control high school student to leave campus, something, frankly, that he might have been going to do anyway. He was threatening to me to such a degree that another teacher decided to move in to help handle him, in order to protect me. I waived him off, but he remained available at a distance if the student had escalated the situation. Even though I was able to handle the situation on my own, I was grateful that the teacher was there. Perhaps just his being there helped.

The student went home where, naturally, he gave his mother a story different from what had actually happened.

As parents, we all want to believe our children, even when we aren't getting the truth. But this case had an extra twist. His parent was a member of the school board for the school district. That led to even more problems.

Along with other teachers and administrators, I have received personal threats against me and my home. Students or others have done things that have put me in danger. The same things have happened to other educators.

From multiple people, I have heard stories of teachers in one school community coming home to find their cats hanging, dead, at their front door. Pet dogs of teachers were also killed and left at their front doors. These things were meant as warnings that the teachers themselves might be next. In this particularly serious situation, the district reportedly had to quietly *evacuate* their entire small school staff before the school year even ended — without notice to the community — because of credible, serious threats against the school staff.

Few schools have situations as serious as that one. But people should understand that teaching can involve far more serious problems than just students talking back to their teachers or not doing their homework.

These are things for which teacher training programs don't prepare new teachers at all. Many professors teaching in such programs are often in denial that such things even happen.

We don't want to lose good teachers and good administrators, but they often need more help than they can get. Educators don't need roadblocks which can put both education and they themselves at risk.

What kind of people stay at a job that can leave them sobbing, that can periodically put them in fear of physical or legal harm, that throws so much in their way that they sometimes don't feel they are doing any good at all, and often doesn't pay enough either?

The answer is that most teachers love and care about their students. They want to help them to learn. Through that learning, they want their lives to be good ones.

It's a sad thing to have to reassure, encourage, and comfort teachers crying on the floor.

25. WHAT ARE "SNOWFLAKES?"

Since many people today haven't yet been introduced to the concept, I'm going to take a moment to talk about this. When I'm done, you'll understand how this has negatively affected education today and how it may do so well into the future. It would be good if this concept has disappeared by the time you're reading this. Right now, I don't see that happening.

The currently derogatory term, "snowflake," has a changing and mixed history. In the world of this book's writing, it refers to a person who is over-sensitive, whose feelings are far too easily hurt, who can't handle and don't accept people with points-of-view other than their own. They may look at themselves as "special" people and expect to be treated that way. But when everyone is special, no one is special.

Words that these "special and unique" people find unacceptable lead to such "snowflakes"becoming uncompromisingly offended. Often, they defend others who are offended by such words and behaviors, even if those others aren't even offended.

Such people and their enablers can create and enforce their own proprietary and constantly changing list of unacceptable, offensive, or "racist" words. Unknown to others, they continually add and condemn behaviors that have been considered benign in the past. It doesn't matter that even "offensive" words and some behaviors have been deemed constitutionally protected by the courts.

Today, "violations" of snowflake demands involve violating vocabulary and behavioral protocols. Violators, even of vocabulary transgressions, are punished — actually punished. This isn't being done by law enforcement or the courts (yet). It is being done by both online and in-person crowds of vigilantes.

Unknowing violations of the constantly changing list of violations may see unknowing violators lose their jobs, endanger themselves and their families, and see their finances destroyed. At times, if someone makes the wrong person "feel bad," that person and others in support have come after the offender in much more concrete ways. Such punishments are entirely extralegal — outside the legal system.

If such unknowing offenders misuse words on the ever-changing list of prohibited words, or if one expresses prohibited beliefs about one thing or another, the pre-judged offender's normal life can be endangered: job, family, money, privacy, and peace.

These snowflake behaviors have often been developed in colleges today, even in so-called conservative ones.

Apologies are constantly demanded for violations by offended people, but not accepted once the apologies are given. These demanded "apologies" are solely meant to demean "violators." They are not meant to put things right so that forgiveness may be granted. Life will not go back to what it had been even after the apologies are given. In fact, an apology is simply an admission of guilt, made to try to save unknowing violators from further attacks and punishment. But it is rarely successful in doing that. Frequently, it has the opposite result.

Offenders can include close family and (now former) friends.

The lives of innocent violators are totally upended for what were, just a few years ago, no issue at all. Such violators are effectively "cancelled." Indeed, this has recently become known as "cancel culture." It is as unjust as it is frightening. Not only does it totally violate rights embodied in the U.S. Constitution, it violates basic human dignity. Those imposing such cancellations are the true criminals. They are enemies of the foundations of the country.

Sometimes it all starts because some of these people were offended by something formerly inoffensive, or otherwise made to "feel bad."

Sometimes the "offensive" words and behaviors didn't even happen, or they happened in some benign context. People may be falsely accused of things they didn't even do. Often, such things weren't even wrong in the first place.

What was normal in the world before (even currently) is now repurposed to all but *ensure* these others are offended. Once offended, once they feel someone has committed some violation of [their] acceptable speech or thinking, no rational discussions are possible with them.

Of course, others can't possibly know what these violations are since they change regularly. They can vary among both "snowflakes" themselves, and their supporters, even including many college professors and administrators who are also intimidated by these people.

Many snowflakes and practitioners of cancel culture are so easily offended that "safe spaces" have been set up for them on college campuses and now elsewhere, including spaces at some companies. These are places snowflakes can go to recover from observed or experienced offenses that made them "feel bad."

Safe spaces? Tell that to the rest of the world.

From where do they get this counterproductive thinking and behavior? In recent times, it has come primarily from schools and universities. Once they are wrongly taught that their ultra-sensitivity is not just normal, but is to be defended in today's society, it is then perpetuated and demanded by others, including by many in the media.

Can anyone imagine an effective military comprised of such people? A superior officer orders them to do something mundane: to clean the barracks, stand inspection, lets them know — and isn't necessarily nice about it — that they aren't doing something right, etc. Perhaps their commanding officer orders them into battle —

but doesn't do it with appropriate courtesy. He makes them "feel bad."

Naturally, they no longer have a reason to do what they are told. After all, their superior didn't talk to them nicely and correctly. The substance of the legitimate order doesn't matter. The substance of the concern or the training doesn't matter. The intent itself doesn't matter. What *is* important is *how* someone said it. If it made the snowflake *feel* bad, it's game over. A superior has no right to talk to them "like that." Might as well just leave! After all, when one makes someone else "feel bad," that's all there is!

Fortunately, battlefield enemies never make anyone "feel bad," do they? Oh wait, they do! Must courtesy and proper words and behaviors now be demanded on the battlefield? Or do we now support military personnel walking off the field and leaving when they feel offended, even intentionally offended, as can often happen in life. An entire military filled with snowflakes? Better to just capitulate in advance of a battle since it will be lost anyway.

But it's not just the military for which people must learn mental and emotional toughness. It's the world itself. Even in (non-military) civilian life, there are countless situations where one learns a new skill or a new job from someone whose priority is not to protect you from "feeling bad." Their only goal is to ensure that the training gets done, that the job itself gets done. They must demand that safety procedures are taught firmly and carried out without compromise. Courtesy and nice words are not always their priority.

The world isn't a courteous and friendly place. "Snowflake" philosophies and behaviors are fully incompatible with the world and with most of the people now in it.

Gently explaining to these oversensitive people that they should understand and do things differently doesn't necessarily make sense to them. After all, it's not how they have grown up. It's not what they've been taught. It's not how their friends think. Even if they understand what you're trying to say, it doesn't mean they'll accept it. It's clear to them that *you* are the problem, not them. Although such people have mostly consisted of students and young adults, those people eventually become the teachers and legislators of the future.

These "snowflakes" should actually be apologizing to others for *their* behavior. The problem is that they don't know they've done anything wrong. How can you apologize when you're absolutely certain that you did nothing wrong?

To make matters worse, even though they don't want to be hurt by others, as per their changing definitions of what hurts them, they have no problem hurting others, even physically. Apparently being protected from "feeling bad" only applies to them and their peers, not to others.

This might seem to involve just a few fringe people. But it doesn't. Here are the serious problems created by it and how it relates to education today:

(1) Snowflakes have often been taught this attitude *in schools*, especially at universities. A snowflake culture is not just acceptable, on too many campuses it is *expected*. Great numbers buy into it. If they don't, they themselves are open to attack.

(2) These ultra-sensitive, highly judgmental students then become parents. They now pass this on to their own children. In fact, instead of pushing back on it, many parents have already learned this new thinking from their own children. They're already passing it on. Once the children of such parents learn this thinking (and feelings) from their parents, and then have it backed up by their teachers and peers at school, we will have a nation of weak, spoiled citizens unable to protect their country and not sure why it's necessary anyway.

(3) I just mentioned that teachers (especially younger ones) can perpetuate this. Why is that? It's because many of our newest teachers have been educated in schools and universities where they themselves have become snowflakes, fully buying in to the philosophy with all of its ramifications. As teachers, they then insist on enforcing its tenets in their students. Why wouldn't they? No student, indeed *no one*, should be made to feel bad by *anyone*

including their teachers, parents, grandparents — pretty much everyone.

Because this is still a relatively new phenomenon, rabid proponents are just now entering the work force as educators. This philosophy and behavior is incompatible with a strong electorate and a strong country. Although such newly trained teachers are spreading out to all levels of education, their breeding ground remains at the university level.

Some have connected this to millennials, but it has spread beyond that one generation. Many people, including the author, have personally seen and endured the things discussed in this chapter.

Newly-minted snowflake teachers are inclined to change history, literally. They are inclined to condemn historical figures who, judged by their new standards, violate their new standards. In other cases, teachers will just skip parts of history with which they disagree, or teach a new form of history — one that never happened. The 1619 Project, discussed earlier, is an example of such historical revisionism. But there are others.

Although this oversimplifies what is happening, statues are torn down and public buildings are being renamed today *in part* because of this philosophy. At more extreme levels, violence itself can be consistent with this philosophy of "don't make me feel bad." They absolutely don't understand that what they expect and are doing is wrong. Many *non*-snowflakes figure they'll just apologize to a snowflake, even if they did nothing wrong. By doing that, they believe that all can move on together in peace. They don't understand that such actions are unlikely to work. Snowflakes will simply take that as an admission of guilt — and respond accordingly.

Education is already in bad shape. Teachers are affecting student behaviors and expectations of others in what are sometimes negative ways. Some parents might think it is they who have been doing things wrong. Many change to match what their child's teachers are teaching.

Snowflake-indoctrinated teachers can teach other teachers as part of teacher training programs. How can things be turned around? There still aren't overwhelming numbers of them yet but, as universities support this thinking as their standard, more will coming. All teachers certainly aren't like this yet. How their numbers might grow in the future isn't known.

The following commentary restates this and offers other insights:

> When generations are raised with a sense of entitlement, often instilled by schools but mistakenly supported by parents, they are less willing to understand self-sacrifice for something greater than themselves, including service to their country. That interior selfishness quickly cuts off anyone who says or does something they don't like or that makes them feel bad.
>
> Children like that used to be called "spoiled." Most would outgrow it. But now that attitude and behavior almost appear to be accepted as normal.
>
> This level and enforcement of entitlement is new. It is doing damage to society, to the country, to everyone around such entitled people, as well as to the young adults themselves along with those who are even younger, but who are growing up under that same umbrella....
>
> Spoiled children have been around forever. What's new are attempts to normalize such (spoiled) entitlement thinking and behavior over a life-time. The question is how much newer generations might also be infected.
>
> That might seem likely as entitled adults become teachers and pass on their expectations, couched as moral imperatives, to their students. If all this becomes the new norm, justifications and defenses of it will emerge in books, seminars, and interviews with "experts." Those disagreeing will be increasingly ostracized. Television and movies now cater to this.

Although we're not there yet, if an entire country eventually accepts this philosophy, it might not be able to recover. How do we know that? We look at the past when radical thinking took over other countries, even empires. Some historians can point to at least part — sometimes a substantial part — of the decline of empires based on changing internal values of their citizens. We've mentioned that before. Those values didn't magically turn back to what had been the earlier strengths of those countries. Once it was allowed to happen, absent something unusual, it was almost always permanent. If what is happening in America today continues, things are not likely to go back to how things were before either.

As I suggested at the beginning, it would be good if this is already disappearing by the time you read this. It's not looking good now. We shall see how things unfold.

26. MANY STUDENTS HAVE DIFFICULT LIVES

In contrast to spoiled snowflakes, there are students about whom we really should be concerned. These are students who actually need our help. They don't always get it because we don't always know they need it.

Earlier, I noted that a legitimate cause of students not doing well is because they don't study enough. They don't do homework or complete other assignments, including work done in class. How can they learn if they don't actually do what it takes to learn! They've got to do at least some work to learn, don't they?

I used to try learning through osmosis, just listening to teachers and being around others who knew everything. Then, at night, I could then become a professional — ready for any test — all in my sleep! Try it! Just rest your hand on a textbook as you sleep at night and, voila!, it's all entered your brain through osmosis! Don't you do the same thing? No?[1]

Let's now look at some examples why real life students didn't study as they should have.

Two middle school or high school students — I can't remember which, at the moment — didn't go home until very late at night. They often didn't get their assignments done. After school, they would immediately spend time at a friend's house instead of going straight home. Homework wasn't getting done. What was the problem with them?

The problem was that they had to wait until later at night before going home. If they went home earlier, their parents could lose their temper at them or blame them for one thing or another that they had not even done. It made things very stressful for the students. Why were their parents so difficult that even their own children stayed away?

They were alcoholics. The students waited long enough until their parents had passed out on the floor before they took a chance to go home that night . When they finally went home, they stepped over the passed-out bodies of their parents before finally going to bed.

I was an administrator at a different school. A teacher complained that one of her 6th grade students kept falling asleep in class. Many students would stay up most of the night playing video games or doing something else instead of doing their homework. Was this student distracted by video games? Why wasn't he doing his assignments? We needed to get to the bottom of this. The teacher was upset that the student didn't appear to be serious about getting his work done, but suspected there might also be some other reason.

Here's what we found: The 12 year old student was trying to stay awake all night to protect his 8 year old sister from getting raped by their father. The boy was exhausted trying to do it.

Those who don't understand that community will have some throw away answer such as, why not just call the police or child protective services? I'm not here to fully explain this other than to say that such answers can be simplistic in complex environments. Of course, we called child protective services to report it. But action to protect children doesn't always happen quickly, sometimes not at all.

"I don't understand!" you say. "Why weren't they out the same day!" If that was your response, you're correct! You don't understand. In some places, things are simply not straightforward. Things don't always work as we would like them to work. In some places, they don't work at all.

As elsewhere, a full discussion of the particular situations in this section is beyond the scope of this writing.

I only tell the story so that you might understand that simply telling a student they aren't studying enough may not be the whole story. Many need some unknown help in their lives.

Depression and mental health issues among teenagers, especially among teenage girls, has been on the rise. This is serious not only because of the hurt and harm to the teenage girls themselves, but because whatever is causing it must be identified, reduced or, as much as possible, eliminated.

These things might be at school. They might be online, perhaps related to interactions on social media. They might be at home. They might be somewhere else.

Such issues might not just be related to the presence of bad things in their lives. They might also relate to the *absence* of things they might need for good mental health and for a normal and, hopefully, happy maturation.

As do adults, many students do have difficult lives. These are not snowflakes. There are no "safe spaces" for them. Schools and educators can't help them all, especially when we don't even know it's happening. I fully believe that educators and schools should not turn their collective backs saying that schools can't solve the world's problems, that their only job is to educate students in a classroom. Sometimes, our students need us for more.

People are often concerned about high school students who might consider dropping out of school. The high school dropout rates are too high.

Parents or guardians don't want that for their children? Right?

Not always.

One high school boy's aunt, with whom he lived, continued to tell him that there was no need for him to finish high school. She had dropped out and felt it was fine if he did it, too. He could then devote his time to working.

Even though his behavior wasn't perfect, I recognized a lot of potential in that student and didn't want to see it lost. A number of times, I personally talked to him to encourage him to stay in school. Not only was he confronting regular encouragement to drop out, but other aspects of his life were challenging, too. Nonetheless, he stayed in school. He did not drop out.

It's true that we can't solve the world's problems. Often, we can't even solve our own. But we should do what we can to help our students, their parents, and the communities that we serve. If we can't, we can't. But our eyes, especially those of administrators, had better be open to provide whatever legal help we can if we are able to do so.

27. HELPING STUDENTS

Here are a couple of stories. I believe that many teachers have similar stories of their own.

For some years, I taught in a self-contained classroom where I taught a variety of subjects primarily including social studies, but also a variety of subjects outside of social studies. The small school had many students at risk of not completing high school. Because I was responsible to teach my students a number of different subjects, I had to find creative ways to teach the material while trying to ensure that they actually learned the material.

In my classes, I personally recorded all of the chapters in the history and government textbooks which I assigned to my students. When I made the recordings, I would stop and record comments and extra teaching about what I was reading to them in order to help them understand the material. I loaned them the tapes of the readings, the additional teachings, and the assignments. Students listened with headphones in the classroom. That way, other students could work on other subjects. I could tell whether they were listening by watching them and knowing how long each tape was. Periodically, I asked about what they were (supposed to be) listening to. They also had to hand in assignments on them.

One 9th grade student had trouble learning overall. He regularly sat close to my desk and listened to the history tapes, conscientiously doing the assignments. Even though academics were difficult for him, he was always respectful and responsive to what he was asked to do. Periodically, he asked questions about what he was reading (hearing).

Our students were not angels. Many were on probation for some crime they had committed. Many were gang members. This student was, too.

One day, he was arrested. His probation officer was a famous man who had done work in the movies. He was tough, but I liked him a lot. He took a sincere interest in the students who were in trouble. He hoped that his tough stance would lead to changed behaviors.

Once, another student violated his probation. It might have been in late November, as I recall. The probation officer told him that he would lock him up again. But it wouldn't be in November. It would be just before Christmas so that he wouldn't be able to spend Christmas with his family.

That was typical of this officer. The bottom line was that those who had him as a probation officer had better stay on the straight and narrow. There was nothing about which to feel sorry for them. They knew what they were doing and brought the consequences on themselves. The probation officer was not just trying to turn them around, he was also protecting the community.

One day, I found that my 9th grade student, an active gang member, had been locked up. He was caught dead-to-rights, on video, selling drugs. The probation officer had known he was involved for some time, but hadn't been able to get solid evidence. Well, now he had it.

The student was to have a hearing at the juvenile detention center sometime later. Court hearings were held in the center, not in the community courts. It was likely he would be locked up for a long while. It was not his first offense.

I asked my principal if I could go to add some comments about him at his hearing. She said that I could go. It wouldn't take too long but, since the hearing was during the day, my students would be watched over by other teachers.

At the appropriate time, I went through security at the juvenile hall detention center and was directed to the room with the hearing. It was a small, narrow room. It was clear that they didn't expect many outsiders there to watch, let alone participate.

Because it was unusual to have a teacher show up — I was actually surprised and disappointed about that — everyone paid attention to me. My student was there. I didn't recognize him at first. As with many gang members, he generally had a bald head. By then, his hair had grown back. It took a moment for me to realize it was the same student.

As the hearing began, the judge asked why I was there. Any extra person stood out like a sore thumb. I was the thumb. In addition to me, the student, the judge, the prosecutor, and the student's defense attorney were also there.

Immediately, after the hearing began, I was asked to speak. I told the court that I was not there to make any excuses for what the student had done. I didn't know much about it and wasn't there to talk about that.

What I was there to talk about was that the student had been respectful and conscientious in my classroom. I wanted the student himself to know that I believed in him. I said as much in court. I told the court that, based on what I had seen for some months, I felt he could potentially have a good life ahead of him if he made the right choices in the future. I felt he should keep up the good things I had seen. I hoped that he might consider that as he spent time locked up. It was a bit of encouragement, an acknowledgement of the good things I had seen in him.

That was all I was there for, just to say what I said. Nothing more.

But it was enough.

The *prosecutor* told the judge that he had never seen a teacher have the interest to stand up for a student. He told the judge he believed that the student — a drug-dealing gang member who was caught on tape doing it — should be released and given another chance. The judge agreed. In no way had I asked or intended that the student get off the hook for what he had done. The defense attorney had said nothing.

Almost before I got back to school, the probation officer was there. The school day had just ended. Most students had already left. The probation officer (remember that I liked him?) proceeded to berate me loudly for getting this drug-dealing student off. I told him that was not why I had gone nor what I intended. I told him that the judge's ruling on the crime (should have) had nothing to with what I had said.

I felt that had the location and situation been different — and he thought he could get away with it — the probation officer would have physically assaulted me…or something more. He was that upset. How dare I be responsible for letting a drug dealer back on the streets! He knew the student. He was clear that this student would re-offend, again!, and eventually be locked up anyway.

A bit shaken, I sat at my desk to calm down.

In the next day or so, the student returned to school. He thanked me for what I had said. (I was indeed very sincere about what I had said about him.) He continued on with his classes.

His girlfriend had tried to get him out of the gang. She consistently supported him, trying to keep him away from bad influences.

The student regularly showed up to his required meetings with the probation officer. I don't remember how long it was for, likely well over a year.

One day, at the end of that time, the probation officer came back into my classroom after school was out. Amazingly to me, he very sincerely apologized to me. He did so with real respect.He didn't beat around the bush saying that he had been wrong. His sincere apology meant a lot to me.

Not only had the student shown up to *every* required meeting with him but, even after he was off probation, he *continued* to stop by. The student had completely changed. I was proud of that student. How could I not be? I think the probation officer himself was, too.

The student married his girlfriend and became a produce

department manager at a community grocery store. One time, much later, I visited him and his family.

Sometimes, it just takes one person to change someone's life. Am I the one who did that? Of course not. The student's own behavior and seriousness as a student — even though he often struggled and was frustrated with his academics — is what created the situation that eventually led to his leaving the gang and turning his life around. His children, some of whom I briefly met, had a good father. I was also able to thank his wife. It's one of the important successes I had as a teacher.

Teachers can positively affect so many students (so many *people*). A note all the teachers got from a different student, with special comments to me, sincerely thanked us for helping and supporting him. He, too, had been involved with that same gang. With his parents, they had moved to a different neighborhood. He began attending a community college. His gratitude, too, has remained with me until today.

What does all this have to do with the death of education? Doesn't it seem these are actually successes? Of course, they are. But the bottom line is, how much did these students actually learn, academically? Was it enough? In most cases, the answer would be no, it wasn't. Sure, I did the best I could in my classes to teach everything possible to my students. But it wasn't enough.

Sadly, in some areas, the students at that school often learned more than many other students, even at much larger schools. Really, though, they all needed much more. The sadness is that few of America's public school students are getting enough education.

Are my standards too high? Absolutely not. They are well within normal expectations for the education of students. Perhaps they should actually be higher.

Such expectations are likely a minimum of what we should want for all of our students. After all, those students will soon become the citizens who run America. They are the people who will take care of us...or we hope that they will.

Even though I taught my at-risk students things that students in more prestigious high schools didn't know, it wasn't enough. The public education system didn't then, and it doesn't now, ensure that enough learning is happening.

And one more thing. Aren't interventions possible at an earlier age so that students don't end up taking these wrong roads? They should be possible, but schools aren't set up that way. Other than some special programs, of which there are very few, we can't run effective interventions for the great number of students who need them. We're told that is not the job of schools and educators. We can and do save some, but we lose far too many others.

***

Okay. I'm on a roll here. Here's another story.

One summer, I was teaching high school history in summer school. Many students had failed U.S. History the semester before and had to retake it. Others wanted to get ahead. This was a school at which I hadn't taught before. You heard about this in two earlier chapters with a few student comments.

The school was strict on attendance. If they caught a student arriving late, the student would be sent to the auditorium where he would be watched over by a staff member.

Why forcing a student to miss a two hour class is a way to punish the student for arriving late made no sense to me. How would that ensure the student would arrive on time in the future? Often, it wasn't even the student who was late. It was the student's parent who got their child to school too late.

I particularly liked these summer school classes. I had put together teaching techniques that I knew worked and could keep my students' attention. More than that, they could actually learn history and the lessons of history and, hopefully, apply them to the world today.

One student spoke up periodically questioning things. It was the sort of questioning that could — and already had — irritated other teachers. It was no problem for me though. I engaged the student and responded to his questions and comments. Even though it may not have been on the specific topic we were on, his comments were always on history. Learning for all students resulted.

Little did I know that he had periodically gotten himself in trouble during the regular school year in various classes, probably by speaking up or becoming frustrated with the way he was forced into the educational box. But it was clear to me that the student wanted even more — more education. I had worked with many students like him before. I enjoyed having him in class and knew how to work with him. The rest of the class did, too.

One morning, he got to class late. He wasn't really late, maybe just a minute or two. I saw him outside the door and moved to get him into class. But the summer school administrator had gotten there just before me. Rather than allowing me to let him into the classroom, the administrator, the summer school principal, took him to the office. I assumed the administrator would have an appropriate talk with him and send him back to class. Since this was not my regular school, I really didn't know the administrator.

But my class said, no. My students told me that the administrator would throw him out of summer school.

What? For being literally maybe two minutes late?

After they convinced me that I should take it seriously, I quickly scrawled a note and had a student immediately take it to the administrator. Most administrators pay attention when a teacher stands up for a student.

This one didn't. He threw the student out of school. He may have had just a couple more weeks until he finished the class. Because he had done well to that point, I was actually willing to give him a lower passing grade regardless of missing the final weeks. But his name wasn't on the final roster. There was no way I could do it.

Why in the world would an administrator throw out a student for something that minor, especially when his teacher, me, *specifically* asked that he be allowed to stay? I won't dispute that the administrator may have had other problems with the student during the school year. I won't dispute that the administrator may have just not liked him. But I had no problem with him. In fact, I considered him an asset to my class, and I was the teacher, not the administrator.

How frustrating are such things to students! And to teachers! That kind of thing takes time, even weeks or months, out of students' lives, never to be given back to them. Two minutes late. A teacher asking that he not be thrown out. Other students in class recognizing the foolishness of what was happening. What was going on?

Sadly, there are many bad administrators. They damage students, learning, and the teachers under them. When I learned that lesson, it ensured that I would not be like that when I become an administrator myself. I can't know for sure, but when I became an administrator, I truly hope that I mostly succeeded.

We all make mistakes. As both a teacher and an administrator, I know that I did, too. But there is really no excuse for some things that go on in schools and that administrators can easily change for the better.

28. ARE WE BUILDING OUR OWN EDUCATIONAL COFFINS?

Teachers are the direct point-of-contact between students and learning. Almost nothing is more important to student learning than a teacher. Yet this key, actually sole cog, is almost never addressed in "reforms." Programs, materials, new textbooks are introduced. But, in most cases, those things aren't what teach students. *Teachers* teach students.

Many teachers have been teaching for many, many years. They have developed their own ways of doing things, their own ways to teach the material. They're happy with what they've been doing and don't want to change. Sometimes they're right. Their ways are very successful. Other times, they aren't very successful at all.

In spite of receiving training in new programs, or being summarily told to implement them, some teachers just don't do it. Some might try, but they often return to what they had been doing before and which, frankly, sometimes works even better.

Some teachers just don't feel like trying something new. It's a lot of work to change lesson plans and ways of thinking. Nonetheless, many do try to implement new programs. Change can shake things up a bit. Sometimes shaking things up is good by itself — though not always.

But, then, there's this: "New" programs are rarely new. They're often mostly repackaged or regurgitated programs from the past under a different name. Those developing them might not even know that. After all, they're new to them, too!

Over the years, programs cycle through education with both the people who literally sell them and the educators themselves who are then trained in them. None of these people have necessarily seen them before. But many aren't new at all.

***

Here's what the people running (or selling) things often say will help: requiring teachers to get even *more* (costly) *training, taking more* (costly) *classes*, or trying some *new* (and expensive) *program*.

In many, the sales people selling such new programs have convinced a district, a school, or the government to buy their program. They have great data for it so, they say, it will do wonders for educating students!

But will it?

A reminder that we're just talking about kindergarten through high school (K-12) teachers here. As we heard some time back, college teachers generally get little or no actual teacher training at all.

In most cases, only teachers at the K-12 level are required to extensively learn teaching skills. Universities may or may not require professors to take any teacher-training classes. K-12 teachers are (correctly) assumed to need more extensive training because they're teaching younger students. Those students need extra care and protection and careful ways to teach them.

But when a professor teaches an adult, who may pay tens of thousands of dollars each year to be educated, that professor doesn't really need to know anything special about teaching. College students will tell you that. Some of their teachers are really good. Others are a mess.

In many cases, college professors don't even do the teaching. Graduate level assistant students do. They, too, often get minimal or no teacher training. These college teachers, most without any training in how to teach, sometimes teach new teachers as part of teacher-training programs.

There are some terrific teachers teaching new teachers. But there are also some terrible ones. Too many. Those aspiring teachers who come into teacher-training programs who have already had experience teaching can often disregard the incompetence of those bad teachers, finish the program, and be good teachers anyway.

But teacher-training students without teaching experience in the real world won't be able to discern good from bad. They won't be able to recognize incompetence. They will learn what's being taught. Only later, when they implement what they were taught, are they likely to find that it's not working.

I don't want to paint all teacher-training schools or professors with too broad a brush. Some really are good and very valuable.

When I was getting my Community College credential, I was *optionally* allowed to take a summer of teacher-training classes offered through UCLA. That would allowed me to get a slightly higher level credential. But it wasn't needed for me to actually teach the classes I taught. I could go on with them regardless.

The teacher-training classes that I took lasted one summer. It was extensive training. I went through with a group of other similar students (a cohort).

It was just one summer. Yet it was some of the best teacher-training I would have. It was far more productive than the later *years* of required teacher-training classes I would complete to fully qualify as a K-12 teacher.

Do years of extensive teacher training (beyond a handful of foundational classes) produce great teachers in the first place? With rare exceptions, they do not.

I hold a firm belief that great teachers are born, not trained. Training certainly helps to form those teachers. It can give them important tools they will need. But it won't create truly great teachers who don't already have that true and special desire to teach within them.

The best teachers, in my view, have a passion for what they do — and they love their students.

***

Too many bureaucrats who are not educators, too many administrators, too many teachers themselves still think that you can just train teachers — K-12 teachers — to think, do, or teach whatever is currently in vogue, whether educational or political.

But you can't necessarily do that. Teachers are their own people with their own thoughts, passions, and beliefs. You can't change them from one concept, belief, or methodology to another at a moment's notice by simply teaching them something new, by "requiring" them to change, to think or teach differently. It's not that easy.

Teachers are human beings, not programmable robots. They can change if they absolutely see something better, something that changes how they sincerely feel, how they understand things. But, in practice, that happens far less often than some would like to think.

Teacher training itself has the same key element that all education has: it relies on the teachers who teach the teachers.

***

Teachers should also be selling their country — its foundational and shared values — its pride. That's what's called patriotism. Frighteningly, that has become a divisive word for some today, even a concept to be condemned, and certainly not to be espoused in classrooms.

Yet how can ANY country survive and thrive without positive love and support from its own citizens?

It can't.

Want to clandestinely destroy and then takeover a country? Destroy the support for that country by its own citizenry. It will then be ripe for the taking.

But all that comes down to *teachers* (and parents, too). These vital teachers are at all levels of education, from kindergarten through the highest levels at universities, as well as in specialized, professional schools.

The survival of America itself is in the hands of teachers. And vast numbers of those teachers are failing the country. Therefore, they're also failing their students. They damage or destroy the dreams and the future of students, our society, and the country. When those are gone, so are our greatest values of Freedom and Liberty.

As we look around, we can see this happening right now. And it may be too late to turn it around. We have seen that the teachers we increasingly have today already come indoctrinated in new generations of thinking and beliefs that are truly destructive of the foundational, democratic principles of America.

We have put ourselves on the path to our own destruction.

The final nail in the coffin might actually come from what is currently a foreign power, but we're building the coffin ourselves. Is it already built?

Although I do not speak of it in this chapter, I remind the reader that the real failure of education is more foundational than what I am bringing up here. It's the failure of teachers to teach, and students to learn, fundamental academics at all levels of education, from kindergarten through college. Some surviving the system might think otherwise — because it's all they know.

Newer generations of both teachers and students did not live through a world war — not through World War II and not through the Cold War from their beginnings. Their understandings of history have been shaped by their own teachers, often by incomplete or erroneous teachings. Today, they are also shaped by news media which, in large part, are failing the population.

What matters here is that we stop building our own educational coffin. Sadly, it's pretty much already built.

Teachers, especially at the college level, much like their students, have always leaned towards liberal politics. Multiple studies have been clear on that. In some colleges, effectively the entire teaching staff resides on just one side of the political spectrum. They shun or force others out.

In past times, most teachers supported America. If it were

threatened, the vast majority would stand up for America — in the past. They may have talked down the government, but they didn't — *most* didn't — talk down America itself.

Many parents today are being brought up by the same deficient, and now fully dangerous, public education system in which vast numbers of outspokenly anti-American teachers freely pass on their animosity towards their own country.

Of course, some teachers do remain strongly patriotic, strongly American.

But there seem to be fewer and fewer of them.

Much of this was extensively discussed in the preface to this book.

Even what have been safe havens for pro-American teachers and students — religious schools and colleges — have even seen some of their own teachers quietly change. After all, by whom were their teachers educated?

Just as education has been destroying the country, education is also the entity that can save it. But who would those teachers be? Do enough of them exist anymore to turn things around?

The path America is on a one-way road. And it isn't leading to the right destination.

***

The damage has already become so severe that some are questioning whether a foreign enemy has been intentionally undermining education in America. Such would be done by quietly weaponizing what have generally been left wing social agendas in schools and in their cadre of educators. These new agendas, unrelated to traditional education, are now damaging students, parents, education, and, by extension, the country itself. If effective enough over a long enough period of time, use of any traditional foreign military force to take over the country could become unnecessary.

Recall that in 1983, A Nation At Risk warned, *"If an unfriendly foreign power had attempted to impose on America the mediocre educa-*

tional performance that exists today, we might well have viewed it as an act of war."

Although it went on to say — as I have said here — that we have done this to ourselves, even the mention of that concern should have awakened us many years ago. That is especially true because the damage being done to the country today extends to areas not even contemplated in 1983.

Although this author is not taking a firm position on this at the moment, the author does believe that this possibility should not be ignored. Even America has long had the capability to quietly affect the politics and beliefs of people in other countries. Others countries have that ability, too.

28a. TRADITIONAL SCHOOLS TEACH TOO LITTLE, TOO SLOWLY

From my personal and professional experiences, both in and out of education, I believe that years of our lives are often wasted by being in inefficient education systems. Young people, especially very young ones, are capable of learning far faster than the slow and inefficient pace that defines traditional schooling.

I'm not suggesting teachers speed up their teaching in order to cram as much as possible into their frustrated students. That's not how this works; that kind of "teaching" won't work. Doing that will have the opposite effect and hurt students. But that doesn't mean that we can't speed up learning anyway. Our students are capable of more — but not how it's being done today.

In *School is dead: An essay on alternatives in education* (1971), Everett W. Reimer, the author, tells us that John Gardner (1912-2002), Secretary of Health, Education, and Welfare in the Lyndon Johnson administration, said that *"everything a high-school graduate is taught in twelve years of schooling could easily learned in two years and with a little effort in one."*

I personally disagree with that. I believe that it would take longer — but far less than the twelve+ years it takes today. We're wasting our children's time by taking so long to teach them — and we're doing it poorly, too.

To accomplish making learning more efficient, the manner and structure of how teaching is done that must be completely re-evaluated. That also means that we had better figure out how to do a better job selecting the teachers we put in front of our children.

Education is critical, whether from a school, from parents, or from life. It's the delivery of that education that is broken. Actually, it's well beyond broken.

***

Too commonly today, schools teach things that are likely to end up hurting our children once they're adults, even on their way to adulthood.

Kip and Mona Lisa Harding homeschooled their ten children. All graduated high school *at the age of 12*.

According to an article of February 2022, here is what happened to them:[1]

(1) The first became the youngest graduate of Auburn University at Montgomery's (AUM). She earned a Bachelor of Science degree in mathematics. She was 17.

(2) Their second child became the youngest member of the American Institute of Architects.

(3) The third became the youngest US Navy doctor at the age of 22. She is now a physician working in Washington.

(4) The fourth was Troy University's youngest graduate with a Bachelor of Science in computer science. He was 17.

(5) The fifth has a counseling degree. He lives in Washington and works as a U.S. sign language translator. He also earned a music degree from Faulkner University at the age of 15.

(6) At age 19, their number six became Alabama's youngest attorney. He works as an attorney in Montgomery, Alabama.

(7) At the age of 18, number seven was, at the time of the report, set to break her brother's record by becoming the new youngest attorney in Alabama.

(8) At the age of 16, number eight was one of Auburn University's youngest graduate students in health science. She is working on getting another graduate degree in horticulture.

(9) At 14 (and at the time of the article), number nine was expected to be a junior at Bellevue University.

(10) At age 11, her brother is a college freshman, also at Bellevue University. He and his (#9) sister are the college's youngest students.

Keeping children out of the workforce, defining them as "children" far longer than had been done in the past, has led to what some might suggest to be a waste of life. This has easily been done by extending the years of what is "required" education.

Then there are schools which have been eliminating their Gifted student programs. Not only are schools failing to educate faster and more efficiently, they're actually dismantling educational programs that do. Gifted student programs address those students who don't do well in regular school programs because they have a special need and ability to move and learn more quickly. Such programs often fall under Special Education programs.

Special Education programs are not necessarily restricted to students experiencing difficulties learning and keeping up in school. Such programs also serve students at the other end of the scale, those who have trouble learning at a slower and unchallenging speed.

Such students become bored and can exhibit behavior problems in class. They might not get high grades because they aren't being challenged — and they don't care. Why would we discontinue such programs to penalize our highest performing students? Does America want to ensure that we always have students who are not educated to their highest potential? (That often happens today regardless of the Gifted programs.)

Really though, we can no longer just let our children loose on the world much earlier than what is happening today without much different preparation. Schools and society are not giving that to them now. But, if things can be made effective again (not at all likely), we might certainly be able to do it again.

With history itself to look at, multiple books give examples of what our currently-defined "children" could do if given the chance.[2] Such opportunities are now gone. That is at least partly due to often unnecessary — effectively wasted — years spent in inefficient schooling, as well as legally restricting "children" from what are now sometimes artificially defined as non-children areas of life. Laws are being passed to "protect" even much older students to ensure they cannot easily start their lives. Admittedly, many today aren't ready to do that both due to immaturity and to simply not being prepared by both school and parents. Nonetheless, young people have more capabilities than are now being developed. As evidence, look again at the Harding family children.

Quoting from J. Allen Weston, executive director, American Homeschool Association, the above mentioned article says, *"Homeschooling takes far less time, giving the children the opportunity to explore things that they are actually interested in."* Further on, the article again reinforces the time efficiency of homeschooling.[3]

An important question is how can we get the same time-efficiency *outside of* homeschooling as many homeschoolers can get *in* homeschooling. Any dramatically new educational design must consider this issue.

Society today wants to "protect" young people far longer than may be necessary when one considers not only the past, but — given a different preparation — their abilities even today.

Many homeschooled children show that such abilities in life are still present at a far earlier age than is now permitted not only by society, but too often by law. "Children" are often kept as children far longer than necessary were an effective and efficient education provided. But that is not being done.

All homeschoolers won't have the phenomenal successes the Hardings had. Many simply wouldn't be able to homeschool. But it can happen far more often than people know. (Almost) all of the properly homeschooled children I have known have been very successful after leaving home and starting college —-that is, if they chose to head in that direction.

The lives of the Harding children have not been wasted. They did not lose years of their lives in the traditional education system — nor did they "lose their childhoods." Instead, they gained life.

There is more on homeschooling in Part Two of this book. However, those interested will find much more and many more stories about homeschooling both on and offline. Perhaps you can discover some homeschooling parents near you. They are often happy to talk to you.

Can we do the same thing on a broader level? Under the current system, we cannot.

***

Education's inefficiency is one of just a handful of reasons why students drop out of school. They're frustrated and they've finally had enough of it.

All children love learning. It's school that becomes the problem.

That inefficiency and waste of life is one of the reasons why strong and competent homeschooling parents can succeed so well. It's also why homeschoolers should not be artificially held back by district or state requirements that often have the effect of pulling the escaping frogs back into the well.

Children, even very young ones, are capable of much more than we give them credit for. We need to stop wasting their time and ours in the current educational design. They can learn all that they need to learn much faster, starting at a very early age.

As an aside and as a seemingly contradictory statement (it's actually not), I do not support current proposals to lower the voting age in America. In fact, I support raising it significantly.

I'm not suggesting simply cutting all children loose willy-nilly. They need a good preparation for life. But that shouldn't take nearly as long as is now required of them.

Note that doing this will not "take away their childhood," unless those teaching the children wrongly unbalance their lives. Even adults need to be a child at times. But fun for many adults also comes from meaningful and exciting work, as well as non-work activities.

Saying that we don't want to take childhood away from our children makes the assumption that life as an adult is so stressful and unhappy that it should be put it off as long as possible.

When we say that, it says a lot about the rest of us as adults. It can also provide an unhealthy example of what purportedly awaits our children.

In reality, life is good. (Well, mostly.)

Like many children, when I was growing up, I was anxious to

get into "the real world" and start doing exciting things! I wasn't bemoaning that I wouldn't have my childhood anymore! I wanted the adventures of life. I got many of them. Some weren't great. Some I really wish hadn't happened. But others were fantastic!

No one ever took away my childhood. Most were there to give me the excitement of life as I became an adult. Frankly, I had felt ready for it far sooner than the system would allow. True, I might not have actually been ready when I had wanted to be. That's what parents and teachers are there for. But it was almost certainly one of the reasons that I dropped out of high school one semester before finishing it. Too many others feel the same way.

According to one article, *"Some students who left public schools in 2020 entered the workforce. About 2 million students dropped out of high school that year, according to NCES* [the National Center for Education Statistics]."[4]

I'm not necessarily suggesting dropping out of high school, by the way. Schools are doing a terrible job preparing students to go out on their own early without finishing school, so most simply aren't ready. (Of course, more time in school might not make things any better anyway.) Nonetheless, in most cases, there are still strong arguments to finish high school, even at a public school.

Regardless of all that, the current education system is dead.

29. OUR COMMUNITIES

Most educators have been taught — and agree — that schools can't fix things outside the school. An educator's job is to provide education. We can't save the world. We can't even save families. That's someone else's job.

But too often, it's no one's job.

As an administrator, I never accepted that reasoning. True, we can't fix everything around us. But, within reason, if we don't at least try to address situations beyond the school that actually affect teaching our students, and unless we support the community, we aren't truly doing our job. By helping families and the community, *we are supporting our students* and the education we're trying to give them…well, within reason.

It might seem strange to say this, but I'm taking a minority position here. Nonetheless, I strongly believe that schools and educators should not be separate from their community. This has to be more than lip service.

We must listen to our communities and they should be listening to the educators who teach their children. *As long as education is served*, it should be a cooperative effort. Both sides should care about the other. Life isn't easy and things don't always work out that way. But, as possible, that should be the goal.

On their end, I don't believe communities should demand, sometimes they shouldn't even expect, attention. They must understand that educators' time and energies are limited. Nonetheless, students and education itself are served when we also interact with parents and the greater community. There are others who feel as I do, but not nearly enough.

A school is an important part of all communities but, in some communities, it is an absolutely critical part of it. Especially in smaller communities, the school can be the center of life.

Some lucky schools have enough money to hire community resource personnel to help parents and as an interface between the school, the home, and the community. Some of those in the job are really great resource people. Others aren't very good at all.

As principal, I tried to attend all significant community meetings local to the school. One Community Leadership meeting involved a number of community entities including members of the city council. As part of the meeting, I spoke to them. A letter sent to the superintendent of a district in which I worked noted my sincere concern for the school's community.

Here is the significant part of that letter:

> *Our Community Leadership invited Mr. Scarpitta to provide an update on [our] school and to discuss ways that we can assist in his work as principal. We were all very impressed with Mr. Scarpitta and his willingness to work with our community to incorporate cultural programs within the school system. Mr. Scarpitta was very energetic and enthusiastic about our students and community. We are very pleased with [the school district] and their decision to hire such a great principal to lead our school. He had many great ideas and a clear understanding of areas that we must work together on improving.*

I have certainly not been perfect... not as an administrator, not as a teacher, and not as a person. Certainly, not all staff or community members liked me. But we can all only do the best we can do. The important thing about the letter they wrote is not me. I quote it so that you can understand how important an officially involved and caring staff, especially administrators, can be to the community and to the positive relationships that can develop between all of them.

By attending community meetings, I put myself on the line to be available for questions or complaints. I could also give the community a report as to what was actually going on at their school. I was straightforward with them. Otherwise, people might listen to disgruntled students or parents and not get accurate information.

Even though attendance at such meetings was not officially part of my job, those running these meetings came to expect my presence and the school reports I provided. The school was not a cold, separate building out of their reach or influence. Because I attended meetings whenever I could, people knew the school was *part of them* and *cared about them*.

I also attended meetings so that I could hear from the community in case there were good suggestions for changes at the school. Even if there weren't any, I was there to listen regardless. I was sincere that I would implement anything good for the school and students that was feasible and possible. The good superintendent at the District listened to me and generally supported these efforts.

By not hiding in order to avoid hard questions, and by providing honest reports, the community knew that I sincerely cared for them and for their children. That's because I actually did. My active presence at community meetings built trust.

As an assistant principal at a different school, I had suggested that the principal should attend upcoming community council meetings, sometimes held monthly. The principal appeared to see it as an unnecessary bother, certainly not part of the job. Whenever I could, I went instead.

A job as an educator should not be "just a job." It's more than that. Fortunately, with the passion that is part of many educators, it usually is. That is especially true in what should be part of good administrators.

29a. A SCHOOL COMMUNITY HEARING

Many years before I was an administrator, I attended a public hearing held at a school in the Los Angeles Unified School District. Changes were going to be made to schools and a hearing had been scheduled to inform parents about what was happening, answer their questions, and listen to their concerns.

A number of parents in attendance were concerned about the coming changes. They attended the meeting to express those concerns. Some asked for what sounded to me like reasonable changes. At least they wanted the district to look into and consider their requests. There was a regional district superintendent, answerable to the main Superintendent, present for the meeting.

That regional administrator ran the hearing for the several hundred people who showed up. I was still a teacher, but I was there with my principal and was separate from the people at the hearing.

Being in the company of my school principal, the regional superintendent assumed that I was an administrator, too. As my principal and I were walking out with him after the meeting, he turned to me in response to some comment I had made supportive of one of the suggestions. He merely smirked at me and said, *"We'll just do what we want anyway,"* or words to that effect.

He had promised parents that he would look into their suggestions to see if something could be done. He had lied. He was just going through the motions. He had no intention to do anything that he didn't want to do. And he didn't want to do anything other than what he had already determined to do before the meeting.

He would not be influenced to even consider the concerns of the hundreds of parents who attended the hearing. There was nothing wrong with the suggestions and concerns the parents expressed. The district would have done well to listen, consider, and see if they could adjust things to address their concerns. But this particular regional district superintendent had no intention of doing any of that. He had held the promised and required meeting. Now he could move on with what he was going to do in the first place.

It was clear to me that the district could not be trusted. I had personally seen other things that had concerned me. Over some years, I learned not to trust those at the L.A. Unified School District. Similar problems exist at other districts across the country. Sadly, some bad districts and some bad superintendents are untrustworthy. They can be really bad.

On the other hand, we can't paint all districts or all unions with the same brush. There are also good districts that support both teachers and administrators. Those who live or work in districts with good and caring leadership should appreciate and support that leadership. They shouldn't expect perfection. We can all make mistakes. But we should be patient with each other.

The kind of behavior I saw may be part of why I became an administrator. Only by doing that could I see whether I could make things better for parents and students — and especially for the teachers. When administrators support teachers, they support students and education overall.

However, I have seen *even worse* outright lies and a lack of caring from teacher *unions*, lying even to the teachers they're supposed to be serving, as well as the public and others. I was a member of unions when I was a teacher and strongly felt that they were not representing me or the situations at the schools, especially in Los Angeles. I remember hearing representations of what they said were things happening at the school and knew that they were, at times, 180 degrees opposite from the truth. Unions are important. But they must possess and display integrity. Too many don't anymore.

Even though it's clear that both some districts and many unions have serious problems and have shown themselves to be untrustworthy, I have also seen good unions, most often in some very small districts, who work well and cooperatively with their district and others. So they shouldn't all be painted — or condemned — with a broad brush. Of course, that also depends on the competence and statesmanship of those involved in both the unions and the districts. Some have brought legitimate improvements to schools and education, not just benefits to their members. Sadly, especially in large districts, that is not always the norm.

Worse are the national teacher organizations, such as the NEA and AFT. Those have become so political as to be worthless as supporters of educators, schools, and the communities. For many decades, they have appeared to be too broken to be fixed.

Public schools themselves should belong to the public, even though the public doesn't have the expertise to run them. There's a hint of that in their title: _public_ schools. But people in positions of power, including politicians, often run roughshod over parents, students, and teachers. I have seen blatant lying on all sides and I am disgusted by it. But I have also seen good superintendents and good people who do as much as they can to further education, who care for both teachers and students.

It's true that sometimes things have to be done that no one likes. It might be forced on a district or a school by a legislature or a court. Perhaps it's something else. Then, no matter how much parents and the community don't like it, there might not appear to be a way out. Sometimes, things we don't like have to be done unless we can change things in a legislature or the courts. That isn't often easy — or even possible to do.

There are also some truly well-meaning parents who might want things done that educators know will only hurt the school and the education of the students.

Nonetheless, there might sometimes be other ways to get good things done. As everywhere, compromises must often be made. Educators should always be open to viable options. But parents and the community must also be open to learning the specific issues and problems faced by schools and educators. They must be open to compromise, too.

***

As possible, parents should be a part of their children's education, providing the support schools and their children often need. But, in places, bad things are happening at some schools. The eyes of parents should be open.

On the other hand, there are things that parents should not be doing:

(1) Parents (and students) should not insist on changing the facts of education itself. They should not decide to change the (actual) facts of history, science, and other academic disciplines. They should not decide that certain subjects, widely accepted as foundational to an educated student, are not important.

For example, parents should not decide that their children don't really have to "waste their time" learning solid language skills — reading, writing, speaking. They should not decide that rules of grammar and language aren't really necessary or important for their child. They should not insist arithmetic not be taught because everyone just uses a calculator app, so why memorize multiplication tables anymore?

Parents should be closely involved in support of their child's school and teachers, but to demand unsupported changes to nearly universally accepted academics is something they should not be doing. Such parents can find other schools which might support non-traditional academics. They can start their own school. They can homeschool. But public schools have a broader responsibility.

I'd better mention that there have been some teachers, administrators, and districts that want to make their own unwarranted changes to the nearly universally accepted facts of education today. These are often based on damaging political or sociological agendas. Today, that is happening nearly exclusively on the "progressive" side.

(2) Parents should not demand their "wonderful" and "truthful" child not receive consequences (be disciplined) when that child exhibits behavior issues that must be brought under control. Parents supporting their out-of-control child — their disrespectful, bullying, defiant child — contribute to dysfunctional schools and classrooms. Teachers and administrators are not always right. But those issues should be worked out without blanket accusations against schools and educators of targeting parents and their children.

(3) Parents should know and mostly agree to follow school rules and guidelines. But there should also be a way for parents to get a reconsideration of such rules if they seem not to be in the best interest of education. Often, formal re-examinations of such school handbooks and procedures happen every year or two at many schools anyway.

Most schools have parent groups that work with the administration to have input and general approval of such rules. Some schools might allow an even broader swath of parents to have input after the initial work on such rules by a parent/administrator group is done.

Really, school rules are generally sensible and similar among most schools. Most have been in place for years. If something seems not to be working, it can be changed — as long as the smooth functioning of the school and its class-rooms are not put at risk. Hopefully, all can work together. All should be firm about keeping dangerous teachings and materials out of schools. But parent representatives should not be unyielding activists determined to get their way regardless of what is best for students and schools.

Although representatives can be strong, they should also have at least a smidge of statesmanship and negotiating skills in them. That should include an ability to compromise. Admittedly, there should be a firm stance against some of the recent radicalized agendas that have crept into some schools. But, absent those, both parents and schools — including administrators and the district — should be willing and able to work together.

But if schools, administrators, teachers, and staff have gone off the deep end — remember the discussion of "dangerous teachings" near the start of this book — then parents need to take strong action to take back their schools — or get their children out of them.

***

Parents should certainly be able to have input, though not always the final word, on many things. Administrators and teachers do need to ensure that the fundamentals of a school and education are not changed for the worse, or thrown out altogether. If that happens, will there even be a school left? However, beyond those basics, parents should certainly be involved and watch over what is happening. Hopefully, those on both sides will be trustworthy and respectful. It's also a good example for our children.

On November 14, 2022, an email was sent out by an organization with this succinct and proper statement of parental involvement in schools:[1]

> *Parents are not demanding they have a say in teaching algebra. They are saying they have a role in determining their child's character formation. They also object when teachers move from education to indoctrination.*
>
> *To be specific, when teachers overstep their boundaries by seeking to indoctrinate children with radical ideas about sexuality* [as just one example], *they need to be called out about it. Children do not belong to the state. And* [public school] *teachers work for the taxpayers.*

As I write these words, there is a push to give parents the right to know what their children are being taught in schools. (Why hadn't they been able to know that before?) Although I strongly support this, it's difficult or impossible to fully implement.

Here's why. Many good teachers often bring in stories and teachings that aren't necessarily part of the class materials. I certainly did that. Such stories and extra materials can encourage, even excite, students about their coming life. They can let students know their teachers better and help them respect teachers' well-rounded life knowledge, not just competence in the subject of the class.

My canary topics are two examples.

Such digressions also give students a break when a class might bog down in difficult material. It can teach students things from a teacher's experience that they might not have otherwise learned. Rather than significantly taking away from the subject of the class, such things can enrich the class and the students.

But because these moments are often unplanned, schools wouldn't be able to give those things to parents as being part of a class. Yet if a parent then took issue with it, they would complain that the story or information wasn't given to them in advance. That can put a chilling effect on teachers wanting to teach something else of value that can enrich the class. Good teachers shouldn't be stopped doing that. So this kind of thing can complicate letting parents know everything that goes on in a classroom. Speaking for me, I would likely have left teaching entirely if my hands were so tied that I couldn't talk about things that weren't necessarily part of the subject of the class.

I often taught some important topics that I knew students would likely never get in other classes — ever. Those topics didn't necessarily deal with the subject matter of the class itself. Yet such teachings can frequently invigorate students and the class itself. They often led to greater learning in the actual subject matter of the course. Almost all teachers periodically do the same thing.

As just one example, my presentations on the atomic bomb would not have fit in a standard outline in all of my classes. Yet, without them, many students would never have learned about them at all.

If a teacher were restricted to teach an unchanging list of approved topics, the class could just as easily be taught by computer — or robot — with only a live person in the room to be sure order was maintained and to answer unrelated questions. Teachers bring important parts of themselves to the classroom. It's one thing that makes teaching exciting and fulfilling for educators.

However, what some teachers are bringing in recently is indeed damaging. That must stop. But where can we draw the lines? Pick good teachers who are sensitive to these things and none of this should be the problem it has become.

That all makes this tough. It wouldn't have been a problem had educators not begun to inappropriately teach their own non-mainstream political and sociological agendas to their classes.

Parents should absolutely know what is being taught at schools. But putting that into effect can become more complicated than it might seem.

Yet proposals are now being put forward to give parents direct power over whether principals can keep their jobs. Although I fully agree that something should be done to more easily counter bad teachers and bad administrators, giving parents too much power over administrators *without safeguards* can also be a mistake.

Fearing for their jobs, many educators will simply back down from administering important student discipline against certain students lest an activist parent personally go after the principal's job. As elsewhere, students and parents with an agenda can and do lie about both teachers and administrators.

Problems don't necessarily always originate with school-level administrators anyway — although they certainly can.

It sounds as though parents would not be given hiring authority, just some authority to fire principals.

However, even though things would not be as simple as many hope they might be, dramatic — but currently impossible — action for substantive change is definitely needed, not just a few fixes at the local level.

Both parents and public education share the blame in what education has become. (So does the government and the media.) However, the bulk of the problems in education today are most often with the education system itself, not with parents.

Parents are correct to be disgusted, even frightened, by what is happening in public schools today.

30. LEGISLATURES, COURTS, AND DISCIPLINE

All schools have misbehaving students. After all, they're children. They're still growing up and learning correct behaviors. Good teaching practices combined with good parenting will normally put such students on the right path.

Most schools do not have students with the serious problems considered in this and past chapters. But enough schools have these problems that I must mention the difficulty teachers and administrators have in protecting students, staff, and the school.

I have already brought this issue up before but, because this is so important and widespread in some districts, I'll add a few additional thoughts. Be patient.

We'll start by considering the inability of administrators at schools, especially in K-12 schools, to remove fully out-of-control or potentially dangerous students from being with other students and school staff. The difficulty in doing so frustrates educators as well as parents whose children must try to function in the same classrooms with such students. In especially serious situations, it puts students and staff in danger. So it becomes important that such students be removed from the school environment.

Yet without a careful, often lengthy process involving meetings, evaluations, reports, and approvals — especially in the case of students designated as having "special needs" — in too many places, administrators are effectively stopped from removing such students from the school in order to protect other students and staff from being physically assaulted. The problem is worse in some places than it is in others.

Special Education students are often wonderful young people. Their teachers are remarkable, too. Few outsiders would be able to have the patience and perseverance that these teachers have to help the students with whom they choose to work.

This country should be proud of the caring and support that we, as a country, actively give to those with special needs — and that's not just at schools. We're not perfect and there will always be complaints. But, compared to so many other places in the world, we generally treat those who need help far better. I am hopeful that we won't see that ever stopping. Both today and in the past, Americans have been a caring people.

Sometimes though, a student might seriously and regularly misbehave. I'm really being kind here because "misbehave" is often too soft a term. This can be a Special Education student or a student who is part of the school's general population. Any student can be a problem.

Sometimes multiple students might misbehave to such a degree as to totally disrupt entire school classes on a daily basis.

But, whatever must be done to get such students under control — or to discipline them — teachers and administrators must sometimes answer to angry parents as to why it had to be done at all. That is even if it may have to be done to protect students, teachers, or others from actual physical harm. Rather than being supportive, many parents will effectively threaten the educators involved. (That's a hint of what might have influenced such students in the first place.)

Administrators and teachers don't have many tools at their disposal. They used to have more but, gradually, some have been taken away. What is left can be effective for some students, but totally ineffective for others.

As mentioned much earlier, no educator wants to call the police on any student. Only very rarely do most schools actually do that.

However, it will surely surprise people to hear that, as mentioned before, some public schools don't have access to any police support *at all* should it be needed, because there is no police readily available in the community. Such schools are on their own.

Some district, state, even federal education officials might say this isn't actually true, that administrators do have ways to remove students. Depending on the jurisdiction in which the school operates, that's often wrong. At times, it's so difficult as to make it almost impossible to remove them without walking on thin legal ice.

The hands of educators are often tied by overly-restrictive laws, procedures, court rulings, or demands from their district or state administrators even when nearly immediate action has to be taken for everyone's safety, including educators, and to save classroom education itself. Suspensions can be limited by law or court rulings to just a few days, when a much more extensive suspension, transfer — even expulsion — might be needed.

I'll quickly add that, especially in the past, there have indeed been situations where schools or administrators have abused an easier process to exclude students from school. I have no doubt that would still occasionally happen. That is important and should be addressed. But the opposite — forcing fully out-of-control or dangerous students to be kept in schools — can be an even worse scenario. (There is more to this, but I'll not go into a full treatise on how suspensions and other discipline work.)

Those writing the laws, putting together consent decrees, or making separate court rulings have rarely had to work in these kinds of classrooms and schools. Although some would say they have, few have actually had to deal with totally defiant and dangerous children. They haven't had to be concerned with their own safety dealing with some of these students, even after teachers and administrators go home.

Legislatures should not be writing laws that can make things worse. They might sound good, but they don't work. Schools need more flexibility. They need more disciplinary and educational tools; they need more support.

Educators should not have to consistently put themselves at risk simply for wanting to educate, help, and care for their students.

***

As I did once before, let me caution that fully expelling a student from school is fraught with other serious issues. Unless there are absolutely no other viable options, it's not a good thing to do. Critically, expelled students are now effectively free to do as they want since they no longer have a structured setting in which to function. Such students can continue to pose a danger. The danger can even increase. In addition, if an alternative school setting isn't available, from where will they get their education?

Admittedly, some students don't seem to care about any of that. However, adults know those student still need education and guidance if they are to later be a positive contributor to American society. Expulsion is not a good option, although sometimes it's all that's left.

In the past, some educators have indeed abused previously broader authority to remove or discipline students. That is why increasingly stronger restrictions were put on educators — and others. But protections to reign in past abuses have now, at times, created untenable situations.

Assuming they're at least minimally cooperative, such students should be given help finding a different facility to serve them. However, not all schools have the resources to find help for such students, especially in smaller communities.

Some educators and readers won't even know what I'm talking about here. They haven't seen such serious issues and can be in denial they even exist. I have personally seen such issues play out. Others have, too.

Sometimes, there is no time for required processes to unfold, yet, while they do, schools are legally forced to wait, to do nothing as things slowly proceed, sometimes at a snail's pace, sometimes not at all. If something terrible were to happen, there would be hearings and inquiries to find out what went wrong and how to stop it in the future.

But we already know the problems and some of the answers right now. They're just not being taken seriously by the right people — primarily legislatures and courts, but sometimes by administrators themselves.

In many places, one can't even get immediate help for concerns over potential student suicides though, again, some with access to the many resources of larger communities will say that isn't true.

But it is.

Those in a position to make changes, but who ignore all this, will be personally responsible when terrible things happen. Unfortunately, they generally don't understand that. They won't think they were responsible and they wouldn't be held "accountable" anyway.

Today, the right people are rarely actually held "accountable" for anything at all. That word is meaninglessly thrown around as if it were an end in itself.

Most of the time, everyone just holds their collective breaths, hoping that nothing happens on their watch.

Along with a few incompetent administrators, even some teachers, the real blame lies primarily with legislatures and courts — especially at the federal level.

Schools should not be expected to function as mental health treatment facilities. Not only is it not their function, but they can't do it effectively anyway. Yet that's the position in which they're often put. I've said this in other places, too.

Whether in or out of schools, the difficulty getting potentially dangerous people — whether or not they're students — confined or assigned to treatment needs to be fixed. Treatment and services are not only needed for them, but also to protect others. Of course, conflicts with constitutional rights and protections must be addressed and that's not always easy. But physical safety and the survival of education need to be brought to the fore.

We don't have to find excuses why bad people do what they do. Sometimes, they've just become bad people. Law enforcement should be given the tools they need to help keep communities safe.

Prosecutors should back them up. Courts should stop letting demonstrably dangerous people back on the streets.

I'm not saying we should lock them up and throw away the key. Those who can be helped, should be helped. But that must be in a safe and controlled environment. I want to help those who need help. I care about them. But schools are not necessarily the place to do that.

These things might be rare, but they're not rare enough. And they seem to be getting worse.

Truthfully, as with education itself, none of this is likely fixable anymore. So this discussion, as with so many other things today, ends up going nowhere.

I recommend the book, *Killers Are Fatherless: The Real Cause Of School Shootings, Serial Killings, and Gang Murders,* also by the author

31. TESTING AND IGNORING WARNINGS

As I mention elsewhere, I strongly support appropriately designed testing (whatever that means) so that we can know what and how much our students are learning. Otherwise we have *no idea* what, if anything, our future adults are learning. If we don't know what our students actually know, we can't make changes to improve how we are teaching them. We are clueless whether they're learning what we're teaching without some sort of standardized testing. We can also have a picture of the level of education in the country. That can even become a national security issue.

Some who design tests might need to reevaluate how they're doing it, but testing is important. Done correctly, as part of class-room instruction, tests and quizzes can be a method of *learning*, not merely a means of evaluation. I talked about this before when talking about math.

I do believe that some minimum educational standards and goals should be set. In my view, states should be handling educa-tion within their state. Among other things, the 10th Amendment to the Constitution appears to leave it to the states. One problem is that many states establish weak or non-existent standards in certain academic areas. That can weaken the country.

On the other hand, there should be flexibility for non-traditional schools as well as for homeschooling so that strong state standards don't interfere with what might potentially be more aggressive or differently-structured — but equally effective — learning designs.

One serious problem (among others) is that many states, districts, schools, and educators will take federally-promulgated, minimum standards as their own standards. They will assume that because they are meeting those minimum standards that they are doing their jobs. Perhaps they are, but that's not always true.

Additionally, we have to consider *who* is setting those standards. Frequently, the standards themselves (and those setting them) aren't up to what are needed.

No matter which "minimum" standards are eventually accepted, people on all sides — educators, parents, community members — will find things they really don't like about them... that is, if they read them at all.

None of this means that all students will or should fit in the same basket. As just mentioned, non-public school students might need different methods of evaluation, different testing. We can't make the assumption that non-public school students are, or even should be, learning the same things at the same pace as public school students. If they wanted to do that, which they don't, their students would effectively be public school students.

In some cases, students *exceeding* set standards are reigned in by state or federal authorities. Both homeschoolers and non-public schools can be forced to meet standards public school students must meet — even if they passed up those standards two years before. As was previously said, many students can learn faster than some educational programs allow. Why should any students be held back — including those at public schools?

Nonetheless, I have no problem testing all students in all educational settings anyway — though generally no more than once or twice a year and hopefully not taking an entire week each time! Data is helpful! If different tests are needed for different school designs, they should be developed in close coordination with the educators involved in those other schools. But testing should not unreasonably interfere with actual education. In recent decades, it sometimes has.

Another problem is that there is often not just one test. There are several totally different tests that teachers might be required to give during the school year. If these tests aren't helping to educate students *(some actually do)*, teachers shouldn't have to waste time on them when time is better spent elsewhere. Schools shouldn't be required to test so often that other things that students need are put aside. As mentioned, some schools and teachers are educating beyond tests which, at times, can actually hold them back. But that's not necessarily the problem.

The real problem is that most times it is the opposite: Students (and therefore schools) are failing at all levels. Most do terribly on those tests. That's one reason these tests are important, to see how far behind the country actually is.

Many people and teachers complain that they have to "teach to the test." In other words, teachers have to teach students what they need to know to "pass" the tests rather than cover other material in class. Is that necessarily a bad thing? Not necessarily. If the tests actually test on what is covered in class, then students are learning what they should be learning anyway. But tests don't necessarily do that.

Teachers need tests not just to evaluate students, but to evaluate themselves and their teaching. If students aren't doing well, teachers can reteach the material or make changes in how they're teaching — at least, those who are willing and able to do so. So classroom tests are evaluative, not merely given so grades can be recorded. On the other hand (there are often several hands), many schools and districts use student testing to evaluate their teachers. Although teachers do need periodic evaluations of varying sorts, the use of student testing to evaluate teachers is fraught with potential unfairness. Regardless, there must also be ways to root out and remove teachers who aren't producing educated students — generally speaking, that is; there are exceptions.

Some teachers choose to work with very difficult students or who have a high number of students who come and go throughout the school year. Those teachers should not at all be held to the same kind of standards as teachers at "regular" schools.

But this isn't the right place to discuss evaluating educators.

Standardized testing is not just so that teachers alone know whether and what their students are learning. Schools and districts need to know that, too. Parents need to know that. States and the country needs to know that, too.

If too many students throughout a school are struggling, good administrators need to discuss with their staff what changes can be made to help. Perhaps things can be scheduled differently. Some teachers might need more support with difficult students, not necessarily because they aren't good teachers, but because the students they have are simply more challenging. That's not the first time I've said that.

Maybe schoolwide activities are interfering. Maybe it's something else. Schools can only consider what to do if they have enough information — through testing — to let them know how their students are doing. I'll add that, for the same reasons, appropriate testing is also helpful with non-public school alternatives, including homeschooling.

On the other hand, some teachers may not always be prepared to teach their classes. Some are burned out or just generally poor teachers. They must be carefully helped to be better — or removed as union contracts allow.

Note that "help" does not mean micromanaging teachers as well as every aspect of what happens in their classrooms. That is almost always counterproductive. But if something truly can be done to support teachers and teaching, it should be done. Sometimes even our best teachers just need some good and regular supportive words.

Of course, things are more complicated than what I said above about testing. But it would be a failing to ignore this issue altogether.

IGNORING WRONGS

Another note regarding testing: When too much is on the line for teachers and schools, some cheat. (Students often try to do that; here I talk about school staff.)

I have personally been aware of teachers (and others) stealing standardized tests in advance to prepare their students, especially special education students, so that they can score higher. Such can be easily done by someone who might have access to the locked area where schoolwide tests are kept. Tests can then be copied and returned so they can be accounted for. Some schools have more secure areas in which to keep tests than others do.

When administrators become aware of such things, some of them ignore it figuring it's just part of what happens. Disciplining staff members is always difficult. Some administrators try to push their responsibility onto someone else.

Speaking of ignoring things, administrators also ignore other things that they should not. In one instance, a member of a school's staff would regularly view pornography on his personal computer, even while overseeing young students at recess or lunch. Periodically, older students became aware of that in his office, although they didn't do anything about it either.

How was this known? Because school district technology people actually saw what he was doing as they remotely accessed computers on the school's network during maintenance of the school's system.

When it was reported to the school principal — there was zero doubt this was happening — nothing was done. Nothing at all. The staff member wasn't even made aware that the administration knew about his daily viewing habits at school.

Some administrators are reluctant to discipline staff out of fear of retaliation by that staff member. So things can be more complicated than what others might think. Regardless, those kind of serious issues should be firmly dealt with. But it doesn't always happen.

At how many schools do such things take place? Hopefully not many, but at far more than people would like to think.

***

Separate from the above, I'll add that, as we should also do for others, sometimes a teacher or staff member — even an administrator — might do something wrong, but be well worthy of a warning and another chance. Except in especially serious cases, no otherwise good educator should be condemned for a single transgression, or even for more than one minor one — depending on what it is, of course. The job is tough enough. Those who are actually good people should be treated as such (within reason) even if they do something wrong — as we all can do at times. Even outside of schools, we should treat each other that way, too. None of us are perfect.

32. GOD IN SCHOOLS

Is it necessary that belief in a god be part of a religion? Although the vast majority of people think that should be obvious, it is not. Courts have ruled that a religion can be defined using a much broader definition. God not required. There are various examples of that in several non-theistic (no god) religions.

America's documents recognize the existence of God, although without defining God or allowing governmental support for one religion over another.

After a variety of lawsuits and court rulings (often involving religions that define themselves, in part, by the absence of a god), schools became concerned. Most became ultra-sensitive about mentioning anything that someone might feel had religious overtones. That not only involved religions, but also the mere acknowledgment of the existence of God.

Outside of foundational federal documents, many states also recognize the existence of God. Here is what California says in the Preamble to its Constitution:

We, the People of the State of California, **grateful to Almighty God for our freedom,** *in order to secure and perpetuate its blessings, do establish this Constitution.* [Emphasis added.]

The constitutions of a number of other states contain similar language. But note that some now redefine such references differently than was originally intended. In that way, they can get around having to actually acknowledge God's existence.

Taking the U.S. Constitution in context with America's other two founding documents certainly suggests to many lay people that God *is assumed to exist*, even by the federal government. After all, God is mentioned in the original founding documents of the country as well as in some state constitutions today.

Congress itself often starts with a prayer. Prayer is still understood by most people as talking to God, although it seems that others can prefer to have a comparatively newer different understanding of that.

But, although the government itself should be able to accept that God exists, the government can't make a law regarding the establishment of religion nor prohibit the free exercise by adherents to them.

Two of the three American founding documents explicitly acknowledge the existence of God — the Declaration of Independence and the Articles of Confederation. The third document, the current Constitution, doesn't mention God by name, but strongly enshrines people's individual rights to believe in and worship God as they see fit. That is found in the First Amendment of the Bill of Rights. Some feel that it is a recognition of God in that it protects the multiple ways to believe in and worship God.

Some feel the Articles of Confederation should be fully disregarded since it was replaced by the current Constitution. However, even though they are no longer legally valid concerning the design and laws of the country. the Articles still provide insights to how the Founding Fathers looked at things — including their acknowledgement of the *existence* of God. Their understanding, also noted elsewhere, was not withdrawn by the Constitution.

Other than in the Bill of Rights, the Constitution takes no position either way as to the existence of God. That leaves the historical and foundational acknowledgement of the existence of God noted in the two earlier documents untouched. That also appears supported by some states.

Part of the context that led to the protection of religious belief in the First Amendment was the persecution of those practicing their religion in England and in much of Europe. People who adhered to religions that did not conform to what was required, acceptable, or at least tolerated by European governments, suffered.

The Founding Fathers of America noted that similar biases against specific religions had crept into the colonies. They moved to stop it and to protect belief in God as well as in the various manners of worshipping God at the time. Their intent was never to protect the absence of religion. It was to protect *actual* religion (traditionally defined). However, some people, seemingly also including many courts, have attempted to dispute and redefine that today.

Religious persecution in England and Europe encouraged many to emigrate to America. Therefore, in America, a belief in God was strongly protected, not unbelief. Non-belief of anything has never been in need of protection. People have always been free not to believe things just as Freedom of Speech does not require us to speak.

***

In the past, public schools were generally respectful of religion. Okay, not always. In the 19th century and beyond, many schools were certainly biased in favor of certain faiths. As we'll hear, that alienated some other religions.

However, well into the 20th century, schools did not exclude culturally-accepted recognitions of God, including Christmas carols and the like. Today, schools tiptoe around such things, often banning them entirely even when not legally required.

Nonetheless, correct understandings of most court rulings (even ignoring the founding documents statements) do not actually prohibit religious talk or activities, even appropriate prayer, so long as they are not actively instigated, promoted — and certainly not *required* — by public school administrators, teachers, and staff.

In the 19th Century, schools frequently included various religious manifestations, including readings from the King James Bible, as part of students' education. That was one reason for the expansion of Catholic schools at the time — to avoid being forced into a protestant-dominated religious program. As part of such school teachings, they sometimes had to listen to a demeaning of their own church's beliefs. Notably, this happened not only in the 19th century, but also beyond.

✱✱✱

Here's a story.

One day, a respected orthodox priest came to see me. I was the principal of the school at the time. He had children in the school and I had spoken to him before. He asked whether he could bless the school. He said the school had been blessed in the past and he asked whether he might be able to do it again. He suggested doing it on a Saturday, as I recall, when it wouldn't bother anyone.

No one mentioned this possibility when I was in principal school — okay, "principal schools" might not actually exist in states. Nonetheless, I saw no reason to say no. After all, I was going to be at school that day anyway. Although not the only religion represented in the area around the school, that particular orthodox church was a respected part of the community.

There was a nice evangelical minister nearby who had been positively involved with some of our students off-campus after school. Had he asked me to bless the school at a time when students and staff would not be impacted, I would have also said yes. The government certainly wasn't forcing anything on students or anyone. In fact, not prohibiting it at a time when no one was impacted appeared to be in full accord with the First Amendment — or so I would think. I'm not sure students (or anyone else) ever knew about it.

After all, if a tree falls in a forest, but no one hears it, did it really fall?[1]

Okay, you win. It probably did.

Regardless, if I had excluded the other minister, that would have appeared to support one legitimate religion over another. That would not have been right. So, as long as it did not disrupt the school — and it didn't — I saw no reason to deny it. It was not a burden on me. My sense was that both the priest and the other locally-involved minister would have supported each other in this anyway.

No one else had ever asked me to bless any school at which I had worked, although I know that it also happens elsewhere.

I accompanied the priest as he blessed each classroom as well as the common area. His blessings were simple and, as blessings go, seemed appropriate.

Although it was not a secret, as far as I know and as I have already mentioned, no one other than the orthodox priest even knew the school had been blessed. The priest was not doing it to make a statement to anyone. He was doing it solely to ask God to bless the school and all within it.

Blessings are widely considered to involve God — even if someone sneezes. People can certainly "bless" something on their own but, without the involvement of God, what does that really accomplish?

One of my good and valued friends — another teacher — was a staunch member of the Freedom From Religion Foundation, a major non-god-believing group. We disagreed on a number of things, but we were friends. He has since died, but I will always be grateful that we were friends.

At one time in this country, people could have significant differences of opinion on almost anything — and still be friends. Newer generations no longer remember, or even know about those times. They need to learn how to be *real* friends even with those with whom they might otherwise have religious, political, or sociological differences.

***

In some small, isolated communities, away from the attentions of non-religion-as-a-religion religions, prayer continues to take place at both official and unofficial school functions. It isn't instigated by school staff, just by the community or by community leaders. Most schools today err on the side of banning anything that might be construed as prayer, lest someone complain — or sue. At remote schools, they don't have much concern about that.

For example, in native communities some elders might be asked to say some *"wise words"* before an event. The speakers of such "wise words" do not launch into a tirade of biblical quotes or invocations of evangelical-specific phrasings (their beliefs are often different anyway). Nonetheless, the reference to a deity is often clear.

Since those words, and the right to use "wise words" by such village elders, are culturally accepted and supported, there are never issues. Remember that it is primarily public school administrators, teachers, and staff who must be careful in direct involvement in such things.

However, even things such as "wise words" might not be permitted elsewhere, or at least they would be closely monitored by people unsure of what someone is *really* doing. Attempts to enforce the increasing dominance of religions that do not believe in God, holding the *non*-existence of God as a core belief, often come from people not even in the community — or state — at all. Such groups might use one or more token individuals as their reason for seemingly trying to put a stop to the mere acknowledgment of the existence of an actual god.

Of course, I'm only passing on my own lay observations here. I'm no lawyer. Debates like this never seem to end. Consult your own constitutional attorney about all this.

There are, of course, beliefs that are widely shared by almost all (traditional) religions. They generally include a basic acknowledgment of the existence of God and an understanding that talking to God (prayer) is not just possible, but is a good thing to do.

Minimally, I think that the country really should clarify its general long-term acknowledgment of the *existence* of God. After all, the existence of God moved to the original colonies hand-in-hand with the country's founding colonists. That acknowledgment is enshrined many national and state documents.

One amendment that I believe needs to be considered for addition to the U.S. Constitution, in further support of America's founding documents, might state something like:

"The existence of God, as traditionally understood at the country's founding, is acknowledged. Although the right to disagree with this acknowledgment is also acknowledged, the right to disagree shall not supersede the right of both internal and external belief in this statement of God's existence."

Okay, it needs a bit of work.

Such an amendment wouldn't mean that people could go around in mixed public settings intrusively praying or proselytizing to other people whether others objected or not. As with other rights, there are, and should be, limitations. After all, you're really not supposed to yell "Fire!" in a crowded theater, as is commonly considered to be an exception to free speech — even though there are many other examples that are actually more legitimate.

There are limits on the rights to peaceably assemble, on religious practice, to petition the government for a redress of grievances, to purchase and use firearms, etc.

However, at the time of this writing, *every* right in the Bill of Rights is under attack. The government itself has been ignoring many rights and protections in the Bill of Rights. That same thing has occasionally happened throughout the history of the country.

Abraham Lincoln was known to have ignored certain enumerated rights, although being president during the Civil War was an unusual situation. However, if things proceed as they are going, the situation today could become one of the most dangerous the country has seen. When we compare the governmental abuses today with those of totalitarian countries, we would be wise to be scared.

Therefore, education may not be the most serious problem facing the country today. However, public education can be involved in supporting, changing, or perpetuating the country's serious problems. It can make such problems worse — or it can make them better.

***

The pendulum has been swinging too far today regarding public acknowledgment of what is sometimes the mere existence of God, as well as of religions themselves. That pendulum needs to be steadied again.

Many public school teachers of world history either bypass or give short shrift to parts of textbooks discussing or comparing various world religions — or they assign readings that are then never discussed in class. After all, adherents to one of the religions discussed might — often with good reason — take issue with a particular portrayal or description of their church in some history books.

Nonetheless, good teachers press forward to discuss the importance of religion in world history as well as providing at least an overview of each of the major world religions. Some have found that risky. But others know that, if they don't talk about world religions, their students will go into the world clueless about them.

In the end today, many students are clueless anyway, or so minimally acquainted with world religions as to effectively be clueless. That's not education.

Then there is the textbook problem (which I think I mentioned earlier) where some textbook authors build in their own religious biases. They might portray the origins or teachings of one or more religions incorrectly. That could be because they have some animus about a religion or because their personal religion disagrees with certain churches. It could also be that the authors never got accurate information about histories of various religions and churches themselves.

Am I suggesting a stronger place for God in public schools? I'm actually only suggesting the elimination of the paranoia of the mere mention of anything dealing with God or religion. I'm suggesting doing away with the near-total divorce in many places of all things God. Doing that isn't even required.

***

Most teachers and administrators are justly proud of their K-12 students who have worked hard and earned a high grade point average. They are proud of those who have won recognitions, who are accepted into colleges, who complete college level courses while still in high school, or who are just really serious students with accomplishments even beyond the expectations of the school. Lots to be proud of! Of course!

But when I finished my work as principal of a small school, I left with special pride in two things:

> *(1) No student dropped out of school while I was principal; and*
> *(2) No student committed suicide.*

Not quite what most principals put on their list, is it? Yet there were specific and multiple students at risk for each of those things. I was told that two students had killed themselves near the end of the year before I arrived. Sadly, that is too common today.

That neither of those things happened while I was there was not by chance. It was directly due to the hard work, concern, and involvement of myself and my staff. These were serious concerns to me and I took students at risk of these things very seriously.

Might the success in those two areas have been because the school had been blessed early in the school year? I don't know. But I certainly don't think it hurt anyone that God had been asked to watch over the school and all those within it.

33. THE LIST

An experienced educator reviewing an early draft of this book, sent me a list with his own criteria which he suggested demonstrates the hopelessness of education. For clarity and acceptability, I have made some slight revisions and clarifications to some of his points. Were time and space available, some could be expanded into their own chapters, even their own books. Others stand alone.

This educator has thirty years of broad experience as a teacher. He has taught multiple subjects and has had professional interactions at dozens of schools, including elementary, middle school, high school, and colleges across four states and in two countries.[1]

Here is The List. I have added my comments after each point he makes.

(1) *Education has failed to produce a critical percentage of educated students.*

My Comments: This statement leads us to ask what a "critical percentage" might be. Is it even important to have a critical percentage? How would this educator — or anyone — define an "educated student?" (We considered that earlier in the book.) Assuming it is a true statement — and we can certainly believe that it is — it would be a continuing indictment of the current education system.

(2) *The experiment of mass education has failed and should be abandoned.*

My Comments: Note that "mass education" simply refers to educating large numbers of people at a time, in a classroom or school, for example. This is an interesting observation. Almost all people today assume that schools in their current form have been around forever (figuratively speaking). That isn't true. The current one-size-fits-all structure doesn't actually fit all. It fails countless students. However, in spite of the deficiencies of the current system, the question naturally arises: What would be the alternative? At this moment, we don't have one.

(3) *America cannot afford the financial costs of maintaining the current system or of more failed efforts as we try to fix it.*

My Comments: Whatever the cost, local or state legislatures just raise more taxes, even though it rarely proves to be enough. Those with an agenda attempt to convince voters to pass propositions or other laws as they are permitted to do. Although we can't afford it — and even though it hasn't worked and likely won't work — America continues to throw more money at the problem. People should ask who is profiting from this. I'm not saying that money isn't important. We will always need money in order to have a successful system — whatever that system is. Effective education isn't cheap.

But money is not the answer to fix the current system. Money has been poured into public education for many years with little or no substantive improvement.

In the coming section, I will have a bit more to say about that.

(4) *Restrictions and accommodations imposed by liberals have made it impossible to teach an honest curriculum.*

My Comments: Note that this educator is not a conservative. He is neither a Republican nor a Democrat. Although this is clearly an observation of politics affecting education, he is not taking the position of a political party in his observation here. He is stating a separate fact, as he sees it. Nonetheless, his concern is currently linked to progressive Democrats.

(5) *Bullies are supported by some administrators. Bullies continue to oppress the majority of children having a detrimental effect on learning.*

My Comments: Recall the earlier section discussing bullying. His statement is misleading. In many cases, administrators do try to suppress bullies. But they are fighting legislative and judicial pronouncements which can sometimes tie their hands. They also fight denials by parents that their "innocent" children could be responsible for bullying along with threats and verbal attacks on educators themselves by some parents of these bullies. I have personally fought this battle. One would think that handling this should be straightforward. Sometimes it is, but nothing is easy. The success of stopping even blatant bullying relies on support from parents, the community, the school district, and the state, as well as any what can be conflicting legislation, also sometimes complicated by court rulings or consent decrees. Yet if serious bullying isn't effectively suppressed, that can open all involved to lawsuits for "ignoring" or supporting the bullies. When bullying can be handled by imposing strong consequences for the bullying, it can be suppressed. But that can't always happen. Is something wrong with this picture? Absolutely yes.

(6) *Some educators don't care about educating children as much as they do about conformity, socialization, and submission to authority in order to make their lives easier.*

My Comments: There is just so much time and stress that even the most patient educator can handle. Working with large groups of children requires that they be under control or everything falls apart. However, in some challenging schools, too many educators are operating on the edge and can move to survival mode. Educators who might appear not to care about educating children have often been beaten down by the system or by a lack of support. Beyond that, my experience is that the vast majority of educators, both teachers and administrators, absolutely do care about the education of their students. Those who don't should be replaced — if allowed by the unions.

(7) *Teachers are usually not qualified to teach. Many are not adequately educated themselves. As such, they cannot serve as role models. Often, they are not creatively flexible. Separately, teachers and administrators are often limited in their ability to exclude or expel chronically disruptive students. In general, teachers are not educated people. They are not "life-long learners." For example, they think that by simply applying teaching "strategies," their students will learn. But many students don't.*

My Comments: When this educator says that teachers "are not educated," he means educated *enough* to be effective teaching students. I do not take a position as extreme as this. However, it's true that many teachers are not as prepared as teachers have been in the past in order to be properly effective in the classroom. (Remember the teacher who didn't know what an atomic bomb was earlier in the book?) If this is true, how could it have happened? Certainly, teachers and administrators today wouldn't think this.

The *only* way this could happen is because the classes and education these educators received weren't good enough. Classes to train teachers how to teach and administrators how to be an administrator would have had to have been broken themselves. Students in those classes can't necessarily know what's missing or whether the material is effective or not. After finishing teacher training programs, teachers assume they were taught what they need to be a good teacher. As mentioned earlier in the book, too many of those classes can be a waste of time.

Poorly prepared teachers — both subject matter and as educators — turn out poorly educated students. Some of those students then grow up to be teachers themselves — after also going through potentially broken teacher (or administrator) training. They then do the same to their students. It's a never-ending cycle. (Truly) educated teachers can create educated students.

I'm absolutely not saying that most educators are poorly educated, whether subject matter or in teaching methodology. But, as possible, the overall competency of the profession needs to improve. (That doesn't necessarily mean taking even more classes.) Sometimes, this has nothing to do with the educators themselves. They, too, are the product of a broken system.

In some schools and colleges, teachers/professors can effectively be given subtle or strong "suggestions" to pass failing students, or to give high grades to low performing students. Both these things happen too often. Sometimes teachers sense their jobs might be on the line. Their untrained and unprepared students then go on into life to become whatever they want — including teachers.

I believe that most teachers really are qualified in the subject area they are hired to teach. However, as pointed out elsewhere, subject matter knowledge and the ability to teach the subject are two different things. Teacher training programs often fail at developing teachers who don't have what it takes to teach in the first place because most teacher training programs are not necessarily designed to do that. There are some qualities in the best teachers that cannot simply be "taught."

(8) *Separate from special education considerations, for various reasons, some students have extreme difficulty functioning for any learning.*

My Comments: Of course, that can be true. However, special schools, programs, and teachers either exist or can be put together to support and teach such students. But, even though such resources *can* be put together, many times they are not. Too many of our children still have unmet needs to support their success in education. Unfortunately, many of those thinking they're providing adequate supporting for them, often aren't. This is not necessarily the fault of individual educators or local schools — although it can be.

. . .

(9) *True education is self-taught. Therefore, mass education isn't needed, just adequate resources.*

My Comments: I disagree with both suggestions in the above statement. However, this might bring to mind the philosophy that was promoted by Carl Rogers (1902-1987), a humanistic psychologist. He has been correctly called, *"one of the most influential psychologists of the 20th century."* Even today, Rogers' writings are influential and compelling.[2] Although some of his work was not always practical to implement in the classroom, I believe that a great deal of his educational philosophies still have merit.

(10) *Many administrators do not seem qualified to administer schools and to support their teachers. Nor do some even appear capable to support and encourage students.*

My Comments: As in all occupations, there are good and bad people. Some administrators are truly competent and caring. Others shouldn't be administrators anymore than some bad teachers shouldn't be teaching. It's can be hard for district administrators to weed out bad school level administrators because district superintendents aren't there to oversee school administrators on a daily basis. It's sometimes hard to know what's actually happening.

On the other hand, some teachers have an axe to grind even with good administrators who set standards to which those teachers object. Other times, good administrators might repeatedly ignore legitimate classroom concerns about some teachers. In some cases, such teachers might unfairly complain to their union or the district. Judging such situations is tough, even if an administrator should actually be replaced. Bad administrators can promote a difficult and stressful school environment for everyone: teachers, staff, and students. Good and caring administrators do just the opposite. But where there is a legitimate problem with an administrator, it's often a serious one.

(11) *School board members are elected by the community. Many school board members not only know little about education and the workings of*

the school or district they oversee, they can also bring an attitude with them that is not supportive of a positive school environment, even at schools that are functioning well.

My Comments: School board members overseeing education can be very effective if they first personally and open-mindedly learn how things are working at the schools and in education, generally. They should get a feel for the difficulties and stresses that educators can be under. They should observe and talk to students to see what is happening with them, too. Rather than making things worse with constant criticism, they can then discuss actual ways to help schools and to make things better. Sadly, some school boards are not there to support the schools, but rather to act on complaints by anyone, including students. Others got on boards to promote their personal agendas that may have little to do with good education.

Too often, board members might listen to complainers, not even hearing and understanding both sides of complaints. That puts educators' jobs at risk since those not protected by tenure can be easily fired even without a chance to defend themselves. Except as relates to district superintendents who are generally hired by school boards, school boards themselves generally don't do any firing. But they can insist on firing or at least strongly recommend it even without, as mentioned, giving an educator a fair hearing.

Recently, as many of us have seen, some school boards don't listen or won't take seriously concerned parents who correctly complain about serious issues at some schools.

In difficult budget environments, when cuts must be made, boards can insist on keeping classes they personally want their children to take, while putting far more critical classes on the chopping block that affect many more students. They should represent the broader community, not just their personal children.

Nonetheless, the concept of school board oversight is important. It allows communities to have some way to try to improve schools, if the boards aren't actually making things worse. They are a backstop when districts and schools aren't educating students.

I have seen school boards correctly question what is happening in schools (earlier, I had noted U.S. Government classes that a school board member brought up), but then be given confusing or non-answers by a superintendent or others.

In many cases, school board members should make themselves more competent not just in what is happening in the schools, but what *should be* happening in schools. They should get at least some minimal training in how schools and education operate.

Classes run by outside agencies can help new board members get up to speed and be more effective. Often, however, such training can also be helpful by bringing in a totally outside perspective on schools and education.

When I have worked with school boards, I took everything they did and said seriously. Sometimes, they had good suggestions. Additionally, it's important for communities to feel they're part of their schools. After all, local schools are *their* schools. Really, though, schools belong to us all. School boards are a direct connection with the community, or they should be.

On occasion, I had to tell them that we couldn't implement some good suggestion they had made due to restrictions from outside legislative, judicial, or district mandates. That can be frustrating for everyone, even for administrators. But it does make board members more knowledgeable about handling some issues in education.

(12) *New immigrant arrivals, often undocumented, can overwhelm schools and resources. Because so much special instruction and support is needed for these new arrivals, often including English language instruction, instruction for those who are already in the pipeline can be seriously damaged.*

My Comments: New immigrants are "mainstreamed" with other students too soon. Depending on how new they are in the country, if they don't speak English or are very weak in it, they immediately need ESL (English-as-a-Second-Language) classes. Those classes should not just focus on language learning. They should also be taught culture, how to interact respectfully with teachers and schools, and what are expected behaviors.

Beyond that, separate classes should be available so that *their parents* can get similar help and support — including ESL classes for them, too. (Previously, I mentioned that I also taught ESL to parents in evening classes.) People new to the country should be given a good start, not just be left on their own to struggle along. That is a sure recipe for problems with many young people. We see that too often.

Support for new immigrant arrivals is often missing. Many times, it's considered someone else's job. That just begs for future problems. One concern with this extra support is money. Additional teachers and resources are needed for all of this. There often simply aren't enough resources without gutting the main education program, even if schools actually want to substantially beef up such support. However, the main education program itself must be made and kept healthy. It's already far weaker than it should be. As mentioned repeatedly, I believe it is very unlikely that we can do this.

Some things in better support of newly arrived immigrants have been tried in the past but were stopped for one reason or another — often for lack of money and resources, including a lack of qualified teachers. But schools and communities should not give up. Support for immigrants is very important. We ask for trouble if we can't provide it.

(13) *Parents without an understanding of their schools, budgeting, or the challenges of education are often given "too much power."*

My Comments: I feel strongly that parents should always be an important part of the education system. However, parents must be open to communication with educators so that each listens to the other. Parents must learn about the problems that exist at schools. In some cases, they might see some of those problems, or the results of those problems, and just become upset with the school without taking the time to learn about the full situation.

Educators themselves are often frustrated with situations that lead to some of these problems, but they have no ability to make changes. They have to function under legislation, court consent decrees, district policies, and state and federal regulations. (I've said all that before.) Some of these issues truly do tie the hands of educators.

Often, parents can get upset with the wrong people. Not always, of course. Some schools and educators can be just plain wrong. On the other hand, as I have said before, none of us are perfect. We need to be patient with each other.

However, parents can also become out-of-control, viciously berating teachers and administrators as they wrongly try to defend their own out-of-control children. Parents must learn that unreasonably defending terrible behavior in their children does not strengthen the character of their children as they gain maturity and grow into adults. It can do the opposite.

One time, when I was the principal, several high school students went on a field trip out of town. I remained at the school. I told the students that I would not tolerate any bad behavior and, especially, any disobedience to the rules and directives of the chaperones with them.

One time late at night, and in full violation of the clearly stated rules, a girl snuck into a hotel room with several boys. (The group was staying at the same hotel.) Most adults know what kind of bad things can happen in situations like that. The chaperones had been crystal clear that there be no mixing of boys and girls at night. There were actually two violations by the same girl, one was after she had already been caught the first time.

When the group returned to school, I immediately assigned appropriate consequences for that behavior. She was generally a good student at school, but she knew that I was not happy with her flagrant violations of what the chaperones had told her multiple times.

The teachers knew her parent would be upset with my consequences for her child — and she was. She came and threatened me with all sorts of things for disciplining her daughter. If the parent wanted to take it up with the district superintendent, so be it. But I refused to undermine my authority, the authority of the chaperones, and set what would be a terrible example to other students who would know they, too, could simply ignore what they were told when away on field trips. I stood my ground.

Teachers later told me they were surprised — and pleased — that I had done that. They said past principals had capitulated to that parent (and others) removing legitimate consequences that had initially been given to students for their bad behavior.

That is not the only time I had to stand firm in the face of parents trying to force the school to accept their children's bad behaviors. Refusing to remove consequences for bad behavior not only sets an example for that student and others, it also supports teachers. When parents win, students then think they can do whatever they want and that their teachers have no real authority over them. They assume their parent will just come in and get us to let them off the hook.

Setting firm, fair consequences for unacceptable behavior is a positive thing all around — except for parents trying to justify such behaviors. Fortunately, not all parents are like that. Many not only support consequences from the school, but will add on their own at home.

Why do administrators and educators have to put up with parents who are not just unsupportive, but who fight to undermine schools with regard to student behavior and other things? We should all be working together!

Parents who work together with schools for the betterment of their children are gold to us. There is give and take, flexibility, and creativity in handling situations with their children because they understand that their children must develop their character so that they will be respectful and respected as adults. Their children will be parents someday.

Character and development of moral standards will not be developed in our future adults unless behavior parameters are set and enforced. Schools don't need parents working against them when our real concern is that our students become even better people as they struggle to grow through what are often some difficult times.

Parents are very important. It is good that they are involved with schools. Schools might consider setting up an evening class or two for parents to help them understand what's happening and how to better interact with the school and its staff. Such classes can guide parents in how to maturely participate with the school. Schools can always be better. But so can parents. Both should learn to work respectfully together.

(14) *Politics has changed the curriculum so that students are no longer part of a national identity or even, in the case of new immigrants, the importance of English as the common language.*

My Comments: This is completely true, but it's fixable — at least it was in the past. I bemoaned the loss of respect and caring for the country — of patriotism itself — in the preface to this book. Failure to build a national identity weakens the entire country. It cuts a vital connection between all who live here. Respect for the freedoms and opportunities this country offers is why most immigrants come here in the first place.

(15) *Change has been tried, but has always failed.*

My Comments: This is absolutely true; many educators agree. We can't merely try to implement changes anymore. They have indeed failed. We have to completely start over, but that is not likely to happen.

Are the issues brought up in this list enough to designate public education to be dead? After all, there may be solutions for most, though not all, of the things on this one educator's list. In conjunction with other observations, including noting the results of the failed system elsewhere, it may indeed be enough.

A FEW MORE WORDS ABOUT MONEY

Before starting *Part Two: Can Anything Be Done?*, let me take a quick moment to consider the issue of money a bit more.

Unions and others make the case that, if we pay teachers more money, we would be able to get and retain higher quality teachers. While sometimes true, it is not true enough to believe that education itself would be greatly improved.

I'm not suggesting that teachers don't need to be paid more. Some districts pay terrible wages. I recommend those educators move to some other district or state that pays better. Even then, with rare exceptions, educators generally aren't paid enough. They should be. In other places, especially where there is a serious shortage of certain educators, or in areas some consider to be less desirable for living, teachers' salaries can be very good. Throughout the country, salaries vary widely.

But, again, the question is whether higher salaries will fix public education today.

In general, they won't.

Is there a way money could actually help education? Sure there is. We could more than quadruple the money given to public schools. After giving some more to teachers and staff, that money could be used to buy more land and then double or triple the number of classrooms. That newly-picked money from local trees would allow the hiring of more teachers and staff for those many new classrooms.

How would that improve things?

Class sizes would be substantially reduced, hopefully cut in half or more. Schools sometimes flaunt having reduced average class sizes by just three, four or five students. But that's far from enough.

Class sizes need to be significantly smaller to allow (good) teachers to more effectively help and encourage struggling students. In some cases, "struggling students" comprise most of the class — and they really do need extra help and encouragement.

On the other end of things, it would allow high performing students to move along even more quickly.

Bad behavior among students is a fact of life in far too many schools. Smaller class sizes can also help to get out-of-control students under better control. Sometimes.

Massive additional money might also allow hiring some family or community liaison staff. If they're competent and motivated, such staff can provide support for the students in the community including personal visits to homes of students.

They can talk with parents. They can also see if they can provide direct help and encouragement for students. They might be able to arrange for, or perhaps personally provide tutoring. They can discover family or other issues impacting students and offer resources to help the family, if the family is open to it.

In communities where English is not the primary language, school-home liaisons can speak the language of the families and also understand their differing cultures. They can then report back to teachers to see if classroom adjustments can be made to support learning. Sometimes adjustments can be made. Others times they can't be.

All this is massively expensive. A budget to *minimally* double classrooms, add an equal number of teachers and staff — which may not be possible to find — and then add a large number of family or community liaison personnel, as well as security officers is a massive cost.

Would we have and be willing to spend the massive amounts of money needed to see these and other things happen at countless American schools today?

We would not. This is all pie-in-the-sky talk.

Such money would likely have to come from significantly increased taxes — or perhaps by planting more money trees.

Why, one might ask, do we need all that massive additional support in the first place? If one looks at other countries, *including China,* one can find (K-12) class sizes *far* larger than classes in America. Yet their academic results far exceed public education in America. Why is that?

One reason is that parents in China and elsewhere aggressively ensure their children study and succeed in school. The culture at schools is such that those not doing well are less respected. Even in lower grades, students are driven to succeed so they can get into better schools at the next level. Peer pressure is for academic success. In America, peer pressure can do the opposite.

It's also attitude. It's an attitude that education is important.

There is a far lower incidence of bad behavior in classes in China. Students work hard to succeed. Once home, they work hard again — studying. Therefore, when teachers teach, students learn. Indeed, parents themselves learn so that they can provide even better support for their children.

Even before they get home, Chinese children might take even more classes *after* school instead of just "hanging out." They might take classes in art or perhaps learn to play an instrument. Most don't consider that to be a negative or burdensome experience at all. Many consider learning to be challenging and enjoyable.

All of that simply isn't happening in most of America. Too many parents do not prioritize their children's learning and success at school. Too many parents don't set strong academic and behavioral expectations for their children, both in and out of school.

Some parents didn't do well in school themselves — or dropped out, as I did. But that hasn't stopped good parents from ensuring that their children succeed. There are countless examples of this, even as mentioned elsewhere in this book.

China is put forth as just one example here. But it's a particularly important one since America is increasingly being left behind today. (Of course, there are some definite disadvantages to education in China, too.)

In general, too many parents, legislators, educators, and courts really don't support an environment of educational success for our children. That is greatly frustrating for devoted educators. We have all seen the results of this for many decades now.

Once again, I'll mention that even students who purportedly do well in schools and colleges often have a lower level of education than they should have, although they and their parents might confidently believe otherwise. They are often successful only by way of comparison — or as determined using the false standard of success-by-good-grades.

Money by itself will not fix public education even if we had a lot more. Much more than that is needed.

Once again, let's move on.

PART TWO: CAN ANYTHING BE DONE?

35. COMMUNITY SCHOOLS

You'll never guess what the title of this chapter actually means. Let's find out.

Are there things we can consider so that we can take a fresh look at schooling? At this point, we don't have enough viable options to let us make a new start. Our hands are pretty much tied to allow us to undertake the total change that is needed. More importantly, we haven't yet decided how to select effective people to put such things together.

Most of the people likely to be chosen are current educational "professionals." By necessity, they are extensively educated and experienced *in the current system.* That makes it very difficult for them to do anything except to set up pretty much the exact same failed system again.

Nonetheless, people with educational experience would be needed. There are good people out there who would love to give it a try. But, as I've repeatedly said, we'll hit roadblocks setting up anything within current legislation, that takes into account court dictates as well as the universities, teacher unions, administrators, and parents.

Pretty much everyone would come on board to argue for continuing the current failed system. Therefore, I don't see a realistic opportunity for people to build a new system. Anything done would be almost entirely based on what isn't working now.

Nonetheless, this chapter will give you some food for thought. It might let you start thinking differently. I'm not telling you that any of the two things mentioned in this chapter would work at all. They likely won't, even if funding were available. Perhaps problems can be addressed and overcome. Perhaps not.

Regardless, what is here does not address the much larger number of students in public schools today. Chapters beyond this one take a brief look at a few other options for learning in traditional public schools. But none will be adequate to replace today's public school system.

One thing I strongly feel about — I've mentioned it before — is that we need to completely overhaul teacher-training and certification. Although there are some good teacher-training schools, most are effectively in business to make money and to keep their staff employed. The more classes someone has to take, the more money they make — or so some say. Other times, governmental or other mandates increase the number or length of teacher training classes.

Money isn't always the reason it happens, but I have to ask myself, why do so many would-be teachers take classes that have little or nothing to do with actual classroom teaching? Why do what should be worthwhile classes fail prospective teachers? Can we condense classes into just a few? Can we do a better job following and actually helping new teachers as they get started?

The mentality still exists that more schooling means better teachers. Even though some classes might be helpful, that's not necessarily the case. It seems to make sense, but we really don't need quantity. We need efficiency in instruction and passionate college professors to deliver that instruction.

We need to do a better job *selecting* those who will eventually be classroom teachers. We need to help and encourage those who seem to be born teachers to get into the field.

I've said all this before.

We certainly want teachers to know their primary subject. That's fundamental. But subject matter knowledge alone doesn't make good teachers. Real teachers need more than that inside of them.

Creating *well-educated teachers*, doesn't necessarily lead to well-educated *students*. The most effective teachers need qualities that are not easily measurable. We'll have to figure that out or we won't have the teachers that K-12 students need.

There are plenty of schools and districts that assign mentors to new teachers to help them as they get going but, too often, it's not of enough real help. Many times, mentors are themselves too busy and, even though they might be good teachers and good people, they can be totally useless for what some new teachers need.

All teacher-training programs generally have one or more required student-teaching assignments. A prospective teacher's teacher then comes out and observes that inexperienced teacher maybe two or three times a semester. Too often, that's only so that a course grade can be given. It doesn't necessarily provide enough substantive help to the teacher-in-training.

Teacher training programs should be much shorter, more intense, and experienced teachers should spend some actual time with brand new teachers as they actually teach — not just visiting briefly for an evaluation. The whole teacher selection and training process needs an overhaul.

Let's look at some non-traditional ways to deliver education to students. When I tell someone that we should put *everything* on the table, most don't really understand that I mean *everything*.

For example, do we actually need students to go to a school building? I'll quickly add that I am NOT talking about distance learning via computer. Even though there are schools that have been successful doing that, I'm not talking about that here.

Students might live in the wilderness or are otherwise many miles from an actual school. There may be a legitimate reason why students can't make it to a physical school building. Online programs to teach such students have been in place in parts of the country for many years now. They have been far more successful than the seat-of-the-pants "distance learning" teaching that schools undertook during the COVID crisis when most educators didn't know what they were doing.

A remote teaching aside: Should we really blame K-12 teachers because they're not good at teaching online? We should not. It may surprise you, but just as are other adults, some teachers really are tech phobic, or at least just minimally competent. When they became teachers, few thought they were going to have to teach remotely online, nor do most teacher training schools provide any training at all for online teaching — although they might do that going forward.

None of that takes into account what are almost always basic weaknesses in online classes, especially for younger students. Many college teachers and students have some experience teaching or taking online classes, but it's not always applicable to younger K-12 students.

So, even though people think that K-12 teachers should be able to handle teaching online, many of them really can't. Even if they learn how, many won't be good at it. That's because they really don't like doing it in the first place.

It's the same with you or anyone else. If you really don't like to do something, you won't be good at it either. And that assumes you know how to do it in the first place.

Teachers aren't super people who can do everything. Many are very good at a number of things but, like any of us, those same teachers can be very bad at other things.

It's really a bit unfair to have expected teachers to be able to handle online teaching when they were just thrown into it. Just as their students were forced into it, so were the teachers. It wasn't what teachers thought they signed up for when they became teachers in the first place.

Although none of this is intended to excuse the failed system of public education, maybe a bit of human understanding might also be called for here.

This isn't to say that teachers are necessarily blameless for the disaster that much of the online COVID-era teaching became. But, neither should they be fully blamed. There is plenty of background blame to go around throughout the public education system.

However, responsibility should fall on teachers for what they were teaching. Many parents were justifiably unhappy, even angry, by what they saw being taught (or not taught) and how it was being done. That's one reason so many pulled their children out of public schools.

Even though there are educational weaknesses in almost all educational alternatives, many parents will never return their children to public schools again.

All sides learned — or should have learned — from the remote educational mess so many had to endure during the COVID pandemic.

One important thing that should have been learned was that children should not have been kept out of school anywhere near as long as they were, especially with such a grossly inadequate remote learning setup.

Later statistics showed that parental fears of their children becoming sick and dying of COVID were not adequately substantiated. The data did not justify the lasting educational, emotional, and social damage done to their children.

Unlike most public schools, after just a very short time out of school, other schools were able to successfully bring their students back into the classroom where life and learning could continue. Some schools never sent their students home at all for more than a few days or so.

COVID was not the Spanish Flu, which had been far more deadly. However, no one knew that when COVID began. Perhaps some of the things done during COVID might be justified during the next — and possibly more deadly — pandemic. Or perhaps the things during COVID wouldn't be helpful then, either.

Let's now return to the consideration of keeping everything on the table in any attempt to redesign education.

If we are actually to consider the current system from the bottom up, we should probably start with the physical school itself. Is a physical school really necessary for teaching our K-12 students? That seems like a pretty basic requirement, doesn't it? (I personally believe that it is.)

Let me give you an example that would have just a small chance — the remotest chance — of working even in very small public schools. Regardless, perhaps this can shake up and expand your traditional thinking about schools.

If classes had maybe just ten or less students, would it be possible to rotate through student homes each day? Teachers would bring the resources from a central location. Educational support personnel at the school can shuttle things out and back if something is needed, even things like printers or forgotten books. But the classes would be held in the living rooms of willing, volunteer parents.

This might be a backup design if a school were to burn down, for example, with no other facilities available. It would be less likely to work in place of a standard physical school itself.

From where would the funds and personnel for all this come, especially for the need of increased staffing? Likely, they wouldn't. After all, a regularly-sized class would have to be split into smaller groups of students. That would require many additional educators.

In small communities, many children have already been in their friends homes so there's likely already a degree of comfort in each setting. The next day, likely the next week, students would rotate to another home. Not all homes would work for this, of course. In the end, it's not likely that any of this might be workable for the long term, but creative options are out there.

Some parents would enjoy taking an active role supporting the teaching in their front room. They could see what's being taught and would likely help out. Involving parents in classes can increase their interest and involvement with their child's learning at home.

Another advantage is that students learn to put their knowledge, skills, and thinking in a place in the real world. Sometimes work in a classroom feels like it should stay in the classroom without real world applicability. But working and rotating through homes of students, or in rotating community locations, has a distinctively different feel. They can even get accustomed to working in an environment when, after going home from a "regular" school, they might otherwise just watch TV or play around on their computer. This might set a different tone for what education can be.

What am I actually saying? No actual school building or student classrooms?

Of course, there would have to be some school facilities. They would be needed for school administration and material support. They would be needed for special classes, such as science labs for science classes. School sports facilities are critical for multiple reasons. But some or all classes themselves could be held in the community, in willing students' parents homes.

Of course, there would be reasons that this won't work. But it's possible that problems might be worked out as they are worked out in a "real" school. Surely we'd run into legislative and legal restrictions. As I've said, multiple times, we can't do any ground up educational redesigns without making significant legislative and court ruling changes. Today, that's impossible. But it's important to wrap your creativity around the true educational rebuilding of what isn't working now.

Do I think we can get rid of school buildings using such a scenario? Actually, I think we would end up having to use physical classrooms as we do now. As an old-fashioned teacher, I like traditional classrooms. But I'm fully open to considering other options. You can also see different options among some charter schools.

I bring these things up so that you can understand that I actually do propose reconsidering education from the ground up. It's very doubtful that you or anyone had thought that I meant to consider actually eliminating physical classrooms and perhaps redesigning traditional school facilities.

Really, I'm not sure this would necessarily work. But, in certain communities, it might.

However, the meat of education itself isn't addressed here and *that's* what we actually need to rebuild.

***

No doubt you're now thinking, *"Ah! That's what the title of this chapter means!"* Community schools!

But no, that's not what it means.

So now I'll talk about Community Schools. Keep your skepticism in check for a few more moments and think a bit differently. Once again, this deals with the location of school instruction, not with the far more important issue of the instruction itself.

It would be highly unlikely that this next scenario might come about on a widespread basis. In addition, getting the absolutely special staff needed for this coming scenario wouldn't be easy. Well, perhaps it might be. But there can be actual danger for some staff in this scenario.

On the other hand, if it worked, it could bring education to students who need special attention, students who have dropped out, students heading in a wrong direction, students living a lost life.

What I suggest next has actually been done at a very limited and personal level by daring K-12 teachers over past decades and beyond who love their students so much that, working on their own, they meet their students anywhere, anytime, in order to help and educate them. They will show up at their homes — or anywhere. I've seen them do that.

Special teachers will find their students in places their students shouldn't be. They can try to bring them away from bad, even dangerous people and places. They can save our young people. Movies are made of such teachers. I personally know one. But I'm talking about something well beyond what a single teacher can do.

Even though their physical safety can be at risk, there are plenty of jobs where people willingly choose to put others first, putting their own lives on the line. Police, firefighters, those in the military, and many others are examples.

Here, we would be turning people into schools. Am I misspeaking?

No, that's exactly what would happen in this scenario. We would need many, many volunteers for this and, as usual, there wouldn't be enough money for all those who would be needed. Nonetheless, let's consider it for a moment anyway.

Each specially selected teacher would have to be fully capable of teaching in a self-contained classroom (meaning to be able to teach effectively *all* subjects to their class of students) — although they wouldn't necessarily be in a classroom. These teachers are the resource, not their books, not their materials, not anything else, although we would still want them to have access to those things when they're needed.

***

Let's see if I can paint a picture of these people in action. They are not simply teachers. They're *self-contained schools.* These schools are made up of a single person — with their students.

Because they're actually *schools,* they'll need to *find* students. *They* have to find them. If they're familiar with particular neighborhoods, maybe even the tougher ones in the city, they might know where to find some. They might already know some of the people in the neighborhoods.

These "schools" must know how to handle themselves. They'll know the risks. They might look where the gangs hang out. They might look where the drug dealers hang out. Perhaps it's somewhere else. But these one-person schools are likely looking for exactly those people to become their students.

***

A small group of maybe seven challenging-looking young people are hanging out together leaning against a building, smoking something, and talking. It's not the kind of group you'd invite over. You can see the bulge of what might be a handgun peeking out of a pocket. There are almost undoubtedly other weapons there, too.

A self-contained school walks up to them. He wears a medium-sized backpack. Talking really fast, he begins:

"Hello, gentlemen! I'm John Sullivan the School."

"You're what?!"

"I'm John Sullivan the School. How many of you have graduated from high school?"

They look at each other. A couple raise their hands. After all, they're proud they made it through.

"Great! The rest of you haven't graduated yet! I'm here to help you!"

"What are you talking about!" the apparent leader with the bulge in his pocket says. *"None of us are going back to that hellhole! So you can just move on!"*

"No problem! You don't have to go anywhere! I'm a self-contained school and we can have school right… *here!"*

"Hey, who are you?!"

"My name is John Sullivan the School. But you can't have a school without students. So I'm going to give you the first opportunity to be my students!"

They give totally confused looks to each other. Here is clearly someone with mental health issues talking to them. Not only is this person not afraid of them, he comes across instantly comfortable being with them. And they don't know a thing about him.

"First thing we'll need to do is figure out is what you'll want to learn first. I've got lots of options for you. They'll all be great. But I'll let *you* choose where we'll start. Some people think they know what atomic bombs are [see how I worked that in?], but they really don't. We can start by looking at some actual videos of them. Don't worry. We can do it all right here. No need to go anywhere. After all, I'm your school and I'm with you now.

"OR! I can teach you a couple things about how our government works…"

Another tough looking potential student chimes in, *"Forget it man. Not interested!"*

The School continues talking, "There's all this stuff in the news and it's really confusing sometimes. So we can start with a bit of that and then talk more as we have time. We can talk about what's happening in the news — but only the interesting stuff. OR! I can teach you how to do math *so fast* that you can make money betting others who can multiply faster! OR! I can help some of you with your writing and English. I can help you become a lot better! We just have to start with a few minutes at a time. No stress. No worries. So what do you think? What's first?"

"Hey, this isn't for me," one says. *"This is stupid!"*

"No problem. We'll work past that. But first, let me tell you why this is important. One day, you'll have children. Maybe some of you have children now. They'll be looking up to their Dad — to *you*. You'll be looking at your cute kids with love — as they will also be looking at you. You'll want to take care of them. Their love for you will be everything to you. I'll talk to you about why all the things I can teach you will help you in your lives, and in the lives of your children — when you have them.

"Speaking of children, when your children's friends later ask them what their Dad does, what will your children tell them? If their friends later ask them if they can come over to their house and bring you, do you want your son, your daughter, to say that you're not home? If they ask what you're doing, do you want them to say that you still have another 15 or 20 years to be locked up? Is that what you want your son or your pretty daughter to tell others?

"I'm here so that they will look up to you with respect and love. I'm here so that you can be with them while they're growing up. You'll be there to love and protect them from the world. You'll be there to teach them the things you've already learned and will be learning now. I bet that sometimes you've been let down in your life, maybe by your own father. Am I right? We've all been let down at times."

One potential student walks away in disgust. He calls to a couple others to go with him. One does. The other stays. The one who followed him looks back as he goes. Will he have second thoughts about leaving?

"But here, I can help you become special people. Really, you already are. But you can have more pride in yourself. Others will respect you — and for the right reasons. After a while some might start asking you for *your* help and advice. That doesn't happen by itself and it's not quick. It takes time and it takes deciding to be that person — especially for your own children who you might have someday. It will also be for your wife, when you have one, who should be your best friend. I can help you. That's what I'm here for.

"I'm John Sullivan the School and I'm your school. Now, shall we get started? Where would you like to start? What would you like to learn? You're my students. Wherever you are, I can be with you. Together, we'll find new things to learn for you. Things can begin to change, starting today."

One of his new students tentatively says, *"Do you have that video on the atomic bomb? I want to see that."*

"I do have it! I'll show it to you right now — but I'll stop it once in a while to tell you even more things about it. Let me get it out."

John Sullivan the School reaches into his backpack and takes out a large screen iPad tablet. As the iPad starts up, he sets up a small, light chair that was strapped to his backpack so that he can sit on it. He grabs a small white board, also in the backpack.

"Looks like I forgot my markers for the white board. Maybe one will show up."

As the iPad finishes starting up and as John Sullivan the School gets the video ready to go, a car pulls up behind him on the street. Someone gets out, goes over to John Sullivan the School and, without a word, hands him a couple of markers for the white board. The School acknowledges the person who, again without a word, gets back in the car and leaves.

"Hey Sullivan, who was that??! How did he know you needed a marker!"

"Hey, I'm not just some guy on the streets! I'm a school! I'm YOUR school! Naturally, I've got support to back me up!"

"Was he listening to you?"

"Everyone listens when a School speaks — just like you're doing! Now let's start the video and get going."

John Sullivan the School starts the video on the iPad. A small, but powerful bluetooth speaker (also in the backpack) ensures the volume is loud enough for everyone to hear.

Indeed, John Sullivan the School does have support. Back at the nearby support offices of Community Schools, he is being quietly monitored both for his safety and so that they can quickly bring him things he might need for his instruction.

The backpack itself contains multiple tracking devices in case it "disappears." The iPad has its own separate tracking device hidden inside its cover. The tablet software also allows tracking.

John Sullivan the School finishes his presentation. All of his students actually watched it with great interest. They listened to John Sullivan the School when he stopped the video to explain more about what they were seeing. He then went on to sneak in a very brief presentation about the government that he had carefully enticed them into hearing.

"Almost lunch time. Anyone want some lunch?"

"Sure! You buying?" one snidely says.

"You're my students now, aren't you? I'll take care of you."

Five minutes later, as he's still talking to his new students who, remarkably, had stayed to hear him, that same car pulls up. He hands John Sullivan the School a box with eight boxes and eight bottles of water in it. John Sullivan the School passes them out and keeps one for himself.

"How's the lunch, guys?"

"Fine. This is very strange. What're we going to do next?"

"We're done for the day. After all, it's just our first day. But I want to be sure I don't forget your names! I'm going to give each of you a card. I want you to write down your name and phone number, your address, too. That way, if you're not here, I can call you to be sure you're not sick and don't need something from me, okay?

"I don't want you to get nervous, but is it okay if I take a quick photo of my new students so I can put your name on them and remember you when I'm back tomorrow? It's just for me. I hope that works for you. Here are the cards."

Albeit a bit reluctantly, they all fill out the cards. Most let him take their picture, but some don't. That's no problem. He'll eventually know and get photos of his students.

"I'll be back tomorrow. If it's raining or something so that we can't meet here, you know the neighborhood. Maybe you can find us an empty building, or one of your homes, so we can go there. Otherwise, we'll just be here again. How's that?"

Looking at each other, they shrug and nod. After all, they weren't bored and they got some free food.

"Let me tell you that there are some other schools around. Don't you dare go to them! *I'm your* school and I'll help you learn things. I'll see you tomorrow!"

Quickly, John Sullivan the School walks away. He wasn't there more than a bit over an hour. He kept their attention. He taught them. He *is* their school. He'll be back. Starting for just a short time, he'll have to gauge how much more he can do each time and still keep their attention.

If he is to succeed, he'll have to be a *real* teacher, perhaps even in the manner of Socrates. (Okay, not quite Socrates.) He'll be passionate. He'll love teaching but, even more, he'll love his students. He'll want to bring them from where he found them forward to a new life. How much success will he have? That's hard to know. But he's on it. He must also take into account the potential dangers in community teaching.

It takes a special person to be a Community School. Fortunately, as with many other opportunities to help people, there are many out there willing to put themselves on the line for something greater than themselves. The Community School support center can provide pay, resources, and support for this special cadre of educators.

The next day, all his students returned — and they brought a couple more with them. John Sullivan the School also has something planned for his two students who already completed high school. After he's done with the second day, he'll invite them to walk with him and suggest that he can get them started with a college class. They won't have to go anywhere right away. He's still their school. After he teaches them for a while (and if he can get them interested enough), he might be able to get a Community College for them: a *Community* College.

***

Within a five-mile radius of where John Sullivan the School found his students, are at least 12 other "schools" just like John Sullivan the School. They've gathered their own students.

It's expensive to have one Community "School" for just six to ten students, maybe even less. Later, a couple of "schools" might come together. *Their students* will find places to meet. Beyond that, the students themselves might one day suggest that they can hang out with their personal "school" in a real school classroom — in a real school.

In the past, special people and special teachers have reached out in communities to bring caring and support to those the regular failing schools weren't reaching. But when those special teachers of the past stopped, it all stopped. They were, after all, just individuals.

But Community Schools, like John Sullivan the School, can set up something that can continue beyond a single individual.

John Sullivan the School and the other Community Schools did not go through the older, dysfunctional program for teacher preparation. They had a much shorter, targeted, and far more effective program. They were all screened for subject matter competence in multiple areas. They were evaluated for their temperament and for their ability to handle difficult situations, difficult students, and difficult questions. They have all volunteered and know what they're getting into. They're excited about making a difference in people whom a regular school (building) can't reach.

These people *are* the Community Schools — and there are lots of them. They are designed for specific scenarios, not for the general student population (pretty sure we'd need a physical building for that — but maybe not).

Would any of this be possible? Likely not — but maybe.

Far more importantly, we must address the vast number of "regular" students. Community Schools won't be able to fix everything that's wrong with education today. We have to consider other options for doing that.

But whatever we do must be alive and passionate. Failed, dead schools must be swept away if we are to save education and the country. Schools must be bastions of learning, not poisoning pits for political or sociological indoctrination.

Those few schools from the old system that never died, that remained alive and healthy, that have continued to serve education and students well, must be supported and preserved. It's good to have options, but only ones that can succeed. There are still some excellent schools around. There just aren't nearly enough to provide the strong counter-balance for the schools that have failed our children and the country.

***

This is just one part of a completely different way to look at what a school can be. It's put forth so that a reader might consider things that haven't been done — even if it's not Community Schools.

Although I personally support physical classrooms, classrooms don't teach students. *Teachers* teach students. Regardless, we must consider all options. Creative options don't have to be used everywhere. But special options for special groups of students can bring great results.

Creativity in designing a living and effective school can help to bring education back. Perhaps it can bring America back.

But the current dead system is protected by legislators, courts, unions, our own experiences, and much more. Those things will prevent the radical changes we must bring about. Taking the full picture into account, we eventually realize that education as we know it today simply isn't fixable.

36. WHAT OPTIONS FOR CHANGE DO WE HAVE?

We have just looked at a couple out-of-the-box ways to get education to students. But neither of those can handle large numbers of students. Perhaps other dramatically new designs might, but what might those be?

Even if there were potentially workable designs, even if there were a strong will for change in the people and in the government so that it could get out of the way in order to make such changes, it's still not likely that substantive change would be made. Even if such changes might appear to be made, schools would likely continue to fail.

There are several reasons for that. One of the most obvious is this dilemma:

Who would be tasked to overhaul the system?

In almost all cases, those tasked to overhaul the system are comfortable and well-experienced in the current system. Those who would likely be tasked to address the problem have already been trained in that failed system. They are people who only know that system and may have been instrumental in maintaining it over the years. They truthfully know only one way to run education.

However, those outside the system know so little about how schools and education work that they're likely to simply duplicate the only education system that they, too, have known — and watch it fail again.

An advantage of those with experience in the current system is that they can more easily recognize what hasn't worked in the past. Then they can try something new. If that doesn't work, they can try something else new again — and again — until substantive education finally takes place in America.

***

Some years ago, I spent time in both the US Army and the US Navy. While I was in the Navy, I knew physician assistants (PAs) who were trained in some advanced medical procedures, including amputations. Since doctors are generally assigned only to the largest Navy ships, PAs are trained to step in to provide some advanced lifesaving medical care. In places where PAs might be assigned, they must be able to handle all emergencies that arise. Communication with licensed physicians is not always possible, especially in wartime. So these non-physicians were well-trained. They were competent. They were able to save lives.

Yet, when they left the Navy, they were at the mercy of state laws and of the influence of the medical community. Not just physician assistants, but also others who were trained, competent, and trusted in the military, are not permitted to do what they did well in the military. Once leaving, using lifesaving medical services for which PAs were responsible in the military, were now specifically prohibited for them to provide. I haven't checked lately, but that's certainly how it once was. Frankly, I'd be surprised if it has changed significantly. Many nurse practitioners are allowed to do things —also quite competently — that physician assistants are prohibited from doing — at least in certain states. Of course, all this might be different now. Things change.

***

There are plenty of good people who are very competent as teachers. It's much easier to give good teachers subject-matter knowledge, than it is to turn someone with good subject-matter knowledge into a good teacher — unless that person already has the ability and passion to actually teach.

But couldn't allowing lesser-educated people in the classroom open the floodgates to letting incompetent people become teachers?

Not if done correctly.

Any changes to teacher recruitment and training must still protect and strengthen subject matter learning for students, not make it worse. The qualifications of those who teach must be observable and strong.

Textbooks are also a mess. Too many purported textbooks today are there to indoctrinate children in the political or social whims and biases of the day, regardless of parental wishes or what should be best educational practices.

The bottom line on everything we've seen is that there is no single change that can "fix" the education system today. The entire system needs to be rebuilt from scratch. Finding the right people to do this is not just tough, it's likely not even possible.

Well-meaning, but misguided legislators have insisted on interfering with schools and education as they pass laws and requirements that they think will fix things, or at least to help make things better. Has involvement by these outside entities helped or hurt things? In a great number of cases, they have made things worse. Some legislation might be needed, but what it might be can't be easily identified now, especially by those without a comprehensive understanding of all that is broken today. And there isn't just one or two things that are broken.

Some recent books believe that the reintroduction of liberal arts or a strong classical education might be the solution to all this. As much as I support classical education — and I do — this is an inadequate answer to what is wrong with education today. Much of a classical or liberal arts education deals with which *subjects* are taught, not necessarily *how* education is being delivered. Furthermore, such options don't fix the extensive public education system where millions of students get their education.

That's a point I need to repeatedly make. Options for your own children aren't options for the country. Only the public school system can educate the vast number of students the country needs to educate.

Can the "how" of teaching be addressed? Is there actually an option as to "how" we deliver education to students? In most cases, what's in place now isn't working.

The will to undertake massive educational changes by those with the power to make such changes doesn't currently exist. If it does, someone's doing a great job hiding it. So the system just repeats itself under the guise of "reforms." So-called new reforms touted by some aren't actually reforms—and they're certainly not new.

Are there effective educational alternatives which can be employed on a wide scale today? There are not. Nonetheless, I'll briefly look at a handful of alternative learning structures. There aren't many here and they absolutely won't fix the totality of failure we have before us. Perhaps they might shake someone up so that they can think about things completely different. Perhaps that might have value.

I do have hope that there may be ways to restructure education so that it can work more effectively. But I'm also fairly confident that any truly dramatic changes wouldn't be allowed to be put into place today. Our hands remain tied.

37. EDUCATIONAL ALTERNATIVES

Really, educational alternatives don't matter. It doesn't matter how good charter or other schools are —- if they're really good enough at all. What matters are the tens of millions currently going to *public schools*. The object isn't simply to let parents take their children out of public schools for some (hopefully) better option. That does nothing to save the tens of millions of children going to public schools who make up the majority of the nation. An entirely new public school system needs to rise from the ashes, one that does not merely replicate the currently dead system.

To many, it seems as though there are many options to public schools for delivering education to students. In reality, there aren't many at all, especially that are easily accessible to most students. Further, none in their current forms appear to be a solution for the dysfunctional public education system of today. Nonetheless, we'll look at a few of them.

But, remember, unless we save the *public school* system, we will lose America. That is happening right now.

ONLINE LEARNING

Not long before the time of this writing, the COVID 19

pandemic, and the country's response to it, seriously affected public education throughout the country. Most public school students were forced to switch to online learning from their teachers. Parents could see first hand how bad the teaching was at their children's schools.

According to one article in January 2023, from 1.4 to potentially as many as two million children left the public school system for the alternatives of charter schools, private schools, and home-schooling. It suggested that most are not likely to return to the public school system.[1]

As mentioned elsewhere, although some educational alternatives are better than today's public school system, most still lack the true educational structure necessary for a solidly and efficiently functioning education system.

Referring to that public education delivered online, that same January 2023 article said, *"Nearly a quarter of Americans, 23 percent, said they were completely dissatisfied with their child's education."*

One parent said, *"For a while, [our kids] were getting homework assigned to them by their teachers...but there was no teaching going on."*

Even though the education system was bad before COVID 19, it became worse during it. Students required to learn "remotely" fell behind. Things are worse now than they were before COVID — and they were bad then.

To say that things are even worse now than they were before the COVID pandemic is beyond bad. It is further evidence of the serious failure of public education in America.

Note that the remote learning that countless students endured during the pandemic was different from other structured and effective online learning methodologies that many schools were already using before the pandemic struck. However, just a small percentage of kindergarten through 12th grade (K-12) students primarily received their formal education online before the pandemic.

The more effective online education that had been provided — and continue to be provided — by some K-12 schools were handled by administrators and teachers who already knew how to teach online courses.

A lot of time had already been spent designing and refining

those courses. They could be conducted one-on-one between a teacher and student, with small online groups, or with (generally small) classes. Teachers involved with such learning had experience and were generally comfortable doing it.

In the most effective cases, properly run online classes can have good student involvement and, hopefully, support from parents who, working with the online teachers, oversee their children's activities and progress.

However, as we already heard, during the COVID pandemic, most teachers were creating online teaching and assignments without the experience or knowledge of how to do it efficiently, and without really knowing what they needed to do.

As we also heard, many teachers weren't comfortable in the new world of online education into which they were thrown. They were learning as they went along. They had to try serving the larger class sizes they had when they met in person. This change was tough for both teachers and students.

Online instruction, especially at the K-12 level, doesn't do well with normally large class sizes, especially classes of immature young people. Even experienced online teachers could have significant problems in this new scenario.

Nonetheless, the pre-existing, online classes designed and taught before COVID, and which continue in many places today, should be differentiated from the far less effective "remote learning" during the pandemic — even though that remote learning also took place online.

Especially important here is that traditional online students themselves have a different attitude, comfort level, and a voluntary buy-in to online learning. That was different from the vast majority of COVID students who were kept at home supposedly learning in an unfamiliar structure. Many COVID-era "remote learning" students effectively became online educational inmates.

In actuality, pandemic-era remote learning was not simply less effective, it was found to do actual damage to students and to their learning progress. Such students lost ground, getting further and further behind in classes that may or may not have been particularly good even when they were taught in actual classrooms.

Effective K-12 online classes are especially important in situations where students are unable to attend school classes in person. In some cases, they can be the only educational connection for students who don't live near enough to a physical school. Students might be many miles from a regular school, perhaps without roads or transportation to get to a school even if they wanted to go. Others might be bedridden or have some other legitimate reason they can't attend a school in person. Such classes may be their only option. An online school itself can be local or it can be many states away.

Let me be clear. Other than for unusual and compelling reasons (the pandemic is likely not one), extended online classes are the wrong way to conduct classes for K-12 students.

Online instruction is more commonly used for university classes that would otherwise be difficult or impossible to attend.

Rural or inaccessible areas such as are found in highly rural states — in parts of Alaska, as one example — can benefit from such online education. Of course, just like students at regular schools, some students do better than others. But many of the pre-pandemic course designs were such that students had a better chance to succeed. Students themselves come to such classes with a better attitude since they understand that other choices don't exist. Experienced online teachers are generally comfortable and proficient teaching online classes, too.

An Aside: I believe that even more can be done online to make specialized courses effective. I have proposed development of online programs that can address particular students, such as those with attention deficit hyperactivity disorder (ADHD) and other issues that can make learning difficult for them. Schools have failed to separately address such students.

It is often hard for them to succeed in the same classrooms run for non-ADHD students. Unfortunately, that is generally all we have at the moment. It is incumbent on educators to develop new approaches to better serve this large population of students. It is not something that can be effectively handled using standard methodologies found in most classrooms. These students can become far more educated than the current system allows. They are often frustrated in the current system.

Using my own experiences, I propose an innovative, specifically-targeted pilot program. It has yet to attract competent technical professionals and educators to develop the program. Students will continue to suffer until their needs are addressed in the public education system.

A March 30, 2023, article reported:

"Millions of US children rely on the [ADHD] medication [Adderall]. The latest estimates suggest that roughly 10% of US children ages 3-17 have been diagnosed with ADHD, according to the Center for Disease Control and Protection, and these numbers may have increased since 2019."[2]

Whatever the actual cause of ADHD, ten percent of US children *is a lot of children.*

Back to online learning...

As long as students can benefit from online classes and can not attend a quality school in person, they shouldn't necessarily shy away from well-designed online learning with competent and experienced teachers just because of the terrible experiences so many had during the COVID-19 pandemic. But that isn't easy to find. Any such K-12 program *must* be well designed, well taught, and its effectiveness carefully and regularly evaluated.

Unfortunately, the educational damage resulting from the COVID-19 pandemic was and continues to be even worse than people know. As part of it, the public has been being lied to — again.

Here's how:

When many educators were asked how long it will take for students to catch up after falling behind online, educators often answered something like, *"A long time!"* ...or, *"We don't really know. It can take a year or more."*

None of that is true. The actual answer is that they will rarely, *if ever,* "catch up." Hear that again: in the vast majority of cases, students will *never* catch up. Some might redefine what "catching up" means in order to proclaim success, but that's simply wrong.

If teachers and schools could so easily teach subjects more quickly, fitting more in a condensed time, they'd be able to do the same thing for their non-pandemic teaching. But only rarely can they do that. The real answer is that, in the vast majority of cases, they can't catch up students.

I've heard this same "catch them up" mantra over my years in education. In almost all cases, it never happens. It's not necessarily the fault of the schools or the teachers. It's simply that it just can't be done. Allotting extra time, extending the school day, or requiring summer school classes are not necessarily workable answers either.

So this talk about "catching up" is nonsense. Topics will be cut out completely. Things they have been "learning" online at home will be considered as having been learned, even though they haven't been, or have been learned poorly.

Those students who are missing a full and adequate education will become our future generations of adults. Those are our next generations of teachers and voters. But they will have holes in their education. Of course, they won't think they have any holes, but they will.

What is so troublesome here is that, when people suggest that students might be able to catch up, parents and the whole country calm down and figure that, while it might be tough, at least it can be done.

But things will be left out or taught poorly, if they are taught at all. Whatever anyone says, within our current system, fully catching up students who are far behind where they should be — can't be done.

CORRESPONDENCE COURSES

Note that, years ago, what were traditional "correspondence courses" were more widely available. As are online courses, they are also part of distance learning. Some are called "distance education courses" or are known by some other name. Although they can be used for standard academic work, I am actually supportive of the hands-on skills students can learn through many of them, especially as offered in some of the smaller non-academic schools and individuals, too.

Some of them are now defined as "online correspondence courses." But there is a different feel working online versus having physical materials at hand for learning. Printed correspondence courses are still commonly in use.

Private individuals or schools would design courses they could then send to students in the mail as lessons. Student complete the lessons and send them back, also by regular mail. The lessons can then be corrected and feedback given to students. For schools that didn't send everything all at once, I was always excited when my own next lessons arrived.

Prices used to be very reasonable. Today, that is not necessarily the case. I commonly recommend against signing up for programs requiring financial aid or financing options, although there can be exceptions to that. Schools of all sorts are generally way too expensive today.

Offline correspondence courses might seem like old school to some, but many can be very efficient. Motivated students have been able to learn the basics of everything from small engine repair to piano tuning to photography to locksmithing to radio broadcasting and much, much more. That was all done without online resources. Even the military has used them.

Once finished, students have been able to set up their own businesses or get entry level jobs — sometimes above entry level. Other students just enjoy learning something fun and new even if never making any money with the skills. Yet people often made fun of these courses. (Do they still?) Apparently, if it's not a serious academic course, it doesn't count as real learning.

Many were efficient enough that they should be again studied as one alternative to standard classes, or at least as substantive supplements. Even though online courses and resources are often used for them today (required course materials would still be sent), there are still some positives to fully offline learning.

As with everything, some courses are better than others. Some aren't worth taking at all, especially those that don't have good support and encouragement for students. Some people have experienced some as scams. Frankly, some more traditionally formatted schools can cross into that area, too. Prospective students should be very careful signing up for these courses — as they should be even for traditional schools.

I myself worked in and completed several such courses. I especially enjoyed this educational format for non-academic and non-required subjects.

One course led to working in an important and exciting job with a skill that I still use today. That was totally unexpected and it was fully because of the self-paced correspondence course that I took. If you're listening to me read this book to you (as an audiobook), you're seeing the results of that correspondence course. I might not be as good as others, but I assure you that I credit much of what I can do to that one course taken well over 40 years ago.

I still have my diploma from that school on my wall, by the way, as I do for another correspondence course. That other course also gave me a skill that I am still able to use today.

Other courses that I took were just really interesting. I took courses to learn skills I wouldn't have thought I could learn. In some cases, people take them because they're just curious. Because these courses are generally lower stress without tight time limits, I found I could benefit more than I had thought. Even those I never finished gave me a broader understanding of whichever subject or skill it was teaching. Sometimes training was helpful even beyond a course that I hadn't even completed.

The better ones come with ongoing and encouraging support from the schools. Many courses are self-paced with broad time limits, although it's good to have some gentle time limits or students would never get around to finishing them.

I completed a military correspondence course to qualify as a Naval postal officer — a job that I never actually worked in. I admit that one was not as exciting, but I enjoyed completing it anyway. Standard military training isn't conducted that way, but the military services do have many courses to choose from. More about military training will be coming up.

. . .

CHARTER SCHOOLS

I support school choice and the charter school is one that is regularly mentioned as an alternative to regular public schools. That doesn't necessarily mean it is the best for you or your children but, unless and until the entire educational system is rebuilt from scratch, it might be.

Check your local charter schools to be sure they are working to educate children rather than primarily being a money-making entity. You might look into getting a group together and start your own — if the local and state laws permit it without requirements that are too onerous.

Charter schools are actually public schools. That's good for some things, bad for others. Depending on state and local requirements, control of these schools doesn't always fully rest with the schools themselves. Be careful that some other entity isn't actually running the new school that you found.

Because foreign powers can sometimes appear to be working too closely with some non-traditional schools — directly or indirectly — be sure your school is an American-controlled school.

In the beginning, charter schools were all about parents in a community getting together with educators and others anxious to try out new things in education. The concept was very exciting when it first got started. However, for a long while now, too many of them have become big businesses, or small businesses, rather than being driven by the original deep passion for innovative teaching and learning. Too often today, some have become corporate or personal money makers rather than what they were intended to be: creative alternatives that are substantively different from traditional public schools.

To get approval for charters from wherever it might be required (usually states or school districts), sometimes means that charter schools don't have enough leeway to truly strike out in distinctively new directions on their own. In some jurisdictions, approvals may not be given unless the charter design isn't too far off from standard public school norms and standards. That can stifle true creativity and run counter to the original intent of charter schools.

Charter schools can be very different depending where they are located. Different states and jurisdictions can treat charter schools differently.

Fortunately, as many parents have found, there are some very good charter schools. If one or more is close to you, and if you can find space in them, take a look to see what your options might be.

But, just because a school is a charter school doesn't automatically mean it's a great school. As with all schools, you must monitor what they are doing and what they are teaching. Also be sure their teachers are whom you want teaching your children.

You can find worthwhile schools of all kinds, even public schools. But, again, there are not enough of them to save education throughout the country today. Nor have most of these, or other schools, significantly departed from the main structure of public schools, even though the instruction itself can be significantly better and their smaller sizes are a major plus. In many cases, standards of student behavior are also better. That, by itself, can improve the learning environment.

Relatively early in the history of charter schools, I designed a full charter to convert the small school at which I taught into a charter school. The school district gave its schools the option to convert to a charter school as one of several choices to choose for school reform. The full school staff supported the effort that I had led at the time.

The principal and I involved ourselves in the burgeoning charter movement at conferences and charter school visits. We held regular meetings, heard suggestions, and had a positive attitude that we could do something different that would make a difference for our students. We were a good group.

But it never made it through the school district's approval process, even though the district itself had offered it as an option.

The unexpected roadblocks that were put in our way by the Los Angeles Unified School District ended our efforts. Charter schools have always had enemies in high places. We fit the parameters they had set but, in the end, their allowed option of conversion to a charter school appeared to be window dressing. It was never approved. We were one of the only district schools to have even pursued that option.

***

Other non-traditional *private* schools are also available although, as mentioned, most are only found in larger urban areas. They include not just Montessori schools, which most people have heard about, but also a number of other non-traditional schools that parents can consider — if they can afford to pay for them. Even when there are government or private subsidies, it might not be enough. And, for some families, the issue of transportation to such alternative schools is sometimes unsolvable.

Montessori schools have been around a very long time and are often available for those who support their philosophy of education. Other schools have a comparatively much more shorter history. As usual, some can be great. Others can be terrible.

Clearly, I strongly support serious changes in education — if such changes are actually possible. But, just because a school is "non-traditional" doesn't necessarily mean it's good. Alternative non-traditional education may or may not provide a good education. If you choose one, research it well, choose very carefully, and continue to evaluate it should you send your children there.

Note that non-traditional high schools don't necessarily put students at a disadvantage in applying for colleges. Of course, that can depend on the quality of their teachers and instruction. But there are always colleges that will accept educated students no matter where they went to school.

However, research where their graduates go before applying anywhere, even to traditional schools.

Always be involved with any school your children attend. That way, you can know what's going on. You might want to volunteer to help out at school to help make things (even) better. When your children are home, keep after them to be sure they're studying and doing their work. *Check it yourself* so you can find out if they're having any problems, but also so you can know what they're (supposed to be) learning.

. . .

PAROCHIAL/RELIGIOUS SCHOOLS

Parochial/religious schools have had a mixed record of success. In most cases, parochial/religious schools must — as required by some states, otherwise by their own rules — recruit staff who are trained and certified educators and who are often experienced in the public sector.

The Catholic school system is the oldest school system in what later became the United States. It has been around since at least 1606 in St. Augustine in what is now the state of Florida. For whatever reason, some give other years as the first Catholic school, even as late as 1783. Regardless, it remains the largest non-public system in the country and the largest parochial school system in the world. As a result, one cannot effectively discuss education and fail to consider the history and record of Catholic schools.

Overall, the Catholic school system has had a very good record of educational success. Catholics run schools from kindergarten through high school and also colleges. Ignoring the omnipresent exceptions, until recent times, its record has been much better than most others, whether public or private religious schools.

However, one change in these schools over the years has been a move away from Catholic nuns, priests, and religious orders as teachers, to lay (non-religious) teachers — though lay teachers often must be practicing Catholics. That is primarily due to the smaller numbers of Catholic priests and religious orders available today.

That has sometimes put Catholic schools at the mercy of hiring some of the same teachers about which this book has elsewhere warned. Others feel that the increasing reliance on lay teachers has benefitted these schools. One finds evidence on both sides of the issue. However, using teachers trained in teacher-training programs under progressive, liberal professors is problematic, especially for religious schools.

This has been exacerbated in recent times by requirements that teachers have state-approved credentials. I assure you that there remain excellent lay teachers who do not have full teacher credentials. Taking at least a couple of methodology classes, without necessarily completing a full credential, can be helpful for almost any teacher. But, until parents can step in to stop it, a subtle progressive indoctrination can still be transferred from some teachers to their students anyway. That has the potential of doing damage to general education, as well as to the religious beliefs and principles still espoused in the majority (no longer all) of Catholic or other religious schools.

A number of well-known colleges began as institutions with a strong Catholic identity, but later moved far away from that earlier Catholic identity. Problematically, some changed to operate in full opposition to some teachings of its own church.

A number of well-known leaders began their education in Catholic schools. In spite of financial and other difficulties at these schools, many Catholic schools have remained stronger than many alternatives. Nonetheless, at times, they can also suffer from academic and other weaknesses.

Unlike public schools, during the COVID 19 pandemic, most Catholic schools remained open to in-person student attendance many months earlier than did most public schools. Some barely closed at all. Therefore, unlike with the remote-learning model embraced by public schools, their students had a much better opportunity to stay current in their education.

Some protestant sects — sometimes openly anti-Catholic — have also set up their own schools. Although some of these schools turn out well-educated students, many do not. Outsiders have had special concerns about some of these later and smaller protestant schools, but issues of concern can occur in any school — private, public, or parochial.

Many smaller religious schools do not have enough solid educational resources, including the money to hire quality teachers. Some are so concerned with the religious calling of the school that non-religious education — English, math, history, government, etc. — may be given inadequate emphasis and teaching. Learning about one's faith is certainly important. But a full and proper education must go beyond that.

Whether one agrees or disagrees with all this depends on one's experience with such schools. Carefully selected, such schools can provide from acceptable to excellent alternatives to other educational options.

. . .

"ALL WE HAVE TO DO" SCHOOLS

There are many "All We Have to Do" schools. People point to successful schools — or what they think are successful schools — and say, "*All we have to do… is to make public schools just like *these* schools and all will be fixed!"

It would be nice if such people were right. They might know of one such successful school. There might even be a chain of many such schools.

It's good to show success in school designs. But to then extrapolate and say that *all we have to do* is to make all schools like this one or that one or like a chain of schools, is usually a fool's errand today.

Consider this. There have been good alternative schools for many decades, actually far, far longer. But we haven't seen their designs significantly influence changes in public schools. Today, there are still many of these schools, but they aren't bringing about the changes in public schools our children and the country need. Some can quietly retain many of the weaknesses that we see elsewhere.

SCHOOL CHOICE

Is "school choice" the answer?

I'm fully supportive of parents having educational options. Hopefully, they're actually better than the school their children are leaving. The problem is that, other than for the students they serve, they're generally not the answer to the broader problems identified in this book.

There are at least two potential problems here.

(1) Some alternative schools, including private and religious schools, can certainly be better — or at least different — from many public schools.

However, such schools are not always better enough. Basic problems exist even in alternative schools. Most such schools generally still function under the same basic educational frame-work as do traditional schools.

In addition, teachers are generally trained in the same teacher-training programs as are public school teachers. That's not necessarily bad. But it's not necessarily good either. Regardless, there really aren't a lot of good alternatives to become a certificated teacher today. (Depending on the state, alternative schools may not even have to hire certificated or traditionally trained educators.)

Our hands are often tied in creating effective alternative schools. State, local, even federal guidelines and restrictions can ensure that some alternative schools can be created too closely mirroring the pattern of the failing schools of today. They are better, but sometimes only by comparison. Too many restrictions can stifle true educational creativity, including allowing a significantly reduced time to fully educate students.

When charter schools began, many state, local, even some federal guidelines and restrictions were waived. Today, many jurisdictions have tightened up on these schools.

Those supporting alternative schools can short-sightedly figure that, because their particular school is good, there's really no problem with education. After all, everyone else can crowd into their school, too. Of course, that is simply false. Such schools can only take a very small number of students compared to what public schools can take.

Regardless, many alternative schools can certainly provide better or specialized education. Parents should absolutely consider them as an option.

(2) There's a second problem with "school choice" as an answer to what ails the current system. In many parts of the country, especially small rural school districts, substantive options from which parents can choose don't exist at all. Public schools may be their only choice.

Those who strongly promote school choice generally live in larger urban areas where multiple options to public schools are available. But they often just think of themselves and of the larger urban area (city) in which they live.

That kind of narrow thinking is disturbing to those not living in areas where other educational choices are readily available. Yet advocates of "school choice" continue to tout it as a solution to the problems of education as though everyone has access to the same options that they have. Just because they have such choices, doesn't mean that everyone else does, too. Others don't have such choices.

Even if another choice is available in a smaller community, it may be just one — and that one may or may not be any good. Further, that single alternative school might just target specific grades or subjects or students, such as only serving lower elementary grades, leaving other students without options. In those cases, parents and educators should work to make their local public schools as good as possible.

A number of states or school districts set up separate small schools for students who are struggling academically or behaviorally. Those schools often target high school students at-risk of dropping out of high school or who are otherwise not functioning well in a traditional school setting. To actually help such students, student-teacher ratios (class sizes) must be *substantially* smaller than those of traditional schools. If ongoing funding can be found, more schools and districts should consider adding on these specialized schools.

The problem is that there are simply not enough of these alternative schools to replace public schools. Should we just abandon the tens of millions of public school students just because we got our own children in a potentially better school? We should not. We must try to save education for the vast numbers of children who either must go, or choose to go, to public schools.

Sadly, as we know, education is now effectively dead. Abandonment of public schools by those comparatively few students who are lucky to have other options isn't necessarily helping the country. It only helps students who have such a school available to them — and can get into it.

Hopefully, it will turn out to be a good one.

LEARN A REAL TRADE

Forgetting college for a moment, there are ways to get out in the world, not be stuck at a desk while life beckons you from afar, and make a difference as you help others who really need what you can do. An important website that promotes this direction in life has this incomplete list: *"...plumbers, electricians, steamfitters, pipefitters, brick layers, farmers, fishers, and a bunch of other skilled workers who help keep our polite society humming along."*

Some people still think that such jobs are low-skill, low -paid, low-respect jobs. Yet a large number of people with their noses in the air can actually make less money, have less job security, and are often unable to do anything as critical to society as these jobs. Those in such trades can directly help people in their day-to-day lives. They can keep help build communities.

Of course, there are trade schools to attend. But, for many trades, there are are still other ways to get many of these skills without attending any school. One just needs guts, tenacity, and a basic willingness to do real work.

Ask around, especially those who are currently working in those fields. As a young guy, I did that before going in the Army. I eventually got the Army job I wanted. Things may have been very different had I not done that. The same thing works for other things you might want to do in life.

As just one solid source to help you get started, see mikerowe-works.org.

✱✱✱

At least temporarily, there is still good news for some students in public schools. Some good schools continue to exist. Many parents with children in those good schools think that the public school system is, overall, still fine. After all, the schools *their* children attend are good. Therefore, many or most others must be, too — or so they think.

As already said, there are indeed still many really fine teachers in almost all schools, whether at top end schools or at schools that are struggling with low performing students. But, as I have also said, there aren't enough of them.

Even outside pandemic times, many of those good teachers have often been frustrated as they try to do their job. They're also frustrated as they look around and see serious deficiencies both in and out of their schools.

As political ideology replaces traditional education (hopefully temporarily), there are fewer teachers who can keep such ideologies out of their classes in favor of actually teaching core subject matter. Such teachers need to be supported, both personally and professionally. More of them are critically needed.

Yet, instead of providing consistent support, many such teachers find administrators, even other teachers, who seem to be working against them.

Overall, education is indeed dead, or at least so broken as to be effectively unfixable unless effective (potentially undiscovered) educational designs, a strong will to do it, and competent reformers are found.

Of course, many people can point to all the things their children can learn at public schools, even at some good schools, that children can't learn at home. Let's look at a few of those things:

From kindergarten through 12th grade, your child's beloved peers can graciously help your child to become skilled in things like lying and treating parents, teachers, and others with disrespect. Older children can develop self-confidence as they become skilled in the art of defiance.

Especially younger children, but also those who are older, can ably demonstrate how to bully other children because it's great entertainment and power over others feels good. Some might even carry that skill into their adult lives.

Those same peers can provide training and help in the free enterprise system as they teach your formerly trustworthy child how to use and sell illegal drugs. Through the example and encouragement of your children's valued peers — their new friends! — your children can learn how to cheat in school and, therefore, learn how to be dishonest in life. (Note that sometimes those friends are found online.)

Your children will be able to broaden their horizons by listening to and learning from these new "friends" rather than from you — even learning valued social skills as they spend time with active gang members at many schools.

Your children can learn creativity as they are shown how to get around school rules and societal laws, to say nothing of basic morality (you did teach that to them at home, didn't you?). They can learn that school — and therefore learning itself — doesn't have to be taken seriously.

They can learn how to have sex with others without parents knowing about it. (In some places, your teenage girl can get pregnant and have an abortion, all without your knowing about that either.)

Your children can also learn where and how to watch "special" movies and programs that even you, as adults, wouldn't watch. (Admittedly, some wrongly-focused parents don't care much about that.)

And, of course, your children can come home and practice new language skills, including new and exciting vocabulary when they get angry with you — perhaps even while threatening you for something you clearly did wrong, maybe by wrongly attempting to provide discipline and other parental guidance.

And there's so much more!

You can see there are many things your children can learn in public schools — but really in many private schools, too. They can't learn those things at home! ...can they?

Don't feel your children will be left out if you send them to one of the good schools out there. Many of those schools are just as capable of providing that same level of "education."

But be reassured once again: Some schools really are good. Seriously. On the other hand, are you sure you can reliably tell which is which?

37a. HOMESCHOOLING

One of my favorite alternatives to traditional education is homeschooling, so I'll give it its own section. I've already mentioned it more than once in this book.

It's important that people know that homeschooling is not home study! Homeschooling is not merely doing school work assigned by a school or teacher to do at home. Sometimes, a student might not be attending the classes a student would normally be attending for whatever reason — including being suspended or an extended illness. Some teachers will regularly send work to do at home. That's would be home study. The school's teachers are still providing the education.

Homeschooling doesn't (normally) involve teachers at school. It's parents who carefully, accurately, and lovingly teach their own children at their own home. It is parents who can assign work, although they can also use one of the homeschooling support companies from where work might come. In the end though, it comes down to parents being in charge.

Certainly, not all parents will feel they're qualified to do that. Many lack the self-confidence to do it even when they actually can. However, there are many companies in the country which provide support to parents for homeschooling. Parents can stay one step ahead of the lessons they will teach. More parents can do this than think they can — even though it can be a lot of work.

"All that's easy for you to say! But some of us have to work so that we can feed our kids! And you just think we can stop everything and starve while we homeschool our kids?! Well then you come over and do it!"

Yes, that's absolutely true. The biggest roadblock to homeschooling is that parents can't be home to do it. They have to work. They might be single parents and are already overwhelmed. This simply isn't an option for many parents. I wish we could do more for them. However, although there are sometimes ways to work it out, education here normally defaults to public (or other) schools.

Regardless, parents should still make the best choices that they can — if choices are even available.

**

An aside. Here's a caution: Leaving children of any age home for regular or extended periods is (almost) always a poor choice today. Yes, there are exceptions, but those exceptions are far less common than trusting parents think. (This comment is not necessarily directed at homeschoolers, but at parents generally.)

**

I've seen really great students come out of competent homeschooling environments, students who went on to do well in college. Homeschooled students can become doctors, lawyers, and anything else they want to be.

Exceptions can be found everywhere, but those who think that competently homeschooled children are missing something or are not up to the same level as traditionally educated children don't understand the quality of education and personal growth that many homeschooled children have. Overall, people who think that homeschoolers are academically missing things are generally wrong. Of course, that assumes the homeschooling is competently done. As elsewhere, including in public schools, it isn't always.

Perhaps the most common criticism of homeschooling is that homeschooled children are not well socialized because they're not around other children. That, too, is wrong. In fact, competently homeschooled children are often some of the best socialized students in any system.

Many homeschooling parents get together with other home-schooling parents to coordinate group activities, including sports. Their children get together regularly. Certain subjects can be taught by parents with expertise in those areas with multiple home-schooled children present. (In the past, some states have inexplicably put restrictions on that practice.)

What are the options for socializing for children who are not homeschooled? Sure, there are wonderful students at public schools. But there are also drug dealers, bullies, students who are totally disrespectful to teachers and staff, and gang members. Is that the socialization you think children should have? Oh sure, your children will only pick the best students at school to hang around. After all, your children were raised to "do the right thing," Right?

Sorry, think again.

As I'll always say, there are exceptions everywhere. But many of the most mature and respectful students that I've seen have been homeschooled. Such children reflect well on their parents.

Some states are very supportive of homeschooling. Some public school districts in Alaska, as one example, officially provide resources to help parents teach their children at home. If parents can't afford it, a district might make computers and other materials available for homeschooling parents. Some even allow parents to send their children to a nearby public school for some classes, if they choose.

For example, supportive districts know that it's not easy for parents to teach their high school aged children science without labs and resources. In some places, districts can allow parents to send their children to their local high school for that science class, or perhaps for some other specialized class. Those districts have an interest in helping all students learn and progress. Public school districts and homeschooling parents can work together for the same goal. That is as it should be.

By contrast, other areas or states have done everything they can to *stop* parents from homeschooling their children at all. They put up barriers, sometimes making things illegal for parents to do. Supposedly to be sure homeschooled children don't fall behind, some districts require homeschooled students to take the same annual (or more often) exams that public school students take to be sure they're progressing as public sector educators think that they should be.

Sometimes, such requirements can hurt students. First, a number of homeschooled students are actually ahead of their public school peers. Requiring the time to prepare for testing materials that are not consistent with a homeschool curriculum can slow things down. In addition, some parents specifically homeschool for religious or other subject-specific reasons. Public school exams don't take those things into account.

In cases where homeschooled students are truly not being taught, options to help them should be available. But there's no reason to penalize students for whom that is not an issue. States and districts should be primarily concerned about their own struggling students at public schools.

There are plenty of resources available to find out more about homeschooling. There are good companies that support homeschoolers nationwide. Online learning and classes often supplement such resources.

In addition, there is generally plenty of help from other homeschooling parents.

Homeschooling is one of the available educational alternatives. But it generally works only if parents responsible for the teaching have the time for it. That often means the parent handling the homeschooling isn't working — although some are able to manage it anyway. It's a lot of work, but it can be very rewarding for all concerned.

Parents should find the confidence that, with support, they'll able to do it. If they can do it well — or mostly well — I recommend it. It can bring parents and their children closer together, too.

37b. COMMENTS ON MILITARY TRAINING

Before we move on, let's take a quick look at one specialized alternative to traditional education programs. Although it's format isn't yet an option to replace traditional education today, it's a long-proven educational design that both public and some private schools should consider when looking at significantly restructuring educational programs.

In the past, military training has been one of the most efficient of all education systems. The military doesn't have time or money to waste on snowflakes or on the tender philosophies-of-the-moment. At least, that was true in the past. Recently, that may be changing.

Some evolving political and sociological ideologies — primarily coming from one political party — have recently been forced on the military. The military continues to be badly damaged by it. Its focus should be on strengthening its fighting ability in order to defend the country and win wars. But that basic focus is currently being preempted by ideology rather than by an actual strengthening of military preparedness.

If the military services significantly and permanently change in response to those outside social demands, it will be to the detriment of the military services and the defense of the country.

***

The military takes the vast majority of its officer corps from college graduates. In the past, they haven't cared what their major was. (Well, in some cases, they did.) Do they just assume that adult college graduates have maturity and other personal attributes because they successfully navigated a college degree program and graduated? In part, they do.

Fortunately, unlike many other employers, they evaluate potential officers in other ways, too. One of the unexpectedly hard tests I took was the entrance exam for potential US Naval officers. I had no problems taking the ASVAB (the Armed Services Vocational Aptitude Battery) many years before. The ASVAB is given to potential enlisted members applying for the military. It helps determine for which jobs they might be qualified.

As a result, I had thought I wouldn't have too much problem with the test for prospective Naval officers. But it was far more difficult. It was truly a different test. I felt relieved, even proud, when I passed it. Tests like that one, which I took many years ago, help to weed out those who lack skills that can be gained in college and in life. I can't speak for that test today — I'm hoping the Navy hasn't lowered its standards — but back then, the test and the screening processes were strong.

I certainly found that test tougher than the LSAT, the Law School Aptitude Test, which I had taken a few years before the Navy test. I spent no time in any advance preparation for the LSAT, yet I did well enough on it to be offered a seat at an ABA approved law school [ABA=American Bar Association].[1]

The military often assumes college graduates have gained some less tangible benefits, including critical thinking skills — whatever those might be understood to be.

How important are specific college majors to the military? Sometimes, they're critical. Other times, they're not at all.

Many years ago, I met a competent military weapons officer, one who was in charge of supervising others handling, as he told me, even nuclear weapons. His college major? Religious Science.

On its own, the military in the past has had some pretty powerful training programs. Therefore, regardless of college major (well, not always), they can train someone in whichever military skills they need. Nonetheless, hearing religious science for a weapons officer did make me nod with some amusement. (He was a good officer.)

Officers who become U.S. Naval Surface Warfare Officers, among vast numbers of other military jobs, may have also completed totally unrelated college degrees.

Because college graduates are normally older, they're likely to have a bit more maturity, too.

Are these things always true?

Making life and death decisions quickly in battle is indeed critical. Some do that far better than others, regardless of their backgrounds. Fortunately, the military has known how to educate its service members. Where they don't do it themselves, they'll farm out the education and training to colleges or other entities which, frankly, aren't necessarily always better.

The sometimes misguided assumption of important college intangibles gained by students isn't restricted to the military. Many large companies, including many in business fields, assume the college graduates they hire have decision-making competence in order to use their subject matter education on the job. Many define that as a "critical thinking" skill.

***

Especially in recent years, those with political or sociological agendas outside the military — and who have authority or influence over the military — have been injecting their agendas directly into our military services. No matter from where such things originate, in the end, such experiments weaken the military and imperil the country. Such meddling hasn't helped education and it's not doing any better for the military. I suggest that, if we want a strong military, meddlers, from wherever they come, would do well to remove past agendas now hoisted on the military services and leave the military alone to do its real job.

But, at the time of this writing, outsiders with agendas aren't leaving it alone. They directly interfere with military preparedness by compelling military members to engage in social agendas that work against a prepared military. In my opinion, military training has deteriorated since such outside social agendas have been forced on the military. Nonetheless, the prior history of its training programs — ignoring the bias of recent agendas having nothing to do with military preparedness — had been good.

***

Many people used to look down on military training. Many continue to do that. But, although you can find good and bad training classes in the military (just as everywhere else), overall, the civilian university system would do well to take a closer look at how the military has been able to successfully educate its personnel in a far, far shorter time. During my own years in the military, I spent about 24 months in a wide variety of military training courses dispersed over a number of years, so I'm not just speaking theoretically here.

Most universities grant some college level credit for certain military training, although it's often not subject matter specific credit. Of course, they rarely consider it to be a replacement for their own *for-profit* college classes that they naturally feel to be far superior to anything the military can do. I'm sure that's sometimes the case. I'm also sure that sometimes it's absolutely not. Of course, one can't always find comparable college and military courses, but sometimes there clearly are comparable courses. Foreign language training is just one example.

For those who might misunderstand, I'll note that not all military training deals with what might be deemed to be skills-of-war, although they all contribute to a prepared military — or they should.

The military can teach in a few months what some colleges and trade schools might take two years or more to do. That's far faster than civilian schools and it's something I've previously discussed.

The military can smoothly and effectively combine their training with follow up on-the-job training (OJT) after students complete their classroom training. They will then work beside others who have longer experience and who can help and further prepare those who have recently completed their military classroom instruction. Just as often, the military feels that some of its training is good enough for trained military personnel to hit the ground running with their new skills.

The military does contract with certain civilian schools to train some of its people. But, for many subjects, some of the best and most efficient schools in the world have been found in the U.S. military. It's concerning that most civilian universities, along with state accreditation standards, don't fully recognize some military experience and schools other than, perhaps, for some often-token elective credit.

We've had a good military in large part due to their training, but also due to the quality of most of our troops. Most of those in America's military possess the virtues of hard work, pride and respect, competence, patriotism, and self-sacrifice. Many of those virtues are missing in civilian college students.

Perhaps I should qualify the above by saying that they *used to* have those qualities. Hopefully, they still do. But today, there are legitimate questions about it.

38. WHAT'S THE BOTTOM LINE?

Both in and out of education, many people try to give us hope. After all, as has happened in the past, things will change for the better in the future. Won't they?

But is such hope warranted today?

It is not.

Consider this:

> If you have something at home that's not working, you have two choices. You can either fix it or, if it's not fixable, you will have to throw it out and get a new one. You won't keep trying to hobble the broken thing together hoping it might work again. Every time you try to fix it, you find that it's still broken. You simply need to replace it with a completely new one that will work better. Often, the new one will be fully redesigned with brand new features the old broken one didn't have.
>
> For many years now, the American Public Education system has simply not been fixable. Stop trying to fix it. We need a completely redesigned system of public education in this country.

If something is found to actually "fix" education, it would be a shock to me. I'd be very happy about it. But, in spite of false reassurances, we haven't even started on the road to do anything effective to fix it. All we hear are nice-sounding platitudes and promises of intentionally confusing reforms that won't reform anything.

Some ask, *"Well, what do you suggest?"* Currently, there really isn't a good answer to that question. One reason is that we're currently restricted in what we can even consider, let alone implement. Therefore, we don't know yet what we will be able to put together when —- and if — we can get the right group of creative minds together to address it.

Many correctly say that "the American people" should have *choice* in education. Choice is good. I support it. But exactly what are these "choices?" Aren't they often choices between multiple broken or inefficient systems? Sure, some are better than others. But the vast percentage of the population is educated at *public* schools, not at these educational "choices."

So definitely support worthy alternatives but, as you heard before, it's the public education system that is particularly dead. Its students — the products of public education — are simply not receiving an adequate education, let alone a strong one — and it's getting worse.

There are so few educators who even see that the problem is this serious. Based on their upbringing and education, they see nothing wrong with education today, or at least nothing that can't be easily fixed. If educators see no serious problem, there is no reason to "fix" anything. After all, it's not broken!

But it is. Negative data and reports on the deficiencies of academic knowledge and skills in our students come out with regularity.

Without a large number of people in the country recognizing that what we have today must be replaced, nothing will get done. In recent years, that number has been increasing. But it's still nowhere enough to demand the wholesale change that is needed.

Even back in 1971, we heard that any workable alternatives to the current system must move *"far enough and fast enough* [away from the current system] *to escape the 'gravitational pull' of the* [current] *school system*, [or] *they will be re-absorbed* [back into the system we have today]."[1]

Even though I disagree (at the moment) with a few of its positions and comments, nonetheless, *School Is Dead* (1971), is an important book. It lets you look at the entirety of the current education system in a new light. Published 12 years before *A Nation At Risk*, it describes the still-existing structure of education that preceded that groundbreaking report — and it wasn't good then either.

Those who have reached this point in the book, without just skipping here, would do well to read *School Is Dead* as you finish the book currently in your hands. It can shake up your thinking enough to think differently about the concept of education — and the near impossibility of replacing it today.

Note that there are other books which also support the observation that education in this country is dead — and has been for many years.

Those who are just waiting for the educational pendulum to swing back again may be naive. The pendulum in educational methodologies does continue to swing from one side to the other. That's why we see the same things come and go over the years as though there has been some great "new" discovery that will significantly improve how we teach or how students learn, especially at the K-12 level. Educators who have been around for a while recognize these "new" methods in slightly different packages being promoted — or required — again and again over the years.

But no "pendulum" exists in the philosophies and beliefs of current educators. There is no "pendulum" as some work to promote new and unhealthy cultures presented to students as the correct way to live and behave. Such things are destructive of students, society, and the country.

Increasingly, what we see today is what we have seen in various dictators over the years. For example, the Stalinists were able to get children to turn in their parents to the government, an action that often led to the imprisonment or death of parents. Early signs of this are already underway in both America and Europe, although it hasn't yet gone as far as that.

The author is very pessimistic that the current situation will turn around and become healthy without a major upheaval in America and elsewhere.

Check the past histories of countries throughout the world. When education is controlled and no longer free, the country loses its basic freedoms.

Because current educators can't see that, they perpetuate what is happening by training the next generation of teachers — their current students — to do and believe the same destructive things — and then passed down to the generations after them.

Education is more just dead today. It's become dangerous to the country, to its former liberties, and to its citizens.[2]

Think there are better places to be, perhaps in other countries? Look closely. You might not find many options anywhere.

America as survived bad things in the past and recovered. But there may be a time and events from which America will not recover. History is replete with countries that no longer exist, with governments and regimes that have been overthrown, often from within.

In the greater scheme of things, America is still a young country. Its survival is not guaranteed. A number of past empires did not survive for 300 years. Even America's Founding Fathers expressed concern that we might not be able to keep our new form of government. Among America's several current crises is that of education.

Related to that failed education system is an increasingly untrustworthy media that are not taking their constitutional right of a free press seriously. That First Amendment protection of the Press was put in place to protect the country, its people, and freedom itself. That free press was put in place to protect us (and the press itself) from possible abuses by the government.

But, with rights, come responsibilities. That is what appears to be ignored by many in the media today. If Americans don't learn actual truths about what is happening, they will only continue to make dangerous decisions based on their lack of accurate information through the media — and through social media.

Among too many is an assumption that reporters and editors of the news, as well as invited contributors and commentators, are more educated and know more than their viewers, listeners, and readers. That isn't necessarily true. Yet reporters and editors are usually even less inclined to change their understandings and positions than are those listening to them.

I've been interviewed a number of times in newspapers, as well as on radio and TV. Not many years ago, a local newspaper was going to do an article on my expertise in controlling a particular kind of invasive weed. I happened to be in their office for a different purpose. I was called over to set up something for a later interview. I spoke only briefly to the reporter who would do the article about when a good time to come in might be.

Instead of setting it up and actually interviewing me, the reporter just wrote the article. In the article, he quoted me. The problem is that he never actually spoke with me about the subject of the article! He literally just made the whole thing up — and printed it! The quote from me (that he made up) gave totally wrong information on the weed.

When I complained to the newspaper publisher, she expressed surprise. She had seen me in the office (on a different matter) and just assumed the reporter must have actually interviewed me. But it never happened. She apologized and offered to have me write something for the paper the following spring, many months after the original article. No correction or retraction was made and the followup piece was never written.

Even in *actual* interviews, my words have been twisted out of context. Perhaps I shouldn't complain. After all, media malpractice isn't unusual. Politicians and others have to fight against this almost all the time. Either their words are twisted, or completely false facts are reported.

Such behavior by the media is more than merely irresponsible. Especially with more serious issues, it damages the country. As I have repeatedly said, Americans need accurate facts if they are to make good decisions as they vote, and even as they live their daily lives. They can't do that if they get false or twisted information — or if news and facts are kept from them altogether.

After people leave school, they get most of their information from the media. For most people, the media is education for adults. It's an ongoing "school." But it's not a particularly good one.

When the media isn't working right, when its biases keep it from reporting balanced news and accurate information, when it makes judgment calls based on personal whims and biases, the country is seriously damaged. When that happens — and it's certainly happening at the time of this writing — voters will be poorly or wrongly informed. In that case, they can't do a good job running their country. Yes, I'm being redundant here.

It's not at all true, as some like to say, that Americans will *"see right through it"* regarding some issue or some wrongly reported "facts."

In order to actually fix it, politicians would need to spend their campaign funds on the actual *unbiased education* of voters — hopefully helped by a real and substantive teacher. Instead, we can look forward to the usual ads we all see before elections as well as a failing news media. So, no, Americans will *not* "see right through it."

It was not truly envisioned that the threat to the country — its people and its freedoms — would come not just from a few ultra-powerful people, corporations, and news media, but also from the people themselves. But that's what seems to be happening.

At the time of this writing, America is not in a good place. Adding to the woes of education is ongoing drug use by many students — and by many parents, too. Parents can affect the education — and future lives — of their children.

Nations, even empires, are temporary. They've always been temporary. However, in the context of history, a still young America has been an experiment from the beginning. To this point, it's worked pretty well — at least compared to countless other countries in the world, including those throughout history. But it's not perfect. No country ever has been.

One thing that has provided a foundation for the country has been a shared education system. (It wasn't there at America's beginning.) For many, many years, public education overtly promoted the specialness of America.

How can any country survive if its own schools don't support it? How can a country survive if its own education system goes so far as to speak badly of it, as too many in education are doing today? If a country's own children don't learn why they should respect, even love, their country, why would those children, as adults, defend and preserve it? They wouldn't. But, in much of public education, that seems to be happening.

Why wouldn't it? So many of today's teachers have themselves been raised in this new and disparaging way of thinking about their country. Regardless of deficiencies in subject matter instruction — of which there are many — development of love and respect for country (patriotism) is critical.

Schools at the K-12 level are a core home to teach and foster these things. Schools have been failing at that. Remember, that is how other countries in history lost themselves. Yet this appears to be the road that America is now on.

The increasing loss of belief in, and respect for God in both America and the world, isn't helping matters either.

In that light, it should also be clear that the political and sociological indoctrination of the moment is continuing to undermine the country's former spiritual health — even if just generically speaking — as well as our formerly shared morality. Previously included as a part of those things, were both the explicit and implicit freedoms and rights of the people. The poisoning may have already gone so far as to make the removal of the things destructive of our previously shared national health not just difficult — but effectively impossible.

Might we be able to recover from this moment as we have at other difficult times in the past?

We shall see.

As I mentioned at the beginning, this book is not simply a warning. There have been enough of those for many decades now. They haven't worked. Formal education, as we have known it, is dead. Without something happening quickly to change or replace it, it appears to many that America, as the world has known it, may be next.

39. CAN WE SAVE PUBLIC EDUCATION?

Okay. So now what? How *do* we realistically save public education?

That...is a good question. Its current structure has become solidly entrenched and is being protected by outside forces.

Once again, here is a summary of some problems:

(1) There has been a widespread takeover of public education by liberal, progressive ideologues — sometimes called the "radical left." They are now operating at all levels of education. All political parties should be concerned about — and reject — the resulting indoctrination of our children as well as adults beyond high school.

(2) There continue to be widespread failures and inefficiencies in the teaching and learning of many or most subject areas, especially in the core subjects. Deficiencies often include inefficient teaching methodologies.

(3) There continue to be broad failures in teacher training. It is generally too long, too expensive and increasingly turns out politi-

cally biased teachers. Beyond that, it doesn't necessarily do its basic job of turning out good teachers.

We must confront the inescapable conclusion that education has become dangerous to the healthy maturity of our children, physically and otherwise.

In the past, schools could not give children a single aspirin (or Tylenol or the like) without parental permission. Today, some schools are putting children on pathways such that they may be given life-altering drugs and surgeries. They have been advising these children not to inform their parents of the pathways on which school personnel wish to put these children. In some cases, district or school guidelines have specifically told school personnel not to inform parents.

When these things are directly brought up to school boards — one February 2023 school board meeting in Maine comes to mind — parents are told that such school-related health issues are "not germane to education."

Damaging political and sociological programs must be banned. These include such radical indoctrinations as Critical Race Theory and the 1619 Project, along with multiple "gender" focused indoctrinations.

Some states and politicians are trying to ban them. Others are not. Some of these things are clearly dangerous for students. They can endanger the physical, mental, emotional, and spiritual (where that still exists) health of our children, particularly in their K- 12 years.

In many places, schools are endangering the health and remnant morality of the country itself.

On the other hand, many people today have become so focused on these political and sociological ideologies that they have forgotten that our basic underlying education itself is broken.

That underlying education has been broken since well before the current ideologies began to take over many schools. Even were we to eliminate such ideologies — which should be done — we would still have a broken education system.

Such ideologies were not in place in 1983 when *A Nation At Risk* warned of *"...a rising tide of mediocrity that threatens our very future as a Nation and a people."* When the report added, *"We have, in effect, been committing an act of unthinking, unilateral educational disarmament,"* it referred to the core of education, not to the political ideologies of today.

In spite of what some others might say, things are not substantively better since *A Nation At Risk* was released.

Therefore, there is a double danger here: ideology and core education. Both must be addressed. The first can be addressed by "simply" getting rid of those destructive ideologies although, with the great number of teachers and administrators supporting these things already permeating schools, an effective ban may no longer be possible. But, under the current system, we can't just replace almost all educators en masse. We don't have any good replacements for them.

However, the second problem — the failure of the core of education — has been going on for much longer. It is even more difficult to resolve. As this book has repeatedly pointed out, it's likely impossible.

✳✳✳

Illiteracy is a danger to the country's survival. In too many places, we see that just 30% of students are reading at grade level, from the very early grades through high school graduates. This is part of the continuing death knell of public (and some non-public) education.

The foolishness of getting away from phonics, memorization, and drills, especially in the lower grades, but even all the way through high school, is just one thing causing major problems today.

But although bringing those things back will be a significant help to learning — they should be brought back *immediately* — they won't be enough to solve the widespread problems in education today. Phonics alone isn't enough for developing higher level reading skills, but it's an absolutely foundational part of the reading process.

If students read poorly, they can't learn anything else. They can't read and understand a history book or books on any other subject. They can't understand even some critical written instructions, including those dealing with safety, to use products at home. Their whole life will be poorer because they can't read a good book, even a novel, beyond those written at low grade levels. They can't read and understand substantive news articles. Many such students can end up on the streets. So will adults. After all, these students grow up. Job prospects become very limited.

Learning to read should begin *well before a child enters pre-school.*

***

The involvement of parents in the education of their children is very important. It is their right. Active awareness and involvement can help protect children from some of today's serious school problems.

As we have seen too often recently, some school boards have involved the police to remove frustrated parents when those parents voice correct educational concerns in a manner with which school board members are uncomfortable.

Understanding, flexibility, and creativity are needed on all sides. However, although parents can generally understand the negative effects of current political and sociological ideologies, they will need a deeper understanding of the core problems of education if they are to be effective in recognizing and judging corrective actions needed to address core learning. Things are difficult even for good educators who might also want change.

Recall for a moment the school community hearing in Chapter 29a where an assistant district superintendent went through the motions of holding a hearing with parents — but didn't care at all what they said. Even though he led them to believe that he would take their concerns and suggestions seriously into account — they believed him — he had lied to them. He was going to do what he wanted to do regardless.

But problems in schools are not simply due to some extremist or uncaring administrators. With fewer and fewer exceptions, the problems permeate the entire system. Nonetheless, because there are still many good and caring educators, including good administrators (outsiders can't always tell the difference), we must be careful not to sweep away the good with the bad.

On the other side, some want to give parents nearly unfettered control over schools and education. That, too, can lead to disastrous results. In too many parts of the country, any authority given to parents will absolutely become politicized or personalized in the communities a school serves.

In such areas, actions taken by parental authority may not have anything to do with education. Parents who are bitter over some corrective action properly taken for their child's misbehaviors will vindictively go after even good administrators and teachers. I have seen that at work and it isn't pretty.

Let's move on.

***

On February 5, 2021, a United States senator told the story of what education has meant to him.

When he was 7-years-old, his parents divorced. He went to live with his grandfather who then raised him. The senator remembered his grandfather reading a newspaper at the table, every day. The boy wondered what was so interesting that his grandfather always read it.

It wasn't until twenty years later that the boy learned that his grandfather couldn't read. He had wanted his grandsons to have a model they could follow in their own lives. He wanted them to understand the power of reading and the power of education. So he "read" in front of them.

> *"It's because of his example, that [my] family went from picking cotton..., to picking a seat in congress. Education is truly the closest thing to magic in America...*

> *"This is the story of America. This is why I think the most important*

issue for us as a nation to close that chasm, the gap between the haves and have nots, it's not focusing on race, it's not focusing on money, it's focusing on education."[1]

Without saving the American Public Education System, America itself will be dead. As repeatedly said, it may already be too late.

If you're in a position to potentially get significant legislative and judicial waivers for the vast majority of education-related requirements, restrictions, consent decrees, and required or "voluntary" guidelines, see me and we can talk. I'll be glad to get involved. Short of that, good luck.

But there is still one more thing. The federal government doesn't even have the constitutional authority to control education. Nonetheless, the federal government regularly forces its way into education anyway. It often holds needed federal funds hostage if states don't do what they say.

Under the Tenth Amendment, power over education belongs to the *states*, not to the federal government. But the ongoing interference of the federal government often seems to control education.

That doesn't mean that, if the states regain their full constitutional control over education, all would be fixed. It wouldn't be. Many states don't know what they're doing concerning education. Most states themselves are a mess.

Although you might think I am, I'm actually not saying that the federal government can't have a productive role in education. There are things the federal government really can do to help. It's just that it has to do it entirely differently from the way it's doing things now. It has to support — and not control or threaten — the states in their work. But is that even possible? Remember, the states don't necessarily know what they're doing either.

***

Many people don't want to believe that public education is actually dead. They want to think positively. It's good to think positively!

But it's not good to ignore decades of data as well as what our own eyes and experience tell us today. Trying to sweep the truth under the rug won't fix education.

Likely temporarily, we still have some fully educated, competent, and patriotic American teachers capable of effectively teaching students at all levels, teachers who will support the core principles of America, pass it to new generations and keep it healthy. But there aren't enough of them. Those who are still with us are often not put in positions where they can make enough of a difference.

Likely also temporarily, there are still some good, caring, courageous, and patriotic American school and district *administrators* who will do everything possible to create an environment where good teachers can actually teach, administrators who will protect, help, and encourage teachers, who will support America and keep it healthy. But there aren't enough of them either. They, too, are often not placed where they can make enough of a difference.

If educators won't support America, especially at the K-12 level, they shouldn't be teaching, nor should they be administrators. Let them travel to other countries to see if there's one they prefer. But don't let them continue to tear down a country that they should be serving as so many educators have done in the past.

What remains of the American Public Education System is effectively dead today. There aren't enough parts that are still alive and healthy enough to save the nation.

The fabric of America is being destroyed in large part because the educational health of the country continues to fail.

As of now, it's not fixable. It's simply not fixable. Even if parents rise up to demand it, effective change is no longer possible.

Without truly massive changes, changes that won't be possible to make, it's already too late. Can good and competent administrators save it? Can non-educators who have no experience in education at all save it? Can all of them working together save it?

Doubtful. But we should give it a try nonetheless.

It will take the involvement of experienced educators. Otherwise we risk repeating the mistakes of the past. It will take educators with substantively different thinking who might offer something totally new, yet workable. Beyond that, we will also need the added involvement of some clear thinkers without the mindset of traditional educators at all.

In most, though perhaps not all cases, those who have risen high in educational administration are the ones who either caused or who perpetuate the ongoing destruction of education in America. So now, it's all that they know.

This is more than simply a matter of missing or weak academic, social, and patriotic education. It's become a national security threat so serious as to likely lead to the loss of America as we have known it. Some look around and see that it is already happening.

The bottom line is that no one has been able to save education and, through education, the country. Now it's your turn to figure it out.

It's a delicate and almost impossible situation.

Don't mess it up.

END

APPENDIX: THE SBAST

This is the full set of questions that comprised the SBAST as discussed in Chapter 10a. It originally took two pages, front and back. Consistent with the original SBAST, the problems here are not numbered. It was a timed test.

Page One:

7+8=	9-4=	7x4=	18÷2=
4+6=	15-7=	5x3=	45÷5=
3+9=	12-8=	8x8=	56÷8=
8+6=	11-6=	3x4=	42÷6=
5+7=	8-5=	14x2=	36÷4=
8+11=	18-9=	7x7=	27÷3=
9+6=	22-7=	3x9=	36÷6=
7+7=	14-8=	2x8=	55÷11=
11+15=	19-6=	4x6=	49÷7=
12+12=	42-24=	3x8=	24÷4=
8+17=	7-3=	8x9=	15÷3=
9+5=	18-12=	7x3=	54÷6=
4+19=	21-14=	4x8=	40÷8=

Page Two:

6+5=	16-9=	3x6=	16÷4=
12+11=	13-5=	7x8=	63÷9=
7+9=	52-14=	10x12=	72÷8=
9+4=	36-11=	12x3=	39÷3=
8+12=	19-13=	9x9=	48÷2=
2+14=	15-6=	15x3=	66÷11=
3+8=	28-15=	7x9=	72÷6=
9+9=	27-27=	9x6=	48÷12=
8+8=	37-12=	5x12=	14÷14=
9+11=	13-7=	11x8=	150÷10=
5+18=	17-9=	9x4=	66÷22=
7+6=	23-8=	8x6=	36÷12=

ALSO BY THE AUTHOR

Other Books by The Author:

Killers Are Fatherless: The Real Cause of School Shootings, Serial Killings, and Gang Murders

Many commentators and others in the media frequently lament the issue of fatherlessness and dysfunctional families, but then blithely move on to discuss other issues important to them, guns among them. Yet those other issues are often of far less importance than the connection of fatherlessness and dysfunctional families. The great number of deaths will continue at the hands of these killers unless this can be far more widely acknowledged and addressed. The failure to seriously address this issue is clear evidence of the ignorance, incompetence — or worse — of both the media and their commentators. This book looks at the issue of fatherlessness and its connection to the vast majority of killers.

The Cartainos: Men of Passion • Men of Stone

Over 12 years in the making, this epic-length true story is the most complete and authoritative work on the journey of this immigrant family ever written. Based on extensive research including original interviews, primary source documents, and eyewitnesses, the stories here will compel you to think about your own life.

Commended by both Britain and the United States for helping to save over 600 lives during World War II, the story of Salvatore Cartaino Scarpitta was told on the popular *This Is Your Life* television series in 1953. He was an adventurer, lover, singer, composer, sculptor, hero, even a judge in the 1932 Los Angeles Olympics. His story leads to the compelling stories of those who followed him. Read this new and unforgettable American classic!

For more, see the Multi-Services Publishing catalog website.

ENDNOTES (WHERE THE FOOTNOTES ARE)

PREFACE

1. This focus group was comprised of 22 students from 16 different countries at New York University in Abu Dhabi. It was conducted by famed pollster Frank Luntz in early 2021.
2. This as a Wikipedia article. Wikipedia is not necessarily known as a reliable source of information, although it is widely used by many and often does have reliable information in it, assuming readers can tell reliable from unreliable. The article here is deemed by the author to be a reliable source for purposes of the discussion here at the time of its access. This article was accessed March 11, 2021.
3. I'll mention that even countries with oppressive dictatorships have people who, for one reason or another, express allegiance, sometimes patriotism for their country. We do not consider that here.
4. NORC was previously known as the National Opinion Research Center and is closely affiliated with the University of Chicago.
5. Articles in a number of other sources also discuss this poll. See the article referenced above at: www.wsj.com/articles/americans-pull-back-from-values-that-once-defined-u-s-wsj-norc-poll-finds-df8534cd?mod=hp_lead_pos9. Accessed 4-9-2023. The full 2023 poll itself might still be at: https://s.wsj.net/public/resources/documents/WSJ_NORC_ToplineMarc_2023.pdf.
6. Of course, you can follow your dreams and be a success in some other countries, too. But in many places, the road to personal independence and success is really difficult, sometimes impossible.

"THIS IS CHAPTER ONE."

1. Lest someone feign confusion, I will often call the United States of America, "America," for short.
2. It's a strange and sad thing to say, but even the word and concept of being an American "citizen" is coming under attack today. Here, I use the word in its traditionally respected sense.
3. As per: web.archive.org/web/20080828192156...edin08.com/uploadedFiles/Issues/A%20Stagnant%20Nation.pdf, accessed 11-29-2022.
4. Lack of proficiency in math is as per *Not One Student Was Proficient In Math In 23 Baltimore Schools: REPORT*, a February 10, 2023 article by Reagan Reese in the Daily Caller. The article quoted data from Project Baltimore. This has also been reported in other sources.
5. See *The Marxification of Education: Paolo Freire's Critical Marxism and the Theft of Education* (2022) by James Lindsay.

1. THE REAL CHAPTER ONE: THE POLITICS OF EDUCATION

1. See the February 10, 2023 article in The Epoch Times, *Missouri Considers Bill to Ban School Encouragement of Child Gender Transition,* by Jackson Elliott, accessed Feb 13, 2023.

1A. DANGEROUS TEACHINGS

1. As found at: pulitzercenter.org/sites/default/files/full_issue_of_the_1619_project.pdf. Accessed 11-9-2022.
2. Among other sites, see: scribd.com/document/466921269/NYT-s-1619-Project-Founder-Calls-White-Race-Barbaric-Devils-Bloodsuckers-No-Different-Than-Hitler-x. Accessed 11-9-2022.
3. Found in: kirkcenter.org/reviews/the-absurdity-of-gender-theory. Accessed Nov 7, 2022. There are many other sources for information on this "theory."
4. As one example, see the March 17, 2023 article in The Epoch Times regarding Elon Musk's March 16, 2023 posting on Twitter. The article is: *Elon Musk: Children Being Fed Transgender 'Propaganda' by Adults.*
5. As per: projectveritas.com/results-and-impact-2022, accessed 1-24-2023. At the time of this writing, multiple investigations into this administrator are underway. No final determination about this is made here.
6. Among other sources, see: nationalpost.com/opinion/catholic-school-has-student-arrested-for-expressing-catholic-beliefs?_gl=1*1ym5gmt*_ga*Mzg4MTQ5OTg4Lj-E2Nzg1MDI3Mzk.*_ga_H792QCFZPV*MTY3ODUwMjc0MC4xLjEuMTY3ODUwMjg3MS42MC4wLjA.&_ga=2.19781560.1674774334.1678502740-388149988.1678502739, accessed 3-10-2023.

2. CAN AMERICA LAST?

1. Victor Davis Hanson made his comments and comparison to China's Cultural Revolution in an *American Thought Leaders* interview on February 14, 2023. Hanson has been a frequent commentator for a variety of media companies. Among other accolades, he was awarded the National Humanities Medal in 2007. Separately, China expert, Gordon Chang, has warned of a possible military first-strike on America from China. He is not alone in that warning.
2. On the statue issue, a significant number of those tearing them down were not doing it for any political or ideological reason. They were just there to destroy things. Many would have also been happy to destroy other things — and any excuse for doing that would have been acceptable to them.

    In those cases, education might not be the problem at all. Well, perhaps for instilling ,some formerly-existing societal morals education may have helped. Sadly, that form of personal development is weak and confusing in today's education system.

    As an incentive to change behavior, some have suggested that conviction and imprisonment for wanton destruction might encourage more thoughtful pursuits from demolition-activists in the future. Perhaps that's just an alternate form of education. But it hasn't seemed to have helped either.

3. Examples include: dailymail.co.uk/news/article-11558067/Woke-Stanford-University-publishes-list-harmful-language-want-eliminate.html; washingtonexaminer.com/restoring-america/community-family/stanford-university-deems-american-harmful-language; nypost.com/2022/12/20/stanford-releases-guide-against-harmful-language-including-term-american; independent.co.uk/news/world/americas/stanford-university-harmful-language-american-b2248833.html; among others, accessed 12—20-2022.

2A. THE DEATH OF COLLEGE EDUCATION

1. This *Just the News* article was found at: justthenews.com/politics-policy/education/zero-gop-professors-nearly-3-dozen-university-departments-across-multiple, accessed 12/8/2022.

2. As per: thecollegefix.com/zero-republican-professors, accessed 12/8/2022. The College Fix is part of the Student Free Press Association, "a nonprofit run by veteran journalists to help beginning [college-aged] journalists."

3. As per: thecollegefix.com/poll-73-percent-of-republican-students-have-with-held-political-views-in-class-for-fear-their-grades-would-suffer, accessed 12-8-2022.

4. As per William Donohue at catholicleague.org/why-are-white-people-so-stupid, accessed 2-8-2023.

5. The Art & Science Group poll isn't long and is worth reading: Politics, Policies, And Student Perspectives – The Impact Of State Social Policies On College Choice, Volume 16 | Issue 1 | March 2023. If still there, it can be found at: www.artsci.com/studentpoll-volume-16-issue-1, accessed 4-2-2023.

2B. WHAT IS AN EDUCATED STUDENT?

1. As per: coursera.org/articles/liberal-arts-majors, accessed 12-5-20223.

3. A NATION AT RISK

1. See Seaborg's comments on the report at: lbl.gov/Publications/Seaborg/risk.htm, accessed 11-28-2022.

2. As per authors James W. Guthrie & Matthew G. Springer in 2009 at: tandfonline.com/doi/abs/10.1207/s15327930pje7901_2, accessed 11-28-2022.

3. See: "A Nation at Risk Revisited: Did 'Wrong' Reasoning Result in 'Right' Results? At What Cost?" (2004) by James W. Guthrie and Matthew G. Springer.

4. See: education.com/magazine/article/america-failing-math, accessed 11-29-2022.

5. See: bipartisanpolicy.org/report/36-years-later-a-nation-still-at-risk-how-we-are-failing-our-young-learners-and-how-we-can-make-it-right, accessed 11-29-2022.

6. See: U.S. Department of Education, A Nation Accountable: Twenty-five Years After A Nation at Risk, Washington, D.C., 2008. At: ed.gov/rschstat/re-

search/pubs/accountable/index.html, accessed 11-29-2022.
7. Found at: edutopia.org/landmark-education-report-nation-risk, accessed 11-29-2022.

4. A DANGEROUS ROAD TO TRAVEL

1. See: *School is Dead* (1971) by Everett Reimer.
2. As a followup, the following year I had Mr. Lenihan for history, which he actually wanted to teach. One time, he called me a buffoon in class that year. It hurt me to this day. Maybe he was right, of course. So I apologize to his memory today for not being totally mature as likely an eleventh grade student. Nonetheless, it never affected how I felt about him as a good teacher in either class and I'm still very grateful to him.
3. See the webpage at: donaldrobertson.name/2018/04/29/was-socrates-a-real-person-and-other-questions, accessed 12-11-2022.

6. NUCLEAR WEAPONS

1. The classes I was teaching were taken in as part of the college's Animal Husbandry Department. Some college classes require proven experience in the subject matter to be hired to teach. Although I never had to separately prove my past experience in order to teach there, an assistant dean at the college had attended a non-credit class I was teaching and (correctly) determined that I was qualified to teach the subject. He hired me. I was indeed qualified to teach the classes that I taught.
2. The correct answer is that you can first recognize an atomic blast by its blinding light, much brighter than the sun. The sound comes after that.
3. One of several articles relating the questioning at this hearing was found at: msn.com/en-us/news/politics/sen-kennedy-stumps-biden-nominee-with-basic-questions-about-the-constitution/ar-AA16LTeE, accessed 2-8-2023.

7. THE HOLOCAUST

1. Containing other results of concern, this poll is found at: polsci.umass.edu/sites/default/files/RaceinAmericaCrosstabsJanuaryNational2023.pdf, accessed 1-16-2023.

9. HISTORICAL REVISIONISM

1. As per T. Carlson, TPUSA Conference, December 19–22, 2020.
2. T. Carlson on February 3, 2021.

9A. AN "INTELLECTUAL PLAGUE"

1. Quoted passages in this section are from Princess Ileana's book, *I Live Again* (1951).
2. Changes due to new scholarship and discoveries, not merely opinions and agendas, are certainly fine and good. But that is not to what we refer here.
3. *Footprints in the Dust: The Epic Voyages of Apollo,* 1969–1975 by Colin Burgess (ed.), Univ. of Nebraska Press, 2010.
4. This quote, which is also seen in other forms, is attributed to George Santayana's (1863-1952) oft-repeated admonition, written in *The Life of Reason* (1905). However, Edmund Burke (1729-1797) is credited by some as having said something quite similar. If true, that would render Santayana's quote a paraphrase of Burke's. With more certainty, and of a certain application in this instance, Burke did say, *"People will not look forward to posterity, who never look backward to their ancestors."* Although Burke has quite a number of excellent insights in his numerous writings and speeches, one of "Burke's" most famous and insightful quotes is, according to multiple sources, likely not even his: *"The only thing necessary for the triumph of evil is for good men to do nothing."* Regardless of who said it, it is often true.
5. Comments in this section are based, in part, on decades of professional experience at multiple levels of education by the author. Princess Ileana and others bring similar perspectives.

10. THE CONFIDENCE OF MATH

1. *The Trachtenberg Speed System of Basic Mathematics* (1960, etc.) by Jakow Trachtenberg, translated & adapted by Ann Cutler and Rudolph McShane. The story of the origin of this method of mathematics is fascinating on its own. At the time of this writing, the availability of this book is uncertain or mixed.
2. As a side benefit, many things in the basics of the Trachtenberg system teach math done substantially in your head, without writing much down. That is a benefit to those students whose minds work very well, but who may not be able to effectively transfer what's in their head to paper. That might include some students with dyslexia. The fewer numbers such students have to write down, the fewer opportunities there are for errors. In my classes, I generally only taught the simplest problems — just enough to create student self-confidence.

10A. MATH: THE SBAST

1. Saying that *"students struggled behaviorally"* puts it euphemistically. Their behavior may have been poor, but it was everyone else who struggled with it: teachers, parents, even other students.

11B. A SATURDAY CLASS

1. It's because many teachers do put in so much extra time and caring without pay that someone should look after them to get them some extra compensation. Supposedly, it's their union's job. Really, it should be the concern of the entire system, including parents and others.

12. WHAT IS FREE ENTERPRISE?

1. Some people interchangeably refer to free enterprise as capitalism. Even though they might appear related, they're actually somewhat different. The term, free enterprise, is certainly more closely aligned to using the term, the free market system. However, depending on to whom you talk, there can be small differences there, too. These terms are more properly explored in a high school or college economics class.

14. THE MEDIA: DO THEY KNOW ENOUGH?

1. Because of the speed and lack of clarity of her remarks, her quote here might be somewhat inexact, although not enough to change its meaning. Her quote comes from several sources, including the Daily Mail.com, reprinted on msn.com, and in other sources.
2. As per Wikipedia, accessed Nov 13, 2022. Wikipedia is not necessarily known as a reliable source for information, even though it is widely used and can indeed have reliable information on it, assuming readers can tell one from another. This article, as well as others referenced in this book, is deemed by the author to be reliable at the time of its access.

18. WHAT DO STUDENTS THINK? PART TWO

1. *Wad-Ja-Get?: The Grading Game in American Education* (1971; anniversary edition: 2021) by Howard Kirschenbaum. Also Rodney Napier, Sidney Simon, and Barry Fishman. The main narrative reads very informally. However, Appendix A shows the depth of its research. Highly recommended, even today.
2. Note that this congresswoman had already actively supported an actual white supremacist who had been convicted of murder. The congresswoman was a Black Lives Matter activist who also supported the Palestinians, but not Israel. Yet she reportedly feels the Pledge of Allegiance is a symbol of racism and white supremacy? What's wrong with this picture?

19. "HIGHER" EDUCATION CAN DESTROY AMERICA

1. John Ellis: Chairman, California Association of Scholars; Distinguished Professor Emeritus, University of California, Santa Cruz; Author: *The Break-*

down of Higher Education.

2. The article is not long. Read it at: www.theepochtimes.com/why-college-degrees-are-working-against-many-job-seekers_4319490.html. Accessed 4-5-2023.

19A. "I HAVE TENURE!"

1. This recommended report can be found here: www.thefire.org/research-learn/academic-mind-2022-what-faculty-think-about-free-expression-and-academic-freedom, accessed 3-2-2023.

19D. DO COLLEGE CLASSES PROMOTE VIOLENCE?

1. This March 29, 2023, article appeared in The Epoch Times: *Michigan Professor Suspended After Suggesting Conservative Campus Speakers Should Be Killed.* Accessed 3-29-2023.

20. CRITICAL THINKING?

1. Cited from Peter Schmidt,"Former Top Official at Education Dept. Criticizes How It Approached College Access," *The Chronicle of Higher Education,* January 9, 2009.
2. "Richard Hersch, 'Going Naked,' *AAC&U Peer Review* 9 (2007):6."

21A. THREATS ENDANGER PARENTS, TOO

1. There are multiple critical ages as children grow up when parents must use a firm hand to correct serious behaviors. Here, I just mentioned one. It was too late, regardless.
2. There are certainly readers who will second guess this situation, coming up with things that might have worked for the father or perhaps had worked for someone they know. They often (wrongly) assume that the same thing will work for everyone. Sadly, such things do not work for everyone. Life isn't always straightforward.

22. VIOLENCE

1. Excerpted from: McMahon, S.D., Anderman, E.M., Astor, R.A., Espelage, D.L., Martinez, A., Reddy, L.A., & Worrell, F.C. (2022). *Violence Against Educators and School Personnel: Crisis During COVID.* Policy Brief. American Psychological Association.
2. Among other reports, see: news-journalonline.com/story/news/crime/2023/02/24/video-shows-matanzas-high-school-teachers-aide-being-attacked-palm-coast-florida/69939938007 and flaglerlive.com/186609/matanzas-ese, accessed 2-24-2023.

24. MANY TEACHERS WANT TO GIVE UP

1. The dog trainer in this story was the author himself. In addition to work as a professional dog trainer, the author also worked for a time as a cat behavioral consultant and ran internationally recognized cat training classes for two years at a community college in Los Angeles, as well as other, more substantive classes.

26. MANY STUDENTS HAVE DIFFICULT LIVES

1. Learning through osmosis with your hand on a book is fake news. To learn something, I recommend doing it in the usual way.

28A. SCHOOLS TEACH TOO LITTLE, TOO SLOWLY

1. Information on the Harding's story is found in a worthwhile article by E. S. Armstrong of February 11, 2022, titled, *"'Brainy Bunch': Parents Homeschool Their 10 Kids With All of Them Graduating High School at 12."* Find it in the Epoch Times: theepochtimes.com/brainy-bunch-parents-homeschool-their-10-kids-with-all-of-them-graduating-high-school-at-12_4210059.html., accessed Jan 2, 2023.
2. As just two sources for this, see *School Is Dead* (1971), by Everett W Reimer, and *Designed to Fail* (2005), by Steve Kellmeyer.
3. As per the article, *Behind the Public School Exodus of 1.4 Million Children,* by Lawrence Wilson, in the Jan 25-31, 2023 edition of The Epoch Times.
4. As per, *Behind the Public School Exodus of 1.4 Million Children,* by Lawrence Wilson, in the Jan 25-31, 2023 edition of The Epoch Times.

29A. A SCHOOL COMMUNITY HEARING

1. Emailed comments from Bill Donohue on November 14, 2022.

32. GOD IN SCHOOLS

1. Yes, I know that's not how people know that piece of tree philosophy, but the point is the same.

33. THE LIST

1. For disclosure, this list was assembled by J. K. Scarpitta, the author's brother.
2. As just one example, see *Freedom to Learn: A View of What Education Might Become* (1969, 1986) by Carl Rogers (1902-1987). A later edition put out after the death of Rogers is also available. (Rogers himself was later reported to have repudiated at least some of his own writings.)

37. EDUCATIONAL ALTERNATIVES

1. The article is, *Behind the Public School Exodus of 1.4 Million Children,* by Lawrence Wilson, in the Jan 25-31, 2023 edition of The Epoch Times.
2. As per a March 30, 2023 article at ABC News online: *Frustration builds around ADHD drug shortage as demand increases* by Emma Egan. *Accessed 3-31-2023.*

37B. COMMENTS ON MILITARY TRAINING

1. Note the requirement for the LSAT for law school admission is being dropped by some law schools. That decision is not supported by other law schools.

38. WHAT'S THE BOTTOM LINE?

1. From *School Is Dead* (1971) by Everett Reimer.
2. Some suggest that a new governmental and socially mandated education may be on the way. Actually, one can point to what appears to be that already happening in multiple states. That movement seems to be growing. If this sounds like one of the countless conspiracy theories proliferating today, it's not. Things really are getting worse. Much can be traced back to the poorly trained students in unbalanced college classes. But it is not just from there. You might be able to find it if you look at today's schools carefully and objectively. Some suggest there is an underlying purposeful design causing and perpetuating it. Others might feel that it's just happening on its own.

39. CAN WE SAVE PUBLIC EDUCATION?

1. These were the words of Senator Tim Scott of South Carolina in a televised interview of February 5, 2021.

Made in the USA
Monee, IL
23 April 2023

32294011R00292